CURRENT APPROACHES TO TELLS IN THE PREHISTORIC OLD WORLD

CURRENT APPROACHES TO TELLS IN THE PREHISTORIC OLD WORLD

edited by

ANTONIO BLANCO-GONZÁLEZ & TOBIAS L. KIENLIN

Oxford & Philadelphia

Published in the United Kingdom in 2020 by
OXBOW BOOKS
The Old Music Hall, 106–108 Cowley Road, Oxford, OX4 1JE

and in the United States by
OXBOW BOOKS
1950 Lawrence Road, Havertown, PA 19083

© Oxbow Books and the individual authors 2020

Paperback Edition: ISBN 978-1-78925-486-0
Digital Edition: ISBN 978-1-78925-487-7 (epub)

A CIP record for this book is available from the British Library

Library of Congress Control Number: 2020944058

All rights reserved. No part of this book may be reproduced or transmitted in any form or by any means, electronic or mechanical including photocopying, recording or by any information storage and retrieval system, without permission from the publisher in writing.

Printed in the United Kingdom by Short Run Press

Typeset by Versatile PreMedia Services (P) Ltd

For a complete list of Oxbow titles, please contact:

UNITED KINGDOM
Oxbow Books
Telephone (01865) 241249
Email: oxbow@oxbowbooks.com
www.oxbowbooks.com

UNITED STATES OF AMERICA
Oxbow Books
Telephone (610) 853-9131, Fax (610) 853-9146
Email: queries@casemateacademic.com
www.casemateacademic.com/oxbow

Oxbow Books is part of the Casemate Group

Front cover: Photo: Marian A. Lie

Contents

1. Introduction: Learning from Prehistoric Tells — 1
   Antonio Blanco-González and Tobias L. Kienlin

PART 1. THE BUILDING-UP OF TELL MATERIALITY

2. Architectural Phases, Use-life Episodes and Taphonomic Processes in Tell Formation:
   An Approach to Neolithic Tell Halula (Syria) — 11
   Miquel Molist, Quim Sisa, Julia Wattez and Anna Gómez-Bach

3. Re-discovering the Neolithic Landscapes of Western Thessaly, Central Greece — 25
   Athanasia Krahtopoulou, Charles Frederick, Hector A. Orengo, Anastasia Dimoula, Niki Saridaki, Stella Kyrillidou, Alexandra Livarda and Arnau Garcia-Molsosa

4. The Old Becomes New: Material Culture and Architectural Continuity on an Anatolian *Höyük* — 41
   Sharon R. Steadman and Jennifer C. Ross

5. Moving Bottom-up: The Case Study of Kakucs-Turján (Hungary) and its Implications for Studies of
   Multi-layered Bronze Age Settlements in the Carpathian Basin — 57
   *Robert Staniuk, Mateusz Jaeger, Gabriella Kulcsár, Nicole Taylor, Jakub Niebieszczański
   and Johannes Müller*

6. Exploring the Bronze Age Tells and Tell-like Settlements from the Eastern Carpathian Basin.
   Results of a Research Project — 73
   Florin Gogâltan, Alexandra Găvan, Marian A. Lie, Gruia Fazecaș, Cristina Cordoș and Tobias L. Kienlin

7. Talking Trash. Reconstructing Activities, Discard and Abandonment at Late Bronze Age Tell
   Sabi Abyad (Syria) — 97
   Victor Klinkenberg

PART 2. THE SOCIAL LIVES OF TELLS

8. Domestication of Tells: Settlements of the First Farmers in Pelagonia (Macedonia) — 111
   Goce Naumov

9. Tells (and Flat Sites) as Social Agents: A View from Neolithic Greece — 125
   Stella Souvatzi

10. Human Activities on a Late Neolithic Tell-like Settlement Complex of the Hungarian Plain
    (Öcsöd-Kováshalom) — 139
    András Füzesi, Knut Rassmann, Eszter Bánffy and Pál Raczky

11. The Practice of Everyday Life on a European Bronze Age Tell: Reflections from
    Százhalombatta-Földvár (Hungary) — 163
    Joanna Sofaer, Marie Louise Stig Sørensen and Magdolna Vicze

12. Social Life on Bronze Age Tells. Outline of a Practice-oriented Approach — 173
    Tobias L. Kienlin

13. Architecture, Power and Everyday Life in the Iron Age of North-eastern Iberia. Research from
    1985 to 2019 on the Tell-like Fortress of Els Vilars (Arbeca, Lleida, Spain) 189
    Joan B. López, Emili Junyent and Natàlia Alonso

PART 3. CONCLUDING REMARKS

14. Then, Now, to Come – A Commentary 211
    John Chapman

1

Introduction: Learning from Prehistoric Tells

Antonio Blanco-González and Tobias L. Kienlin

This book focuses on one of the most appealing and intriguing phenomena in prehistoric Eurasia: The occurrence of bulky artificial mounds, made of deeply stratified occupation layers, sometimes walled or ditched and inhabited by agropastoral communities. Tell is a frequently used Arabic place name for these massive hills, derived from the Assyro-Babylonian *tillu*, meaning a heap of ruins (Liverani 2016, 4). The conspicuous nature of these prehistoric settlements readily has attracted the attention of scholars since the beginnings of scientific archaeology in the late 19th century. Subsequent regional surveys and modern excavations in the 20th century highlighted their sharp contrast with the more common types of prehistoric habitats, namely 'normal' fortified settlements – often on hilltops – and open flat sites. Indeed, throughout later prehistory people often left behind only scattered and scanty traces of their domestic and everyday life and death. Remains generally consisted of underground features, debris of wooden and daub buildings, insubstantial tombs and occasional earthen and stone monuments. Against this background, multi-layered sites protruding from their surroundings stand out as a distinctive and somehow extreme case of household archaeology vis-à-vis other more ubiquitous yet elusive outcomes of social life.

Tells and tell-like sites are known worldwide and occasionally arose from the earliest Neolithic. Thus, in the Indus Valley human-made hillocks such as Mehrgarh (Pakistan) are the result of the prolonged accretion of occupation layers and mud-brick rubble on the same spot (*c*. 6500–2800 BC); within the Americas, the Amazonian Basin shows 3rd and 2nd millennium BC mound-building pastoralists living in conspicuous *sambaquis* made of shells and dwellings and 1st millennium AD bulky earthworks (7–8 m high) such as Teso dos Bichos (Brazil) within the so-called Camutins group; and further north flat-topped Mississippian platforms (*c*. AD 1000–1650) such as the enormous Monks Mound in Cahokia (Illinois, USA) housed elite residential quarters and ceremonies (Scarre 2018, 341, 663, 678–681). As with our study area in the Old World, this phenomenon also bloomed from the Early Neolithic onwards, and again tell-living only occurred during specific timespans and was circumscribed to certain foci, especially some parts of Anatolia, the Middle East and Southeastern Europe. Such eye-catching cases have never gone unnoticed. Thus, beyond the most successful academic designation of 'tells' they have received assorted folk names in diverse languages – *e.g. tepe, höyük, chogha, magoula, toumba, obrovci, turuñuelo, motilla, etc.* Setting aside funerary tumuli, these habitats represent a heterogeneous casuistry, as this volume tries to demonstrate.

This topic is relevant because key issues in later prehistory have a direct impact on it: The lifestyles and subsistence strategies of their occupants – whether semi-permanent or fully sedentary; the formation dynamics leading to such accumulations – entailing ways of building, refurbishing, refuse managing and abandoning domestic structures; the character of this sort of settlement archaeology, where subsoil burials and votive deposits are frequent – whether mundane and prosaic or highly ritualised; or the kind of socio-political organisation behind them – whether villages of egalitarian farmers, gathering places, aristocratic residences or even capitals of territorial polities – to name just a few. Above all, these interpretive frameworks have been shaped by national scholarly traditions. Thus, the archaeological analysis of tells often fall within too compartmentalised ways of doing archaeology, backed by an array of long-held assumptions and research agendas (Kienlin 2015). This is especially so in the case of two of the most insightful academic traditions on tells: Neolithic and Bronze Age archaeologies in Southwestern Asia and Southeast Europe, which have produced exhaustive overviews on the subject and brought forth competing or complementing strands of tell studies (*e.g.* Chapman 1989; Wilkinson 2003; Rosenstock 2009; Hofmann *et al.* 2012; Matthews 2014; Fischl & Kienlin 2019).

Beyond these research hubs, tell archaeology is far less established despite the striking commonalities between the targeted material records. In sum, this version of prehistoric settlement known as tell epitomises crucial and hotly debated questions in current archaeological agendas. However, such scholarly traditions remain entrenched within their research procedures and discussions, and they rarely benefit from advances in comparable sites in prehistoric Eurasia to move beyond their comfort zones.

The idea of this volume stems from co-editors' shared interest in such distinctive sites and their research challenges. It was prompted by the realisation that there is an inexhaustible body of evidence and a wide array of intellectual approaches and fieldwork strategies. However, a quick survey of recent literature allows identifying ideas and assumptions that deserve a closer critical look. It is also noticeable that prehistoric tell-dwelling communities are too often tackled from narrow local perspectives or discussed within strict time- and culture-specific frameworks. These efforts encounter similar problems time and again, follow comparable lines of reasoning and as a result tend to repeat arguments and discourses, sometimes already discredited by other colleagues. The benefits of tackling tells from a wider spatial and temporal scope have not been fully explored. As a response to such pitfalls, an overview of tell archaeology transcending scholarly borders from a decidedly comprehensive and comparative perspective (Smith & Peregrine 2012) might help to identify promising avenues of enquiry, trigger debate and contribute to establishing an updated and critical picture of the subject.

The above concerns and ideas led the co-editors to undertake a twofold initiative: a) the research stay of one of us (ABG) in November 2017 at the Department of Prehistoric Archaeology of the University of Cologne (Germany), that allowed us to work together on this topic; and b) the co-organised session held at the 24th Annual Meeting of the European Association of Archaeologists at Barcelona (5–8 September 2018), which focused on cutting-edge methods and fresh theories to tackle multi-layered and tell-like sites in Eurasia during the later prehistory. This volume is the result of both opportunities to exchange standpoints and experiences; its core comprises a selection of some of the most remarkable contributions to the EAA Barcelona session. In addition, the book includes invited chapters to round out under-represented areas and periods in the EAA session with relevant research programmes in the Old World.

Of course, our modest aim here is not to solve any shortcomings, but to clearly pinpoint some of them and spotlight viable and promising lines of advance, as cases of good practice whose collation may boost cross-fertilisation. Therefore, the *leitmotiv* in this volume is that there is a great

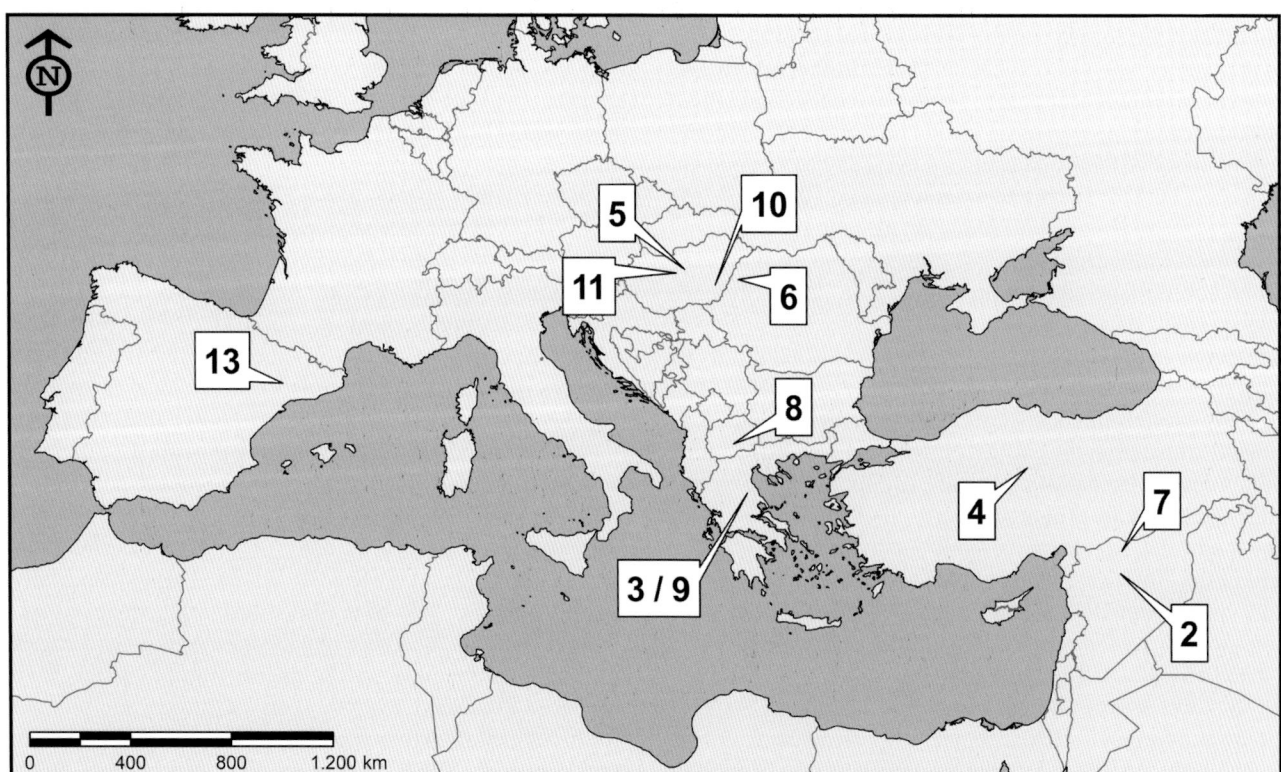

Figure 1.1 Location of study areas covered by papers in this volume, indicating chapter number (cartographic base: Natural Earth).

potential to learn from such archaeological manifestations from a decidedly integral or cross-field approach. To do so, a key point in our joint endeavour has been to explore the topic from other angles, envisaging tells as the material outcomes of cross-cutting dynamics impacted by comparable underlying forces irrespective of time and space. Thus, the book was designed to assemble a representative range of ongoing theory- and science-based fieldwork projects on this kind of site. With the explicit aim of encompassing a rich variety of social and material dynamics, the volume's scope entails an extended diachrony – from the Earliest Neolithic up to the Late Iron Age – and covers a large region – from Iberia in Western Europe to Syria in the Middle East – including periods and areas beyond the customary hotspots of tell archaeology (Fig. 1.1). To our knowledge, these flexible and wide-ranging parameters, intended to convey the actual variability under such an umbrella, are unparalleled when discussing tells. In outline, this volume aims at offering a fresh snapshot of tells as a transversal phenomenon, whose commonalities and divergences are poorly understood yet may benefit from cross-cultural and inter-scholarly comparison.

In order to follow such an extensive course, the book takes a case-based approach. It draws upon a variety of ongoing and stable – long or medium-term – fieldwork projects, led by international and local teams working on tells across the northwestern part of the Old World. These contributions are disparate both in their theoretical foundations – from household archaeology, social agency and formation theory – and in their research strategies – including systematic geophysical survey, micromorphology and high-resolution excavation and dating. Contributors have been asked to present synthetic overviews of their research programmes delving into their first-hand experiences. The commissioned chapters address key questions such as: What discursive or embodied social practices (*e.g.* kinship patterns, commonality, subsistence, defence, maintenance or abandonment chores) contributed to their characteristic superimposed stratification in contrast to those held on flat sites? What are these massive sites made of (*e.g.* everyday refuse, feasting or ritual deposits, sun-dried mud or stone building detritus)? How can we measure and correlate time with sedimentation rates/accumulation trajectories using 'micro-archaeology' science-based methods (micromorphology, taphonomy)? How did these sites relate to mobility/sedentarism and high-/low-density aggregation dynamics? How might excavation and survey datasets support sounder social interpretations? What cultural rationales, notions of relatedness, sensory experiences or arenas for social negotiation may have afforded such archaeology (in terms of cosmology, genealogies, history making and cultural memory, monumentalisation, movement and perception, legitimation of ownership claims)? The next section briefly presents the contributors' responses.

A varied case-based collection to learn from tells

The core of this volume is divided into two parts, with six contributions each drawing on case studies, and a third part with some concluding comments. There is a series of recurring themes addressed by different authors and, to a certain extent, the division of Parts 1 and 2 is conventional, since these interests and topics run through both sections. Chapters in every part are organised in chronological order to convey the idea that these cross-cutting issues transcend habitual fields of study.

Part 1 *The building-up of tell materiality* deals with the physical aspect of tells, a classical theme only very recently tackled by robust science-based methods. This section is opened with the essay by M. Molist, Q. Sisa, J. Wattez and A. Gómez-Bach (Chapter 2), who present their fieldwork at Early Neolithic Tell Halula (Syria), where they have carried out a fine-grained analysis of the site stratigraphy, including sedimentological and geoarchaeological studies that have revealed significant information to approach formation processes. This approach has allowed them to differentiate between building/refurbishing phases (earthen household and monumental architectures), occupation layers (everyday activity episodes) and taphonomic processes. Chapter 3 presents a concise summary by A. Krahtopoulou, C. Frederick, H. Orengo, A. Dimoula, N. Saridaki, S. Kyrillidou, A. Livarda and A. Garcia-Molsosa of their research on the exceptionally rich case of Neolithic Thessaly. Their project challenges scholarly stereotypes and pushes forward the understanding of Neolithic settlement dynamics and social use of space via interdisciplinary landscape fieldwork (remote sensing, geoarchaeological survey data, excavations on both tells and flat extended sites) and new analyses of existing datasets (using photogrammetry and radiocarbon-dating). S. Steadman and J. Ross contour in Chapter 4 the trajectory of the small *höyük* of Çadır (Turkey) over four millennia, from the Late Chalcolithic to the Late Iron Age. Their essay shows how different communities successively occupying the same sectors of the tell led to a striking continuity in both architecture and domestic inventories. The authors explore the motivations for such cultural decisions and outline the influences of earlier material culture on subsequent dwellers. The next contribution, co-authored by R. Staniuk, M. Jaeger, G. Kulcsár, N. Taylor, J. Niebieszczański and J. Müller (Chapter 5), presents the 'Kakucs-Turján Archaeological Expedition' on this Bronze Age multi-layered settlement in Hungary and shows how interdisciplinary research – combining non-invasive and geoarchaeological surveys with thorough stratigraphic excavations – provides key insights into its complex life-histories. This contribution has wider implications for the study of Bronze Age tells throughout the Carpathian region. In Chapter 6, F. Gogâltan, A. Găvan, M. Lie, G. Fazecaș, C. Cordoș and T. Kienlin present the project

'Living in the Bronze Age tell settlements', implemented in Western Romania, which also involved both non-invasive surveys – which targeted 46 multi-layered Bronze Age sites, several ditched – and excavations at the sites of Toboliu and Sântion. This part closes with V. Klinkenberg's paper (Chapter 7) on Tell Sabi Abyad (Syria), an impressive Late Bronze Age outpost of the Assyrian army, whose material culture and ways of deposition suggest the frequent rearrangement of spaces and cast doubts on the overused notion of *in situ* assemblages.

Part 2 *The social lives of tells* delves more into the interpretive problems of tells and encompasses an array of theoretical proposals suitable to this goal. This section of the book starts with the contribution by G. Naumov (Chapter 8) on the Early Neolithic of Pelagonia (Macedonia) drawing on recent excavations in the tell of Vrbjanska Čuka, which epitomises the notion of domesticity and ancestral rootness in wetland settings, in an attempt to emphasise lineages and genealogy within a house ideology based on intensive agricultural production. S. Souvatzi argues in Chapter 9 for approaching tells in terms of social relations, as ever-changing units of sociality far from static, and as the physical embodiment of time and history. Her examination of tells and non-tells from Neolithic Greece exposes the traditional over-emphasis on the contrasts between both site categories, which has curtailed a more nuanced recognition of actual variation. To rebalance the analysis, she explores the interconnection between each other as diverse ways of social integration and kinship organisation and proposes a multi-scalar approach that characterises tells as variable vehicles for change, fully endowed with social agency. Chapter 10 by A. Füzesi, K. Rassmann, E. Bánffy and P. Raczky discusses the case of Late Neolithic Öcsöd-Kováshalom (Hungary), a complex aggregation over 3–5 hectares with a central tell and seven smaller activity clusters divided into concentric zones. This team envisages the monumentalised site as a social arena for the repeated negotiation of social networks in a sort of *lieu de mémoire* representing taskscape configurations. The subsequent contribution by J. Sofaer, M.L.S. Sørensen and M. Vicze (Chapter 11) challenges conventional narratives of cyclical house biographies from their excavation at Bronze Age Százhalombatta (Hungary). They propose a more detailed approach to under-estimated habitual practices of 'dynamic maintenance' that were part and parcel of tell materiality resulting in 'the messiness of everyday life', including disruptions and spatial reorganisations. T. Kienlin offers in Chapter 12 a novel perspective on the sociality, materiality and space of tells, centring his attention on the Bronze Age in the Carpathian Basin. His anti-essentialising account draws on practice theory and particularly on the intellectual frameworks of A. Giddens and Th. Schatzki and takes the archaeological elaboration of J. Barrett as an inspiration to build a robust alternative beyond mainstream grand narratives. Finally, Chapter 13 presents the imposing Iron Age fortress of Els Vilars (Spain) researched by the late Joan López – who sadly passed away while finishing this essay – E. Junyent and N. Alonso. The open-area excavation of the whole tell, a one-off oversized walled enclosure occupied for 400 years, and a large multidisciplinary programme allow a minute account of the site's itinerary and its preponderant role within its landscape.

The last section of the volume (Part 3) includes the insightful remarks by J. Chapman (Chapter 14), who participated very actively in the EAA Barcelona session. In his illuminating essay Chapman reflects on several distinctive features in this anthology. He underlines his amazement at the diverse range of perspectives and concerns among the 13 case studies, as an eclectic timemark of the early 21st century where theoretical and 'atheoretical' contributions coexist. In his view the very definition of tell is challenged throughout the book and tends to dissolve when faced with an extended array of cases beyond the classical ones. From the landscape dimension of tells, Chapman highlights the potential of palaeo-hydrology as a relevant location factor. He also identifies geophysical approaches to site anatomies as the strongest contributions in the volume, coupled with the microscale and intra-site focus, which are yielding fine-grained biographies of both daily chores – deposition and fragmentation patterns, maintenance and abandonment – and extraordinary and communal actions – building of earthen banks, ditches, ramparts, *etc*. Both strands reveal once more an unexpected variability, and demand more theorisation, even a new language. Finally, the four misrepresented themes remarked on by Chapman – yet touched upon in several chapters – are: A direct comparison between the Neolithic/Chalcolithic and Bronze Age/Iron Age cycles; an adequate attention to gender relations; the role of ancestors and social memory; and the agency of tells.

Towards a cross-cultural comparison

This final section intends to synthesise, from a comparative approach, some major points in the state of the field out of the collection of essays that the reader will find in the following pages. These are not new topics or ideas, but the matching of eclectic cases, often distant in time and space – and so far even considered alien and incommensurable – may facilitate fresh insights and lead to habitual arguments being put in perspective.

Thus, a first point is the input of this book in the ongoing debate on why prehistoric tells should occur at all, with diverse contributing factors being assessed. Among them, environment/climate versus culture has been intensively discussed (Rosenstock 2009; Gyucha *et al.* 2013). In this regard, there is wide consensus on refusing any sort of geographic determinism and underscoring the material linking to the past as a key political and symbolic mechanism of tell-building societies. Drawing on a comparative perspective, we should also highlight cultural aspects, because of such interrupted long-term patterns as the above-mentioned case of the Amazonian Lowlands (Scarre 2018) – Middle and Late Archaic *sambaquis* (*c.* 3500–1500 BC) and Arawak mounds of the Camutins group (*c.* AD 600–800) – or in the Carpathian Basin, where we have the cycling of Late Neolithic and late Early to Middle Bronze Age tells with a long hiatus in terms of tells in between (Parkinson 2002; Kienlin 2015, 33), both trajectories without obvious climate oscillations corresponding to their tipping points.

A second point, highlighted by J. Chapman in his comments, is the broad heterogeneity of the contributors' intellectual settings, with some essays theoretically informed – especially in Part 2 – and other more down-to-earth proposals leaning toward culture-historical concerns. In our view, far from being optional choices, these trends are heavily constrained by the state of play in every period and region, and they speak volumes of differences in scholarly background and track record, empirical legacy and fieldwork investment within different research communities. In addition, this may seem a good proxy of the international milieu of archaeologists, where the processual versus post-processual dispute makes little sense, and where many Eurasian regions still demand basic research in terms of functional, cultural and temporal characterisation.

Another crucial point is the transformation of tells as a research topic, which is expanding its definition and meanings, as this book tries to demonstrate, and Chapman notes in his chapter. Thus, several essays (Chapters 3, 5, 6, 9) provide a more nuanced reassessment of tells as a not so distinctive site type as long-held dualistic typologies would have it. This redefinition in particular affects the protruding versus horizontal sites, a traditional classification that these authors contribute to undermine after considering similarities between both archetypes. We should also add that, in terms of taphonomy and preservation vagaries, many sites in the tell-like category are in fact heavily affected by agriculture, as is demonstrably the case of recently assessed cases (*e.g.* Kienlin *et al.* 2018). We are not trying to bump them up into proper tells, yet they warn us that the picture of 'flat' tell-like sites we get is biased as well. In addition, the images emerging from modern geoscience-based surveys (Chapters 3, 5, 6, 10) and open-area excavations (Chapters 2, 8, 10, 11, 13) support the realisation of ample site variability within definite prehistoric landscapes, often including ambiguous cases, *i.e.* multi-layered or tell-like sites. In any case, all these contributions invite us to call into question any purportedly universal scale of variation based on restrictive and mostly context-specific – *i.e.* hardly interchangeable – criteria such as stratification depth, number of layers or phases, compactness of buildings, *etc.* All in all, these developments may lead to envisage a wider continuum of site modalities between the traditional clear-cut extremes. The grey zone between the black and white ends of this spectrum of variation is increasingly better characterised as fieldwork makes progress.

The inclusion in this book, under a flexible concept of tell, of case studies from diverse subfields of archaeological practice will be an obvious issue for most readers. Indeed, this volume aims to contribute to expanding the horizon of knowledge by addressing the subject from complementary and even contradictory angles, under the philosophy of learning from each other. Thus, the collection of these assorted cases should not conceal clear divergences in scholarly interests and approaches between contributions. The bottom line behind such diversity of scopes is the entrenched split between research traditions based on antiquarian prejudices – still very much in keeping with the old Three Ages System – and reproduced by the sociology of academia. However, contrary to the dual divide denounced by J. Chapman in his essay, we unfortunately envisage an even more fragmented and introspective panorama, with a threefold division: a) the centuries-old research field of Neolithic/Chalcolithic tells; b) the theoretically lively and controversial Bronze Age; and c) the Iron Age, almost a newcomer in debates on tells. As has been adequately discussed (Kienlin 2015), Neolithic/Chalcolithic tell narratives often adopt an ascending or bottom-up perspective, attentive to the microscale and framed with topics such as culture, identity and symbolism, so akin to postmodern viewpoints (*e.g.* Chapman 1997a; 1997b; Bailey 1999). By contrast, the Bronze Age has been more frequently addressed from a descending or top-down approach, *i.e.* departing from the socio-political structures and trying to reconstruct long-term processes. This procedure entails the elaboration of grand narratives in political and economic terms, where tells are understood within social landscapes of competition and conflict, populated by aristocracies and inequality (Kristiansen 1998; Earle 2002; Earle *et al.* 2012). The third 'paradigm' entertained here is the Iron Age, whose concept of tell is often used as a hackneyed trope, without pursuing its practical or heuristic consequences further. This is the case of Western and Central European prehistory, where tell is a mere descriptive label to stress the distinctive nature of some long-lived settlements and their massive materiality compared to their contemporary insubstantial counterparts. Cases in point are the Hallstatt D stronghold of the Heuneburg, Germany (Harding 1978, 110–116; Vandkilde 2007, 166–167) or Bronze Age fortresses (Martín *et al.* 1993) and Early Iron Age built-up settlements in Iberia (Álvarez-Sanchís 2000; Armada & Grau 2018). In interpretive terms, despite the increasing number of alternative stances (*e.g.* Moore & Armada 2011; Currás & Sastre 2020) this archaeology too often represents an exacerbation of the sort of discourse and concerns allegedly foreshadowed during the Bronze Age. This reasoning is frequently favoured by protohistorians and ancient historians. Indeed, in mainstream accounts of the 1st millennium BC, the atomised landscapes of integrated and hierarchical polities feature prominently (*e.g.* Kristiansen 1998; Vandkilde 2007). Since these scholars are very likely to be tempted to seek nucleated and stable centres of power and their ancillary and ephemeral nuclei, predictably tells and non-tells are prone to be subsumed under such logic.

The above threefold outline has some bearing on themes intersecting this volume. The first thing to note is that thorough descriptions focusing on the 'everyday' in the meantime may be found in the research of the Earliest Neolithic tells right through to the Bronze Age. These contributors often display what may be perceived as broadly processual leanings towards the natural sciences, from the reconstruction of prehistoric landscapes and climate down to household practices by micromorphology, *etc.* Accordingly, in this respect their inference procedure is more akin to the ascending or bottom-up one and aimed at highly-textured accounts and bold readings. This perspective seems to be gaining momentum over top-down approaches, yet there is still a divide in terms of listening to the evidence and to what interpretative framework this focus on the micro-scale is linked to. Thus, various contributions here resort to scientific methods to delve into themes such as the economy and subsistence of tell-dwellers or the architecture and formation processes of tells, but also to more interpretive issues such as demarcation, experience, motivation, identity or symbolism (Chapters 2–6, 8, 9, 11, 12). These concerns are often still found rather on the Neolithic side, and they clearly have affinities towards broadly speaking post-processual approaches. In this sense, good post-processual archaeology, such as the contextualised understanding of social practices and their material conditions outlined by J. Barrett (1994), imposes much higher demands on the archaeological data at hand than processual 'checklist' archaeology (*e.g.* Renfrew 1973a; 1973b). The same holds true for current macro-histories and large-scale narratives (*e.g.* Kristiansen & Suchowska-Ducke 2015), often still found instead on the Bronze Age side and largely aloof from the actual material remains of past social lives. A widely held perception associates methodological advances with broadly speaking processual archaeology and its current successors (*cf.* González-Ruibal 2014; Kristiansen 2014). However, it is the detailed reconstruction of past social practices, invariably bound to practical understandings and the expedient manipulation of a material world, that requires the more fine-grained excavation techniques and scientific analyses – a prominent example being, of course, I. Hodder's fieldwork at Çatalhöyük, irrespective of his ensuing interpretations (*e.g.* Hodder 2006). That is to say that with a practice-oriented approach, we are certainly not moving up some ladder of archaeological inference towards the more abstract and impossible to know. However, it is also necessary to acknowledge that we often still lack data applicable to the detailed accounting of past social practices and material arrangements that are aimed at.

By contrast, contributors working with later periods (Chapters 7, 13) and also with the Bronze Age more widely (several papers delivered in the EAA session, yet regrettably not included here) may have strong hints and reasons – ramparts, specialised sites, military paraphernalia, written sources, *etc.* – to embrace a top-down perspective in terms of political economy, with fortification and centralisation as chief arguments. Our point here is that these readings might also benefit from considering traditionally downplayed aspects under the wide banner of moral economy – *i.e.* the moral values and agencies cited in J. Chapman's chapter. Examples of these disregarded topics may be the cohesive dimension of some fortified sites in terms of their temporal depth, as communal landmarks or places of refuge and defence for scattered populations, or the very notion of building upon the superimposed remains of forebears as a way of anchoring identities. We should not forget that centripetal and levelling ethical mechanisms are always present in society and are – and were – even more crucial in highly ranked, unequal and integrated polities (Scott 2009; Currás & Sastre 2020). Another unchallenged aspect in accounts on 2nd and 1st millennia BC tells is the supposedly unproblematic and taken-for-granted nature of their physicality. Their vertical building-up is indeed regarded as the straight reflection of long-lasting stability coupled with the cumulative – and almost inadvertent and natural (?) – side effect of building with earthen and stone architecture. Thus, contrary to the vibrant interpretive atmosphere surrounding Neolithic and Chalcolithic sites, the layers, deposits and assemblages from Bronze and Iron Age tells are often envisaged in utilitarian terms as socially deactivated debris and trash. However, we are only finding what we are looking for. No parallels – or counterexamples – are sought in terms of lifestyles, household dynamics, waste management or building and abandoning practices in earlier periods. This would contribute to challenging the misleading rampant familiarity of the Bronze and Iron Ages, as denounced decades ago (Hill 1993) and still very apparent in current literature. To a certain extent, the shorter the archaeologists' time distance with their subjects, the weaker and more blurred their otherness.

Final remarks

The state of affairs of tell archaeology condensed here faces a classical problem of equifinality. We can recognise sites from different prehistoric periods and regions with similar morphologies, which might or might not be the result of concurrent social and taphonomic dynamics, and we should untangle them. We need to characterise the idiosyncrasy of their trajectories using diverse lines of information and responding to an even more extended array of queries. The mobilisation and exploration of cross-field topics and untested avenues of enquiry is promising in this regard. However, in order to facilitate cross-fertilisation and cross-cultural comparisons between tells, we need to recover comparable samples and records, processed with similar procedures and responding to shared research questions. The increasing implementation of advanced non-invasive geophysical methods or thin-section microstratigraphy are already contributing to provide us with standardised, more accurate and analogous pictures of biographies and anatomies of tells or semi-micro-palimpsests of their landscapes. Yet these new dimensions of the material record require a deeper theorisation, since the mere accumulation of information is unlikely to make any breakthrough. To start bridging the gap between academic subfields we should transcend parochial context-dependent parameters (*vide supra*) and assess key transversal phenomena such as demographics and household patterns, maintenance and abandonment cycles, physical demarcation, defence, history making or ancestor linkage. In this vein, we may resort to kinship theory, as demonstrated by S. Souvatzi with the Greek Neolithic (Chapter 9) or pay adequate attention to social practices (Chapters 11, 12). In this way we may expect to overcome current pitfalls and gain deeper glimpses into the alterity of these fascinating sites referred to here as tells.

Acknowledgements

The research stay of ABG at the University of Cologne was generously funded by the Deutscher Akademischer Austauschdienst (German Academic Exchange Service). We are very grateful to the organising committee at the EAA Annual Meeting at Barcelona for accepting to include our session in their tight schedule and for facilitating things during that event. This volume is the outcome of a huge collaborative enterprise, only possible thanks to the commitment, enthusiasm and effort of 40 internationally renowned scholars, friends and colleagues from ten countries. A special thank you is due to Joan López and Natàlia Alonso for their generosity and involvement with this project in especially difficult times. John Chapman invigorated debates and kindly accepted to act as a discussant for this book. The editorial tasks went more smoothly thanks to the extra help by Alexandra Găvan and Gian-Luca Paul, and Ian Copestake with the English proofreading. We would also like to thank Julie Gardiner and Jessica Scott from Oxbow Books for their encouragement and technical support during the edition and production of the volume in the tough circumstances of early–mid-2020.

References

Álvarez-Sanchís, J.R. (2000) The Iron Age in western Spain (800 BC–AD 50): An overview. *Oxford Journal of Archaeology* 19(1), 65–89.

Armada, X.L. & Grau, I. (2018) The Iberian Peninsula. In C. Haselgrove, K. Rebay-Salisbury & P.S. Wells (eds), *The Oxford Handbook of the European Iron Age*, 1–43. Oxford, Oxford University Press.

Bailey, D.W. (1999) What is a Tell? Settlement in fifth millennium Bulgaria. In J. Brück & M. Goodman (eds), *Making Places in the Prehistoric World. Themes in Settlement Archaeology*, 94–111. London, University College London.

Barrett, J.C. (1994) *Fragments from Antiquity. An Archaeology of Social Life in Britain, 2900–1200 BC*. Oxford, Blackwell.

Chapman, J. (1989) The early Balkan village. *Varia Archaeologica Hungarica* 2, 33–53.

Chapman, J. (1997a) Places as timemarks – the social construction of prehistoric landscapes in eastern Hungary. In J. Chapman & P. Dolukhanov (eds), *Landscapes in Flux. Central and Eastern Europe in Antiquity*, 137–161. Oxford, Oxbow Books.

Chapman, J. (1997b) The origins of tells in Eastern Hungary. In P. Topping (ed.), *Neolithic Landscapes*, 139–164. Oxford, Neolithic Studies Group Seminar Papers 2.

Currás, B.X. & Sastre, I. (2020) *Alternative Iron Ages. Social Theory from Archaeological Analysis*. Oxford, Routledge.

Earle, T.K. (2002) *Bronze Age Economics. The Beginnings of Political Economies*. Boulder CO, Westview.

Earle, T., Kiss, V., Kulcsár, G., Szerényi, V. & Polányi, T. (2012) Bronze Age landscapes in the Benta Valley – research on the hinterland of Bronze Age centres. *Hungarian Archaeology e-journal* 1–4.

Fischl, K.P. & Kienlin, T.L. (2019) *Beyond Divides – The Otomani-Füzesabony Phenomenon. Current Approaches to Settlement and Burial in the North-eastern Carpathian Basin and Adjacent Areas*. Bonn, Universitätsforschungen zur Prähistorischen Archäologie 345.

González-Ruibal, A. (2014) Archaeological revolutions. *Swedish Archaeological Review* 22, 41–45.

Gyucha, A., Duffy, P.R. & Parkinson, W.A. (2013) Prehistoric human-environmental interactions on the Great Hungarian Plain. *Ethnologie* 51(2), 157–168.

Harding, D. (1978) *Prehistoric Europe*. Oxford, Elsevier-Phaidon.

Hill, J.D. (1993) Can we recognise a different European past? A contrastive archaeology of later prehistoric settlements in southern England. *Journal of European Archaeology* 1, 57–75.

Hodder, I, (2006) *Çatalhöyük. The Leopard's Tale*. London, Thames and Hudson.

Hofmann, R., Moetz, F.-K. & Müller, J. (2012) *Tells. Environmental and Social Space*. Bonn, Universitätsforschungen zur Prähistorischen Archäologie 207.

Kienlin, T.L. (2015) *Bronze Age Tell Communities in Context – An Exploration Into Culture, Society, and the Study of European Prehistory. Part 1: Critique. Europe and the Mediterranean*. Oxford, Archaeopress.

Kienlin, T.L., Fischl, K.P. & Pusztai, T. (2018) *Borsod Region Bronze Age Settlement (BORBAS). Catalogue of the Early to Middle Bronze Age Tell Sites Covered by Magnetometry and Surface Survey.* Bonn, Habelt.

Kristiansen, K. (1998) *Europe Before History.* Cambridge, Cambridge University Press.

Kristiansen, K. (2014) Towards a new paradigm? The third science revolution and its possible consequences in archaeology. *Swedish Archaeological Review* 22, 11–34.

Kristiansen, K. & Suchowska-Ducke, P. (2015) Connected histories: The dynamics of Bronze Age interaction and trade 1500–1100 BC. *Proceedings of the Prehistoric Society* 81, 361–392.

Liverani, M. (2016) *Imagining Babylon. The Modern Story of an Ancient City.* Berlin, De Gruyter.

Martín, C., Fernández-Miranda, M., Fernández-Posse, M.D. & Gilman, A. (1993) The Bronze Age of La Mancha. *Antiquity* 67(254), 23–45.

Matthews, W. (2014) Tells in archaeology. In C. Smith (ed.), *Encyclopedia of Global Archaeology.* New York, Springer.

Moore, T. & Armada, X.L. (2011) *Atlantic Europe in the First Millennium BC. Crossing the Divide.* Oxford, Oxford University Press.

Parkinson, W.A. (2002) Integration, interaction, and tribal 'cycling': The transition to the Copper Age on the Great Hungarian Plain. In W.A. Parkinson (ed.), *The Archaeology of Tribal Societies,* 391–438. Ann Arbor MI, International Monographs in Prehistory.

Renfrew, C. (1973a) *Social Archaeology: An Inaugural Lecture.* Southampton, University of Southampton.

Renfrew, C. (1973b) Monuments, mobilization and social organization in Neolithic Wessex. In C. Renfrew (ed.), *The Explanation of Culture Change: Models in Prehistory,* 539–558. London, Duckworth.

Rosenstock, E. (2009) *Tells in Südwestasien und Südosteuropa. Entstehung, Verbreitung und Definition eines Siedlungsphänomens.* Remshalden, Urgeschichtliche Studien II.

Scarre, C. (2018) *The Human Past. World Prehistory and the Development of Human Societies* (4th edition). London, Thames & Hudson.

Scott, J.C. (2009) *The Art of Not Being Governed. An Anarchist History of Upland Southeast Asia.* New Haven CO, Yale University Press.

Smith, M.E. & Peregrine, P.N. (2012) Approaches to comparative analysis in archaeology. In M.E. Smith (ed.), *The Comparative Archaeologies of Complex Societies,* 4–20. Cambridge, Cambridge University Press.

Vandkilde, H. (2007) *Culture and Change in Central European Prehistory. 6th to 1st millennium BC.* Aarhus, Aarhus University Press.

Wilkinson, T.J. (2003) *Archaeological Landscapes of the Near East.* Tucson AZ, University of Arizona Press.

PART 1

THE BUILDING-UP OF TELL MATERIALITY

2

Architectural Phases, Use-life Episodes and Taphonomic Processes in Tell Formation: An Approach to Neolithic Tell Halula (Syria)

Miquel Molist, Quim Sisa, Julia Wattez and Anna Gómez-Bach

Introduction

Fieldwork carried out at the site of Tell Halula, a settlement in the middle Euphrates valley (Syria), has allowed detailed analysis of the stratigraphy, together with a study of the sedimentological composition and other analytical approaches to the formation of the tell. In this contribution, the main characteristics of these processes are analysed and discussed, differentiating above all between architectural phases (earthen architecture with both domestic and monumental evidence), occupation levels (life/activity episodes) and taphonomic dynamics.

Like any tell-type site, Tell Halula is the result of the complex combination of the ruins of architectonic constructions and deposits of anthropogenic remains resulting from several human occupations over a period of time. In turn, these remains have been subject to natural and human modifications in the form of post-depositional alterations.

Due to the circumstances occurring in the formation of this type of site, where most of the sediments are of human origin, they become an important source for the study of past societies and their close relationship with the surrounding environment. In addition, tell-type sites also contain natural deposits, which can be studied to identify possible environmental or climate indicators that might have affected the human groups that occupied them. Therefore, both aeolian and hydrological agents should be considered because, as well as contributing to the accumulation of natural sediments, they can cause the alteration of the site through erosion (Davidson 1976; Rosen 1986). It is therefore essential to discriminate between the natural and anthropic formation processes (Butzer 1982; Schiffer 1987).

The study of the formation of tells has been approached from different perspectives through geoarchaeological techniques. First, some studies have focused on the architecture and, to be more precise, on the type of building materials. This is because the structural characteristics are important to understand the growth and development of the site at the same time as they offer a way to understand human interaction with nature as regards the use of natural resources, as well as to determine the post-depositional processes that might have affected the record (Goldberg 1979; Rosen 1986; Love 2013; Marchiori 2015; Sapir *et al.* 2018).

Second, other research has studied the formation of this type of site at a regional or *extra-site* scale, focusing on the evolution of the landscape, the geomorphology and environmental conditions with comparative studies that include such techniques as Geographic Information Systems (GIS), geochemical analysis of sediments and microstratigraphy, in which the role played historically by humans is left in the background (Liebowitz & Folk 1980; Bar-Yosef 1993; Barton & Clarke 1993; Akkermann *et al.* 2005; Maghsoudi *et al.* 2014; Ullmann *et al.* 2019).

Another important kind of study is linked to the different uses given to the site in order to characterise the activity areas and understand the phases and strategies of occupation that took place. The objective is to ascertain the tell formation processes at a smaller or *intra-site* scale. The main analytical technique in this case is the micromorphology of soils, often complemented by other geochemical, biochemical and sedimentological techniques (Wattez & Courty 1996; Matthews *et al.* 1997; 2014; Shillito & Matthews 2013; Sedov *et al.* 2017; Koromila *et al.* 2018).

Thus, the geoarchaeological study of tell formation processes may involve many approaches and strategies, depending on the problems to be addressed and the questions to be solved. This does not exclude the overlapping of different analytical techniques.

In the present study, the formation processes of the site of Tell Halula will be approached through the contrast between the use of space, in terms of structural or building remains and the use and degradation of those remains. The stratigraphic and microstratigraphic formation of the settlement will be described together with the architectonic phases that have been identified, their characteristics, use and process of abandonment and/or reuse. Two parts of the settlement displaying completely different formation processes have been chosen; the first consisting of domestic architecture and uses, and the second formed by large architectonic structures with a communal use, dated to the second half of the 8th and first half of the 7th millennia BC.

Brief presentation of Tell Halula

The middle valley of the River Euphrates is known as one of the areas in the Near East with the most interesting archaeological record informing about the neolithisation process. The archaeological site of Tell Halula is in this valley, about 150 km to the east of the modern city of Aleppo (Syria). It was discovered by archaeological surveying in 1989. From 1991 to 2011 a stable scientific project concentrated on excavating a part of the site and performing a detailed archaeological analysis enabling a historical interpretation of the social, economic and cultural development of the human group that lived in the settlement. No excavations have been carried out in recent years because of the war, but the analysis and studies based on the archaeological record obtained previously have continued.[1] In this way, the excavation and research project has been able to characterise the main occupations and define the different types of use, such as the architectonic structures, the economic system, including the definition of the plant and animal domestication processes, and technological transformations. The archaeological excavation, covering about 2500 m², has differentiated 38 occupation phases[2] with several thousands of stratigraphic units identified, and has documented a practically continuous occupation from 7800 to

Figure 2.1 General view of the site.

5700 BC. The analysis of the remains, including relative and absolute dates, has allowed those anthropic occupations to be matched to the following periods: middle and recent phases of the Pre-Pottery Neolithic B (PPNB); Pre-Halaf phase of the Pottery Neolithic (PN); and the Neolithic–Chalcolithic transition (Halaf culture) (Molist 1996; 2013; 2016).

The site is currently in the form of an artificial hill, roughly circular in shape, covering about 8 ha and about 11 m in height in the southwest, the highest part of the tell (Fig. 2.1). The southern slope is steep, whereas the western, eastern and northern sides are gentler. One of the first objectives of the excavation was to determine the stratigraphic sequence and attempt to define the surface areas of the different phases. This work, during the 1990s, achieved an initial characterisation of the formation of the stratigraphic sequence, the anthropic area and the post-depositional processes it had suffered. At a methodological level, this first fieldwork phase included geoarchaeological studies[3] in addition to the classic archaeological excavation methods of prehistoric sites.

The fieldwork carried out since 2000 has focused on excavating some of the occupation phases over a wider area to understand the human occupations in some periods more extensively. In the course of the whole project, both biotic and abiotic remains in the material record were subjected to different kinds of analyses and studies.

Within the objectives of this chapter, we would like to note that the study and characterisation of the architectonic techniques and constructions have been constant during the project, partly because of their importance for an ethnographic and archaeological understanding of the settlement but also influenced by their good state of conservation. A faithful reconstruction has been made for the PPNB period, consisting of a habitat layout with houses joined together on an east–west alignment. The standardised habitation unit was made of rectangular pluri-cellular houses. In more recent periods, standardisation was lost both in the type of buildings and in their arrangement. The houses were more dispersed, with large open spaces between the habitation units. Circular or *tholos*-type constructions appeared between the mid-7th and 6th millennia as habitat and/or domestic structures complementary to the rectangular houses that continued in use (Molist *et al.* 2014; Molist 2016; Molist & Gómez 2018). New methodologies for the study of adobe as the main building material have documented a differential use depending on the architectonic purpose and have examined the resistance and robustness of earth-based building materials (Marchiori 2015).

Study of Tell Halula in the PPNB period

The stable excavation and research project has allowed the study of a large sample of the archaeological record at the site. Bearing in mind the objectives of the present paper, it will concentrate on the two most representative site formation processes. On one hand it will study the geoarchaeological processes in the domestic areas in the PPNB occupation and on the other hand it will refer to the monumental or collective constructions corresponding to the late PPNB and the PN or Pre-Halaf periods (Fig. 2.2).

Tell formation in domestic areas in Sector 2/4 at Tell Halula

The site of Tell Halula is located on Upper Eocene terrain and largely delimited by two permanent water-courses, the Wadi Abu Gal Gal and the Wadi el Fars, tributaries of the River Euphrates, which flows less than a kilometre away. The Eocene materials at the base of the tell consist of very light-coloured shaley limestone with remains of crinoid, globigerina and miliolid fossils (Álvarez 2013, 25). The natural terrain is divided by practically vertical fractures aligned north–south and the dynamic actions of external geological agents have formed semi-desert plains towards the north and west. The Quaternary deposits in the area correspond to the terraces that the *wadis* (*i.e.*, discontinuous riverbeds) have left over the Upper Eocene bedrock. They are very homogeneous, formed by slightly rounded pebbles from the erosion of Eocene and Miocene materials. This geological basement, which can be clearly identified around the whole settlement, is the sedimentary foundation for the archaeological deposits. In the southern part of the settlement (Sector 2/4) the archaeological levels consist of the accumulation of the building ruins still *in situ*, the sedimentary mass from the destruction/erosion of part of the buildings and the anthropic layers produced by the activities of the community. However, this composition varies in the areas outside the habitat, where some disperse remains and/or accumulations of building materials may be found, but the high volume of biotic elements and/or remains result in a different sedimentary characterisation. The excavation and study of these layers has allowed the reconstruction of architectonic structures, the observation of strata produced by the deterioration and destruction of part of the houses (normally the upper part and the roof), and also sediments associated with human activities. The identification of a structural association of the different strata has enabled approaching their temporality at an archaeological level. To summarise, the remains of the human occupations with their corresponding anthropic activity create an accumulative sedimentary deposit in synchronic and diachronic terms. The final result is the product of the successive deposition and subsequent erosion of materials corresponding to human occupation over long periods of time.

In general, the archaeological levels belonging to the oldest phases are relatively homogeneous since in most cases all these strata are associated with domestic buildings and daily life. The best-known levels correspond to

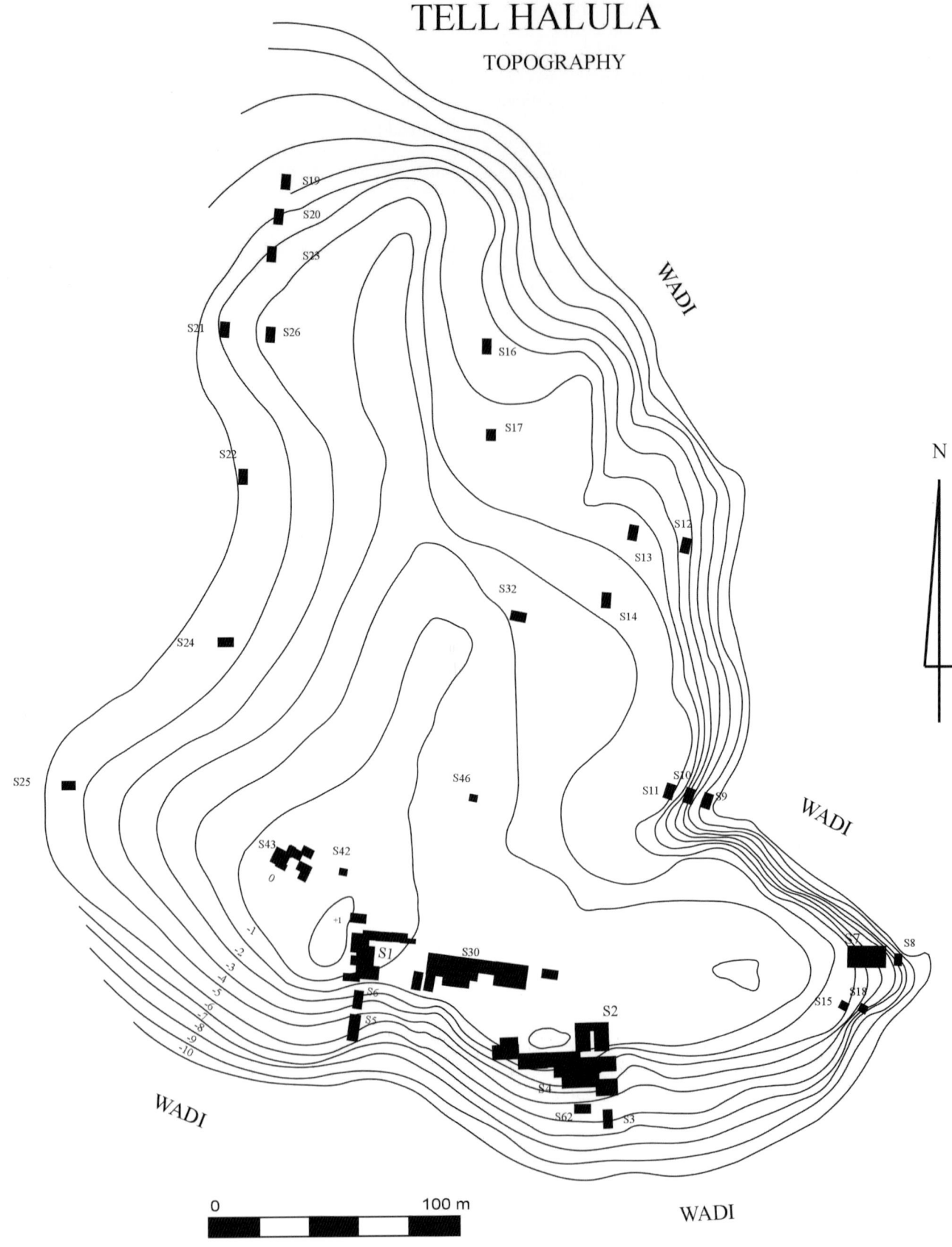

Figure 2.2 Tell Halula topography and sectors.

Figure 2.3 Example of the superposition of domestic areas in Sector 2/4.

the Middle PPNB (Sector 4), a period characterised by the rapid and continual superimposition of domestic buildings, with the conservation of levels between 1 m and 1.5 m thick (Fig. 2.3). These attest to the sequence of superimposition and reconstruction of each domestic unit above the remains of the previous construction. The continuity in the new buildings is particularly significant, as the orientation of the constructions is maintained, and the previous structures are partially reused. Together with the ruins of the buildings themselves, the levels include occupation, destruction and abandonment strata. The destruction and abandonment levels may in turn be altered (removed, filled with sediment, …) for the next building phase.

The successive accumulation of archaeological levels in the same area and sector has led to a total number of 14 layers being identified, all displaying great continuity. However, two factors of change must be mentioned. First, from the palaeo-ethnographic perspective, the documentation of variations and transformations in the use and the architectonic changes in the structures indicate the progressive 'use-life' of the level. Thus, inside the buildings it is usual to find repairs and/or reconstructions of the floors, hearths and ovens (raised structures) and changes in the layout (or the final abandonment) of interior domestic elements (benches, doors, alcoves, silos, *etc.*). In outside areas, it is difficult to establish the stratigraphic relationship, and indirectly the chronological association, of each precise stratum with a particular building. In this regard, the juxtaposition of different outer 'decapages' with the walls allows a correct association and is of great help in the overall analysis, especially as most of the archaeological remains (particularly bones and chipped lithic artefacts) are usually concentrated in the outer areas.

In the upper archaeological levels in this sector, the uniformity is lost, and the strata are superimposed in a more irregular way, even though no natural layer (aeolian deposits, erosion, *etc.*) indicates a temporary abandonment of the area. In the study that has been carried out, the explanation is linked to changes in the use of the area, which becomes much more disperse, and in the architecture, with less investment in labour and technology. Thus, the evidence of habitation, while unequal, is characterised by both rectangular and circular houses, built on a stone base and using earthen building materials, and with beaten earth floors. These are associated with habitation and activity spaces for the different human groups. The strata are thinner, indicating a very different abandonment pattern than in the previous sectors. This may be regarded as sporadic, with few episodes of intentional filling-in and also with precarious conservation of the use and abandonment levels.

Finally, in the upper part of the tell, Sectors 2, 30 and 38–49 have been excavated over a wide area, albeit unequally, and have revealed a long sequence that began in the Pre-Halaf (*c.* 7000 BC) and continued until the late Halaf (5300 BC). This large surface is in the southern half of the upper platform of the tell and exposed to serious edaphological and anthropic phenomena. Crop fields and aeolian and hydrological erosion have affected much of this upper part of the site.

Micromorphological study of the sedimentary and architectonic process in domestic buildings

An initial micromorphological study of the sediments was performed (Wattez & Courty 1996) through the analysis of thin-sections of sedimentological samples extracted without disturbing the materials. It is based on the differentiation of micro-stratigraphic units corresponding to natural or anthropic facies, using the well-established descriptive criteria for this type of research (Bullock *et al.* 1985; Courty *et al.* 1989; Stoops 2003). In this way, it is possible to ascertain the nature and history of each of the levels identified in the field.

The sampling consisted of extracting discontinuous blocks of earth, marking their orientation and without disturbing them. The aim was to evaluate the quality of the sedimentary information and obtain an overall view of the mode of occupation in the transition from the Middle PPNB to the Pre-Halaf Pottery Neolithic in Sectors S1 and S2/4 (Wattez & Courty 1996). Here we shall analyse the blocks from Sector 2/4 characterised by domestic architecture dated to the older occupation. A total of ten samples were taken both from outer areas associated with domestic structures and from the interiors of buildings (Fig. 2.4). As can be imagined in the case of a tell-type site, the strata sampled at Tell Halula display a high degree of anthropisation and the natural facies are restricted to the units subjected to destructuration of anthropic sedimentary features by pedological phenomena. Biological activity is also evident, mainly insect cavities, while crystallisation of soluble salts and carbonates resulted from humectation-desiccation cycles, which caused fragmentation of the original sedimentary matrixes.

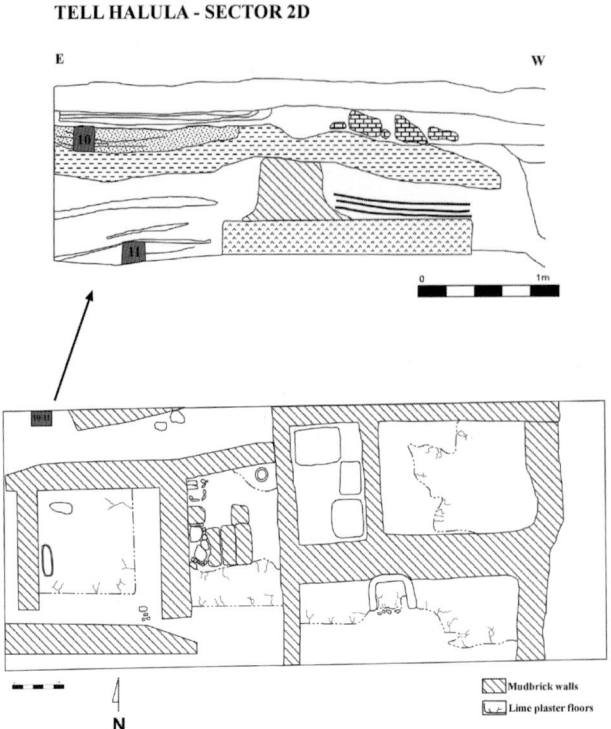

Figure 2.4 Situation of some of the micromorphological samples (Ha-10, Ha-11) taken from the domestic area.

Two main types of strata formation have been differentiated in the anthropic facies. Some are due to the preparation, planning and regularisation of the area and others are the result of their use. In the case of the outer areas, the study revealed a continual sequence and alternation of the two facies with short episodes of abandonment between them, when pedological features tended to appear. The preparation and planning of the outer spaces are characterised mainly by soils that have received some form of treatment. This made them into constructed floors with remains of earthen building materials. Three general types of surfaces can be differentiated. First, some floors consist of levels of well mixed and compacted silt and clay, sometimes with plant materials as cohesive matter and occasionally remains of herbivore coprolites, which attest to the use of raw material from habitation levels. Second, in a very similar way to these floors, large accumulations of plant materials and phytoliths are concentrated in a laminated layer, suggesting a floor with a plant cover in the form of matting. On occasions, accumulations of carbonates and coverings of very fine clay are caused by water circulation, either during cleaning and maintenance activities or because of the climatological factor. Finally, floors in outer areas were very occasionally covered with a layer of lime. The remains of building materials were disintegrated by biological activity and human action in the maintenance and preparation tasks during times of reoccupation. The use facies appear as activity surfaces with large accumulations of waste. To a greater or lesser extent, they contain remains from fires (bones, charcoal and ash), coprolites, lumps of detritus and plant remains. Biological alterations are observed most frequently in this type of strata. Trampling is also seen and, together with the orientation and laminar structure of the micro-remains, it attests to frequent use episodes of the area. Unlike the outer areas, use facies are not found in the house interiors. Instead, the interiors are characterised by a continuous sequence of constructed floors that indicate the different phases of occupation and episodes of repair and maintenance. Floors made with compacted clay and covered with lime have been detected, some of them with a vegetal cover. No remains of waste have been observed, which demonstrates frequent maintenance work.

Tell formation in areas of monumental architecture or collective work in Sectors 1 and 7

The open-air occupation areas associated with monumental constructions are located in Sectors 1 and 7. This type of deposit and structure is not common at Neolithic sites in the Near East, and therefore their formation will be analysed here. They have been described in previous works, but their formation and development have not been analysed and interpreted before. The first point to note is the absence of evidence of monumental structures on the surface. Therefore, the initial objective of the first excavations (1991 and 1992) was to study the most recent occupations at the site, based on the assumption that the latest and/or most significant historical occupations would be located in the upper part of the tell (Sector 1) and in the confluence of the two rivers that flow around the settlement (Sector 7).

Thus, Sector 1, in the south-western part of the tell, was excavated over a total surface area of 185 m². It revealed a new and interesting stratigraphic sequence, 4.5 m deep without reaching the natural base of the tell, and established continuity in the occupations from the recent PPNB to the Final Halaf period (Fig. 2.5). The most significant feature in this area is a monumental constructive element, interpreted as a large terracing wall (E 101) that was 3.2 m high from the base of the excavated area and dated to the start of the recent PPNB. The 20 m long excavation in this sector allowed to determine its morphological and construction characteristics. It was built with large stone boulders only slightly pre-shaped but well-laid in irregular rows that become gradually smaller near the top. The whole wall is very stable. It is orientated on a south-north alignment with a slight curve towards the west (see Fig. 2.6) and has an average thickness of 60 cm. In the profile in Sector 1 it is clearly inclined towards the west.

The excavation revealed the contact between the archaeological deposits and Structure E101 on its eastern or outer face in its whole height. The strata do not include any built

Figure 2.5 Sector 1 – Structure E101.

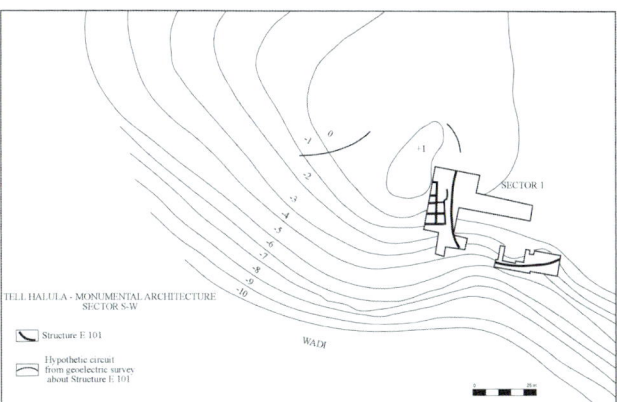

Figure 2.6 Location of the monumental architecture and geoelectric survey.

series of habitation levels and domestic buildings like those in Sector 2/4 described above. For this reason, it has been interpreted as a terracing wall, because it was built against a wall face formed by old domestic occupations (Fig. 2.7). The question is therefore: what was this large terracing structure for? The answer obtained in the first studies is that it was supporting a large building, located to the west or interior of the wall and above the high platform, which can be related stratigraphically with the start of the construction of the great wall. This is a pluri-cellular rectangular building with beaten earth floors whose stone basements still survive. Although the floor plan is not complete, it was dated both relatively (by the stratigraphy) and absolutely and this has shown that it was coetaneous with the building of the large wall. This archaic and specific occupation was followed by a reoccupation and reuse of the same area during the 7th and 6th millennia BC, when the construction remained in use. Therefore, towards the east, outside the wall, a compact sequence of exterior floors has been documented, with abundant evidence of anthropic activity, whereas on the upper part of the platform further occupation levels consist basically of beaten earth floors and a large number of pits. The same type of evidence (exterior floors and pits) continues to form the main archaeological evidence of more recent occupations in the upper part of the site belonging to the Halaf culture. A circular construction or *tholos* has also been documented. A final occupation, with remains of a rectangular building, belongs to the time of the Final Halaf. To be more precise, the stratigraphy and occupations in this sector are conditioned by the existence and reuse of the great wall (E101), which, with a height of over 3 m, formed a platform built at the end of the Pre-Pottery Neolithic phase (late PPNB) and which continued in use throughout the 7th and 6th millennia. This north-to-south wall separated the strata corresponding to later occupations on the eastern and western sides of the wall and which differ over 1 m in height.

Two complementary actions were taken to obtain a fuller understanding of the constructions, the sedimentary processes and ultimately the appearance of the area in the Neolithic. They consisted of geo-electrical surveying in the northern part of Sector 1 and another excavation area in the south, aligned towards the east (Sector 30 west). These would allow to establish the possible continuity of the terracing and its stratigraphic characterisation. The results were very interesting because the geo-electrical signal indicated a south–north dividing line which may be interpreted with much precaution as the continuation of the wall towards the north (Valdés *et al.* 2013). The evidence obtained in the extension of the excavation in the southeast is more solid. It documented the continuation of the wall (E101) although its state of conservation is worse as only the last rows of stone blocks have been preserved with their associated strata. It is interesting that the wall curves towards the eastern part of the settlement. Additionally, the excavation in the outer part of

structures and instead had likely been formed by open-air tasks; *i.e.* exterior floors with evidence of anthropic activities (see *infra*). A section at the southern end of the wall showed that it had been joined on its western face to a

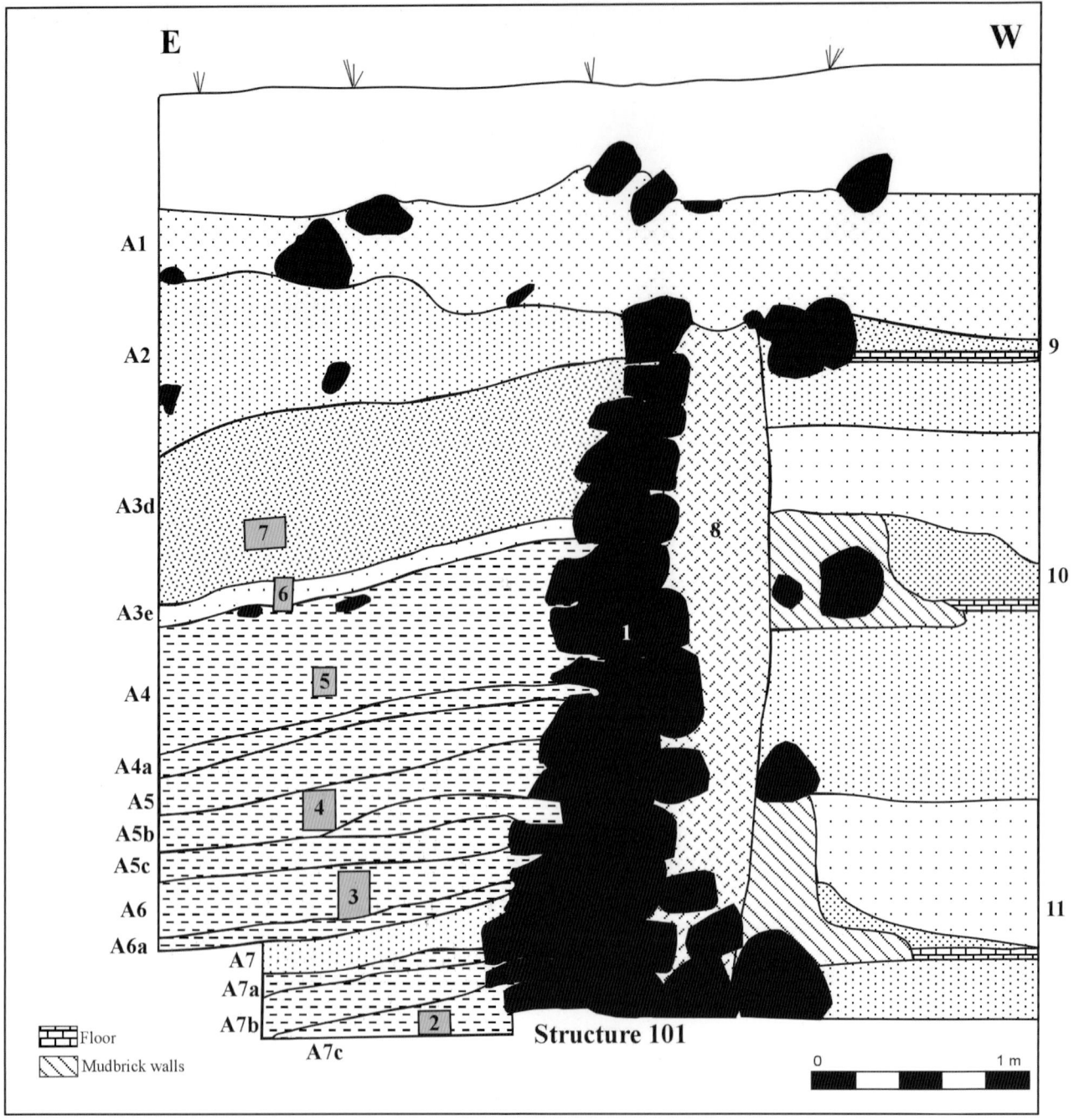

Figure 2.7 Profile of the structure E101. 1: Structure E101; 2–7: micromorphological samples; 8: trench of E101 cutting the previous domestic structures; 9: complex pluri-cellular building located on top of the artificial terrace; 10–11 superimposition of previous domestic structures cut by E101.

the wall, to the north of it, revealed a series of archaeological deposits that, like in Sector 1, covered the 7th and 6th millennia BC but which included constructions. Two stone walls were discovered (equally preserved in few rows), each of them as a repair or reconstruction of the initial terracing wall. The stratigraphic evidence and elements of relative chronology (archaeological materials in the associated strata) indicated their construction in one case in the late 7th millennium BC and in the other during an indeterminate time of the Halaf period. Thus, the evidence indicated that the area originally had a totally different morphology from its current appearance. It would have been characterised by a high part of the settlement both in the west (Sector 1) and in the south (Sector 2/4), partly supported by the large terracing wall (E101) (Fig. 2.8). Outside the wall, a depression or lower open space would have been used for diverse domestic activities (see *infra*). The area would have been first arranged in this way at the end of the 8th millennium and would have lasted for over a millennium, with a substantial difference. Although towards the west (Sector 1) the wall is stable and was not repaired, in the south it had to be rebuilt on different occasions. It should be noted that this area has suffered most erosion, even today, because of its location next to the *wadi*.

The occupations dated to the first quarter of the 7th millennium BC (Pre-Halaf, *c.* 6700 BC) display other interesting evidence of monumental structures with complex formation processes. This has been found in Sector SS7 (excavated surface area of 228 m^2) defined generally as an area without domestic habitation. Stone alignments were identified as walls (Walls E10, E6 and E4). These are dry-stone walls, preserved to an average height of 1.30 m, in one of which a gate or access area was observed. They were built with medium-sized stones, which had not been shaped, and they have been interpreted as a perimeter wall enclosing the settlement (Molist 1996; 1998) (Fig. 2.9). This interpretation is based on the great difference in the nature of the archaeological deposits on the eastern or outer side of the wall and on the western or inner side. Thus, while the strata on the eastern side are formed by an irregular amalgam of diverse unconnected materials and can be interpreted as the consequence of the erosion and destruction of constructions, the interior strata consist of a series of open-air levels and beaten-earth floors, over a base of small pebbles and with numerous reuses. After documenting them all and grouping together the different archaeological strata in this area, a series of 13 levels has been determined, characterised by phases of use and abandonment. In those interior open areas, with a pebble pavement, a structure that had been dug into the ground but also constructed has been interpreted as a channel. Evidence has been found in different levels, but the best-preserved remains are from the lowest layer. It is a small shallow channel that has been followed over a length of 22 m. It was faced with clay, with a small layer of pebbles at its base, and a cover of flat limestone slabs has been documented. This shows that it was carefully finished, and its importance is attested by three repairs to

Figure 2.8 Detailed view from the east side of the Structure E101.

Figure 2.9 Sector SS7. Walls E10, E6 and E4 and channel.

it. It is regarded as a drainage channel probably for waste water using its gentle slope from west to east, that is, from the interior towards the exterior (Molist & Gómez 2018, 33). This construction is particularly important because it is new evidence of large-scale structures, in this case for the flow of water, but at the same time it acted as boundary. Evidence of pedogenesis has been observed in this channel, including sedimentation of carbonate deposits, precipitation and dissolution of organic material and the formation of secondary materials, like sulphates and nitrates. These are currently being studied.

Contribution of micromorphology to the study of sedimentary/architectonic processes

The micromorphology of floors has contributed to the study of sedimentary processes in areas of monumental architecture through the analysis of six samples taken in Sector 1B, from the southern section corresponding to the external or eastern face of the structure (E101). They were collected in sequence in order to characterise the different uses of the area during the PPNB-Halaf transition.

Two phases have been identified for the oldest period (recent PPNB), contemporaneous with the construction of the great wall (E101). The first of these displays fragments of earthen building materials, in this case unbaked adobe, whereas the second attests to an area of transit shown by trampling. In this way, building materials may have collapsed and then the area became a transit place. The fact that this sample comes from the base of the wall suggests that the previous architecture was demolished before the construction of the wall. However, the previous buildings may have deteriorated and collapsed naturally. Significant biological activity observed in the remains of building material would have contributed to its disintegration and fragmentation.

The Pre-Halaf levels have revealed a long sequence with four different uses of the area. In the first phase, the presence of areas of transit is clear because of the evidence of trampling on a surface that was not prepared for walking, as it is not a constructed floor. The presence of aeolian deposits is seen in the characterisation of the sediment, as well as archaeological micro-remains, and these are typical of outside areas. Among the pedological features, the crystallisation of carbonates is the consequence of humectation/desiccation phenomena. The second phase again corresponds to an outside area. In this case, the presence of plant remains increases, above which another transit level was established, with which they became altered and mixed. In addition, the appearance of accumulations of herbivore coprolites suggests the area was frequented by animals even though the surfaces do not display the specific organisation typical of barn areas. The function of this area changed later as it contains accumulations of plant remains, with no evidence of animal activity. Finally, the last phase exhibits the same kind of evidence as the record in the second phase. Still in the times of the Pre-Halaf occupation, the information from the third sample reveals a change in the formation of an unprepared floor through the mixture of clay and silt with the presence of archaeological micro-remains, testifying to the use of raw materials from nearby habitation levels. Above it, a series of remains reflect diverse types of domestic activities that finish in what has been interpreted as a phase of abandonment, owing to the absence of archaeological material and the deterioration caused by biological activity.

In the Early Halaf, accumulations of waste include small bone fragments, charcoal from the combustion of wood and herbaceous plants, phytoliths, fragments of burnt building materials and even some coprolites. These were compacted and altered by an upper level used for transit which caused the compression of the underlying levels. Micritic layers cover the remains and contribute to the cementation as a consequence of dissolution/reprecipitation processes associated with the circulation of carbonate-rich water. These phenomena are accompanied by the growth of lenticular-shaped crystals in the pores. Finally, the last phase in this period is represented by more waste, but this time connected with combustion activity, as suggested by the state in which the archaeological micro-remains appear.

Lastly, in the Middle Halaf period, a series of superimpositions and alternation of outside floors and waste from domestic activities has been documented. Again, these floors do not exhibit much effort made in their preparation, as they are characterised by a heterogeneous mass from proximate habitation levels. This alternation is repeated as many as three times to finish with an episode of abandonment attested by destructuration under post-depositional processes such as biological activity and humectation and desiccation cycles.

This study has helped to understand in detail the different uses of the area over time, as a consequence of the continual reoccupation of a part of the site characterised by the large structure E101, which has greatly influenced the form acquired by the modern tell.

Discussion

The detailed description and analysis of the two types of formation processes in the tell, depending on the nature of the anthropic occupations and constructions, demonstrates the complexity of the sedimentary dynamics at the settlement of Tell Halula. At a methodological level, the different techniques and methods used in our analysis have complemented one another. The classic stratigraphic study of deposit formation at a macro level (in a generalist archaeological approach to the composition and nature of the strata) has been supported by more specialised analyses, a micromorphological study in this case. The comparison in dialectic terms of the data from this double approach undoubtedly helps to attain a more complete interpretation. The architectonic study of built structures is also important even though in the archaic periods building techniques and spatial arrangements can be regarded as very simple. Thus, earth-based architecture is very particular and needs specific attention. It is doubtlessly important to refer to ethnoarchaeological research and studies on traditional building techniques.

The two systems involved in the formation of archaeological deposits documented at Tell Halula should be compared with those at other sites. However, a direct comparison will not be possible. The first formation process, the conjunction of structures and domestic activities, is definitely the most common one, observed at most ancient settlements in the Near East. Indeed, this type of process has been identified at numerous Neolithic sites in this region. Without attempting to be exhaustive, Cafer Hoyuk (Molist & Cauvin 1991; Cauvin *et al.* 1999), Abu Hureyra (Moore *et al.* 2000) and Sabi Abyad II (Akkermans & Verhoeven 2000) are some of these sites where a similar process has been documented.

In contrast, complex processes that involve monumental architecture are less common. The comparison with similar formation processes in the Near Eastern Neolithic reveals greater variability, probably because of the powerful influence of the 'constructed element' generating a complex sedimentary process. One case involves monumental constructions that are interpreted as community buildings with structural elements of diverse functions (enclosing walls, embankments, pits, *etc.*). Recent finds in PPNA and early PPNB settlements are very illustrative, such as Göbekli Tepe and Jerf el Ahmar as the best-studied examples (Schmidt 2011; Stordeur-Yedid 2015). A second case has been documented at such settlements as Tell Magzaliya (Bader 1989), Khirokitia (Le Brun & Le Brun 2009) and Jericho (Kenyon 1957; Kenyon & Holland 1982), which are magnificent examples of complex processes whose stratigraphy is open to a revision or new interpretation. This has been carried out in the case of the latter site (Bar-Yosef 1986). At Tell Halula, in contrast, the study has been approached from the perspectives of both macro- and micro-stratigraphic analyses. This has rendered detailed documentation of pre-depositional, depositional and post-depositional processes in the different spaces, which will enable an overall understanding and vision of the life of the whole tell.

In sum, the aim of this essay has been to analyse and establish the formation process through the information provided by the macro- and micro-stratigraphic studies of a farming settlement. It has also revealed evidence of the great technological ability and social organisation of the inhabitants, especially in the quality of the architecture and the planning of the anthropic space. In this regard, the diversity of access to and management of hydrological resources, as described above again shows the organisational ability of the community. The management of permanent maintenance activities went beyond the private sphere on technological, symbolic and social levels. Research at the settlement of Tell Halula has allowed to infer some aspects that can be regarded as particularly interesting for the understanding of anthropic and natural phenomena. The study has given priority to the stratigraphic evidence at macro and micro scales, but we are aware that an overall analysis of the formation of the tell requires the consideration of several other variables. The first of these is a detailed chronological framework as precise as possible for the different construction phases and the abandonment/sedimentation episodes, as well as for the duration of each archaeological period. The project carried out a first approach and also possesses a generic chronological framework (Barceló & Faura 1999; Molist 2013), but a new study with an updated radiometric series is in progress. Second, a more detailed palaeoenvironmental study will be necessary as part of future research. This way, it will be able to relate geoarchaeological observations with climate changes, such as periods of drought, *etc.* The complexity of Neolithic settlements in the Near East requires a line of research that can approach both the formation and sedimentation processes of the tells and the uses and social characterisation of their spaces.

Notes

1. The Tell Halula Archaeological Project has been made possible thanks to the assistance and collaboration of the Syrian General Directorate of Antiquities and Museums, and the Spanish Cultural Heritage Institute (Ministry of Education, Culture and Sport) and the Ministry of Economy and Competitiveness (HAR2016-78416-P), as well as the Palarq Foundation. Finally, the GRAMPPO/SAPPO research group is supported by the Universitat Autònoma of Barcelona and the Generalitat de Catalunya (2017 SGR-1302).

2. The term 'occupation phase' corresponds to the terminology used in the analysis of the stratigraphic sequence. Thus, from a smaller to larger scale, the stratigraphic unit is the basic element in the record and in the analysis of the excavation. These units are grouped into occupation phases, depending on their context, characteristics and composition. They define a precise moment in the human presence consisting of the construction, use and destruction of a built space. Following this scheme, the occupation levels in each sector of the excavation are numbered with Roman numerals (I, II, III, *etc.*) from the most recent to the oldest. The correspondence between the occupation levels between the different areas of the excavation have enabled a definition of the occupation phases for the site as a whole based on chronology, archaeological record, *etc…*

3. We are very grateful for the contribution of the geoarchaeological reconstruction carried out in the 1995 and 1996 fieldwork by Marie Agnès Courty and Julia Wattez. Dr J. Wattez has continued to be linked to the project and the present study includes some of the conclusions of her micromorphological analysis.

References

Akkermann, O., Bruins, H.J. & Maeir, A.M. (2005) A unique human-made trench at Tell es-Sâfi/Gath, Israel: Anthropogenic impact and landscape response. *Geoarchaeology* 20(3), 303–327.

Akkermans, P.M.M.G. & Verhoeven, M. (2000) *Tell Sabi Abyad II – The Pre-Pottery Neolithic B Settlement*. Leiden, Nederlands Historisch-Archaeologisch Institut.

Álvarez, A. (2013) Reseña geológica de la zona de Tell Halula. In M. Molist (ed.), *Tell Halula. Un poblado de los primeros agricultores en el valle del Éufrates*, 24–30. Madrid, Ministerio de Educación, Cultura y Deporte.

Bader, N.O. (1989) *Earliest Cultivators in Northern Mesopotamia: The Investigations of Soviet Archaeological Expedition in Iraq at Settlements Tell Magzaliya, Tell Sotto, Küll Tepe*. Moskow, Nauka.

Barceló, J.A. & Faura, J.M. (1999) Time series and neural networks in archaeological seriation. An example on early pottery from the Near East. In L. Dingwall, S. Exon, V. Gaffney, S. Laflin & M. van Leusen (eds), *Archaeology in the Age of the Internet. CAA97. Computer Applications and Quantitative Methods in Archaeology. Proceedings of the 25th Anniversary Conference, University of Birmingham, April 1997*, 91–102. Oxford, Archaeopress.

Bar-Yosef, O. (1986) The walls of Jericho: An alternative interpretation. *Current Anthropology* 27(2), 157–162.

Bar-Yosef, O. (1993) Site Formation processes from a Levantine view point. In P. Goldberg, D.T. Nash & M.D. Petraglia (eds), *Formation Processes in Archaeological Context*, 11–32. Madison WI, Prehistory Press.

Barton, C.M. & Clark, G.A. (1993) Cultural and natural formation processes in Late Quaternary cave and rockshelter sites of Western Europe and the Near East. In P. Goldberg, D.T. Nash & M.D. Petraglia (eds), *Formation Processes in Archaeological Context*, 33–60. Madison WI, Prehistory Press.

Bullock, P., Fedoroff, N., Jongerius, A., Stoops, G. & Tursina, T. (1985) *Handbook for Soil Thin Section Description*. Wolverhampton, Waine Research.

Butzer, K. (1982) *Archaeology as Human Ecology: Method and Theory for a Contextual Approach*. Cambridge, Cambridge University Press.

Cauvin, J., Aurenche, O., Cauvin, M.-C. & Balkan-Atli, N. (1999) The Pre-pottery site of Cafer Höyük. In M. Özdoğan & N. Basgelen (eds), *Neolithic in Turkey*, 87–103. Istanbul, Istanbul Arkeoloji ve Sanat Yayinlazi.

Courty, M.A., Goldberg, P. & Macphail, R. (1989) *Soils and Micromorphology in Archaeology*. Cambridge, Cambridge University Press.

Davidson, D.A. (1976) Processes of tell formation and erosion. In D.A. Davidson & M.L. Shackley (eds), *Geoarchaeology: Earth Science and the Past*, 255–266. Boulder CO, Westview Press.

Goldberg, P. (1979) Geology of Late Bronze Age mudbrick from Tel Lachish. *Tel Aviv* 6(1/2), 60–67.

Kenyon, K.M. (1957) *Digging up Jericho*. London: Benn.

Kenyon, K. & Holland, T.A. (1982) *Excavations at Jericho. Vol. 4. The Pottery-type Series and Other Finds*. Jerusalem, London British School of Archaeology in Jerusalem.

Koromila, G., Karkanas, P., Hamilakis, Y., Kyparissi-Apostolikad, N., Kotzamani, G. & Harris, K. (2018) The Neolithic tell as a multi-species monument: Human, animal, and plant relationships through a micro-contextual study of animal dung remains at Koutroulou Magoula, central Greece. *Journal of Archaeological Science* 19, 753–768.

Le Brun, A. & Daune-Le Brun, O. (2009) Khirokitia (Chypre): la taille et les pulsations de l'établissement néolithique précéramique, nouvelles données. *Paléorient* 35(2), 69–78.

Liebowitz, H. & Folk, R.L. (1980) Archaeological geology of Tel Yin'am, Galilee, Israel. *Journal of Field Archaeology* 7(1), 23–42.

Love, S. (2013) Architecture as material culture: Building form and materiality in the pre-Pottery Neolithic of Anatolia and Levant. *Journal of Anthropological Archaeology* 32(4), 746–758.

Maghsoudi, M., Simpson, I.A., Kourampas, N. & Nashli, H.F. (2014) Archaeological sediments from settlement mounds of the Sagzabad Cluster, central Iran: human-induced deposition on an arid alluvial plain. *Quaternary International* 324, 67–83.

Marchiori, C. (2015) *Arquitectura en tierra de la prehistoria y la protohistoria del Próximo Oriente. Estudio arqueométrico del adobe en los yacimientos de Tell Halula, Yumuktepe y Tell Tuqan*. Unpublished PhD Thesis, Departamento de Prehistoria, Universitat Autònoma de Barcelona.

Matthews, W., French, C.A.I., Lawrence, T., Cutler, D.F. & Jones, M.K., (1997) Microstratigraphic traces of site formation processes and human activities. *World Archaeology* 29, 281–308.

Matthews, W., Shillito, L.M., Elliott, S., Bull, I.D. & Williams, J. (2014) Neolithic lifeways: microstratigraphic traces within houses, animal pens and settlements. In A. Whittle & P. Bickle (eds), *Early Farmers: The View from Archaeology and Science*, 251–280. Oxford, Oxford University Press.

Molist, M. (1996) *Tell Halula (Siria). Un yacimiento neolítico del valle medio del Eufrates. Campañas 1991 y 1992*. Madrid, Instituto del Patrimonio Histórico Español.

Molist, M. (1998) Espace collectif et domestique dans le néolithique des IXéme et VIIIéme millénaires B.P. au nord de la Syrie: apports du site de Tell Halula (Vallée de l'Euphrate). In O. Aurenche & M. Fortin (eds), *Espace Naturel, Espace Habité en Syrie du Nord. (10e–2e millénaires av. J.C.). Actes du colloque tenu à l'Université Laval (Québec) du 5 au 7 mai 1997*, 115–130. Lyon, Maison de l'Orient méditerranéen.

Molist, M. (2013) *Tell Halula. Un poblado de los primeros agricultores en el valle del Éufrates*. Madrid, Ministerio de Educación, Cultura y Deporte.

Molist, M. (2016) Tell Halula (Aleppo). In Y. Kanjou & A. Tsuneki (ed.), *A History of Syria in One Hundred Sites*, 54–56. Oxford, Archaeopress.

Molist, M. & Cauvin, J. (1991) Les niveaux inférieurs de Cafer Höyük (Malatya, Turquie): stratigraphie et architectures (fouilles 1984–1986). *Cahiers de l'Euphrate* 5/6, 85–114.

Molist, M. & Gómez, A. (2018) Las estructuras construidas para la gestión del agua en los primeros poblados del neolítico del próximo Oriente: Aportación desde el estudio del asentamiento de tell Halula (Valle del Éufrates, Siria). *Anejos a Cuadernos de Prehistoria y Arqueología* 3, 27–36.

Molist, M., Gómez, A., Bofill, M., Cruells, W., Faura, J.M., Marchiori, C. & Martín, J. (2014) Maisons et constructions d'habitation dans le Néolithique. Une approche de l'évolution des unités d'habitat domestiques à partir des documents de Tell Halula (Vallée de l'Éuphrate, Syrie). In J.L. Montero (ed.), *Redonner vie aux Mésopotamiens. Mélanges offerts à Jean-Claude Margueron à l'Ocassion de son 80e anniversaire. Cuadernos Mesopotámicos 4*, 97–116. Ferrol, Sociedad Luso-Gallega de Estudios Mesopotámicos.

Moore, A.M.T., Hillman, G.C. & Anthony, J. (2000) *Village on the Euphrates: From Foraging to Farming at Abu Hureyra*. Oxford, Oxford University Press.

Rosen, A.M. (1986) *Cities of Clay: The Geoarchaeology of Tells*. Chicago IL, University of Chicago Press.

Sapir, Y. Abraham, A. & Faust, A. (2018) Mud-brick composition, archaeological phasing and pre-planning in Iron Age structures: Tel 'Eton (Israel) as a test-case. *Archaeological and Anthropological Science* 10(2), 337–350.

Schiffer, M.B (1987) *Formation Processes of the Archaeological Record*. Albuquerque NM, University of New Mexico Press.

Schmidt, K. (2011) Göbekli Tepe: a Neolithic site in southeastern Anatolia. In S.R. Steadman & J.G. McMahon (eds), *The Oxford Handbook of Ancient Anatolia (10,000–323 BCE)*, 917–933. Oxford, Oxford University Press.

Sedov, S.N., Aleksandrovskii, A.L., Benz, M., Balabina, V.I., Mishina, T.N., Shishkov, V.A., Şahin, F. & Özkaya, V. (2017) Anthropogenic sediments and soils of tells of the Balkans and Anatolia: composition, genesis, and relationships with the history of landscape and human occupation. *Eurasian Soil Science* 50(4), 373–386.

Shillito, L.M. & Matthews, W. (2013) Geoarchaeological investigations of midden-formation processes in the Early to Late ceramic Neolithic levels at Çatalhöyük, Turkey ca. 8550–8370 cal BP. *Geoarchaeology* 28, 25–49.

Stoops, G (2003) *Guidelines for Analysis and Description of Soil and Regolith Thin Sections*. Madison WI, Soil Science Society of America.

Stordeur-Yedid, D. (2015) *Le village de Jerf el Ahmar: Syrie, 9500–8700 av. J.-C. L'architecture, miroir d'une société néolithique complexe*. Paris, CNRS.

Ullmann, T., Lange-Athinodorou, E., Göbel A., Büdel, C. & Baumhauer, R. (2019) Preliminary results on the paleolandscape of Tell Basta/Bubastis (eastern Nile delta): An integrated approach combining GIS-based spatial analysis, geophysical and archaeological investigations. *Quaternary International* 511, 185–199.

Valdés, L., Reina, J., Muñoz, R., Pujana, I. (2013) Prospección geofísica en Tell Halula (Síria). Campaña de 1995. In M. Molist (ed.), *Tell Halula. Un poblado de los primeros agricultores en el valle del Éufrates*, 94–111. Madrid, Ministerio de Educación, Cultura y Deporte.

Wattez, J. & Courty, M.A. (1996) Modes et rythmes d'occupation à Tell Halula. Approche géoarchéologique (premiers résultats). In M. Molist (ed.), *Tell Halula (Siria). Un yacimiento neolítico del valle medio del Eufrates. Campañas 1991 y 1992*, 53–67. Madrid, Instituto del Patrimonio Histórico Español.

3

Re-discovering the Neolithic Landscapes of Western Thessaly, Central Greece

Athanasia Krahtopoulou, Charles Frederick, Hector A. Orengo, Anastasia Dimoula, Niki Saridaki, Stella Kyrillidou, Alexandra Livarda and Arnau Garcia-Molsosa

Introduction

In 1889, just eight years after the incorporation of Thessaly into the young Greek state, the Head of Antiquities of the Archaeological Society of Athens, Christos Tsountas, launched his first field campaign in the archaeologically unexplored region. While excavating a Mycenaean *tumulus* at Marmariane, east Thessaly, he noticed that the surface archaeological material on the 'tomb' was distinctively different from the expected Mycenaean. Intrigued, Tsountas opened several test-trenches, exposing several metres of cultural deposits that looked definitively older, most probably from the earlier Bronze Age. Fascinated, he surveyed several neighbouring mounded sites. Many exhibited even older surface material culture, convincing Tsountas that the Neolithic, a period already known from elsewhere in Europe, was indeed present in Thessaly (Tsountas 1900; 1908; Gallis 1979a, 3).

The sounding at Marmariane thus marked the beginning of tell-research in Thessaly (and Greece). Importantly, Tsountas's pioneer expedition demonstrated for the first time that the earthen mounds (locally known as *magoúles*) that litter the lowlands of Thessaly may contain superimposed remains of prehistoric lifeways and/or cover later single or multiple graves. Interestingly, it also provided the first record of the post-abandonment use of prehistoric settlement mounds for funerary purposes.

Tsountas's subsequent horizontal and extensive open-area excavations at Sesklo and Dimini, coastal Thessaly, test-trenches at several other tell sites, and extensive reconnaissance of the Thessalian landscapes resulted in the publication of his landmark regional synthesis (Tsountas 1908) that laid the foundations of Neolithic research in Greece (Kotsakis 2006; P. Halstead 2006). Building on this work, Wace and Thompson (1912) introduced the region to the international scholarly community and Thessaly has been the focus of an impressive amount of Neolithic research ever since. Most scholarship, however, has focused on eastern and southern Thessaly, whereas the western basin and the mountain ranges that border the region to the west has received far less attention (Andreou *et al.* 1996; Krahtopoulou 2019a).

Strikingly, regardless of the shifting research interests, themes and narratives of all major national theoretical and methodological approaches to the Neolithic during the last 100 years, relevant field research has almost exclusively targeted medium- and high-visibility mounds. Inevitably, prominent tells became the dominant and powerful lens through which Neolithic settlement and society in Greece were perceived until late in the 20th century (Andreou *et al.* 1996; Kotsakis 1999; 2005; 2006; P. Halstead 2006), when flat sites, another form of settlement organisation and possibly perception of place and the landscape, started to become increasingly archaeologically visible, first in the north of the country (*e.g.* Andreou & Kotsakis 1986; Grammenos 1991; Pappa & Besios 1999; Pappa 2008; Ziota 2014; Karamitrou-Mentessidi *et al.* 2015) and later in Thessaly (see Toufexis 2017; Krahtopoulou 2019a and references therein).

For most of the 20th century, extensive landscape reconnaissance and rescue excavations, usually of limited scope and scale, produced a striking settlement pattern. The marked regional contrasts in settlement density are clearly revealed by a recent Neolithic site inventory compiled by the *Innovative Geophysical Approaches for the Study of Early Agricultural Villages of Neolithic Thessaly* (IGEAN) research project that reported 342 documented tells throughout Thessaly (http://igean.ims.forth.gr/). Eastern Thessaly exhibits an exceptionally dense settlement pattern, whereas most of the meagre 55 Neolithic sites reported for western Thessaly are concentrated in the southern part of the region; the rest of the western plain appears tantalisingly empty. This odd, nearly suspiciously clear, contrast has been long recognised (Papadopoulou 1958; Halstead & Jones 1980; P. Halstead 1984) but, as we argue below, has not been scrutinised thoroughly. Therefore, for more than a century western Thessaly has been, almost routinely, treated as a Neolithic backwater (Souvatzi 2008; Krahtopoulou 2019a) and has been largely disregarded in regional syntheses and broader Neolithic narratives.

Here we argue that this persistent regional picture is heavily biased and misleading. By integrating new, important evidence assembled by the ongoing interdisciplinary landscape project *Long Time, No See: Land reclamation and the cultural record of central-western plain of Thessaly* that focuses on the Kambos area of the plain of Karditsa, with information from very recent rescue excavations and the high-resolution multi-proxy re-reading of the stratigraphy of previous excavations at Prodromos, we will maintain that the Neolithic of western Thessaly was a much richer and more interesting world than hitherto assumed.

Western Thessaly: The setting

Located in the heart of mainland Greece, Thessaly, the largest lowland of Greece, currently comprises one of the most intensively cultivated and productive provinces of the country (Fig. 3.1). The region is surrounded by impressive mountains

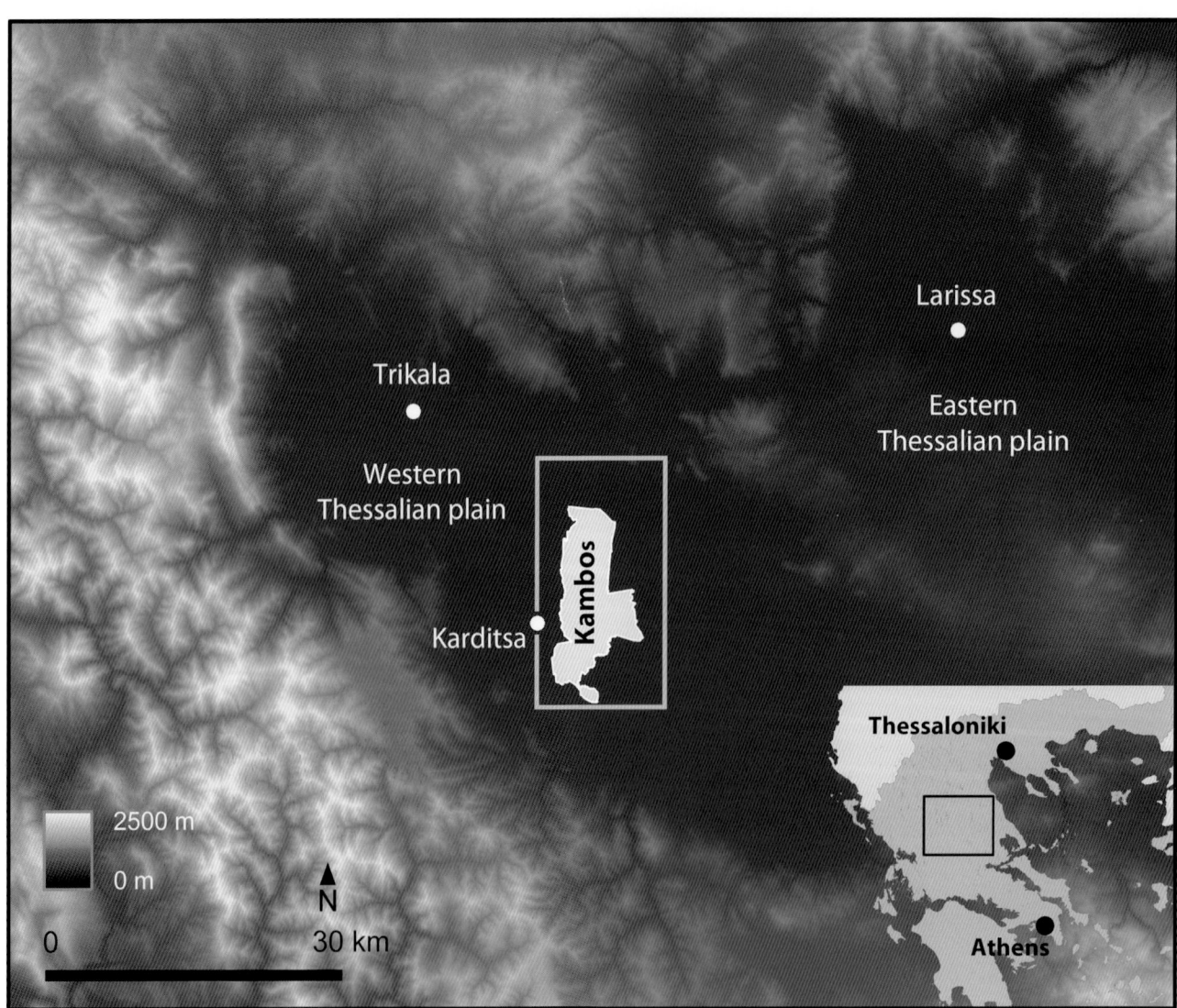

Figure 3.1 Map of Thessaly and location of the Kambos.

(1000–3000 m a.s.l.), while in the interior, Pliocene and Early–Middle Pleistocene tectonism have created two large subsiding basins of different altitude. The higher and fragmented Larissa Basin to the east and the lower, continuous Kalambaka – Trikala – Karditsa – Pharsala Basin to the west are separated by the northwest-southeast trending Middle Thessalian Hills or Revenia (Caputo & Pavlidis 1991).

The western basin, totalling c. 6100 km^2, is bordered by a mountainous-hilly zone and the lowlands (up to 200 m a.s.l.) occupy an area of 2309 km^2. Lying between the geotectonic zones of the internal and external Hellenides, western Thessaly exhibits great geological variety. The fringes of the plain comprise various Alpine and post-Alpine formations, whereas Quaternary lacustrine and fluvial deposits more than 550 m in depth occupy the lowlands (42% of the region). The Peneios River, originating in the Pindus Range, and a powerful, well-developed, complex and extended network of tributaries drain the entire western basin (Apostolidis & Koukis 2013, 408, 414).

The municipal unit of the Kambos region, the focus of this chapter, occupies an area of 90 km^2 in the heart of the western Thessalian alluvial plain, next to Karditsa, the capital of the Karditsa prefecture (Fig. 3.1). The Kambos, and much of the western plain, is currently devoted to intensive, irrigated cultivation of cash-crops, mainly cotton and maize. But this was not always the case.

Visions of a landscape unpromising for modern farming and … Neolithic archaeology

In the wake of the devastating World War II and the following Civil War that ended in 1949, most of the farmers of the Kambos practised small-scale rain-fed subsistence agriculture in small, fragmented and dispersed plots cultivated by hand and/or with plough animals. They grew a diverse spectrum of cereals and pulses and kept modest numbers of domestic animals. A limited network of dirt paths and roads connected villages, whose inhabitants accessed their fields and other taskscapes by foot, horse and cart (H. Halstead 2019, 5; Krahtopoulou *et al.* 2020a; P. Halstead forthcoming).

At that time, permanent and/or seasonal wetlands and marshlands covered large parts (c. 100 km^2) of the Karditsa Plain (Prontzas 1992, 66, 81), and the Kambos setting. Seasonal flooding and waterlogging of fields resulted often in localised poor harvests and/or crop failure (P. Halstead forthcoming), as well as seasonal disruption of movement and, therefore, of various activities performed across the landscape. Despite the tangible seasonal risks, and contrary to the dominant Western ideology that perceived wetlands as unhealthy wastelands to be eliminated (Prontzas 1992; Idol 2018), the people of the Kambos considered permanent and seasonal bodies of water as valuable assets, integral to their pre-mechanised lifeways (P. Halstead forthcoming). Tells were called 'islands' (*ansiá* in the local dialect) and those situated close to areas of seasonal inundation were typically used as animal pens. Predictably, people and animals took refuge on tells during exceptionally heavy rainfall and flooding.

Until the late 1960s, therefore, the rural population of the Karditsa plain lagged behind their eastern Thessalian neighbours in infrastructure, agricultural technology, income and living conditions (Prontzas 1992; H. Halstead 2019, 6). Importantly, tangible poverty largely reinforced earlier views that linked economic hardship with social backwardness (*cf.* Prontzas 1992) and strongly underpinned a self-perception of 'otherness'. Most crucially, perhaps, the allegedly hostile and unhealthy environmental conditions of the mid-20th century were certainly not compatible with the widely accepted view that links Neolithic settlement choice, especially during the earlier phases, with optimal natural settings and availability of prime agricultural land (*e.g.* Demoule & Perlès 1993). In essence, it appears that for most of the 20th century, powerful social and environmental images, narratives and preconceptions of the recent past infiltrated archaeological thought and practice and the western Thessalian plain was overwhelmingly considered as exceptionally unpromising for Neolithic settlement and archaeology alike (Krahtopoulou 2019a).

Land reclamation and the archaeological record of the Kambos

To further complicate matters, in the late 1960s–early 1970s, the Greek State sponsored and executed a large-scale land reform programme (in Greek *anadasmós*), in order, firstly, to create new and profitable agricultural land, suitable for intensive and specialised – *i.e.* mechanised, irrigated – farming and, secondly, to secure an economically sustainable future for the impoverished rural population of the lowlands of Karditsa. Agricultural modernisation involved massive land reclamation and redistribution, as well as associated infrastructure and water management works. In less than five years, the landscape of the Kambos was profoundly and irreversibly remodelled (Fig. 3.2); wetlands were drained, a new road network and a modern irrigation system were established, old fields were reshaped and new ones were created, the land was flattened and the soil was shifted locally to fill in old streams and other topographic depressions. At the same time, the ways in which people and animals experienced and interacted with the land, the landscape and the environment were abruptly and violently abolished (Orengo *et al.* 2015; H. Halstead 2019; Krahtopoulou *et al.* 2020a).

Although there is no doubt that much was gained by the *anadasmós*, much too was lost (H. Halstead 2019, 6), including mounded archaeology. Many archaeological sites, tell settlements and burial mounds alike, were either completely erased or partially levelled during, or in the years after land reclamation works (Fig. 3.3) (Orengo *et al.* 2015;

Figure 3.2 Top: land reclamation and land flattening process; bottom left: the landscape around the modern village of Makrychori in 1945; bottom right: the same part of the landscape in 2015.

Figure 3.3 Prodromos I: The LTNS team survey the levelled tell.

Krahtopoulou 2019a; Krahtopoulou *et al.* 2020a). Ironically, several Neolithic *magoúles* were rescue- or test-excavated in the 1970s by the staff of the Greek Archaeological Service (*e.g.* Chourmouziadis 1971a; 1972; Gallis 1979), in order either to prevent further destruction by levelling or to justify rejection of applications to do so (Krahtopoulou 2019a).

This was the context for the investigation in the early 1970s (Chourmouziadis 1971a; 1971b; 1972; 1973) of Early Neolithic Prodromos I and Plateia Magoula Prodromos (or Prodromos II), two of the most widely referenced tells of the Greek Neolithic for early architecture (Plateia Magoula Prodromos), secondary manipulation of the dead (Prodromos I), early pottery and anthropomorphic imagery (Prodromos I and Plateia Magoula Prodromos).

Catastrophic levelling, strongly suggesting differential preservation and visibility of mounded archaeological sites, on the one hand, and the important discoveries of the Prodromos excavations, implying an extremely interesting and potentially rich western Thessalian Neolithic, on the other, provoked initiation of the ongoing (2014 to present) landscape project *Long Time, no See: Land reclamation and the cultural record of central-western plain of Thessaly* (hereafter LTNS), under the auspices of the Ephorate of Antiquities of Karditsa, Hellenic Ministry of Culture and Sports.

Moving from wider landscapes to specific sites and employing integrated research methodologies and a wide range of analytical tools, LTNS aims at reconstructing and understanding the long-term cultural landscapes of the Kambos region. Research workflow combines Remote Sensing (RS), Geographic Information Systems (GIS) and archaeomorphological analysis with extensive and intensive surface survey, off- and on-site geoarchaeology, palaeoenvironmental, bioarchaeological and material culture studies, absolute dating, archival and ethno-historical research and finally evidence from old and very recent rescue excavations carried out in the region (Orengo *et al.* 2015; Krahtopoulou *et al.* 2020a).

Our integrated, innovative approach is resulting in the identification, mapping and characterisation of an unprecedented and still growing number of mounded archaeological sites (settlements and tombs) and negative off-site features (road and field systems), the vast majority of which were previously unknown (Orengo *et al.* 2015). Rigorous ground-truthing by extensive surface survey of over 200 'places of archaeological interest' with a striking site detection rate of 93% confirms RS-based interpretations and demonstrates that the catastrophic agricultural levelling of the recent past has seriously compromised an impressive 77% of the mounded archaeological record of the area. Most importantly perhaps, preliminary results of intensive survey of levelled Neolithic settlements indicate that, despite removal of a substantial part of the archaeological deposits, meaningful insights can still be gained into their nature, extent and temporal and socio-cultural associations (Dimoula *et al.* forthcoming; Krahtopoulou *et al.* forthcoming).

Reclaiming the Neolithic of the Kambos

To date, RS-based landscape reconstructions, surface survey and rescue excavations have identified 25 Neolithic sites (Table 3.1 and Fig. 3.4), including 22 tells and three flat sites, that form 65 % of the prehistoric settlement record of the Kambos area. Only six sites, all tells, were previously documented (Krahtopoulou *et al.* forthcoming). Unsurprisingly, RS and extensive surface survey have detected sites with fairly clear topographic expression, whereas all flat settlements in the Kambos and elsewhere in western Thessaly have been located in the context of very recent large-scale developer-funded infrastructure projects and small-scale private works (Krahtopoulou 2019a and references therein). Most tells (14) have been severely damaged during the last 50 years and all flat sites identified so far are buried under locally substantial alluvial deposits.

According to relative pottery-based chronological assessments (Dimoula *et al.* forthcoming) and limited radiocarbon dating (Karagiannopoulos 2016; Krahtopoulou *et al.* 2018; Krahtopoulou 2019a), the Kambos record spans the entire Neolithic.[1] Seven fairly unevenly distributed sites comprise the Early Neolithic (6500–5980 BC) settlement record of the study region. Interestingly, four tells cluster around the modern village of Prodromos. On available relative chronological evidence, Prodromos I has been established during the Early Neolithic I and is the earliest site identified to date in the study area. All Early Neolithic sites continue to the Middle Neolithic (5980–5500 BC), when another nine tells and one flat site appear to have been established for the first time, resulting in a relatively dense settlement pattern, with sites distributed more evenly across the landscape. The total number of tells (10) decreases during the Late Neolithic (5500–4500 BC) and two newly established flat sites extend the settlement record of the Kambos zone. The Final Neolithic (4500–3300 BC) is characterised by a sharp decrease in site numbers (4). Finally, four additional tells, exhibiting highly weathered and/or eroded surface material, are presently characterised as 'broadly Neolithic'. On current evidence, tells and flat sites coexist in western Thessaly since at least the Middle Neolithic, exhibiting diverse and complex spatial, temporal and, presumably, social relationships, especially during the Late Neolithic (Krahtopoulou 2019a).

Bearing in mind the notoriously poor surface visibility and limited diagnostic potential of the earliest Neolithic pottery assemblages, especially monochrome wares (Dimoula 2014 and references therein), and the substantial loss of tell deposits due to levelling, the Kambos record exhibits clear diachronic habitation throughout the Neolithic. Only one site, Magoula Agios Ioannis Prodromos and its possible 'satellites' span the entire Neolithic (Halstead & Jones 1980; Karagiannopoulos 2016). Notably, several tells are short-lived and/or single-period, while all flat sites are single-phased (Krahtopoulou 2019a).

The spatial patterning on Neolithic sites deserves further attention. A closer look at the results of the photointerpretation and archaeomorphological analysis (Orengo *et al.* 2015, fig. 8) and the updated Neolithic map of the Kambos (Fig. 3.4) indicates uneven spatial distribution of sites, with large voids especially to the north and the west of the study area. Interestingly, all sites (15) checked to the west of the modern village of Prodromos date exclusively to the late historical and medieval periods. Furthermore, numerous trial sections for small-scale private construction projects in the western part of the modern village of Myrine (see Fig. 3.4) revealed substantial alluvial deposits and in one case, Bronze Age remains (3rd–2nd millennia BC) were found buried under 3 m of alluvial sediments (Krahtopoulou *et al.* forthcoming). The only Neolithic site identified to date in the western zone of the Kambos region (Table 3.1, 18 and Fig. 3.4, 18) belongs to the flat type and was also concealed by alluviation.

Although tells still dominate the settlement record of the Kambos and indeed Thessaly, the chance discovery of many buried sub-alluvial flat sites, randomly scattered along the course of newly constructed motorways and other infrastructure projects in the study area and throughout Thessaly (see Toufexis 2017; Krahtopoulou 2019a), proves that non-tell

Table 3.1 The Neolithic sites of the Kambos.

No	Site name-modern village	Type	Preservation	Dating*	Method of archaeological exploration/Reference
1	Magoula Megala Leivadia – Makrychori	Tell	Levelled	MN	Extensive surface survey
2	Magoula Vaiou Kalamara – Makrychori	Tell	Partially levelled	MN–LN	Extensive surface survey – test excavation (Gallis 1979b)
3	Magoula Pouliou – Myrine	Tell	Upstanding	EN–MN	Extensive surface survey
4	Agia Varvara – Myrine	Flat	Sub-alluvial	MN	Rescue excavation (Krahtopoulou 2019b)
5	Magoula Semou – Myrine	Tell	Levelled	EN–MN	Extensive surface survey
6	Prodromos 11 – Prodromos	Tell	Levelled	EN–MN	Extensive surface survey
7	Prodromos I – Prodromos	Tell	Levelled	EN–MN–LN	Extensive and intensive surface survey – rescue excavation (Chourmouziadis 1971a)
8	Prodromos II (Plateia Magoula Prodromos) – Prodromos	Tell	Upstanding	EN–MN	Rescue excavation – Stratigraphic investigation (Chourmouziadis 1971a; 1972)
9	Prodromos 9 – Prodromos	Tell	Levelled	MN–LN	Extensive and intensive surface survey
10	Prodromos 7 (Magoula Koukouli or Rovoli) – Prodromos	Tell	Levelled	MN–LN	Extensive and intensive surface survey
11	Prodromos III (Magoula Agios Ioannis Prodromos) – Prodromos	Tell	Upstanding	EN–MN–LN	Test excavation (Halstead & Jones 1980)
12	Prodromos Primary School – Prodromos	Tell	Upstanding	MN–LN–FN	Rescue excavation (Chatziaggelakis & Karagiannopoulos 2012; Karagiannopoulos 2016)
13	Babtzelis plot – Prodromos	Tell	Levelled	LN–FN	Rescue excavation (Chatziaggelakis 2007)
14	Magoula Agios Nikolaos – Agios Theodoros**	Tell	Upstanding	N	
15	Magoula Rizava or Aggeli – Agios Theodoros	Tell	Partially levelled	EN–MN	Extensive surface survey – test excavation (Krahtopoulou et al. 2018)
16	Voulgarolakka – Agios Theodoros	Flat	Sub-alluvial	LN	Rescue excavation (Krahtopoulou et al. 2020b)
17	Magoula – Stavros	Tell	Partially levelled	MN	Extensive surface survey
18	Iera Moni Koronas – Stavros	Flat	Sub-alluvial	LN	Stratigraphic investigation (Krahtopoulou et al. forthcoming)
19	Magoula Ptelopoula 2 – Ptelopoula	Tell	Levelled	LN	Extensive surface survey
20	Magoula – Melissa	Tell	Partially levelled	N	Extensive surface survey
21	Magoula Agios Nikolaos – Ptelopoula**	Tell	Upstanding	N	
22	Magoula – Ptelopoula	Tell	Levelled	N	Extensive surface survey
23	Magoula – Ptelopoula	Tell	Upstanding	MN–LN	Extensive surface survey
24	Magoula Apostolou Sitatira – Ptelopoula	Tell	Partially levelled	MN–LN	Extensive surface survey
25	Karnomagoula – Ptelopoula	Tell	Upstanding	MN–LN–FN	Extensive surface survey (Orengo et al. 2015)

* EN: Early Neolothic; MN: Middle Neolithic; LN: Late Neolithic; FN: Final Neolithic; N: broadly Neolithic
** Sites uncultivated for a very long time; No visible surface material

settlements were a rather common feature of the Neolithic landscapes of Thessaly and implies that many more non-tell sites are likely to be discovered in the future.

Recent geophysical prospection of numerous tell-sites in coastal Thessaly demonstrated significant variability in their extent, layout and spatial organisation during the Neolithic (Sarris et al. 2017). Additionally, recent excavation and analytical evidence provide nuanced insights into formation processes and practices performed within the confines of early Middle Neolithic Koutroulou Magoula, a tell site situated at the southwestern edge of the western Thessalian plain. The substantial, nearly 5 m thick, cultural sequence was created in less than 200 years by vertical rebuilding of detached houses, made of mudbricks on stone foundations, regular middening and, probably, *in situ* animal penning in alternating open and roofed areas (Hamilakis *et al.* 2017; Koromila *et al.* 2018).

In an attempt to understand the formation and use of tells, LTNS focused on one of the earliest sites of the Kambos, Plateia Magoula Prodromos.

Plateia Magoula Prodromos re-visited

Background to the site

Plateia Magoula Prodromos (or Prodromos II) (hereafter PMP) is located *c.* 6 km northeast of the modern city of Karditsa and 1.4 km north-northeast of the modern village of Prodromos (see Fig. 3.4). The visible part of the mound presently stands approximately 5.6 m above the levelled surrounding terrain (Fig. 3.5).

Following persistent requests to level the mound, Giorgos Chourmouziadis, an emblematic figure of Neolithic archaeology, undertook rescue investigations at PMP in the early 1970s. Regrettably, the excavation was never fully-published and two general, preliminary reports, lacking stratigraphic and contextual information, are the only records available (Chourmouziadis 1971a; 1972). According to these reports, excavation in the centre of the mound revealed

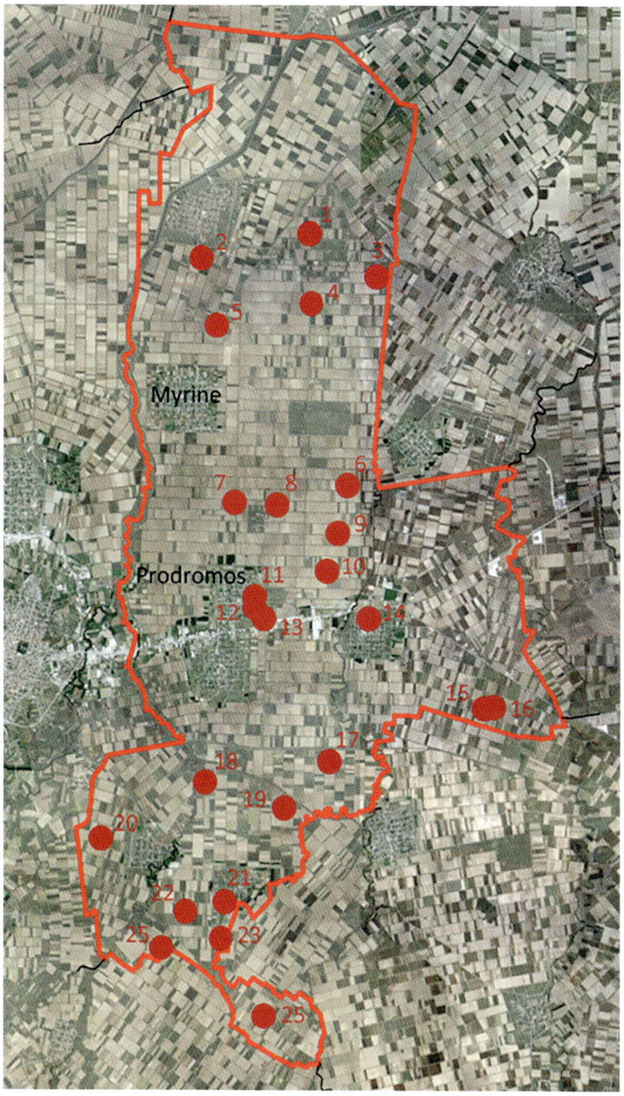

Figure 3.4 The Neolithic record of the Kambos: 1. Magoula Megala Leivadia; 2. Magoula Vaiou Kalamara; 3. Magoula Pouliou; 4. Agia Varvara. Myrine; 5. Magoula Semou; 6. Prodromos 11; 7. Prodromos I; 8. Prodromos II (Plateia Magoula Prodromos); 9. Prodromos 9; 10. Prodromos 7 (Magoula Koukouli or Rovoli); 11. Prodromos III (Magoula Agios Ioannis Prodromos); 12. Prodromos Primary School; 13. Babtzelis plot. Prodromos; 14. Magoula Agios Nikolaos. Agios Theodoros; 15. Magoula Rizava or Aggeli. Agios Theodoros; 16. Voulgarolakka. Agios Theodoros; 17. Magoula. Stavros; 18. Iera Moni Koronas; 19. Magoula Ptelopoula 2; 20. Magoula. Melissa; 21. Magoula Agios Nikolaos. Ptelopoula; 22. Magoula. Ptelopoula; 23. Magoula. Ptelopoula; 24. Magoula Apostolou Sitatira; 25. Karnomagoula.

Figure 3.5 Orthophotograph (top) and Digital Surface model (bottom) of Plateia Magoula Prodromos.

ten successive habitational phases that, on material culture evidence, span the Early Neolithic through to the beginning of the Middle Neolithic. Trial trenches at the edges of the *magoúla* exposed little cultural material (Halstead & Jones 1980, 95).

The major find of the PMP excavation was the remains of a wooden feature, made of beams, branches, planks up to 0.3 m wide and wooden pegs interpreted by the excavator as the collapsed roof of a fairly large (10 × 10 m) building (Chourmouziadis 1971a). Fascinated by this rare find and hoping to discover more organic remains, Chourmouziadis extended the excavation but only revealed traces of extensive destruction by fire; he concluded that, if present, organic materials must have also been destroyed. Based on the examination of the structural remains unearthed, he suggested that the presumably closely spaced buildings of PMP were large, rectangular, made of wattle and daub and divided internally by low walls, constructed in the same technique (Chourmouziadis 1972).

The multi-proxy investigation

On visual inspection, all profiles of the stratigraphic sequence of the large (15 × 5 m) trench opened at the centre of the tell in 1970, except for the eastern one, exhibit a remarkably uniform stratigraphy, consisting of a series of alternating light- and darker-coloured beds. The eastern exposure comprises a basal burnt wattle and daub structure, overlain by a relatively thick mineral bed and multiple stratified layers that visually resemble those exposed in all other profiles of the old excavation trench (Fig. 3.6).

LTNS adopted a high-resolution, multidisciplinary and multi-proxy approach with the aims of, first understanding the vertical development of the tell and, secondly addressing issues central to current Neolithic debates, such as the timing and duration of occupation, origin of deposits, use of space, range of activities performed on- and off-site, local vegetation and environmental conditions, land use, and environmental and/or anthropogenic disturbances. To this end, the stratigraphy of the old trench was documented photogrammetrically, in order to obtain a highly accurate framework for the integration of all data subsequently gathered. The stratigraphic section was then sampled systematically for sediment, micromorphological, pollen and non-pollen palynomorphs, archaeobotanical, anthracological, archaeomalacological, animal bone and pottery analyses and for radiocarbon dating. Photogrammetry was also employed for the high-precision recording and integration of all samples taken from the stratigraphic section. Although photogrammetric reconstruction and several analyses are still in progress, sedimentological, preliminary micromorphological and dating evidence suggest an extremely interesting site biography.

The entire *c.* 4.2 m thick sedimentary sequence exposed in the western and northern profiles of the old excavation trench was described in the field and then sampled for physical and chemical characterisation, using 2.5 cm plastic palaeomagnetic cubes. The suite of 138 bulk sediment samples collected was analysed for magnetic susceptibility, particle size distribution, organic carbon and nitrogen content, as well as for the determination of the stable carbon ($\delta^{13}C$) and stable nitrogen ($\delta^{15}N$) isotopic composition of the soil organic matter.[2]

Moreover, 14 micromorphological blocks were extracted from the east, west and south profiles. Two blocks, MB9 and MB14, taken from the west and east profiles respectively, were selected for further micromorphological analysis. Two large-format (*c.* 14 × 7 cm) micromorphological thin sections were produced following standard procedures (Murphy 1986) and studied under both a large-field stereo-binocular microscope and an optical polarising microscope at magnification from × 25 to × 500, following standard methodologies and guidelines (Bullock *et al.* 1985; Courty *et al.* 1989; Matthews 1995; Stoops 2003).

The temporal framework for this study was established by a suite of 11 AMS radiocarbon dates, ten from short-lived seeds and plant macro-remains at the NERC Radiocarbon Laboratory, University of Oxford, UK and one assay from oak charcoal at DirectAMS Radiocarbon Dating Service, USA. All dates obtained were calibrated, using Calib 7.2 and the IntCal13 calibration curve (Reimer *et al.* 2013). The temporal aspect of the tell was modelled with statistics, using OxCal v. 4.3.2. (Bronk Ramsey 2017) and the IntCal13 dataset (Reimer *et al.* 2013) (Table 3.2 and Fig. 3.7).

Preliminary results

On available radiocarbon evidence, PMP was established by 7405±57 BP (6418–6201 cal BC: Early Neolithic I – II transition) and was abandoned shortly after 7160±37 BP (6086–5931 cal BC: Early Neolithic III – Middle Neolithic I transition). The duration of the 3.2 m thick anthropogenic sequence is 255±70 years, in other words, between 185 and 325 years, indicating that PMP was a fairly short-lived site. Having established the timing and duration of occupation and/or use of the tell, we resorted to detailed sediment analysis and limited micromorphological evidence to gain insights into formation processes, internal structure and use of space at PMP. The results of sediment analysis will be discussed here in four groups exhibiting slightly different attributes (Figs 3.8 and 3.9).

The 3.2 m anthropogenic sequence was built on an Ab-Bw-C soil, formed within Holocene alluvial deposits. The fining upwards basal Group 1 sediments exhibit increasing magnetic susceptibility and organic carbon. The $\delta^{13}C$ values of the buried A soil horizon (−26.2 to −26.5‰) are consistent with organic matter derived predominately from arboreal (C3) vegetation, whereas the $\delta^{15}N$ exhibits values between 5.5‰ and 6‰. Stable isotopic values are

Figure 3.6 The stratigraphy of the historical excavation trench: western, northern and southern profiles (top); eastern profile (bottom).

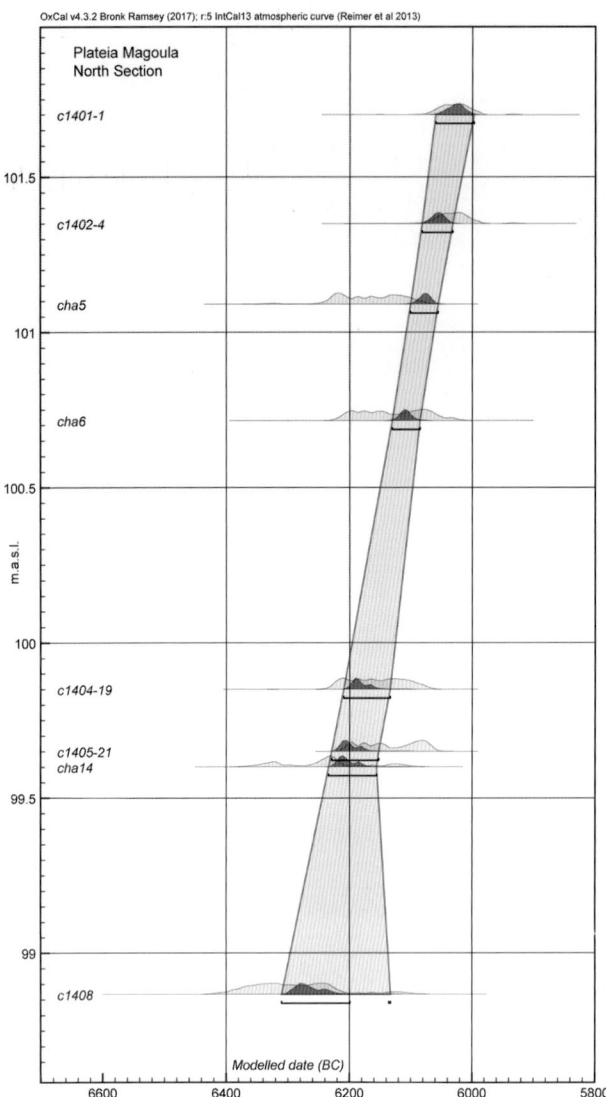

Figure 3.7 Plateia Magoula Prodromos: statistically modelled dates, excluding the date from the burnt structure, exposed at the eastern profile (sample ID 505).

Table 3.2 The AMS dates from Plateia Magoula Prodromos.

LTNS ID	Lab code	Area	Depth m.a.s.l.	Sample type and species	^{14}C age BP	Calibrated date (BC) from	to	%	Modelled date (BC) from	to	%
c1408	D-AMS 017802	North profile	98.867	Charcoal *Quercus deciduous*	7405±57	6418	6201	95.4	6319	6239	95.4
505	OxA-36551	East profile	99.57	Seed *Triticum monococcum*	7395±35	6387	6213	95.4	6242	6185	95.4*
cha14	OxA-36438	North profile	99.6	Charcoal *Erica*	7367±35	6367	6098	95.4	6240	6183	95.4
c1405-21	OxA-36587	North profile	99.65	Seed *Triticum monococcum*	7257±37	6211	6062	95.4	6235	6179	95.4
C1405	OxA-36429	South profile	99.718	Charcoal *Fraxinus* sp.	7333±34	6323	6077	95.4	6226	6174	95.4
c1404-19	OxA-36586	North profile	99.85	Seed *Triticum dicoccum*	7306±33	6230	6078	95.4	6214	6180	95.4
c1403	OxA-36428	South profile	100.198	Charcoal *Fraxinus* sp.	7333±34	6323	6077	95.4	6182	6147	95.4
cha6	OxA-36137	North profile	100.715	Seed *Triticum monococcum*	7253±40	6220	6034	95.4	6136	6096	95.4
cha5	OxA-36552	North profile	101.09	Seed *Triticum monococcum*	7326±37	6251	6072	95.4	6101	6060	95.4
c1402-4	OxA-36585	North profile	101.35	Seed *Triticum monococcum*	7164±35	6082	5985	95.4	6082	6032	95.4
c1401-1	OxA-36584	North profile	101.7	Seed *Triticum monococcum*	7160±37	6086	5931	95.4	6054	5994	95.4

*Not included in the radiocarbon calibration model

slightly heavier in the pedogenically unaltered sediments that underlie the buried palaeosol.

The earliest phase of the Neolithic occupation (Group 2 deposits) is characterised by fairly massive, alternating darker- and lighter-coloured beds that exhibit considerable small-scale particle size variation, indicating sediment additions from an array of subtly variable texture sources. Overall, the darker-coloured beds exhibit elevated magnetic susceptibility values and organic carbon content. According to preliminary micromorphological analysis of the MB9 thin section from the upper part of Group 2 deposits (Fig. 3.10), the organic material of the darker-coloured beds studied comprises ashes, notable burnt wood fragments and other charred plants, burnt bone, and burnt aggregates from probable cooking installations, including possible lime

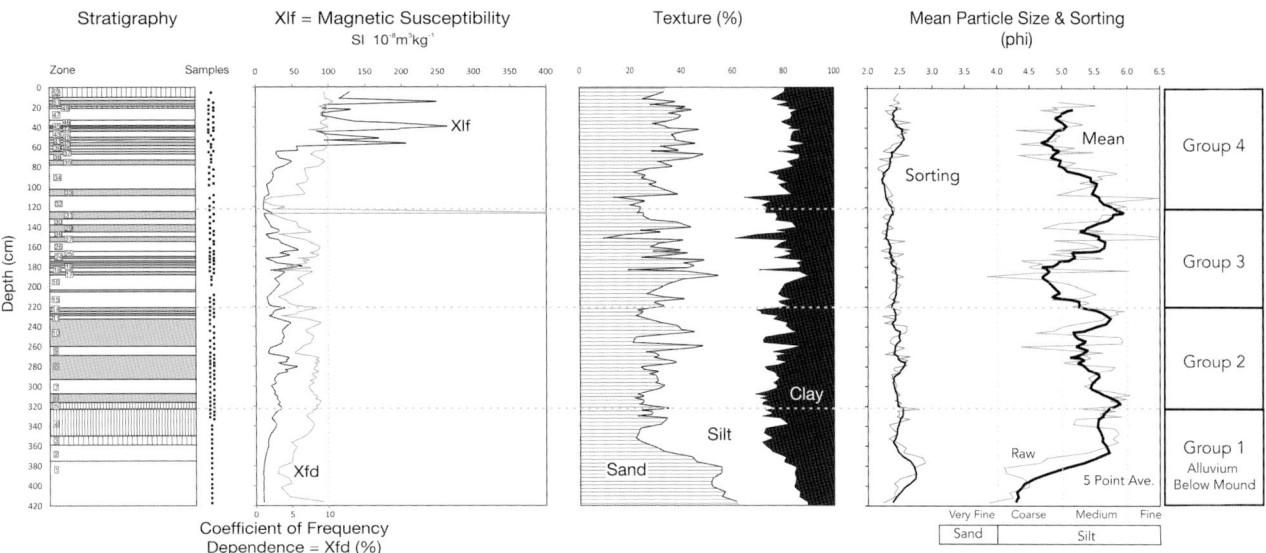

Figure 3.8 Graphic illustration of the Plateia Magoula Prodromos composite stratigraphy (north and west profile) and depth variation in the magnetic susceptibility (heavy line is the 3 point running average), texture, mean particle size and sorting.

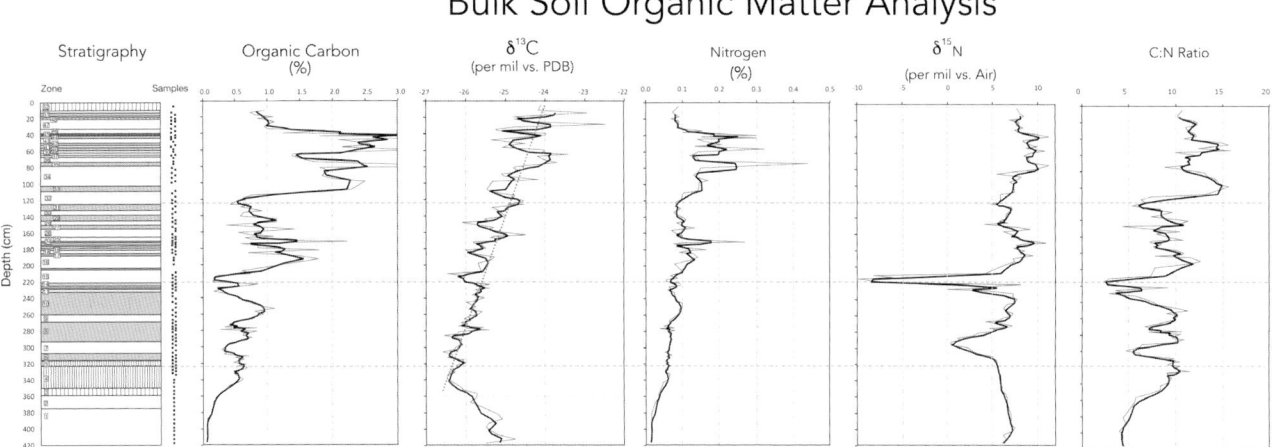

Figure 3.9 Graphic illustration of the Plateia Magoula Prodromos composite stratigraphy (north and west profiles) and results of bulk soil organic matter analysis (heavy line is the 3 point running average, light line is the raw data).

plaster fragments. The range of residues present therefore is compatible with the elevated magnetic susceptibility and organic carbon values observed and, most probably, indicate dumping of debris associated with food preparation, cooking and consumption events and structures in open-air spaces (Banerjea *et al.* 2015). Carbon isotopic composition ($\delta^{13}C$ values) becomes gradually heavier and bears little relation to the trend observed in the organic carbon. Finally, the nitrogen content gradually increases but shows no clear relationship to the stratigraphy, whereas the $\delta^{15}N$ content is strongly patterned.

The majority of Group 3 deposits are thinly bedded and exhibit slightly more variation in particle size than underlying Group 2 sediments. Overall, the organic carbon content increases markedly, with the base of the unit exhibiting the highest values that then decline throughout the deposit. Moreover, the $\delta^{13}C$ content increases from bottom to top, showing a rather cyclical pattern. The nitrogen content is also elevated in the lower beds and decreases somewhat towards the top of the unit, a pattern mirrored by the $\delta^{15}N$ content.

With the exception of the fairly thick lower beds, most of Group 4 deposits are thinly bedded and exhibit a high variability in particle size. Overall, these generally coarsening upwards sediments are slightly sandier than underlying beds. The organic carbon content of Group 4 sediments

Figure 3.10 Plateia Magoula Prodromos. Top: photo of the western profile showing location of MB9, scan of the thin section (13.5 × 5 × 6.5 cm) and microphotographs showing burnt bone (top) and wood fragment (bottom). Bottom: photo of the eastern profile showing location of MB14, scan of the thin section (13.5 × 5 × 6.5 cm) and microphotographs showing charred and siliceous plants.

steps up to almost double that of Group 3 average and the $\delta^{13}C$ continues to gradually become lighter, ending around −24‰, in other words it shifts *c*. 2‰ comparing to the basal palaeosol. Nitrogen and $\delta^{15}N$ values peak in the middle part of the unit. The most striking feature of Group 4 sediments however, is the remarkably high magnetic susceptibility values in the top 60 cm of the profile, indicating either a significant change in sediment source or a marked change of activities performed on site in the transition from the Early to the Middle Neolithic.

The eastern profile of the old excavation trench exhibits a more complex stratigraphy (Fig. 3.10). According to field observations, the base of the exposure comprises three successive floors, overlain by a thick layer of collapsed burnt daub. A radiocarbon date on carbonised einkorn seeds, recovered from a cache associated with the collapsed daub, dates destruction by fire to 7395±35 BP (6387–6213 cal BC) during the Early Neolithic II. Preliminary micromorphological observations indicate that the basal compact and possibly trampled floor is overlain by multiple finely laminated layers of *in situ* accumulated charred and siliceous plants, with or without occluded carbon, that may represent burnt fuel or burnt food-processing residues and imply food preparation and consumption in a roofed area (Matthews 1995; 2010; Banerjea *et al.* 2015). After destruction by fire, the structure was buried with a thick fill brought in from the surrounding landscape. Overlying sediments consist of alternating light- and darker-coloured beds that look, at least macroscopically, very similar to the deposits comprising the anthropogenic sequence exposed in all other profiles.

Discussion

The stratigraphic, analytical and dating evidence presented here, in conjunction with the close re-reading of the published accounts of the early 1970s excavations, offers a significant, albeit not necessarily conclusive, new understanding of the history of the site.

Although the horizontal extent, density and layout of Early Neolithic II PMP remain unknown, it is very likely that the burnt structure exposed in the east of the trench examined here correlates with the extended destruction level uncovered by Chourmouziadis (1972) immediately to the north. On available evidence, a residential use can be suggested for this occupation phase; people laid successive floors, stored grains, prepared, cooked and consumed food inside wattle and daub buildings.

The spatio-temporal correlation and role in the early built environment of PMP of the wooden feature interpreted by the excavator as the collapsed roof of a probable large wattle and daub house (Chourmouziadis 1971a) is much harder to pin down. Intriguingly, this feature was preserved unburnt, inviting at least two alternative interpretations: a) that it pre-dates Early Neolithic II and is perhaps associated with the, at present architecturally elusive, initial Early Neolithic I–II phase, suggested by the earliest radiocarbon date obtained from the base of the anthropogenic sequence; b) that burnt and unburnt debris are contemporary and the wooden feature miraculously survived the fire that destroyed the rest of the buildings.

What is certain however, is that after destruction by fire the Early Neolithic II building, exposed at the eastern end of the old excavation, was not replaced vertically; instead, it was intentionally buried and its life-cycle ended. Although it is presently unclear whether this pattern applies to the entire Early Neolithic II built environment of PMP, a profound change in the organisation and use of space followed destruction, at least in the part of the site investigated. Current stratigraphic, sedimentological and preliminary micromorphological evidence indicates substantial deposition into an open space. The lack of any evidence indicating the presence of structural elements (*e.g.* pits, postholes, walls, *etc.*) in the stratigraphic sequence is striking. Interestingly, the only architectural remains reported by Chourmouziadis (1971a; 1972) are those confined to the lowermost levels of the tell sequence. Unfortunately, the small area of the old excavation still exposed precludes any definitive argument as to whether residential areas were reorganised and relocated following destruction and closure or whether this event marked the formal end of habitational practices at this site. It is interesting to note that another three Early Neolithic sites are situated in close proximity to Plateia Magoula Prodromos, forming perhaps a broader interconnected settlement and/or activity complex. It is too early to speculate as to the role these four contemporaneous sites might have played in the construction of the early Neolithic landscape and way of life, but a degree of mobility and perhaps fluidity in the use of space and practices performed on- and off-site cannot be precluded (Kotsakis 2005).

Returning to PMP, overall, the most pronounced feature of the highly stratified depositional sequence of the site is the persistent, almost cyclical, alternation of more- and less-organic deposits. In terms of geometry, the lighter-coloured, less-organic beds range from sheet-like layers to discrete semi-lenticular piles (flat bottom, convex top, thinning to the edges), suggesting that they were brought into the site as dumps of sediment. Repeated deposition of organic-rich sediments on the other hand, implies activities that generate considerable amounts of organic material (*e.g.* disposing of human and animal waste, domestic cooking, animal penning, burning of different materials, various pyrotechnological processes, *etc.*). Understanding the nature and the possible range of these activities is still in progress. The only micromorphological sample as yet subjected to preliminarily analysis suggests that accumulation of organic material within Group 2 sediment is associated with food preparation and cooking debris. But how representative this single sample is of the 3.2 m anthropogenic sequence remains at present unclear. Moreover, chemical and isotopic data reported here only hint at the origins of the organic material deposited in PMP. Arguably, a more refined understanding of the range of practices associated with organic-rich residues and materials incorporated into the sedimentary matrix should await further micromorphological and other bioarchaeological (*e.g.* Bogaard *et al.* 2013; Vaiglova *et al.* 2014), chemical and biomolecular analyses.

Despite the limitations highlighted above, some interesting broad trends can still be discerned. The organic carbon of the deposits appears to vary inversely to the introduction of earthen fills from the surrounding landscape. It is likely therefore, that the build-up of organic matter was one of the driving forces behind the introduction of new sediment into the mound, reflecting perhaps hygienic tolerance. The dramatic increase observed in Group 4 sediments on the other hand, may indicate a radical change in the source of the organic matter introduced into the sedimentary matrix towards the end of the site occupation. One of the most intriguing trends in the organic matter analysis is the gradual shift towards heavier values in the stable carbon and nitrogen isotopic composition through time. From the start of the settlement to its abandonment the $\delta^{13}C$ shifts from *c.* −26‰ to −24‰ and the $\delta^{15}N$ changes from *c.* 3‰ to 5–8‰, trends that may indicate an increasing presence of cereals in the organic matter contributed to the site and may hint at intensive land management practices (*e.g.* Bogaard *et al.* 2013; Vaiglova *et al.* 2014), or increased presence of dung in the matrix (*e.g.* Koromila *et al.* 2018; Portillo *et al.* 2019), implying perhaps changes in the species composition (Shahack-Gross *et al.* 2008) and/or an increasing herding range, or yet another change in the use of space at PMP.

The emerging evidence, however, indicates that the remarkable, nearly cyclical, deposition of organic debris and of large volumes of mineral sediments hauled or burrowed from the surrounding or underlying landscape, constituted a distinct, perhaps communal, social practice sustained throughout the life-history of the site, however residential or otherwise its function.

Conclusions

The new discoveries and data reported in this chapter undermine traditional stereotypes and interpretations and allow a new reading of the Neolithic landscapes of the Kambos region. It is now clear that western Thessaly has long remained on the periphery of Neolithic discourse due to the striking concurrence of: a) long-established research traditions, focus and priorities; b) unsubstantiated projection into the Neolithic of powerful social and environmental notions and images of the recent past; c) catastrophic landscape modifications in the 1970s; and d) locally heavy Holocene alluviation.

Contrary to earlier assumptions, fresh evidence demonstrates that the Neolithic forms a dominant component of the prehistoric landscape of the Kambos area. The settlement record spans the entire Neolithic and comprises tells and flat sites that coexisted, from at least the early 6th millennium BC. All flat sites were single-phased; many tells were occupied for only a few centuries and less than a handful developed into the iconic sites that inspired theoretical discourse and preoccupied research agendas until late in the 20th century. Tell building is not necessarily the result of exclusive habitational use and of long-term vertical replacement of closely spaced substantial mudbrick houses. The persistent, possibly deliberate, accumulation of materials and sediments in extensive open spaces, as reported for Early Neolithic Plateia Magoula Prodromos, may also have led to rather substantial vertical deposition and tell formation.

In recent years, we have learnt a lot about the Neolithic of Thessaly. Arguably there is much more to be learnt. The work presented in this chapter highlights the great potential of integrated multiscale and multidisciplinary research to expand our understanding of Neolithic lifeways in the Kambos region, and beyond and to illuminate the complex and dynamic practices and interactions that operated within the wider Neolithic social milieu.

Acknowledgements

We would like to thank Drs Antonio Blanco-González and Tobias Kienlin for the stimulating session in the 24th Annual Meeting of the EAA and for editing this chapter. This research was undertaken with permission of the Hellenic Ministry of Culture & Sports. Research was funded by the Institute of Aegean Prehistory (INSTAP), the Mediterranean Archaeological Trust (MAT) and the NERC-AHRC National Radiocarbon Facility (NF/2017/17). We are grateful to Prof. Paul Halstead for commenting on an earlier draft of this chapter, Dr Llorenç Picornell-Gelabert for identifying wood for radiocarbon dating and to Domna Isaakidou, Anna Karligioti and Georgia Kasapidou for valuable assistance during fieldwork. Special thanks to Kostas Palaiochoritis for his refreshing view of the Neolithic.

Notes

1. This chapter uses the chronological framework for the Neolithic of Thessaly proposed by Reingruber *et al.* (2017).
2. The soil organic carbon and nitrogen content and the stable isotopic composition of the soil organic carbon were determined by Bruce Barnett at the Keck Palaeoenvironmental & Environmental Stable Isotope Laboratory at the University of Kansas, USA. All other sediment analyses were conducted by Dr Charles Frederick at the Geoarchaeology Laboratory at Austin, Texas, USA.

References

Andreou, S. & Kotsakis, K. (1986) Diastaseis tou chorou stin kendriki Makedonia: apotiposi tis endokoinotikis kai diakoinotikis choroorganosis. In *Amitos. Festschrift to M. Andronikos*, 57–88. Thessaloniki, Aristotle University of Thessaloniki.

Andreou, S., Fotiadis, M. & Kotsakis, K. (1996) Review of Aegean Prehistory V. The Neolithic and Bronze Age of northern Greece. *American Journal of Archaeology* 100, 537–597.

Apostolidis, E. & Koukis, G. (2013) Engineering-geological conditions of the formations in the Western Thessaly basin, Greece. *Central European Journal of Geosciences* 5(3), 407–422.

Banerjea, R., Bell, M., Matthews, W. & Brown, A. (2015) Applications of micromorphology to understanding activity areas and site formation processes in experimental hut floors. *Archaeological and Anthropological Sciences* 7(1), 89–112.

Bogaard, A., Fraser, R., Heaton, T.H., Wallace, M., Vaiglova, P., Charles, M., Jones, G., Evershed, R.P., Styring, A.K., Anderson, N.H., Arbogast, R.-M., Bartosiewicz, L., Gardeisen, A., Kastrup, M., Maier, U., Marinova, E., Ninov, L., Schäfer, M. & Stephan, E. (2013) Crop manuring and intensive land management by Europe's first farmers. *Proceedings of the National Academy of Sciences* 110(13), 12589–12594.

Bronk-Ramsey, C. (2017) Methods for summarizing radiocarbon datasets. *Radiocarbon* 59(2), 1809–1833.

Bullock, P., Fedoroff, N., Jongerious, A., Stoops, G., Tursina, T. & Babel, U. (1985) *Handbook for Soil Thin Section Description*. Wolverhampton, Waine Research.

Caputo, R. & Pavlidis, S. (1991) I neotektoniki domi kai ekseliksi tis Thessalias. *Deltio Hellinikis Geologikis Etaireias* 25, 119–133.

Chatziaggelakis, L.P. (2007) I Epochi tou Charlkou sti ditiki Thessalia. *Thessaliko Imerologio* 52, 1–48.

Chatziaggelakis, L.P. & Karagianoppoulos, Ch, (2012) Prodromos Karditsas. Neotera stoixeia apo ti Magoula ston Agion Ioanni. *AETHSE* 3, 85–96.

Chourmouziadis, G. (1971a) Dio neai engatastaseis tis archaioteras Neolithikis eis tin Dytikin Thessalian. *Archaiologika Analekta eks Athinon* 4(2), 164–175.

Chourmouziadis, G. (1971b) I diakekosmimeni kerameiki tis archaioteras Neolithikis periodou eis tin Thessalian. *Archaiologiki Efimeris* 1971, 165–187.

Chourmouziadis, G. (1972) Anaskafes eis ton Prodromon Karditsis. *Archaiologiko Deltio* 27, 394–394.

Chourmouziadis, G. (1973) *I Anthropomorphiki Eidoloplastiki tis Neolithikis Thessalias: Provlimata Kataskevis, Typologias kai Ermineias*. Volos, Etaireia Thessalikon Erevnon.

Courty, M.A., Goldberg, P. & Macphail, R. (1989) *Soils and Micromorphology in Archaeology*. Cambridge, Cambridge University Press.

Demoule, J.-P. & Perlès, C. (1993) The Greek Neolithic: a new review. *Journal of World Prehistory* 7, 355–416.

Dimoula, A. (2014) *Proimi Kerameiki Technologia kai Paragogi. To Paradeigma tis Thessalias*. Thessaloniki, Altintzis.

Dimoula, A., Saridaki, N., Vliora, E. & Papadias, G. (forthcoming) Ta mystika tou Kambou – I meleti tis kerameikis. *AETHSE* 6.

Gallis, K. (1979a) A short chronicle of the Greek archaeological investigations in Thessaly, from 1881 until to the present day. In J. Pouilloux (ed.), *La Thessalie*, 1–30. Lyon, Maison de l' Orient et de la Méditerranée.

Gallis, K. (1979b) Proistorikos oikismos Makychoriou (agros Vaiou Kalamara). *Archaiologiko Deltio* 29, 568–567.

Grammenos, D. (1991) *Neolithikes Erevnes stin Kendriki kai Anatoliki Makedonia*. Athens, Archaeologiki Etaireia.

Halstead, H. (2019) Reclaiming the land: Belonging, landscape and *in situ* displacement on the plain of Karditsa (Greece). *History and Anthropology*. https://doi.org/10.1080/02757206.2019.1696325

Halstead, P. (1984) *Strategies for Survival: An Ecological Approach to Social and Economic Change in the Early Farming Communities of Thessaly*. Unpublished PhD Thesis, University of Cambridge.

Halstead, P. (2006) *What's Ours is Mine? Village and Household in Early Farming Society in Greece*. Amsterdam, University of Amsterdam.

Halstead, P. (forthcoming) Georgoktinotrophia kai trofi. Apo tis paradoseis ton Karagkounidon stis praktikes ton archaion. In V. Koziou (ed.), *Proceedings of the 5th Diethnes Ethologiko Synedrio ton Thessalon Karagkounidon*.

Halstead, P. & Jones, G. (1980) Early Neolithic economy in Thessaly – some evidence from excavations at Prodromos. *Anthropologika* 1, 93–117.

Hamilakis, Y., Kyparissi-Apostolika, N., Loughlin, T., Carter, T., Cole, J., Facorellis, Y., Katsaroy, S., Kaznesi, A., Pentedeka, A., Tsamis, V. & Zorzin, N. (2017) Koutroulou Magoula in Phthiotida, central Greece: a Middle Neolithic tell site in context. In A. Sarris, E. Kalogiropoulou, T. Kalayci & L. Karimali (eds), *Communities, Landscapes, and Interaction in Neolithic Greece*, 81–96. Ann Arbor MI, International Monographs in Prehistory.

Idol, D (2018) The 'Peaceful Conquest' of Lake Kopaïs: Modern water management and environment in Greece. *Journal of Modern Greek Studies* 36(1), 71–95.

Karagiannopoulos, Ch. (2016) Prodromos Karditsas, Magoula Agios Ioannis. A prehistoric settlement in the western Thessalian plain. In Z. Tsirtsoni, (ed.), *The Human Face of Radiocarbon. Reassessing Chronology in Prehistoric Greece and Bulgaria, 5000–3000 cal BC*, 381–393. Lyon, Maison de l' Orient et de la Méditerranée.

Karamitrou-Mentessidi, G., Efstratiou, N., Kaszanowska, M. & Kozlowski, J.K. (2015) Early Neolithic settlement of Mavropigi in western Greek Macedonia. *Eurasian Prehistory* 12(1–2), 47–116.

Koromila, G., Karkanas, P., Hamilakis, Y., Kyparissi-Apostolika, N., Kotzamani, G. & Harris, K. (2018) The Neolithic tell as a multi-species monument: human, animal, and plant relationships through a micro-contextual study of animal dung at Koutroulou Magoula, central Greece. *Journal of Archaeological Science Reports* 19, 753–768.

Kotsakis, K. (1999) What tells can tell: social space and settlement in the Greek Neolithic. In P. Halstead (ed.), *Neolithic Society in Greece*, 66–76. Sheffield, Sheffield Academic Press.

Kotsakis, K. (2005) Across the border: unstable dwellings and fluid landscapes in the earliest Neolithic of Greece. In D. Bailey, A. Whittle & V. Cummings (eds), *(Un)settling the Neolithic*, 8–15. Oxford, Oxbow Books.

Kotsakis, K. (2006) Settlement of discord: Sesklo and the emerging household. In N. Tasić & C. Grozdanov (eds), *Homage to Milutin Garašanin*, 207–220. Belgrade, Serbian Academy of Sciences and Arts.

Krahtopoulou, A. (2019a) Current approaches to the Neolithic of Thessaly. *Archaeological Reports* 65, 73–85 https://doi.org/10.1017/S0570608419000048

Krahtopoulou, A. (2019b) Aftokinitodromos Kentrikis Elladas – E65. Neolithikos oikismos sti thesi 'Myrine-Agia Varvara'. *Archeologiko Deltio* 70 (2015), 717–721.

Krahtopoulou, A., Dimoula, A., Livarda, A. & Saridaki, A. (2018) The discovery of the earliest specialised Middle Neolithic pottery workshop in western Thessaly, central Greece. *Antiquity* 92(362), E5. https://doi.org/10.15184/aqy.2018.54.

Krahtopoulou, A., Orengo, H.A., Palaiochoritis, K. & Stamati, A. (2020a) Anadasmos kai politismiko topio ston Kambo tis Karditsas. *AETHSE* 5, 167–179.

Krahtopoulou, A., Sofianou, F., Alexiou, N., Papakosta, C., Charouli, M., Kostopoulou, F. & Christoforidi, E. (2020b) Apo ti Neoteri Neolithiki sti Mesi Epochi tou Chalkou stous Mavrachades kai ston Agio Theodoro tis Karditsas. *AETHSE* 5, 127–140.

Krahtopoulou, A., Orengo, H.A., Dimoula, A., Garcia-Molsosa, A., Palaiochoritis, K. & Saridaki, N. (forthcoming) Ta mystika tou Kambou – i Neolithiki *AETHSE* 6.

Matthews, W. (1995) Micromorphological characterisation and interpretation of occupation deposits and microstratigraphic sequences at Abu Salabikh, Southern Iraq. In A.J. Barham & R.I. Macphail (eds), *Archaeological Sediments and Soils: Analysis, Interpretation and Management*, 41–74. London, University College, Institute of Archaeology.

Matthews, W. (2010) Geoarchaeology and taphonomy of plant remains and microarchaeological residues in early urban environments in the Ancient Near East. *Quaternary International* 214(1–2), 98–113.

Murphy, C.P. (1986) *Thin Section Preparation of Soil and Sediments*. Berhamstead, A.B. Academic Publishers.

Orengo, H.A., Krahtopoulou, A., Garcia-Molsosa, A., Plaiochoritis, K. & Stamati, A. (2015) Photogrammetric re-discovery of the hidden long-term landscapes of western Thessaly, central Greece. *Journal of Archaeological Science* 64, 100–109.

Papadopoulou, M. (1958) Magoulitsa. Neolithikos oikismos para tin Karditsan. *Thessalika* I, 39–79.

Pappa, M. (2008) *Organosi tou Chorou kai Oikistika Stoixeia stous Neolithikous Oikismous tis Kendrikis Makedonias. D.E.Th.-Thermi-Makriyalos*. Unpublished PhD Thesis, University of Thessaloniki.

Pappa, M. & Besios, M. (1999) The Makriyalos Project: rescue excavations at the Neolithic site of Makriyalos, Pieria, northern Greece. In P. Halstead (ed.), *Neolithic Society in Greece*, 108–120. Sheffield, Sheffield Academic Press.

Portillo, M., García-Suárez, A., Kjimowicz, A., Barański, M.Z. & Matthews, W. (2019) Animal penning and open area activity at Neolithic Çatalhöyük, Turkey. *Journal of Anthropological Archaeology* 56, 1–16.

Prontzas, V. (1992) *Oikonomia kai Gaioktisia sti Thessalia (1881–1912)*. Athens, National Bank of Greece Cultural Foundation.

Reimer, P.J., Bard, E., Bayliss, A., Beck, J.W., Blackwell, P.G., Bronk-Ramsey, C., Buck, C.E., Cheng, H., Lawrence-Edwards, R., Friedrich, M., Grootes, P.M., Guilderson, T.P., Haflidason, H., Hajdas, I., Hatté, C., Heateon, T.J., Hoffmann, D.L., Hogg, G., Hughen, K.A., Felix-Kaiser, K., Kromer, B., Manning, S.W., Niu, M., Reimer, R.W., Richards, D.A., Scott, E.M., Southon, J.R., Staff, R.A., Turney, C.S.M. & van der Plicht, J. (2013) IntCal13 and Marine13 radiocarbon age calibration curves 0–50,000 years cal BP. *Radiocarbon* 55(4), 1869–1887.

Reingruber, A., Toufexis, G., Kyparissi, N., Anetakis, M., Maniatis, Y. & Facorellis, Y. (2017) Neolithic Thessaly: radiocarbon dated periods and phases. *Documenta Praehistorica* XLIV, 34–53.

Sarris, A., Kalayci, T., Simon, F.X., Donati, J., Cuenca-García, C., Manataki, M., Cantoro, G., Moffat, I., Kalogiropoulou, E., Karampatsou, G., Armstrong, K., Argyriou, N., Dederix, S., Manzetti, C., Nikas, N., Vouzaxakis, K., Rondiri, V., Arachtoviti, P., Almatzi, K., Efstathiou, D. & Stamelou, E. (2017) Opening a new frontier in the study of Neolithic settlement patterns on eastern Thessaly, Greece. In A. Sarris, E. Kalogiropoulou, T. Kalayci & L. Karimali (eds), *Communities, Landscapes, and Interaction in Neolithic Greece*, 27–48. Ann Arbor MI, International Monographs in Prehistory.

Shahack-Gross., R., Simons, A. & Ambrose, S.H. (2008) Identification of pastoral sites using stable nitrogen and carbon isotopes from bulk sediment samples: a case study in modern and archaeological pastoral settlements in Kenya. *Journal of Archaeological Sciences* 35, 983–990.

Stoops, G. (2003) *Guidelines for Analysis and Description of Soil and Regolith Thin Sections*. Madison WI, Soil Science Society of America.

Souvatzi, S.G. (2008) *A Social Archaeology of Households in Neolithic Greece: An Anthropological Approach*. Cambridge, Cambridge University Press.

Toufexis, G. (2017) *Oikistiki Drastiriotita kai Organosi tou Chorou stous Oikismous tis Neoteris Neolithikis sti Thessalia. Paradeigmata apo tous Oikismous ston Profiti Ilia Mandras, Makrychori, Galene kai Rachmani*. Unpublished PhD Thesis, University of Thessaly.

Tsountas, Ch. (1900) Anaskafai en Thessalia. *Praktika tis en Athinais Archaiologikis Etaireias* (1899), 101–102.

Tsountas, Ch. (1908) *Ai Proistorikai Akropoleis Diminiou kai Sesklou*. Athens, Vivliothiki tis en Athinais Archaiologikis Etaireias.

Vaiglova, P., Bogaard, A., Collins, M., Cavanagh, W., Mee, C., Renard, J., Lamb, A., Gardeisen, A. & Fraser, R. (2014) An integrated stable isotope study of plants and animals from Kouphovouno, southern Greece: a new look at Neolithic farming. *Journal of Archaeological Science* 42, 201–215.

Wace, A.J.B. & Thompson, M.S. (1912) *Prehistoric Thessaly*. Cambridge, Cambridge University Press.

Ziota, Ch. (2014) O oikismos tou Kleitou Kozanis sto evritero physiko kai anthropogenes perivallon tis Neoteris kai Telikis Neolithikis periodou. In E. Stefani, N. Merousis & A. Dimoula (eds), *Ekato Chronia Erevnas stin Proistoriki Makedonia 1912–2012*. Thessaloniki, Archaiologiko Mouseio Thessalonikis.

4

The Old Becomes New: Material Culture and Architectural Continuity on an Anatolian *Höyük*

Sharon R. Steadman and Jennifer C. Ross

This paper will present several examples of material culture continuity at Çadır Höyük – continuity that does not seem to be grounded in ancestry or cultural permanence, but that appears based in the experience of this particular place, a small tell in a fertile valley of central Anatolia (Fig. 4.1). These examples speak to a specific set of material culture practices that were periodically revived, and materials and ideas that were, themselves, reused, recycled, and occasionally reconceived. It is possible to see these practices in terms of limitations: a limited set of resources, or an interruption in supplies due to political and economic crises. But the tell, or in Anatolian parlance, the *höyük*, also provided opportunities and affordances; as archaeologists, it is important for us to keep in mind that ancient peoples did not necessarily experience limitations and changes in terms of loss or absence.

While archaeologists and others have recently written about the phenomenon of 'place memory', rooted in particular landscapes, or in the creation of monumental or structural markings that would evoke memory and imagination over generations (Bachelard 1958; Heidegger 1977; Harmanşah 2013; 2014), what we see at Çadır Höyük is perhaps a more mundane form of memory: a continuity of technological choices that related to resources, socio-economic and political circumstances, and aesthetic perceptions. The first two examples consider ceramic traditions at the site, while the third draws on a long-lived architectural pattern.

The site and excavations

Çadır Höyük ('Tent Mound') is located in the Yozgat Province of central Anatolia (Turkey). It sits on a natural rise surrounded by a landscape ideal for agrarian production. A river, several streams, and many nearby springs provide ample fresh water. Major north–south and east–west trade routes converged at a point approximately 15 km to the northwest at least as early as the 1st millennium BC and were likely in operation for millennia before. At least two clay, and several chert, sources were accessible to Çadır residents; obsidian and metals were also regularly obtained, likely from the trade routes just described. The resources available to Çadır residents ensured that the location would enjoy a long history of occupation.

Excavations began at Çadır in 1994 following an intensive site surface survey. Surface collections suggested that the prehistoric occupation of the mound – the Late Chalcolithic, *c.* 4000–3000 BC – was limited to the lower southern slope; succeeding periods including the 2nd and 1st millennium BC were to be found primarily on the eastern and northern slopes, but also on the upper southern slope. Byzantine occupation, unsurprisingly, rested on the mound summit. Excavations have borne out these initial assessments of the spatial placement of occupation through the millennia (Fig. 4.2). A deep sounding, excavated from 1994 to 2000, provided a radiocarbon date of around 5200 BC (Middle Chalcolithic), at a depth of several metres below the present Late Chalcolithic (*c.* 3800–3700 BC) exposure. Excavations on the mound summit have suggested the site was abandoned during the major Seljuk incursions onto the plateau, in the 13th or early 14th century AD. The *höyük*, therefore, was continuously occupied for over 6000 years.

Excavations of the prehistoric occupation have described four major cultural phases. The earliest yet exposed, known as the 'Agglutinated' phase *c.* 3800/3700–3600 BC (Steadman *et al.* 2017; 2019a), presents a farming/herding settlement structured in Eastern and Western Compounds, bisected by a street. The street leads into the interior of the settlement, to what is likely a Northern Compound, not yet revealed. Following the Agglutinated is the 'Burnt House/Omphalos Building' phase *c.* 3600–3200 BC (Steadman *et al.* 2017; 2019a; 2019b). The street still separates the

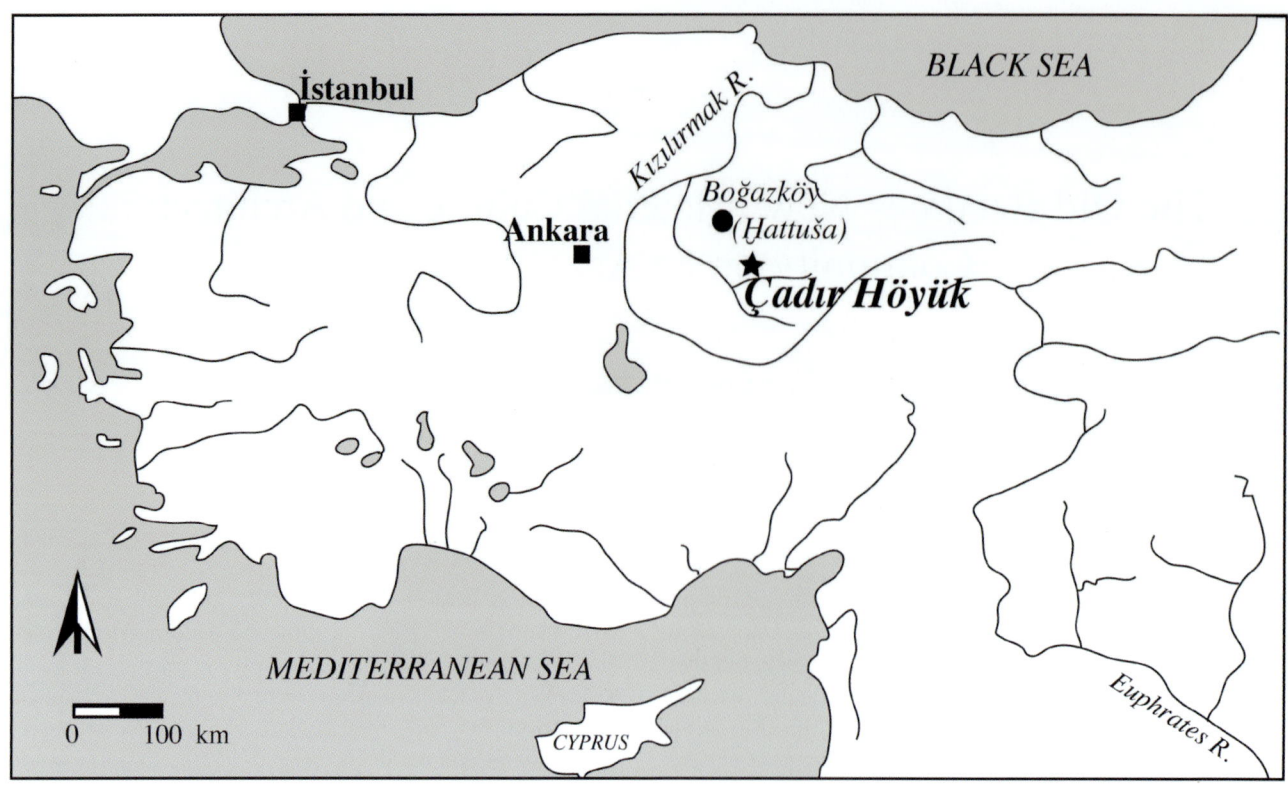

Figure 4.1 Top: map showing location of Çadır Höyük; bottom: view of Çadır Höyük mound looking south.

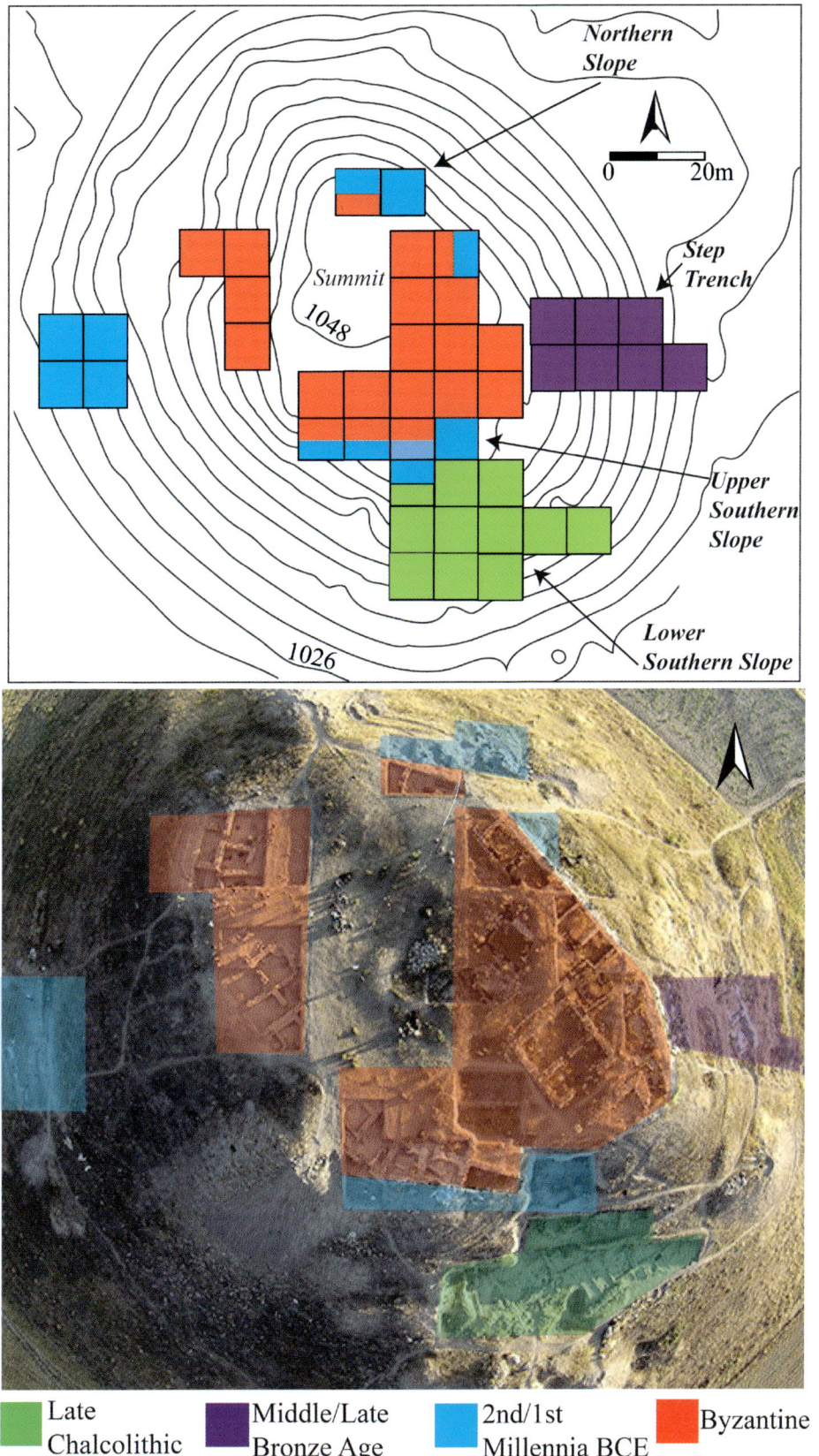

Figure 4.2 Top: topographic map of mound with location of trenches (colours indicate chronological occupational periods currently represented in trenches); bottom: aerial of mound with periodization colours superimposed.

compounds. The Eastern Compound now consists of a large residence (the Burnt House) with associated courtyards, and an area behind it where ritual activities likely occurred. The Western Compound is industrial, providing an area for major ceramic production activities and a structure, the 'Omphalos Building', for the distribution of ceramics. To the north, residents lived on an 'Upper Town' terrace approximately 1.2 m above the 'Lower Town' Eastern and Western Compounds.

The third 'Transitional' phase, *c.* 3200–3000 BC sees major changes in the Lower Town with residents building smaller structures with storage pits and hearths attached (Steadman & McMahon 2015; Steadman *et al.* 2015). Their purpose seems to have been for temporary shelter and possibly for storage. The Eastern Compound begins to fall into disuse at this time. On the other hand, the Northern Compound in the Upper Town shows a vibrancy once found in the Lower Town. Ceramic production and general habitation moved to the Upper Town.

The fourth and final 'Early Bronze I' prehistoric phase (*c.* 3000–2800 BC) features distinct trajectories for the Lower and Upper Towns (Steadman *et al.* 2019a; 2019b; 2019c). The Lower Town is largely abandoned, while residents in the Upper Town built an impressive external (defensive?) wall (Fig. 4.3); most of the domestic occupation moved inside the wall – as yet unexcavated – and some of the industrial activities remain in place, now outside the large wall. At the end of the millennium residents moved away from the outer, more accessible areas into an interior, more protected, living situation. The Lower Town was never again occupied and remained open and accessible to those who came later. This is evident by the presence of an Early Bronze II pit, a 2nd millennium BC Hittite silo and Hittite pits, and 1st millennium BC Late Iron Age pits, all scattered across the area.

After the Early Bronze I occupation of the southern slope, habitation over the next millennium or so (*c.* 2800–1600 BC) moved to other areas of the mound, primarily the eastern slope where Early Bronze III (*c.* 2800–2000 BC), Middle Bronze, and early Hittite (*c.* 2000–1650 BC) cultural and architectural remains abound. Residents returned to the southern slope in the 2nd millennium BC, likely in the Old Hittite period, *c.* 1600 BC, when they built a large 2 m wide wall encircling their settlement (excavated in eastern and northern slope trenches). In the 15th or early 14th century the wall was rebuilt, expanded to 3 m in width around the settlement, with the addition of a mudbrick platform in the upper southern slope portion. From the building of these walls onward, occupation continued on the upper southern slope, stretching from the mid-2nd millennium BC to the Hellenistic and early Roman periods (4th–3rd centuries BC).

Of these many post-Chalcolithic cultural phases, the most germane to the present discussion are the Late

Figure 4.3 View of Upper Town (looking west) showing substantial Early Bronze I wall.

Bronze Age (1500–1200 BC) and Early Iron Age periods (1200–900 BC). By the 13th century BC the Hittite Empire, an ethno-linguistic group that spoke an Indo-European language, had controlled much of the Anatolian plateau for several centuries. Çadır rests within the orbit of the Hittite centre, with the imperial capital, Ḫattuša, just 70 km distant. Hittite ceramics, present at Çadır in southern, eastern, and northern slope excavations, are most often recognised based on mass-produced, highly standardised ceramics, often called 'drab ware'. Hittite rule, attested across central and southern Anatolia until around 1200 BC, is marked by incorporation into a semi-centralised system of resource extraction, taxation, and religious practices. At Çadır, participation in the imperial economic system is evinced in the presence of mass-produced drab ware, as well as a very small number of Hittite fine wares. The period is best represented in excavations on the eastern slope, where the remains include both fortification walls and likely domestic buildings.

By the early 12th century BC, the Hittite Empire had collapsed, and the Early Iron Age period commenced. Even prior to its collapse, however, in the late years of Hittite power, the political grip of the Hittite government on its territories faced challenges on various fronts, and this seems to have led to some loosening of control over ceramic production. At Çadır, these changing circumstances resulted in new local industries. Atop the massive mudbrick fortification wall and adjoining platform are several phases of reuse of an industrial installation, interpreted as a locale for remelting copper-bronze alloys; before the decline in centralized Hittite power, it is likely that Çadır provided metals as tax payments to Ḫattuša, but now residents likely kept the supply for themselves. Associated with this installation is an array of wheel-made pottery – relatively little of it typical Hittite drab ware – as well as handmade forms.

By the Early Iron Age, whatever trickle of goods that had been attainable from trade networks during the last stages of the Hittite Empire, had disappeared, and Çadır residents clearly 'made do' with what was locally available. On the upper southern slope, people changed their industrial endeavours to textile-based activities, including what appears to be leather-working and felt production, presumably in response to localised forces of supply and demand (Ross *et al.* 2019). Architectural features from the Early Iron Age are limited to low walls and a large number of shallow depressions and deeper pits, many of them with a finely plastered surface, periodically reapplied. The Early Iron Age residents also sought out other ways to make up for a dwindling of resources. Included in these innovations was a new, or renewed, direction in their ceramic production.

Ceramic revivals

As nearly all archaeologists have experienced, ceramic styles at a long-lived site may change drastically, and often unpredictably. Changes can be attributed to a wide range of causes: technological developments, foodways, culture contacts, resources, and other needs. Among the aspects of pottery that change are the methods of manufacture, predominant forms, decoration, and raw materials.

At Çadır, occupied by pottery producers for more than 6000 years, such changes are evident in each period. But of particular interest are earlier production methods, vessel shapes, and decorative techniques originating in the Late Chalcolithic that were revived several thousand years later, in the Late Bronze Age and Iron Age. This revival follows the period of political control by Hittite imperial power.

Late Chalcolithic ceramics at Çadır: Setting the stage

The Late Chalcolithic pottery at Çadır Höyük is entirely handmade; construction techniques include pinching, coiling, and, for large vessels, attaching two slabs together. Ceramics are quite consistent throughout the first three phases with regard to surface treatment, which included applying a slip, and burnishing most vessels to a very high gloss. This is accomplished by letting the slipped vessel dry to leathery hardness. A tool, in the case of the Late Chalcolithic usually a smoothed bone or stone, is then used to polish, or 'burnish', the exterior and often the interior of the vessel. The burnish marks are often visible after firing, known as 'pattern burnishing'.

The earlier Late Chalcolithic kilns at Çadır were 'updraft' kilns (Fig. 4.4); the fuel, likely a combination of dung and plant materials, was placed at the base of the kiln and the resulting smoke exited the kiln through the top of the chamber. Firing regularly took place in a lower-temperature 'reduction' atmosphere in which oxygen is largely denied to the surface of the vessels; this was often combined with an oxidising atmosphere allowing oxygen to reach the surface. Reduction atmospheres produced black surfaces – sometimes with mottling – while oxidation atmospheres produced more vivid colours including reds and oranges. More neutral colours, such as buff and brown, were also achievable.

In the Agglutinated phase the most common colour on the exterior of vessels was black; interiors, if burnished, were either black or sometimes one of the other colours noted. Often interiors were left unburnished and presented the natural clay colour (post-firing). The most common shapes (Fig. 4.4) consisted of small- and medium-sized open bowls, jars with flared rim, closed-mouth pots, accompanied by large storage vessels and standard cooking pots. Exterior surface decoration was rare and consisted almost exclusively of incised geometric patterns.

The Burnt House/Omphalos phase sees the continuation of these forms, with the addition of many more shapes and sizes as befits an expanding economy. Residents preferred a wider range of colours on their vessels as well, most of which were burnished to a high gloss, with an increase in reds, oranges, and buff/buff-yellows on exteriors and interiors, though black remains the most common colour for exteriors and occasional interiors. Decoration included white-painted stripes applied after firing, as well as the application of red ochre-based paint, also post-firing, on both exteriors and interiors.

In the Transitional/Apsidal phase residents returned to the smaller assemblage of shapes and forms found in the Agglutinated phase. Burnishing was not as carefully completed in this phase, and buffs and neutral browns became common, with fewer reds and oranges. This may indicate the abandonment of updraft kilns, perhaps turning to pit-firing – a more easily-built fire installation. Incised decoration continued, red ochre paint was rarely applied, and white paint largely disappeared. In the Early Bronze Age I period in the Lower Town burnishing was far more uncommon and plain ware ceramics were low-fired and friable; in the Upper Town the assemblage is consistent with that of the Transitional/Apsidal phase.

Figure 4.4 Top: View of Late Chalcolithic Omphalos Building phase with updraft kiln; 1. kiln for ceramic production; 2. area for ash dump from the kiln; 3. storage building; bottom: examples of Late Chalcolithic pottery including buff, red, and black burnished bowls, jars and cups.

A casual visitor to the Late Chalcolithic and Early Bronze villages at Çadır would observe a ceramic assemblage that was primarily black-burnished, with a few other colours (red, orange, yellow, buff) scattered among the shiny black sherds. Indeed, this is what the Çadır team observed in our 1994 surface survey, and likely what Hittite and Iron Age builders of the silo and pits in this open area also dug up as they created their features.

Stylistic revivals: The Late Hittite and Early Iron Age periods

In the later 13th century, as noted above, the late Hittite Empire metal-working industrial installation, atop the Hittite wall, was used to recycle copper-bronze objects, presumably into new tools. Associated with this installation is an array of wheel-made pottery (relatively little of it is typical Hittite drab ware), as well as handmade forms (Fig. 4.5).

The latter include jars, jugs, and bowls with an external surface that is highly burnished. Some pieces, additionally, featured incised patterns, while a number of bowls had a red or orange-burnished slip on their interior surfaces. These decorative choices recall the predominant Late Chalcolithic methods for vessel decoration, also applied in that period to handmade vessels.

To produce the black burnished surface, as was the case in the Late Chalcolithic, potters had to fire vessels in a reduction atmosphere, rarely attested in the Middle and Late Bronze Age in this region. It is possible that these vessels were fired in open pits rather than updraft kilns, or that significant changes were introduced to firing methods within kilns, returning to methods more like the 4th millennium BC products described above. The large number of handmade vessels may indicate a 'decline' or reversion to earlier manufacturing methods, as well as, perhaps, a loss of full-time work for potters as Hittite power waned. The use of black burnish continued into the Early Iron Age.

Other older traditions reappeared in the Early Iron Age. In central Anatolia, this phase is typically regarded as transitional, and even as a period of decline, due to the withdrawal of state power. At Çadır, occupation from the Late Bronze Age to the Early Iron, and subsequent Middle Iron Age, was continuous on the south side of the mound, indicating that, while political power may have been discontinuous, residential occupation remained strong. The ceramic assemblage offers a view into the adjustments made by Çadır's inhabitants to new socio-political and economic circumstances.

As noted above, black burnish continued to be one form of ceramic decoration in the Iron Age; both handmade and wheel-made vessels were produced in the Early Iron Age. In 2005, H. Genz drew attention to the appearance of painted decoration and specific forms and features of Early Iron Age ceramics at several central Anatolian sites, including Çadır. Genz (2005, 76–78) attributes these features, which are notably different from Hittite precedents, to the revival of a local tradition of handmade painted pottery that went back to the Early and Middle Bronze Age in this region. Unfortunately, the materials available to Genz from Çadır came largely from non-random surface collections; excavation since that time has not uncovered significant quantities of these features – dotted triangles, horseshoe-shaped handles, beak spouts, and basket handles – *in situ* in Early Iron Age contexts.

Further excavation has, however, indicated one additional area of continuity from the Hittite ceramic repertoire: the prominence of a burnished red slip, applied to a variety of vessel types. Red slip occurs in the Late Chalcolithic at Çadır (described above); it is also a feature of Early Bronze Age pottery (EB II) in central Anatolia (Orthmann 1963; Steadman 2011) and reappears on both mass-produced and fine pottery of particular forms under the Hittites. The red slip of the Early Iron Age at Çadır is, however, distinct from that found at the site under the Hittites: The Iron Age examples are often a red-pink colour, while Hittite slip tends to be orange-red to brick red. In addition, the red slip of the Early Iron Age occurs on handmade vessels, both fine and coarse. On coarser, thicker-walled bowls, it co-occurs with the impressions of burnt-out chaff, which is otherwise rare among vessels of this period.

By the Middle Iron Age, most vessels at Çadır were again wheel-made. Here, too, red slip appears; at this time, the quality of the ware, and the slip colour, returned to an orange–red hue. Middle Iron Age vessels were typically well-fired, with a consistent, grit-tempered paste, likely indicating a return to specialist manufacture.

Ceramic continuity in decoration or form across millennia at Çadır Höyük provides suggestive evidence for the revival of local technological and decorative practices that were embedded in socio-political and economic structures. Locally-available resources played a role in the choices made by ceramic producers, but so did their knowledge of and access to the products of previous generations at their long-lived site.

Figure 4.5 Examples of Late Bronze Age pottery.

Ceramic reuse

Another category of evidence where we see the renewal of ceramics at Çadır comes from the common practice of ceramic recycling, specifically reusing ceramic sherds for a variety of purposes. This is a phenomenon known worldwide, for all periods of ceramic production – including present-day (Sullivan *et al.* 1991; López Varela *et al.* 2002; Korobkova *et al.* 2008). In part, the ubiquity of ceramic reuse derives from the ubiquity of ceramics themselves – produced nearly everywhere, suitable materials are available, and susceptible to breakage, but durable even afterward. Transforming a sherd into a 'tool' for some other use is also expedient; one of the most common forms, a roughly rounded piece with a hole in the centre, could be produced in a matter of minutes (U.-D. Schoop, pers. comm.).

But people also chose (and choose) to reuse sherds because of certain qualities of the original piece and in order to fulfil specific needs. This aspect of reuse is especially evident at Çadır, where sherd tools, or 'worked sherds', are found in all levels, from the Late Chalcolithic to the Byzantine period. Different forms, and different types of modification, prevail in the various periods, indicating an intentionality that deserves more attention than simply labelling a piece as a 'spindle whorl' or 'jar stopper'. Instead, we must be open to seeing the needs, functions and the practices in which these objects participated.

Tell sites like Çadır are, almost by definition, massive sherd dumps, and may include some features that served as literal trash pits for ceramics. With each subsequent occupation, the availability of broken ceramics increased; slopes, especially, were good sources for reusable sherds. At Çadır, we have found that residents sometimes retrieved vessels of earlier phases for reuse, though in general they seem to have been recycling their own pots, or those of the recent past. Substantial amounts of reused dirt, including broken ceramic materials, were also moved from the mound to the Byzantine terrace for use as construction fill.

For a better sense of ceramic reuse at Çadır, we can examine the patterns of worked sherd forms and frequency in Late Bronze Age (Hittite and post-Hittite) and Early–Middle Iron Age contexts in different occupational areas on the mound. In the Hittite levels on the eastern slope, a variety of worked sherds were recovered, dominated by pieces that could easily be held in the hand, in shapes ranging from triangles to trapezoids to circles, often with breaks intentionally chipped from both sides to create a 'sharp' edge (Fig. 4.6). Others had been worked to form a point, while still others had surfaces, or edges, smoothed from use. A few also had holes, or attempts at holes, one of the most recognizable modifications. These forms and modification types are, in fact, found in all phases at Çadır. Joining them, though, is a form specific to the Hittite levels: reused storage jar handles, still attached to body sherds that had been abraded along the edges and, often, the inside surface. Plaster adhered to the surfaces of these objects; we posit that they served a specific purpose related to construction, mixing and/or spreading, and maybe even burnishing, coats of plaster on walls and floors.

By the final years of the Hittite Empire, Çadır residents had built the aforementioned industrial installation on the southern slope of the mound. This area, in contrast to the eastern slope, and despite its likely function in metal recycling, contained very few identifiable worked sherds. In the Early Iron Age, when the area was repurposed for production of simple textiles (including maybe felt) and leather, the typical range of modified sherd forms occur; the majority were small in size and featured some form of point or sharpened edge. Finally, in the Middle Iron Age, the textile industry in this area of the site flourished, as attested by several clay loom weights scattered across areas with heavily plastered, shallow depressions – for soaking

Figure 4.6 Examples of worked sherds likely used as tools.

or dyeing wool? – and paving that connected them. Worked sherds in these contexts are of the widest possible range of forms – though none like the Hittite jar handles reappear here. Large numbers of reused sherds with central holes, or pieces broken when a hole was made, are prevalent, and must have supplemented spindle whorls and loom weights of more traditional types, made specifically for that purpose.

The enticement of ancient walls

It is difficult for archaeologists to imagine what was visible to those who occupied the site in the past. Reconstructions of excavated remains present what past peoples lived in and used, rather than what they saw out their windows. Like all tell residents, Çadır's inhabitants encountered and reused the architecture of previous periods on a regular basis. They also recycled older architectural designs and concepts, and when these failed, they innovated solutions.

In the Çadır team's experience, walls are the clearest indicator that later occupants were well aware of what earlier residents had built. The Çadır Höyük mound is an entangled nest of used and reused walls that protected those who lived within them. There are numerous instances of walls at Çadır being reused, often by individual builders using those created a generation or two before. In the Late Chalcolithic domestic areas of the Lower Town, residents regularly reused the bases of earlier walls for later structures across the four phases, perhaps simply for purposes of efficiency, but also effecting a persistence of place (Hackley *et al.* 2018). Profiled here are three instances in which it must have been an institutional decision – by the settlement as a whole, or the governing elites – to reuse walls built sometimes hundreds of years, even a millennium, in the past.

Bronze Age 'bonanza'

Excavations on the eastern slope of the Çadır mound, in an area known as the 'Step Trench', have, over many years, revealed a remarkable reuse of pre-existing walls spanning the Early to the Late Bronze Ages. While there were a few instances of simple 'stone robbing', more often builders used previously standing structures as foundations for their own walls (Steadman & McMahon 2015). This certainly indicates that these Bronze Age builders were *aware* of earlier walls, and that these walls were, at least in part, visible to them, but also that builders *trusted* these walls to undergird their own construction. This suggests both knowledge about building techniques, and a certain level of faith in the architects and builders of the earlier walls.

The earliest extant wall in the Step Trench is near the easternmost end of the area and is an Early Bronze III (*c.* 2300–2000 BC) fist- and head-sized stone perimeter wall, perhaps a foundation of a larger wall, or a revetment meant to stabilise the area's slope. At some point in the early 2nd millennium BC (in the Middle Bronze Age, henceforth MBA), residents used this wall as a footing for one arm of their MBA gated entry into the settlement. The MBA builders removed some of the stones (likely using them in their own wall) and placed a hard-packed mud layer on the remaining stones. They then constructed their 1.2 m wide gate arm with its foot resting on the Early Bronze Age perimeter wall (Fig. 4.7a, b). As can be seen in Figure 7a, another wall runs across the MBA gateway, effectively blocking it. This wall dates to the Old Hittite period (*c.* 1700–1600 BC). We made these discoveries in our 2002 excavations.

We did not return to this excavation area until 2012, when we significantly expanded operations. Between 2013 and 2014, a Bronze Age 'bonanza' of wall building was revealed (Fig. 4.7b). The other arm of the MBA gate was revealed (Fig. 4.7b:1); it had been heavily robbed in antiquity, likely by the Old Hittite wall builders. The Old Hittite wall was a casemate structure between 1.5 m and 2 m wide (Fig. 4.7b: 2); it was constructed in a zig-zag pattern to accommodate the mound's slope. We also discovered the continuation of the Early Bronze III wall (Fig. 4.7b: 3) which had been bolstered and used by the Old Hittite wall-builders.

A couple of centuries later, perhaps around 1400 BC, the Hittite residents began construction of a new casemate wall, this one 3 m in width (Fig. 4.7b: 4). These builders used the Old Hittite wall as a foundation for their own wall and added a squared tower (Fig. 4.7b: 5) which was a normal element of Hittite Empire walls. The Hittite Empire wall builders even constructed a staircase (Fig. 4.7b: 6) from the earlier Early/Middle Bronze Age wall to their Hittite Empire period tower.

The Step Trench revealed a wall building process that spanned nearly 1000 years, from the late 3rd to the later 2nd millennium BC, likely sponsored by elites or town elders/leaders. Builders, in their efficiency and wise employment of labour, made judicious use of standing walls that were still visible and viable, and removed and reused stones from unneeded or unstable earlier walls. Such actions today would be deemed environmentally-conscious conservation; in the 2nd millennium BC it must have been sensible, perhaps even thoughtful, pragmatism.

Hittite ingenuity

The Early and Middle Bronze Age wall structures discussed above are not found anywhere but the eastern slope Step Trench. The two Hittite period walls, however, are found on both the northern and southern slopes of Çadır's mound. The Hittite Empire (later) wall was first excavated in 2005 on the northern slope; the underpinning Old Hittite wall was revealed in our 2018 excavations (Steadman *et al.* 2019c), resting directly under the later and larger wall in an exact reproduction of how builders handled wall construction in the eastern slope portion. The rather monumental nature (for Çadır) of the northern gate and wall likely results from its

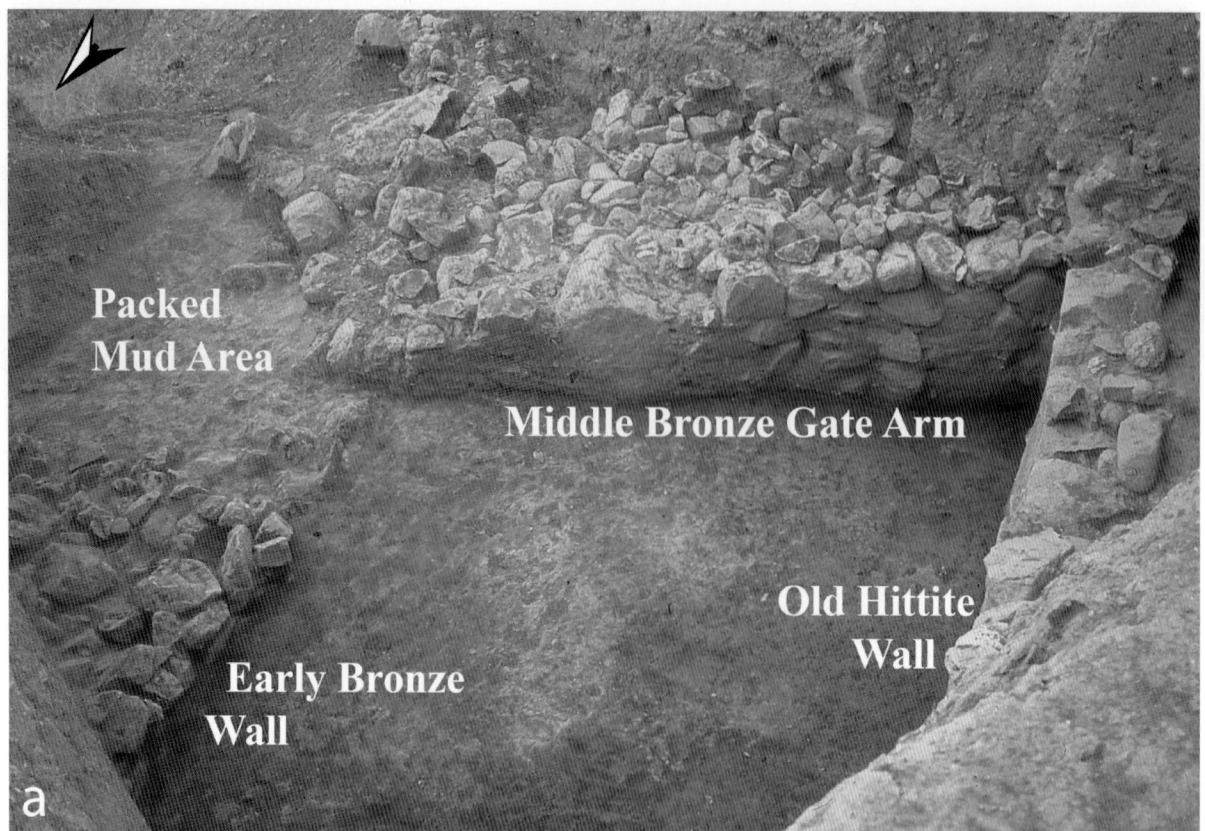

Figure 4.7 a. Close-up of Step Trench excavations showing Middle Bronze gate wall set atop Early Bronze III wall, with Old Hittite wall blocking gated Middle Bronze entry; b. aerial view of entire Step Trench; 3. Bronze Age walls showing progression of wall-building from EB III wall; 1. used by the Middle Bronze Age gate arms; 2. used by the Old Hittite casemate wall; 4–6. used by the Hittite Empire casemate wall, tower and staircase.

position facing Ḫattuša; the sight of it would greet emissaries from the Hittite capital.

The southern slope construction presents a different circumstance. As described above, the upper southern slope, with Late Bronze and Iron Age levels, rests on the earlier Early Bronze I and Late Chalcolithic Upper Town occupation. At the end of the 4th and into the early 3rd millennia BC, in the Early Bronze I period, most residents appear to have rejected Lower Town living and moved 'uptown' and behind the large 2 m wide mudbrick perimeter/defensive wall (see Fig. 4.3). We do not know if the interior Upper Town continued to be occupied after the Early Bronze I period as it rests under the later Hittite/Iron Age occupation. We do know that the Old Hittite and Hittite Empire residents made use of the Early Bronze I wall. In the Old Hittite period builders prepared the Early Bronze wall by smoothing its top and then laying down a plaster surface; upon this they built their Old Hittite mudbrick wall (Fig. 4.8).

Approximately two centuries later, as they had on the eastern slope, the Hittite Empire residents rebuilt their town wall on the southern slope. Once again builders smoothed the top of the Old Hittite wall and laid a plaster surface, upon which they constructed their new and likely much more extensive wall. On the upper southern slope, they added the mudbrick platform described above (Fig. 4.9). This is the platform that served as a work space for residents in the final century of the Hittite period and into the Early Iron Age occupation.

As was the case on the eastern slope, Hittite builders assessed the stability of earlier wall remains and found them sufficiently reliable to serve as foundation(s) for their new walls. How such evaluations were conducted are likely questions present-day archaeologists will never answer. Was there a 'wall whisperer', a specialist who was the go-to person when it came to large-scale renovations? One can imagine a singular individual spending the morning carefully tapping, testing, even drilling, the Early Bronze and Old Hittite walls to assess their ability to hold a later and even larger construction. Alternatively, the collection of labourers involved in building these walls may have all been knowledgeable about setting viable foundations. Certainly, when our team is in the field, it is often our fellow workers from the local village, rather than we 'trained archaeologists', who are the first to identify a wall foundation or a mudbrick floor. What we can document is that those 2nd millennium BC Hittite wall builders were correct; their two walls, based upon a 3rd millennium BC wall, remained standing for over three more millennia.

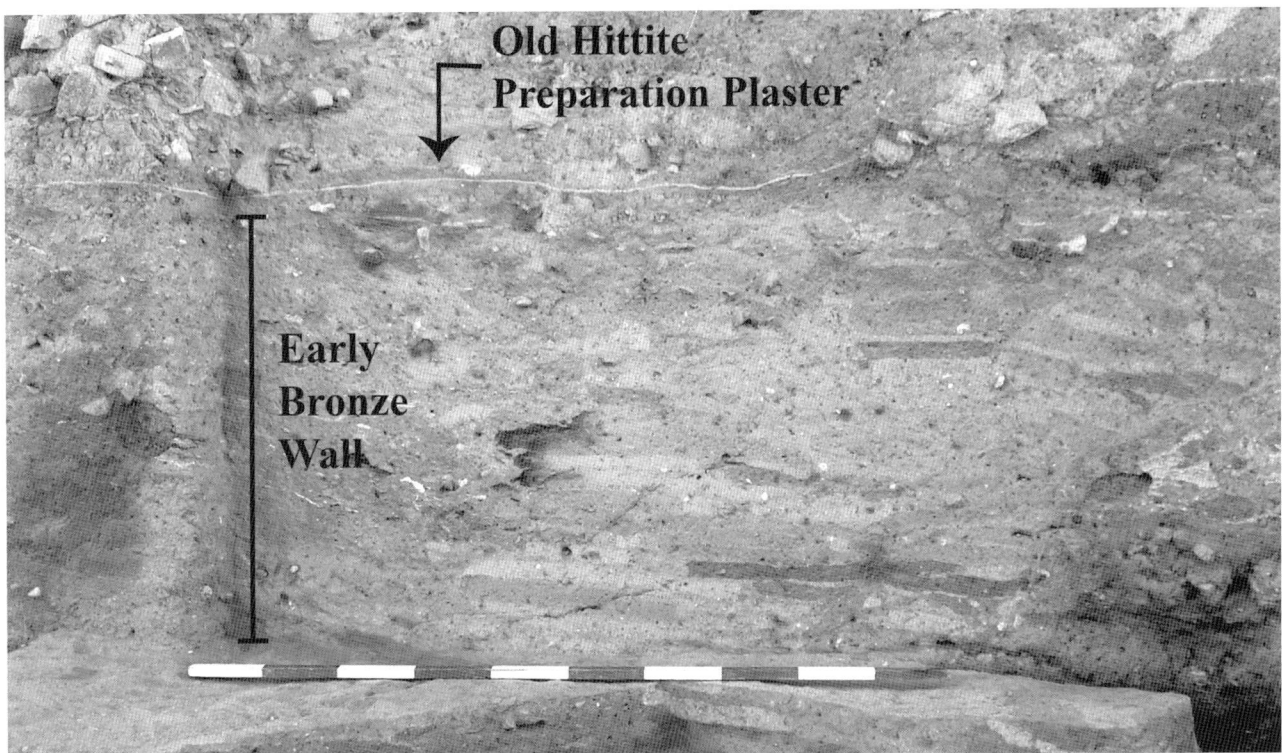

Figure 4.8 View of north section in Upper Town area, showing the major Early Bronze perimeter wall (see Fig. 4.3), the top of which was smoothed and plastered by the Old Hittite wall builders.

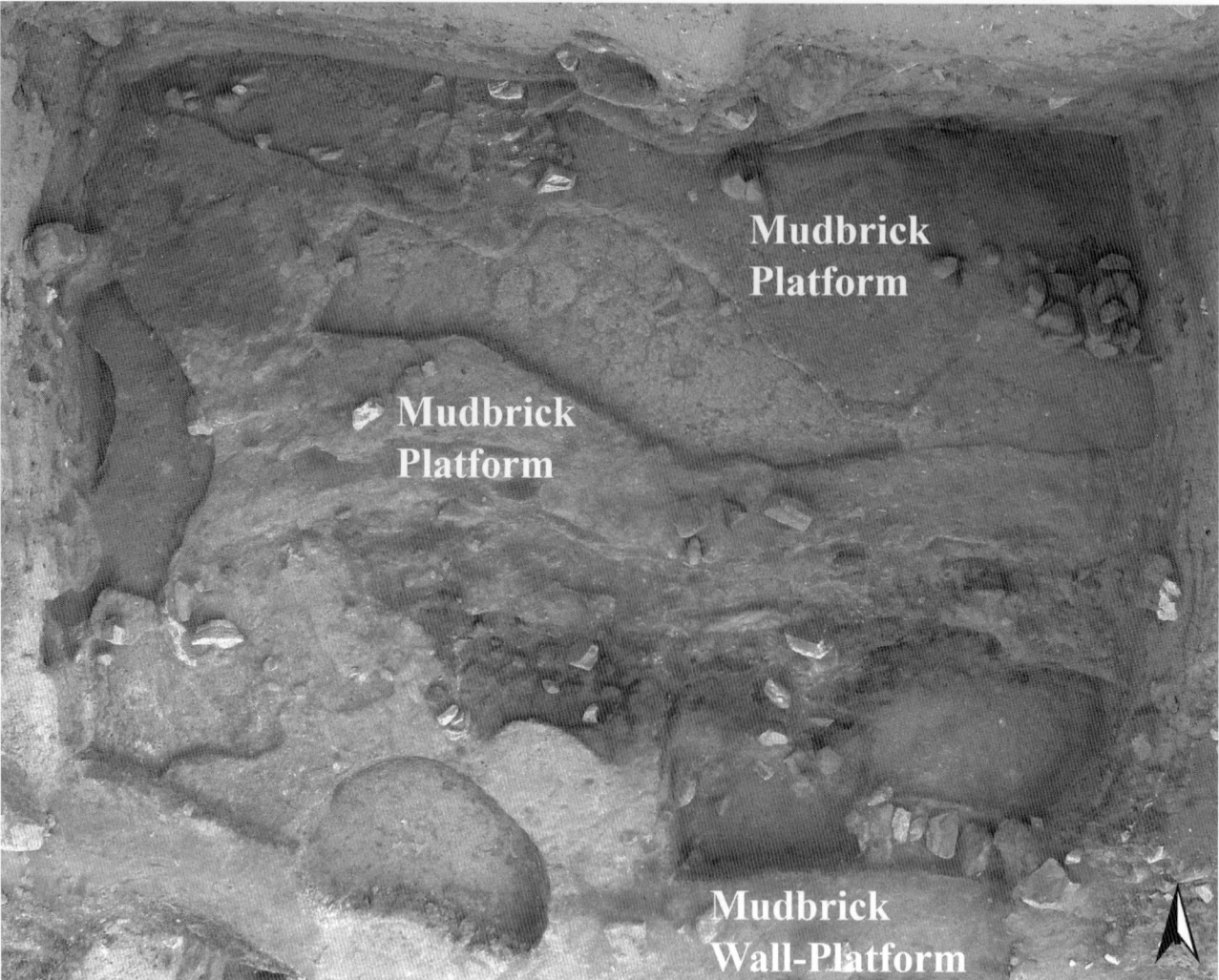

Figure 4.9 Aerial view of Upper Southern Slope excavations showing the Hittite Empire mudbrick wall and platform, trenched and pitted by very Late Bronze Age and Early Iron Age industrial activities.

Byzantine resourcefulness

The third episode of wall reuse mentioned here occurs over two millennia later, in the Byzantine period (10th–11th centuries AD). Detailed analyses of Byzantine wall-building at Çadır have been published elsewhere (Steadman *et al.* 2015; 2019c; Cassis *et al.* 2019) and thus only a summary is necessary here. At some point in the 10th or 11th century AD, Byzantine residents built a substantial defensive wall surrounding the mound summit (Fig. 4.10). There may have been some urgency regarding wall construction, given that both Arab and Seljuk (Turkic) incursions into Byzantine imperial lands had taken place over the previous century or more; additionally, mercenaries who had broken away from the Byzantine army, were also at large across the countryside (Steadman *et al.* 2017; Cassis *et al.* 2019).

As had the Hittites before them, the Byzantine builders made consistent use of previous architecture, in this case, both the Late Iron Age stone walls that girded gateways and passages into the 6th–3rd centuries BC settlement on the eastern and northern slopes, and the Late Roman/Early Byzantine (*c.* 7th–9th centuries AD) walls on the southern summit. The archaeological team was not surprised to see this Byzantine use and recycling of earlier walls as this seemed to be a virtual 'Çadır norm' given past examples. What *was* startling was what the Byzantine builders did when previous architectural remains were absent, or the slope of the summit edge prevented them from using older structures.

Byzantine wall builders innovated a series of wooden 'deadmen' – wooden poles laid horizontally to underpin a foundation – and packed mud 'boxes' to support their

Figure 4.10 Aerial view of Çadır Höyük summit with black arrows pointing to exposed sections of 10th–11th century AD Byzantine defensive wall; in most cases the wall makes use of earlier (e.g. Iron Age, Late Roman, Late Antique) architecture as a foundational support system.

massive stone and mortar wall (Fig. 4.11a). Where Late Iron Age architecture fell away, posts in the lowest levels of the wall, or even underneath the mortar, take up the duty of stable foundational support. However, even the deadmen were not deemed strong enough for at least one area of the mound, near the north-eastern corner. Here the Late Iron Age builders had a courtyard flanking one of their gated entries into the settlement, creating a gap in stone or mudbrick architecture. The Byzantine wall builders constructed 'boxes' to support the wall foundation here (Steadman *et al.* 2015). Each box consisted of packed mud encased in a mat which was plastered (Fig. 4.11b). The wall rested directly on the box, which appears to have served its purpose, as the Byzantine wall still stands today.

These Byzantine building techniques have not been observed elsewhere in Anatolia (Cassis *et al.* 2019). This Byzantine resourcefulness may stem from the necessity to build the defensive wall in something of a hurry, but more likely derives from a millennia-long pattern of recycling and reuse of previous skilled builders' creations and the innovations necessary to bridge the gaps in them.

Figure 4.11 a. View of 10th–11th century AD Byzantine wall (looking west) showing where deadmen posts were inserted to support the wall's foundations; a 'box' is located under the wall on the right side of the photo; b. close-up of 'box' seen on right side of photo 11a (arrows point to outside of box); boxes were filled with packed mud, encased in matting and plastered, and served as supports for the Byzantine wall foundations.

Conclusion

The material culture and architectural continuity at Çadır Höyük stem from a variety of motivations that include necessity, convenience, pragmatism, and not least, a deep faith in the quality of past work. The first two rationales, necessity and convenience, are deeply intertwined. Scarce resources in the Late Hittite and Early Iron Age resulted in reuse and recycling of what was available: what was available was conveniently located downslope at Çadır, and perhaps most tells. A pragmatic approach can be found in the (re)construction of stone walls. What archaeologists regularly call 'robbing' of earlier walls was, at the time of building, a savings on labour; why go several kilometres to haul back heavy stones when they are available a few metres down the mound? However, as was the case at Çadır, a judicious 'robbing' was undertaken so as not to eradicate the stability of what came before. The revival of Late Chalcolithic ceramic types in the Late Hittite and Early Iron Age periods, and the reuse of earlier architecture, with the reconceptualization of how to address 'gaps' in past constructions, both speak to a faith in the past.

The confidence placed in builders and artisans who lived centuries, even millennia, before seems remarkable, but perhaps not for tell residents. The intimacy residents of all periods experienced with their particular place generation after generation, seeing the same 'remains from the past' downslope, from their own childhood to old age, may have produced feelings of familiarity and even devotion, eliciting deep ties with ancient creators of what lay beneath their feet. The compilation of ancient, recent, and new in such close vertical proximity is largely unique to tell sites, producing the fascinating circumstance of revival, reuse, and renewal found on a *höyük* in central Anatolia.

References

Bachelard, G. (1958) *The Poetics of Space.* Paris, Presses Universitaires de France.

Cassis, M., Lauricella, A.J., Tardio, K., von Baeyer, M., Coleman, S., Adcock, S.E., Arbuckle, B.S. & Smith, A. (2019) Regional patterns of transition at Çadır Höyük in the Byzantine Period. *Journal of Eastern Mediterranean Archaeology and Heritage Studies* 7(3), 321–349.

Genz, H. (2005) Thoughts on the origin of the Iron Age pottery traditions of Central Anatolia. In A. Çilingiroğlu & G. Darbyshire (eds), *Anatolian Iron Ages* 5, 75–84. Ankara, British Institute.

Hackley, L.D., Selover, S. & Steadman, S.R. (2018) The persistence of social and spatial memory at prehistoric Çadır Höyük. *International Journal of the Constructed Environment* 9(4), 1–20.

Harmanşah, Ö. (2013) *Cities and the Shaping of Memory in the Ancient Near East.* Providence RI, Brown University.

Harmanşah, Ö. (2014) *Place, Memory, and Healing: An Archaeology of Anatolian Rock Monuments.* London, Routledge.

Heidegger, M. (1977) Building, dwelling, thinking. In D. Krell (ed.), *Basic Writings*, 323–339. New York, Harper Collins.

Korobkova, G.F., Mandryka, P.V. & Volkov, P.V. (2008) Stone and ceramic tools from Ush-Shilka-2, a hill-fort of the Early Iron

Age. *Journal of Siberian Federal University. Humanities and Social Sciences* 1, 70–76.

López Varela, S.L., van Gijn, A. & Jacobs, L. (2002) De-mystifying pottery production in the Maya lowlands: Detection of use-wear on pottery sherds through microscopic analysis and experimental replication. *Journal of Archaeological Science* 29, 1133–1147.

Orthmann, W. (1963) *Frühe Keramik von Boğazköy aus den Ausgrabungen am Nordwesthang von Büyükkale*. Berlin, Wissenschaftliche Veröffentlichungen der Deutschen Orient-Gesellschaft 74.

Ross, J.C., Steadman, S.R., McMahon, G., Cannon, J.W. & Adcock, S.E. (2019) When the giant falls: Endurance and adaptation at Çadır Höyük in the context of the Hittite Empire and its collapse. *Journal of Field Archaeology* 44, 19–39.

Steadman, S.R. (2011) The Early Bronze Age on the Plateau. In S.R. Steadman & G. McMahon (eds), *The Oxford Handbook of Ancient Anatolia (10,000–323 BCE)*, 229–259. Oxford, Oxford University Press.

Steadman, S.R. & McMahon, G. (2015) Recent work (2013–2014) at Çadır Höyük on the North Central Anatolian Plateau. In S.R. Steadman & G. McMahon (eds), *The Archaeology of Anatolia: Recent Discoveries (2011–2014)*. Vol. 1, 69–97. Newcastle upon Tyne, Cambridge Scholars Publishing.

Steadman, S.R., McMahon, G., Ross, J.C., Cassis, M., Şerifoğlu, T.E., Arbuckle, B.S., Adcock, S.E., Alpaslan Roodenberg, S., von Baeyer, M. & Lauricella, A.J. (2015) The 2013 and 2014 seasons of excavation at Çadır Höyük on the Anatolian North Central Plateau. *Anatolica* 41, 87–124.

Steadman, S.R., Şerifoğlu, T.E., McMahon, G., Selover, S., Hackley, L.D., Yıldırım, B., Lauricella, A.J., Arbuckle, B.S., Adcock, S.E., Tardio, K., Dinç, E. & Cassis, M. (2017) Recent discoveries (2015–2016) at Çadır Höyük on the North Central Plateau. *Anatolica* 43, 203–250.

Steadman, S.R., Hackley, L.D., Selover, S., Yıldırım, B., von Baeyer, M., Arbuckle, B.S., Robinson, R. & Smith, A. (2019a) Early lives: The Late Chalcolithic and Early Bronze Age at Çadır Höyük. *Journal of Eastern Mediterranean Archaeology and Heritage Studies* 7(3), 271–298.

Steadman, S.R., McMahon, G., Arbuckle, B.S., von Baeyer, M., Smith, A., Yıldırım, B., Hackley, L.D., Selover, S. & Spagni, S. (2019b) Stability and change at Çadır Höyük in Central Anatolia: A case of globalization? *Anatolian Studies* 69, 21–57.

Steadman, S.R., McMahon, G., Şerifoğlu, T.E., Cassis, M., Lauricella, A.J., Hackley, L.D., Selover, S., Yıldırım, B., Arbuckle, B.S., von Baeyer, M., Heffron, Y., Tardio, K., Adcock, S.E., Dinç, E., Özger, G., Selvi, B., Offutt, S. & Hartley, A. (2019c) The 2017–2018 seasons at Çadır Höyük on the North Central Plateau. *Anatolica* 45, 77–119.

Sullivan, A.P. III, Skibo, J.M. & van Buren, M. (1991) Sherds as tools: The roles of vessel fragments in prehistoric succulent plant processing. *North American Archaeologist* 12(3), 243–255.

5

Moving Bottom-up: The Case Study of Kakucs-Turján (Hungary) and its Implications for Studies of Multi-layered Bronze Age Settlements in the Carpathian Basin

Robert Staniuk, Mateusz Jaeger, Gabriella Kulcsár, Nicole Taylor, Jakub Niebieszczański and Johannes Müller

Introduction

This article outlines the investigation of the Middle Bronze Age settlement in Kakucs-Turján as a bottom-up research project studying communities inhabiting the Carpathian Basin in the first half of the 2nd millennium BC (Fig. 5.1). The method is based on the identification and classification of material culture related to the formation of a particular archaeological site which, subject to question-oriented analysis, is used for the construction of socio-cultural models. First, it is argued that the bottom-up method provides the means of generating comparable, cross-site results, while maintaining their historical particularities. Secondly, the developed models provide grounds for investigating inter- and intra-regional patterns. Lastly, the method provides the means for considering the interplay between particular historical processes and long-term historical trajectories. A historical overview of the development of Middle Bronze Age research is presented, aimed at providing perspective on how research on tell and multi-layered settlements was tied to the historical development of archaeology in the Hungarian[1] part of the Carpathian Basin.[2] It is argued that a historical perspective on the formation of the prevalent frameworks enables contextualisation of the relations between the analysis of archaeological finds and the formulated interpretations in former research. Such a critical analysis is necessary in order to integrate previous findings into present-day analytical projects, especially due to the increasing complexity of the questions raised by modern-day research.

The bottom-up model applied throughout the excavation of Kakucs-Turján is outlined on the basis of the underlying research principles, the implemented methodology and an overview of recent findings. The recognised threads of the investigation are then used in an exploratory sense as a tool for structuring follow-up research along human–environment relations, local histories and interregional processes.

Methodological development of Hungarian Bronze Age tell archaeology

Culture-historical archaeology is considered the primary form of archaeological practice in Central and Central-Eastern Europe, where it is characterised by an extensive inclination towards the study of material culture, limited (if any) theoretical framework, and an ever-persisting reliance on the 'archaeological culture' concept (Laszlovsky & Siklódi 1991; Trigger 2008; Bertemes 2011). In historical terms it is often associated with the so-called German school of archaeology, despite increasing evidence that the principles and execution of continental research has undergone changes related to state histories since the mid-20th century and, considering the historical circumstances of the discipline formation, only partially represent the historical trajectory of the region (Childe 1929; Neustupný 1991; Kadrow 2011; Rączkowski 2011). The latter case is illustrated by the Hungarian archaeological practice, where the paradigm shifts within the culture-historical perception of archaeology are well-linked to the changing socio-political situation. Beyond understanding the particularities of archaeological research in one country, such an investigation provides an opportunity to understand how archaeological sites, in this instance tells, are used in scientific investigations and how the established perspectives undergo change. Attempts at characterising the shifts in research perspectives were already made on various occasions with an emphasis on describing the history of research in Hungary (*e.g.* Banner 1956; Laszlovsky & Siklódi 1991) or serving as a point of departure for the discussion of new results (*e.g.* Sørensen & Vicze 2013, 160). In this particular instance, it provides the possibility to outline a refined model which focuses primarily on the explicit scientific investigation of the site.

Before discussing which theoretical principles of Hungarian research on Bronze Age tells were established and how they underwent change, it is important to consider how archaeological research and Central European Archaeology specifically (Harding 2009; *cf.* Gramsch 2011), deal with reimplementing old findings into new statements regarding past communities. Rather than investigating the discussion of the outlined theoretical principles, consideration of the responses to previous results provides a contextualised observation on how scientific discourse was structured in a particular research milieu. The cumulative nature of archaeological research, where the findings of the preceding generations of researchers are incorporated into new scientific ventures, is expressed in at least four forms of implementation of past results.

First, the existing findings justify not only the initial assumptions but validate the need for investigating previously recognised patterns and trajectories (*e.g.* Vicze 2011). In this sense, the research follows the established paradigm and verifies its validity by applying the developed principles in a previously unexamined setting. Secondly, the existing findings are explicitly reaffirmed as supporting the proposed scientific project with the main emphasis made on previously unexplored aspects (*e.g.* Sofaer 2015). As such, it is either assumed that research was preceded by re-evaluation of the initial findings or that the determinations representing the point of departure for further research are legitimised by the fact of their publication. The shift is made towards the contribution made by the novelty of the applied method and

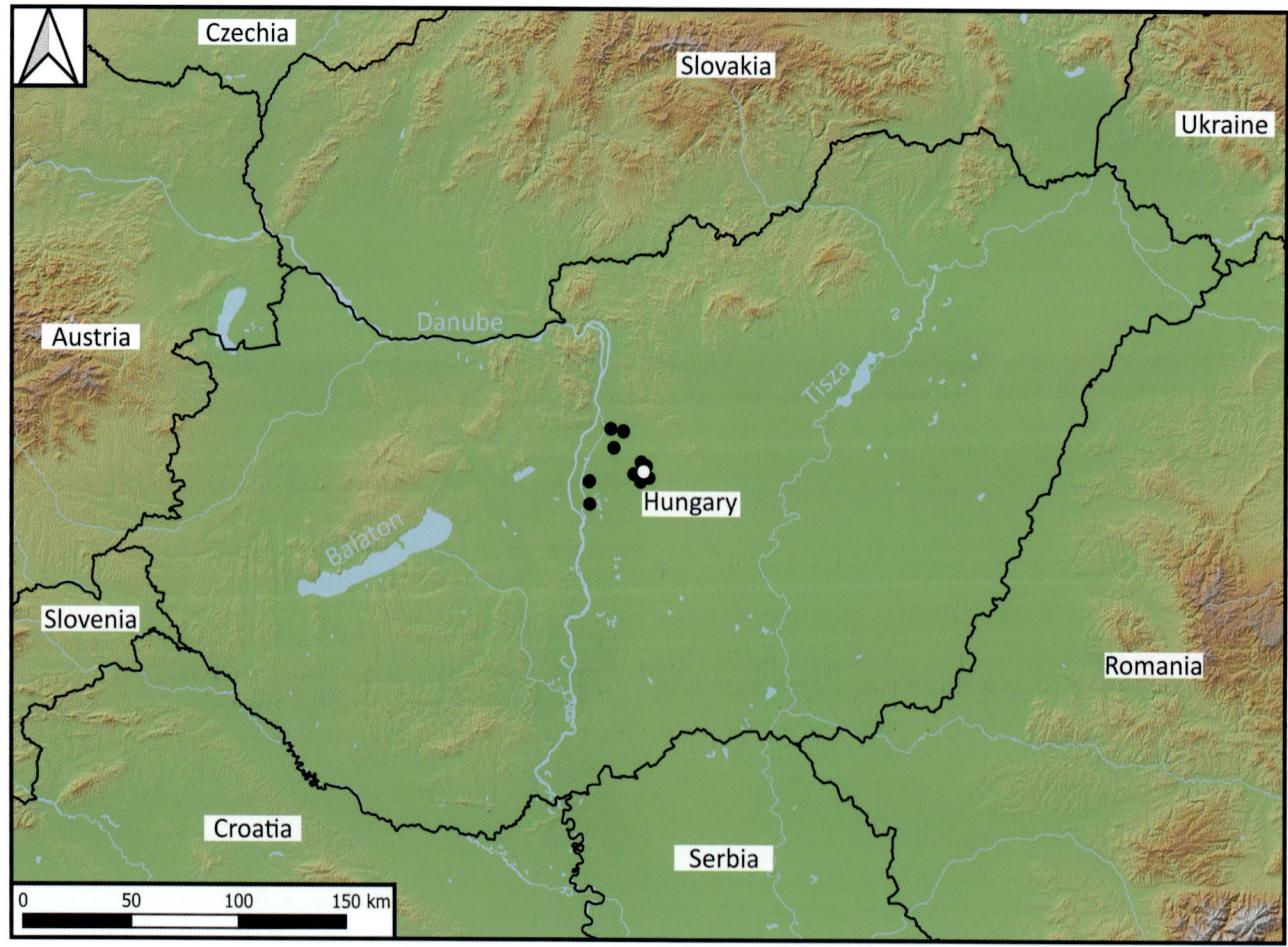

Figure 5.1 Present-day borders of Hungary and the location of the Kakucs microregion. Black dots: Early and Middle Bronze Age settlements, white dot: Kakucs-Turján.

its impact on the state of knowledge. Thirdly, the incorporation of the preceding results into the new research projects is characterised by a critical overview of particular findings, which in itself is considered the reason for the formulation of a particular research project. In this particular approach it is often explicitly stated that there is a need to address and correct the logical fallacies of preceding research as the essential step towards the advancement of the discipline, and a necessary one towards formulation of sound, new directions in research (*e.g.* Szeverényi & Kulcsár 2012; Jaeger 2016). In this case, the change of the results is often characterised by a change in the applied perspective, which is argued to be a more viable representation. Lastly, a selective approach, where only particular aspects of the past research are used, favours the importance of the investigated problem rather than adherence to the existing determinations (*e.g.* Kreiter 2007). The results – usually expansive in both fields since they alter the state of departure by venturing into previously unrecognised aspects of the framework, while providing an additional case study in the investigation of a particular problem – represent a separate, instrumental form of reimplementation of old findings.

While all responses to the integration of the past results can be anticipated to occur simultaneously, their emergence can be considered as representative in the change of the discourse by reaffirming, exploring, negating or selecting the relevant scientific field. From the perspective of the current investigation, it is worth considering whether such changes were implemented in the discourse from early on, or represent a recent development tied to contemporary projects. Since the majority of the investigations were conducted by local archaeologists it requires consideration of the historical process related to the formation of archaeology as a scientific discipline and its ties to the socio-political changes in the 20th century (Laszlovsky & Siklódi 1991, 272).

Pre-World War I

The time period 1802–1914 represents the long century of antiquarian interests, focusing primarily on the collection of finds, and associating archaeology with object-oriented interest (Bóna 1975, 20). This temporal delimitation overlaps with the impact of the French Revolution, the Napoleonic Wars, the Spring of Nations, and finally, the formation of the Austro-Hungarian Empire (Molnár 2001; Fig. 5.2A), *i.e.* the long century of establishing the nation as the entity to be equated with state-formation; a common thread in the history of European archaeology (Jones 1997, 2; Sommer & Gramsch 2011, 10). The post-revolutionary industrial investments, including railway construction, draining of swamps and regulating the flow of the Danube (Cartledge 2011, 251), certainly contributed to the increasing frequency of recovering archaeological objects by means of circumstantial finds. Although based on collections, both amateur and professional, the position of archaeological research was becoming increasingly well-established as indicated by the formulation of specific research groups, *e.g.* the Archaeological Committee of the Academy of Sciences (1858) or the presence of continuously published journals (*Akadémiai Értesítő* or *Archaeologiai Közlemények*), not to mention the increasing infrastructure of museum institutions (Vékony 2003, 17–18). From the perspective of Bronze Age research, the significance of the period for the prehistory of Hungary was associated with the presentation of the findings from the tell in Tószeg (Vékony 2003, 19). The effort of individual collectors culminated in the Hungarian Millennial Exhibition, which served as a foundational event for the cultural significance of archaeological research for archaeologists and citizens alike (Vékony 2003, 19; Barenscott 2010). The final stage of the research period is represented by the increasing discussion of methodological aspects, *i.e.* the implications of stratigraphic excavations and the usefulness

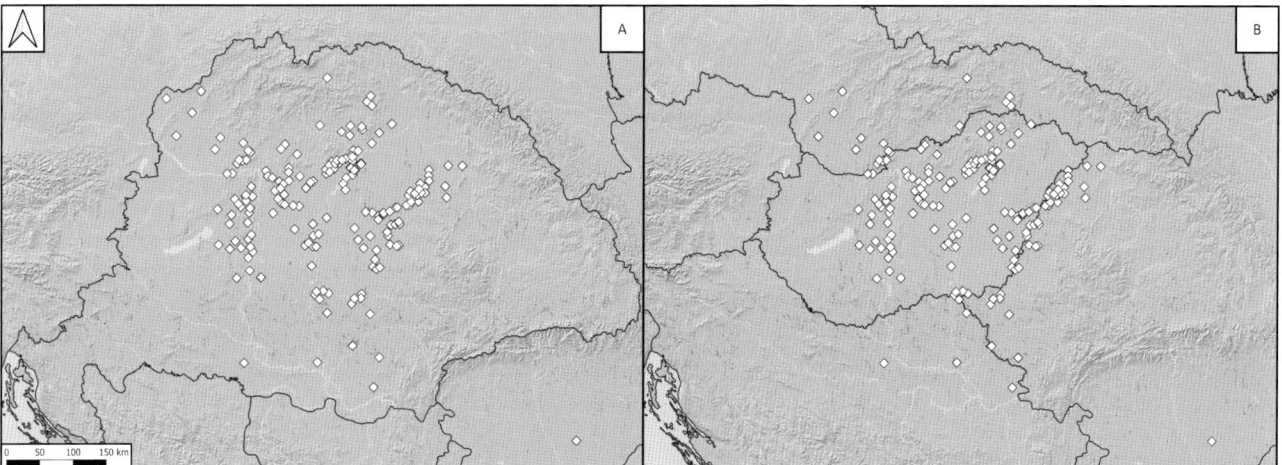

Figure 5.2 Changes of state boundaries in the first half of the 20th century. A – state borders c. AD 1900; B – state borders c. AD 1930.

of the typological method (von Márton 1912, 180). In this sense the initial standpoint, despite the differences in the types of archaeological sites encountered in Hungary, and the scientific origins were similar to other European, find-based and description-oriented standards.

Between the wars

The trajectory of the Hungarian school of archaeology was altered by the outbreak of World War I and further affected by the post-war peace treaties resulting in the changes of political borders in light of the Treaty of Trianon (1920), with archaeological institutions and researchers finding themselves as citizens of other states (Macartney 1937; Molnár 2001, 262; Vékony 2003, 19; Cartledge 2011, 325; C.G. Kiss 2013, 25; Fig. 5.2B).

Despite the deep political changes, this time-period represents the formation of archaeological theory and the increasing refinement of field archaeology (Bóna 1975, 20–21). The former is linked to the first European grand narrative of V.G. Childe in which, beyond presentation and the discussion of archaeological finds linked to the flow of the Danube, an emphasis is made explicitly on formulating the principles behind the study of prehistoric material culture and its link to social processes (Childe 1929). The explicit outline of the theoretical principles behind the investigation and interpretation of archaeological finds emphasised the normative aspects of culture, where the link between material culture and social life was governed by the principle of pursuing invariable deposits of material culture (Childe 1929, vi–vii; Kadrow 2017, 174). Integration of the paradigm with the universally considered aspects of social life (*i.e.* movements of people or methods of diffusion) was constrained towards re-enforcing the underlying statement. From a local perspective, the application of this approach was incorporated in the works of F. Tompa (1937) in his consideration of Bronze Age archaeology in Hungary. The principles of the archaeological work were based on a positivist perspective on material culture, where tells represented static and non-transformed fossils of past reality to a degree that findings from one particular settlement could be used as explanatory for the entire cultural area. Furthermore the archaeological findings and the established typo-chronological cycles were immanently objective and direct evidence of concrete cultural groups (Tompa 1937, 63–66). The positivist approach to archaeological studies was further justified by a specific form of scientific discourse: the interpretation of reports from other sites were not viewed as contradictory, in the sense of requiring the re-consideration of the recognized principles such as the existence of well-defined social groups across large geographical areas. Instead, the identification of similar findings was used to validate the chronological observations made on the basis of etically-viewed stylistic similarity. This form of archaeological inference emphasized the significance of archaeological sites for understanding archaeology, and the primary focus on using site-based archaeology to formulate statements on chronological characteristics. In this sense, the primary epistemological tool and analytical method of archaeological work was equated with excavations. However, as will be shown later, this particular paradigm, similarly to the antiquarian approach, was also to undergo change.

Post-World War II

As destructive as World War II was on the demographics and material culture of Hungary, the borders of the state remained unchanged. Instead, the pre-World War II research paradigms underwent changes of a non-linear trajectory. The separation of archaeological studies into excavation-based investigations and material culture studies are an example of this direction (Bóna 1975, 21).

Excavations of large tell settlements formed two approaches to settlement archaeology: characterisation studies at Tószeg-Laposhalom (Csalog 1952) and question-formulating investigations at Békés-Várdomb (Banner 1956). In both cases the positivist and normative perception of archaeological finds was reinforced, with the latter example clearly linked to the open formulation of statements drawing on urbanisation, construction, social structure, craftsmanship, and interaction. The limited scope of the investigation and its direct tie to a specific archaeological site represented a development of the characterisation-based studies (Banner & Bóna 1974).

Beyond localised investigations, attempts at formulating a holistic approach required explicit formulation of principles behind archaeological studies. Reliance on a materialistic perspective of the past reality used particular material evidence to directly reconstruct the social process they were formed in and the cultural influences involved in their constitution (Kalicz 1968). The principal role of archaeological theory was to provide the means of making associations and reconstructing the dynamics of the otherwise static archaeological finds (Kalicz 1968, 7). The applied method was the reconstruction of the historical positioning of finds, which, if done properly, would allow forming a dynamic perspective on universally considered aspects of human culture. As such, the investigation of material culture found on archaeological sites is linked to the study of past human groups where the delimited material principles are considered representative of actual social groupings.

The latter point was further emphasised in the works of I. Bóna, where the identification of real-life human groups was the primary research question and where the history of Bronze Age was related to the cycles of cultural formation, interaction and disintegration (Bóna 1975). The previously identified archaeological cultures were directly correlated with groups of people self-identifying themselves because of the material culture differences (Bóna 1975, 15). Further methodological principles following this premise were flexibly used as means of precisely characterising the chronological stages of group-formation, spatial delimitation of such entities, and, in anthropological terms, the means of change, *e.g.* conflict, migration and, last but not least, diffusion (Bóna 1975, 16). Application of the method resulted in a specific interpretation of the archaeological record where, instead of site histories representing the primary tool of archaeological inference, the primary entity became an *a priori* defined ethnic group which was then used to both 'sort' the distribution of other ethnic groups (in this particular example such an entity was the Vatya culture) and objectively reconstruct the historical trajectory. While similar in principles to G. Kossinna's *Siedlungsarchäologie*, this particular paradigm-shift in Hungarian archaeology occurred more than 50 years after the formulation of such principles in German archaeology (*e.g.* Heyd 2017, 350). While it provided the means and stimuli towards the investigation of multiple archaeological sites and expanding the state of knowledge on tell archaeology, the emphasis on precisely defined constellations of finds as indicators of ethnic uniformity would result in confusing interpretations of tell sites. Since pottery was linked to specific cultural groups with well-defined historical formations and trajectories, the occurrence of interchanging styles on tell sites would imply regular ethnic replacements and almost a constant state of conflict without any architectural evidence of such (*e.g.* Bóna 1992). From an epistemological perspective, this thread of the Hungarian school of archaeology should be linked to the personal transfer of post-World War I experience and the post-Trianon history of Hungary, where places previously recognised as historically Hungarian, became subject to other states. The emphasis on a group-centered perception of particular places rather than accentuating the historical development of archaeological sites remains problematic in archaeological research since the precise identification of groups and communities keeps being conceptually and empirically challenging (*e.g.* Jones 1997; Sørensen 1997; Kadrow 2017). However, the historical perspective on the possible formation of such a process highlights the significance of investigating cultural change as an internalized process (Minta-Tworzowska 2011). The other accomplishment of this direction was aggregating finds into distinct groups, which remains the hallmark of Central and Eastern European archaeology.

The discussion on the development of theoretical principles of Hungarian archaeology after World War II emphasised the highly empirical nature of the research, where the development of the archaeology was not necessarily linked to uncovering new ways of thinking about the past but finding evidence of it (Laszlovsky & Siklódi 1991). To a degree this particular direction is linked to the discontinuities in the institutionalisation of scientific life, where archaeological schools of thought are not linked to administrative units but particular individuals. The instability of institutional life is rather well-documented considering the post-World War I political changes, post-World War II casualties, and the impact of the subjection to the politics of the Soviet Union (Vicze 2011, 13). What is significant is that the situation and the multiplicity of perspectives towards Bronze Age archaeology began increasing towards the end of the 20th century. However, considering the global development of archaeological theory and the formulation of the principals of processual archaeology in the English-speaking world (*e.g.* Binford 1962; Clarke 2015), both the scope of the investigations and their integration with non-archaeological theory was rather limited.

Post-1990

The political change brought by the fall of the Soviet Union and the rapid process of transformation introduced new forms of engaging in archaeological practice (Milisauskas 1990). Beyond changes related to the political and economic organisation of archaeology, the establishment of long-term scientific collaborations resulted in the formation of pluralistic approaches to the Bronze Age. The common thread is represented by an emphasis on inter-regional connections between former, culture-historically constrained archaeological entities (*e.g.* Czebreszuk 2003; Fischl *et al.* 2013a; Ling *et al.* 2014). The shift towards investigation of long-distance ties facilitated the need for high-resolution definitions of local processes, as well as the ambiguity of the results provided by field archaeology (Jaeger & Czebreszuk 2010; Kienlin 2010; Găvan & Gogâltan 2014). Both trends are visible in the studies of Bronze Age tell settlements indicating the departure from normative perspectives characterising research until the end of the 20th century.

The structural opposition of local and broad processes is tied to the reformulation of grand narratives with a clear stating of the Bronze Age societal trajectories triggered by the pursuit of wealth and amplified by reliance on anthropological models (Kristiansen 1998; Kristiansen & Larsson 2005). Within this spectrum tell sites represent not a historical particularity as an occupational form practiced by historically-specific groups but the consequence of the pendulum of world processes, where adaptation of institutional principles of Mediterranean societies is exemplified, among others, by interpretation of archaeological sites as static reflections of past social structures (Kristiansen & Larsson 2005, fig. 1).

Accentuation of the historical particularities in the Carpathian Basin is provided by an increasing number of case studies, where site-specific or regional investigations represent the backbone of model construction (Gogâltan *et al.* 2014; Kienlin *et al.* 2018; Rassmann *et al.* 2018). The over-arching archaeological similarities of site-characteristics and the contemporaneity of phenomena indicate the importance of local processes of interaction prior to the structural assertion of ties with the Mediterranean.

Within this structural opposition, the position of Hungarian archaeology is central to the acquisition of information and materials on archaeological sites, increasing awareness of the heritage-related aspects of archaeological practice and maintenance of international cooperation. The former is exemplified by exploration of anthropological perspectives of material culture (Fischl *et al.* 2013b), site-specific investigations (Endrődi & Reményi 2016) and pursuit of new topics within archaeological research (Kreiter 2007). Common thread of these investigations is the adherence to the principles established in the interwar or post-war period. These statements are used as concepts subject to verification or falsifying, indicating that the pursuit of new frameworks is secondary to provision of new results. In other words, the development of the discipline is examined from the perspective of new findings rather than the focus of how they were obtained, as shown by the variability of theoretical approaches used in different investigations organized primarily by an expressed interests in a particular time-period, or sometimes, geographic area (*e.g.* V. Kiss 2011; Kulcsár 2011; Vicze 2013). In this sense, post-1990s Hungarian archaeology represents a shift from a monolithic pursuit of individual interests towards an exploration of previously unacknowledged or unavailable, due to the historic circumstances, aspects of the Bronze Age.

Based on this historical overview it is possible to formulate important guidelines for future research on Bronze Age tell archaeology: The links between historically specific groups of people and tells is extrapolated based on the similarity of material culture, not empirical observations; site-specific investigations allow development of regional anthropological models; the significance of the natural environment is understated; last but not least, in order to provide a coherent socio-cultural model, it is necessary to consider both local and broad scale processes.

Kakucs-Turján: The aims of the project and the methodology

The Kakucs micro-region in the Middle Danube Valley was selected for this investigation based on observations of the research history (cf. Fig. 5.1). The study area is characterised by a geographical offset from large tell settlements (Kulcsár *et al.* 2014), the presence of Early Bronze Age occupation (Kulcsár 2011) and the variability of settlement organisation (Szeverényi & Kulcsár 2012). This point-of-departure stands in opposition to the existing narratives of centralized models (Earle & Kristiansen 2010) and reinforces the increasing consensus regarding the non-economic principles of social interaction in the 2nd millennium BC (Kienlin 2012; Brück & Fontijn 2013) by investigating the constituents of a particular settlement landscape (Jaeger *et al.* 2018b). From this perspective, the Kakucs-Turján settlement represents a unique case study of architectural planning, where the settlement organization is archaeologically recognised as comprising of internal and external ditches, household space and architectural structures related to everyday existence.

While the temporality of the ditch systems and the inter-relation of their construction with the inhabited areas remain open, the investigation opens the possibility of considering the dynamics of Bronze Age settlement systems in the 2nd millennium BC as a crucial factor in understanding human–environment relations, local histories and inter-regional processes. These three foci are used as commonalities related to the anthropological perspective of settlement life which can be used to integrate large-scale social phenomena in the Bronze Age. These foci allow for a narrative-driven organisation of the analytical part of the research aimed at characterisation of the selected settlements and the discussion of their anthropological significance by structuring the methodological inquiries towards the particular threads of settlement histories. However, rather than being a manifestation of the inherent properties of the material record, they are considered as approaches to data acquisition, which can be later integrated towards formulation of a holistic perspective (Fig. 5.3).

Human–environment relations focus primarily on conceptualising the properties attributable to the physical aspects of the social space. In this particular case, they were investigated by means of geoarchaeological methods. The local histories aspect focuses on investigating small-scale, high resolution and site based interactions, primarily via field archaeology. Lastly, the focus on inter-regional processes is oriented towards the characterisation of large-scale, long-term phenomena. The focus on legacy data is twofold: in many cases it involves consideration of the past narratives and consideration of the findings related to valuable resources, *e.g.* bronze and amber. Having outlined the contents of the specific foci, it is necessary to outline the findings related to concrete sections in order to highlight a holistic bottom-up approach to the settlement in Kakucs-Turján.

Human–environment relations

The study of human–environment relations is linked to understanding the relationship between Bronze Age communities and their landscape. The following questions were outlined towards achieving this goal:

1. What are the components of the settlement landscape?
2. How did the inhabitants of the settlement alter their environment over the course of the settlement duration?

Answering these questions was based on the application of non-invasive geoarchaeological methods: the analysis of satellite imagery, magnetometric prospection, targeted coring and sediment analysis (Pető *et al.* 2016; 2018; 2019; Niebieszczański *et al.* 2018; 2019).

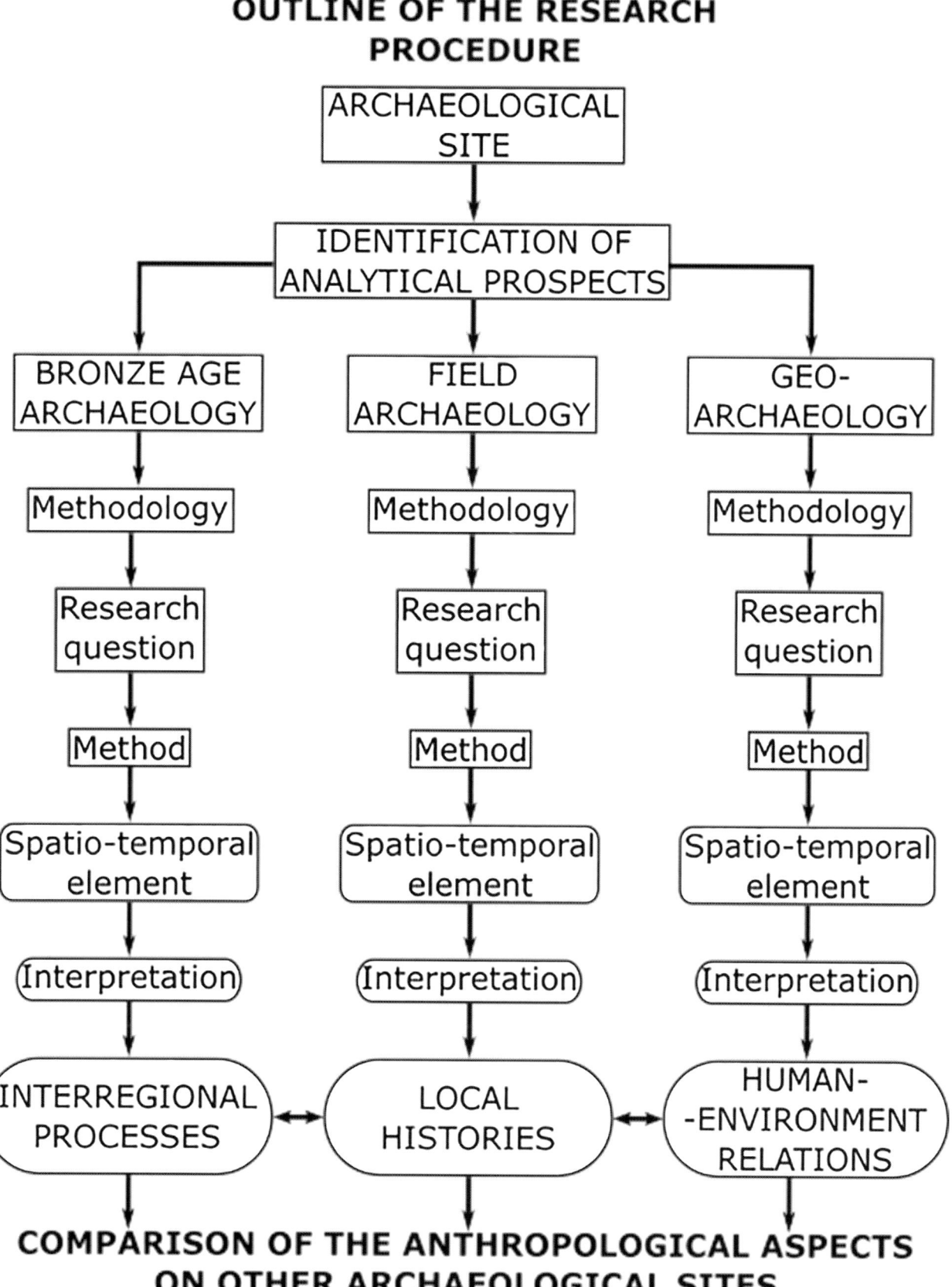

Figure 5.3 The bottom-up methodology of the Kakucs-Turján investigation.

The settlement structure, initially classified as bipartite due to the evidence from satellite imagery (Fig. 5.4), was verified using geophysical methods. These indicated the presence of a tripartite structure with a system of internal and external ditches and three primary occupation areas (Fig. 5.5). The distinctiveness of the three occupation areas lead to a classification into zones A, B, and C (Fig. 5.6). The geophysical prospection indicated the presence of shared characteristics, *i.e.* household- and pathway-like anomalies primarily in zones A and B. The anomalies related to area C were limited to pit-like ones suggesting spatial differences of settlement use. In addition, 16 house-like structures located in zone A were documented in the geophysical imagery, regularly distributed around the central feature. Due to the structure of this occupation zone, it is not clear to what extent the geophysical anomaly can be used to distinguish structures related to particular settlement layers. The exact nature of the spatial separation by the ditch-system remains open, due to the observed discontinuities of the ditch outlines, which potentially could signal the presence of access points, and the unclear chronology of the different ditch segments.

The structural similarities were further investigated on the basis of coring transects. These showed that the settlement was established upon a natural elevation. The settlement landscape of zone A was characterised by thick deposits of anthropogenic refuse and debris, while zones B and C were devoid of such characteristics. This indicated that the tell-like characteristics of the site were spatially restricted, and that middening behaviour was a form of waste disposal that was of limited significance.

The investigation of the ditches by means of ground-penetrating radar (GPR) and electrical resistivity tomography (ERT) revealed their large scale: *c.* 12 m wide and with an excessive depth of 4.5 m. The selected cores comprised both anthropogenic and natural deposits, suggesting infilling and natural erosion related to the post-abandonment stage of the settlement. While the constant presence of water is still under investigation, a hypothetical argument for such an interpretation is presented by the circular anomalies

Figure 5.4 Kakucs-Turján: satellite imagery of the site.

Figure 5.5 Kakucs-Turján: magnetometric prospection.

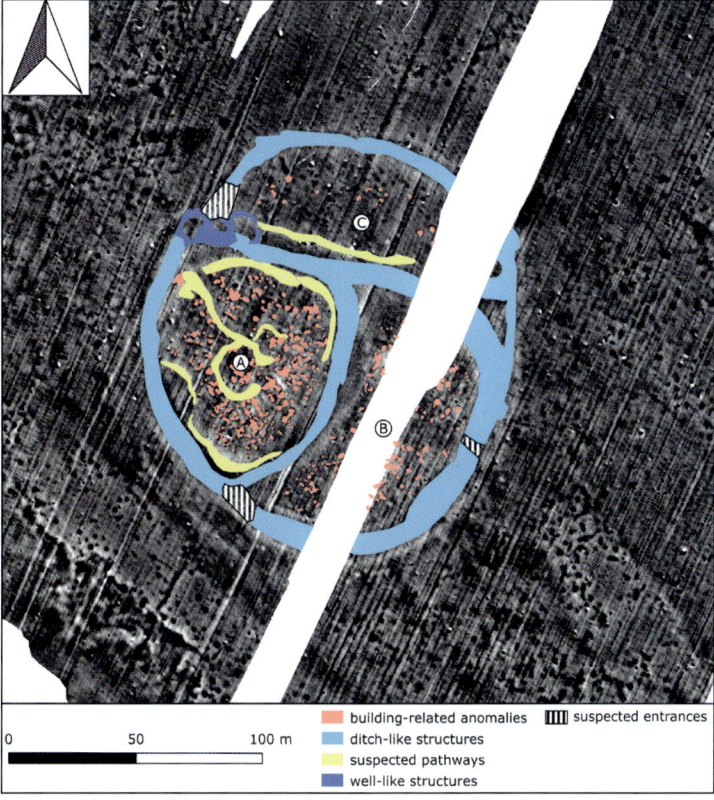

Figure 5.6 Kakucs-Turján: magnetometric prospection with the interpretation of magnetic anomalies.

documented in the northwestern part of the settlement at the intersection of internal and external ditches. The depth of the features which generated the anomaly exceeds the depth of the ditches (*c.* 5 m) and, assuming that the water was present in the ditches, would indicate a hydrological system for maintaining water flow.

The current stage of the investigation shows that the present-day landscape of the Kakucs-Turján settlement is substantially different from its original state. Initially, the settlement location was likely chosen due to the natural elevation and was transformed into a tell-like settlement due to the practiced waste disposal strategies. Whether used for water flow or not, the construction of the ditches permanently altered the landscape of the settlement through the formation of large-scale divisions between areas, firmly separating the natural and cultural landscape.

While the human–environmental relations of the inhabitants exceeded the landscape modification for settlement practices, *e.g.* economic or subsistence processes, the evidence at hand shows the impact human populations had on the transformation of the natural landscape. From a broader perspective, the widespread presence of such practices is well-established in the Carpathian Basin (Kienlin *et al.* 2018) and, if investigated in detail, could provide a possibility for cross-regional investigation of landscape impact.

Local histories

In order to explore the anthropogenic constituents of the occupation layers documented in zone A, an excavation area of *c.* 110 m^2 was outlined around the best-preserved structure anomaly. The excavations aimed to answer the following questions:

1. What was the occupation history of settlement zone A?
2. What material constituents of the settlement can be documented?
3. What information can be obtained on architectural, subsistence and economic practices?

While the two primary questions are directly linked to field archaeological questions, the last one is aimed at extending the investigations towards the social processes during the Middle Bronze Age in the Middle Danube Valley.

The excavation seasons 2013–2016 showed that the constituents of the archaeological deposits identified by means of coring allow only a general characterisation of the archaeological deposits. In order to properly identify their sequences it is necessary to conduct stratigraphic excavations. Beyond the ploughzone, 11 settlement phases datable to the Early and Middle Bronze Age were documented in zone A (Table 5.1), indicating the long-term history of the settlement in Kakucs-Turján (Jaeger *et al.* 2018a).

The earliest stages of the settlement (phases 1–3) were characterised by the presence of rudimentary architectural structures, reduced to regularly distributed postholes and large waste-disposal pits. Based on their size and distribution, it is plausible that their construction severely limited the possibility of maintaining adjacent occupation due to the destruction of the natural soil. The number of such pits indicates that occupation was rather intensive during this settlement stage.

The formation of a tell-like occupation practice, *i.e.* the superimposition of waste disposal and household construction and abandonment stages, occurred directly after phase 3 and lasted until the end of the documented habitation sequence (phases 4–10). During this time-period,

Table 5.1 *Phasing of the Kakucs-Turján settlement, respective characteristics, chronology and position within the local periodization scheme (after Jaeger et al. 2018, table 1).*

Local periodisation scheme	Absolute dating cal BC (2σ)	Occupation type	Phase
Migration Period	–	workshop	Kakucs 12
Bronze Age–Iron Age	–	–	hiatus
MBA3	1752/1676–1751/1640	deep pits	Kakucs 11
	1760/1696–1756/1686	levelling	Kakucs 10
MBA2	1777/1706–1768/1705	household destruction	Kakucs 9
	1813/1739–1802/1731	household	Kakucs 8
	1844/1749–1827/1745	levelling	Kakucs 7
MBA1	1903/1879–1752	household destruction	Kakucs 6
	–	household	Kakucs 5
	–	levelling	Kakucs 4
EBA3/MBA1	–	settlement activites	Kakucs 3
EBA3	–	waste disposal	Kakucs 2
EBA1-2	–	household remains	Kakucs 1

two well-documented household phases took place. The older structure was subject to extensive post-abandonment destruction, significantly affecting the possibility of studying its internal organisation. The later structure correlated well with the anomaly documented on geomagnetic imagery. In both instances, the overall positioning of the households showed spatial overlap, indicating that basic knowledge on the architectural parameters of the earlier construction was taken into consideration.

The final documented occupation stage was characterised by extensive pits cutting through the entire stratigraphic sequence of the settlement (phase 11). Their volume and specific beehive shape suggest that they represent large storage structures dug into already-deposited strata. Based on the available evidence, the abandonment stage of the entire settlement and the possible reasons for this event are unclear. No evidence of large-scale destruction and rapid abandonment was documented, nor was there any clear indication of the settlement undergoing a decline. This is most likely due to the constant agricultural use of the area and the destruction of the archaeological data due to modern ploughing.

From an architectural standpoint, both households comprised thick clay floors (in some instances measuring up to 20 cm), and wattle and daub walls (as evidenced by the extensive daub deposits and lines of postholes). However, architectural structures were not restricted to houses and their interiors: Investigation of the archaeological deposits showed the differences in the site formation processes between household and non-household structures, *e.g.* pathways (Niebieszczański *et al.* 2019). The differences between the mixed cultural deposits found inside and outside the houses show that waste disposal outside the household structures was characterised by an increased presence of phosphorous, zinc, copper, and manganese elements, suggesting that consumption and disposal occurred directly in front of the occupied structure, most likely directly opposite the main entrance. The different elemental content could be linked to small-scale accumulation of remains linked to consumption or metallurgy. However, no major furnace

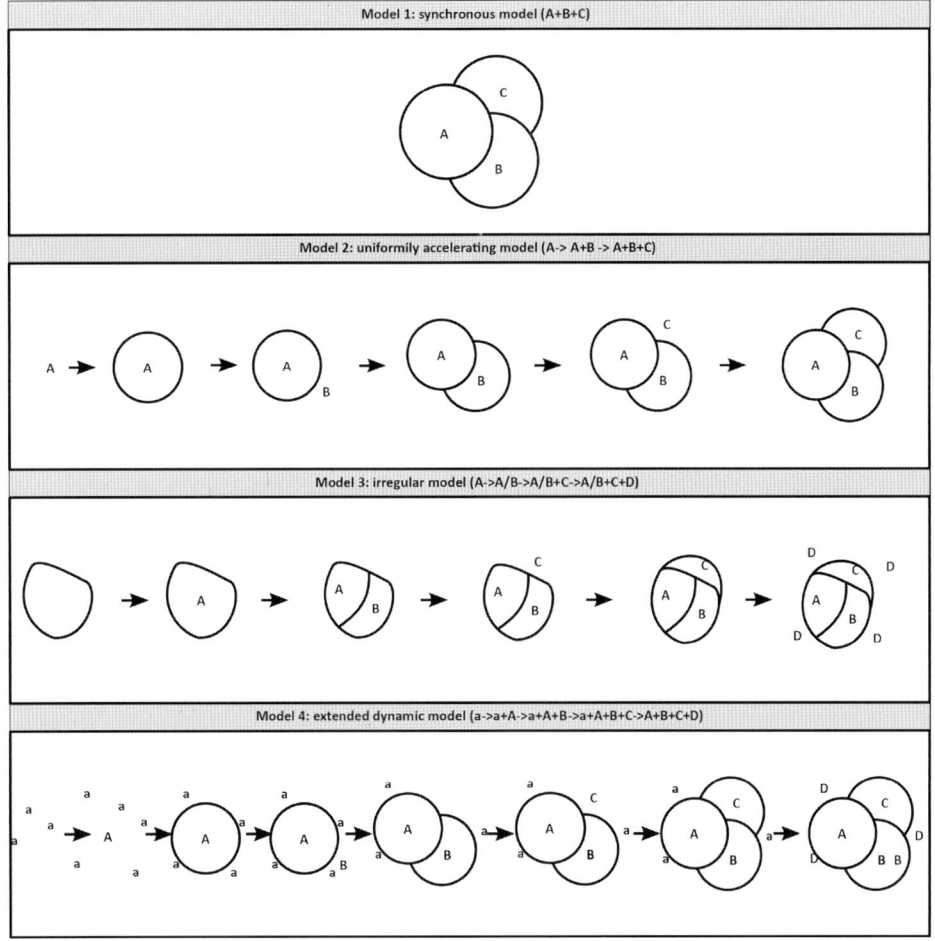

Figure 5.7 Possible scenarios for the formation of the Kakucs-Turján settlement (after Staniuk (in press)).

installations which could be related to on-site metallurgical activities were observed.

From a socio-economic perspective, the households were characterised by the presence of internal or external storage pits and the use of firing installations, *e.g.* hearths or ovens. Evidence of consumption is related to widely distributed macro-botanical and zooarchaeological remains found in almost all documented contexts (Biller 2018; Filatova *et al.* 2018). Investigation of the botanical remains shows reliance on agricultural produce, namely cereals and legumes. The animal economy was based on domestic animals, with sheep/goat and cattle representing the majority of the documented animal remains. From a material culture perspective, the site was continuously used for the consumption and storage of produce as indicated by the presence of both small and large vessel forms (Staniuk 2018a).

Based on the evidence discussed, it is clear that throughout its history the settlement of Kakucs-Turján and its inhabitants were actively engaged in the formation of a specific occupational lifestyle linked to the established landscape. The exact sequence of changes is yet unclear, with an instantaneous formation of the archaeologically recognised settlement structure representing only one of the few possible scenarios (Fig. 5.7).

Due to differences between non-tell and tell-like forms of occupation, the single instance formation of the full site represents a highly unlikely scenario (model 1). Other possibilities include the formation of a single settlement area, later encircled by a single ditch, and an even later encircling of the entire area (model 2); the initial encircling of the area chosen for habitation, and its subsequent division over the course of settlement history (model 3); or the formation of the settlement as a consequence of a long-term process of population aggregation resulting in the transformation of a central part of an otherwise non-centralised system (model 4). Apart from model 1, non-centralised aspects of site formation processes are argued for.

The selection of the excavation area, focusing primarily on verification of the household-related anomalies, is a first step towards the study of such settlements. Based on the investigation it is clear that formation of the specific landscape form was a long-term process, already taking place after a successful first occupation stage (phases 1–3). The evidence of agricultural subsistence, *i.e.* cereals, legumes, and animal husbandry, could imply that the formation of a specific landscape, based on waste disposal, was related to limiting the impact of settlement spread towards agricultural areas. Linking such concepts to the large-scale changes, such as the construction of the ditch system and the division of the settlement, requires further attention to clarify the situation. However, it does point to the dynamics of settlement involved in archaeological site formation processes. The latter is especially evident for the comparative investigation of the architectural differences.

The subsequent obliteration of the archaeological deposits due to further construction was documented as the destruction of architectural structures (phases 6 and 9) or infilling of the standing remains with waste (phases 4, 7, and 10). Considering the impact of the permanent state of destruction, the perception of tell sequences as well-preserved temporal records has to be treated with caution. Comparison of different settlement histories will require understanding both the temporal positioning of houses as well as the identification of the most suitable contexts for investigations. The latter aspect is directly linked to the third focus of the methodological approach: interregional processes.

Inter-regional processes

The subsequent generations of the Kakucs-Turján settlement were not an isolated community of the Bronze Age Carpathian Basin. Whether involved in the intra-regional exchange of objects and ideas, as evidenced by the assemblage of non-local ceramic objects (Staniuk 2018b), or inter-regional contacts, as shown by the presence of locally non-available resources such as amber, bronze and gold (Jaeger 2018), the distinct generations were always part of a broad network of interactions, together with their particular historical trajectories. The essential aspect of such trajectories is the temporal scale since it provides the means of positioning the particular settlement stages in a broader context. The reliance on typo-chronological studies derived from burial archaeology is problematic due to regional differences in funerary practices and the grave goods deposited. Thus, inhumation sepultures typical of Eastern Hungary did not deploy the large storage vessels common in household inventories (Thomas 2008), while the cremation burials found in Central Hungary have a highly-standardised inventory (Vicze 2011). Such studies are primarily useful from the standpoint of comparative datasets and require constant re-evaluation in the sense of expanding the spatial scope. In order to develop such perspectives it is necessary to obtain absolute dating of the sites tied specifically to the stratigraphic sequence (*e.g.* Drașovean *et al.* 2017). From this perspective, the primary research question was: How was the development of the Kakucs-Turján settlement linked to the formation of the tell-like occupation form?

The radiocarbon sequence for Kakucs-Turján was modelled on the basis of dated botanical macro-remains collected from the second half of the occupational sequence, representing the developed stage of the tell-like occupation, *i.e.* phases 6–11. The modelling itself was achieved with the Sequence and Phase functions of Oxcal 4.3 (Bronk Ramsey 2017).

Overall, the radiocarbon dating shows that the settlement was already intensively used in the 19th century BC, with the stratigraphic evidence suggesting that the formation of the tell-like form of occupation happened *c.* 2000 BC, while the site history can extend as far back as 2400 BC. From this perspective, the formation of the site and the communities inhabiting it were integrated into the larger process of the resettling of the Middle Danube Valley after a long period of impermanent occupation (Kulcsár 2013). From this point of view, the transition from Early to Middle Bronze Age occupation practices in the Carpathian Basin has to be perceived as a dynamic period of social and agricultural changes, which resulted in the formation of the persisting landscape. The establishment of a tell-like occupation, even on relatively small settlements, at such an early point suggests the rapid spread of such forms of occupation, which was not necessarily linked to well-established trade routes or power structures, but was directly linked to widely-practiced forms of land occupation.

The contextualised examination of the inter-regional processes and the specific temporal links is a major step towards understanding the 2nd millennium BC beyond typo-chronological classification, and towards understanding the trajectories of change related to large-scale phenomena, such as the spread of metallurgy and its reception among communities of the European Bronze Age (Earle *et al.* 2015) or demographic processes and their socio-environmental impact (Müller 2015).

Conclusions

From a historical research trajectory towards the identification of new problems in studying multi-layered fortified settlements, the investigation of the social processes in the 2nd millennium BC requires the implementation of data from different sources (legacy data and historical studies) and different excavations (contemporary expeditions). In all instances, the attained results rely upon the complimentary presentation of the analytical methods and their reproducibility. As shown by the study of the historical trajectory of tell research in the Carpathian Basin, the increasing multiplicity of approaches increases uncertainty related to the achieved results: While working with the same type of archaeological deposits, different research foci provide different insights on the social formation and the history of particular communities. Integrating results between different investigations will provide the means to identify commonalities between different areas and the developed findings. In order to achieve such a goal, it is necessary to explicitly tie the specific research stages, which in the case of the findings discussed here is related to the outline of the methodological approach of the Kakucs-Turján investigation and its implementation, to analytical and interpretative purposes. From the perspective of the investigated area, the challenges of incorporating findings of past researchers will prove essential in the upcoming years. While contemporary approaches represent selective perspectives, their explicit formulation and the deployment of a bottom-up approach to the study of social processes is, in our opinion, the key towards shifting study from tells as an inevitable result of occupation towards the social processes resulting in their formation.

Acknowledgements

The financial support for the project was provided by a National Science Centre of Poland (NCN 2012/05/B/HS3/03714); Hungarian Academy of Sciences, National Cultural Fund 3234/261; Lendület/Momentum Mobility Project LP2015-3 (2015–2016); the post-doc project 'Transforming Landscapes of Fortification in the Bronze Age of Central Hungary' (JMA 1013 06 685 20) and PhD-position 'Tradition and Practice – Study on Pottery, Chronology and Social Dynamics of the Hungarian Bronze Age' (GSC608).

Notes

1. While the emphasis is placed on the Hungarian part of the Carpathian Basin in a political sense, this is not to say that it represents the only discussion taking place on the methodology and history of Bronze Age tell archaeology in Central and Central-Eastern Europe (*e.g.* Medović & Medović 2011; Bátora *et al.* 2012; Lie *et al.* 2018). Due to historical circumstances, the discussion on tell-related archaeology in the Carpathian Basin has become split into particular schools; this paper deals specifically with just one of these.
2. The maps used in this publication are partly based on the following source: © EuroGeographics for the administrative boundaries.

References

Banner, J. (1956) Research on the Hungarian Bronze Age since 1936 and the Bronze-Age Settlement at Békés-Várdomb. *Proceedings of the Prehistoric Society* 21, 123–143.

Banner, J. & Bóna, I. (1974) *Mittelbronzezeitliche Tell-Siedlung bei Békés*. Budapest, Akadémiai Kiadó.

Barenscott, D. (2010) Articulating Identity through the Technological Rearticulation of Space: The Hungarian Millennial Exhibition as World's Fair and the Disordering of Fin-de-Siècle Budapest. *Slavic Review* 69, 571–590.

Bátora, J., Behrens, A., Gresky, J., Ivanova, M., Rassmann, K., Tóth, P. & Winkelmann, K. (2012) The Rise and Decline of the Early Bronze Age Settlement Fidvár near Vráble, Slovakia. In J. Kneisel, W. Kirleis, M. Dal Corso, N. Taylor & V. Tiedtke (eds), *Collapse or Continuity? Environment and Development of Bronze Age Human Landscapes. Proceedings of the International Workshop 'Socio-Environmental Dynamics over the Last 12,000 Years: The Creation of Landscapes II (14th–18th March 2011)' in Kiel*, 111–130. Bonn, Habelt.

Bertemes, F. (2011) Prehistoric Archaeology in Central Europe. In A. Gramsch & U. Sommer (eds), *A History of Central European Archaeology. Theory, Methods and Politics*, 41–55. Budapest, Archeolingua.

Biller, A.Z. (2018) Archaeological results of the pits from Kakucs-Turján. In M. Jaeger, G. Kulcsár, N. Taylor & R. Staniuk (eds), *Kakucs-Turján. A Middle Bronze Age multi-layered fortified settlement in Central Hungary*, 159–173. Bonn, Habelt.

Binford, L.R. (1962) Archaeology as Anthropology. *American Antiquity* 28, 217–225.

Bóna, I. (1975) *Die mittlere Bronzezeit Ungarns und ihre südöstlichen Beziehungen.* Budapest, Akadémiai Kiadó.

Bóna, I. (1992) Bronzezeitliche Tell-Kulturen in Ungarn. In W. Meier-Arendt (ed.), *Bronzezeit in Ungarn. Forschungen in Tell-Siedlungen an Donau und Theiss*, 9–41. Frankfurt am Main, Museum für Vor- und Frühgeschichte.

Bronk Ramsey, C. (2017) Methods for Summarizing Radiocarbon Datasets. *Radiocarbon* 59, 1809–1833.

Brück, J. & Fontijn, D. (2013) The Myth of the Chief: Prestige Goods, Power, and Personhood in the European Bronze Age. In H. Fokkens & A. Harding (eds), *The Oxford Handbook of the European Bronze Age*, 197–215. Oxford, Oxford University Press.

Cartledge, B. (2011) *The Will to Survive. A History of Hungary.* London, Hurst & Company.

Childe, V.G. (1929) *The Danube in Prehistory.* Oxford, Clarendon Press.

Clarke, D.L. (2015) *Analytical Archaeology.* London/New York, Routledge.

Csalog, J. (1952) Die Ausgrabungen in Tószeg im Jahre 1948. *Acta Archaeologica Academiae Scientiarum Hungaricae* 2, 19–33.

Czebreszuk, J. (2003) Amber on the Threshold of a World Career. In C.W. Beck, I. Loze & J.M. Todd (eds), *Amber in Archaeology. Proceedings of the Fourth International Conference of Amber in Archaeology in Talsi 2001*, 164–179. Riga, Institute of the History of Latvia Publishers.

Drașovean, F., Schier, W., Bayliss, A., Gaydarska, B. & Whittle, A. (2017) The Lives of Houses: Duration, Context, and History at Neolithic Uivar, Romania. *European Journal of Archaeology* 20, 636–662.

Earle, T. & Kristiansen, K. (2010) Introduction: Theory and Practice in the Late Prehistory of Europe. In T. Earle & K. Kristiansen (eds), *Organizing Bronze Age Societies: The Mediterranean, Central Europe and Scandinavia Compared*, 1–33. Cambridge, Cambridge University Press.

Earle, T., Ling, J., Uhnér, C., Stos-Gale, Z. & Melheim, L. (2015) The Political Economy and Metal Trade in Bronze Age Europe: Understanding Regional Variability in Terms of Comparative Advantages and Articulations. *European Journal of Archaeology* 18, 633–657.

Endrődi, A. & Reményi, L. (2016) *A Bell Beaker settlement in Albertfalva, Hungary (2470– 1950 BC).* Budapest, Budapest History Museum.

Filatova, S., Gissel, C. & Filipović, D. (2018) The plant economy at the Bronze Age site of Kakucs-Turján. In M. Jaeger, G. Kulcsár, N. Taylor & R. Staniuk (eds), *Kakucs-Turján. A Middle Bronze Age multi-layered fortified settlement in Central Hungary*, 175–187. Bonn, Habelt.

Fischl, K.P., Kiss, V., Kulcsár, G. & Szeverényi, V. (2013a) Transformations in the Carpathian Basin around 1600 BC. In H. Meller & F. Bertemes (eds), *1600 – Kultureller Umbruch im Schatten des Thera-Ausbruchs? 4. Mitteldeutscher Archäologentag vom 14. bis 16. Oktober 2011 in Halle (Saale)*, 355–371. Halle (Saale), Landesamt für Denkmalpflege und Archäologie Sachsen-Anhalt.

Fischl, K.P., Kiss, V. & Kulcsár, G. (2013b) Specialised Households in the Carpathian Basin during the Early and Middle Bronze Age. In B. Rezi, R.E. Németh & S. Berecki (eds), *Bronze Age Crafts and Craftsmen in the Carpathian Basin. Proceedings of the International Colloquium from Târgu Mureș 5–7 October 2012*, 9–22. Târgu Mureș, Editura Mega.

Găvan, A. & Gogâltan, F. (2014) 'Zentrum und Peripherie?'. Der bronzezetiliche Tell von Pecica 'Șanțul Mare' (Kreis Arad, Rumänien). In B. Nassel, I. Heske & D. Brandherm (eds), *Ressourcen und Rohstoffe in der Bronzezeit. Nutzung – Distribution – Kontrolle. Beiträge zur Sitzung der Arbeitsgemeinschaft Bronzezeit auf der Jahrestagung des Mittel- und Ostdeutschen Verbandes für Altertumforschung in Brandenburg an der Havel, 16. bis 17. April 2012*, 26–40. Wünsdorf, Brandenburgisches Landesamt für Denkmalpflege und Archäologisches Landesmuseum.

Gogâltan, F., Cordoș, C. & Ignat, A. (2014) *Bronze Age Tell, Tell-like and Mound-like Settlements on the Eastern Frontier of the Carpathian Basin. History of research.* Cluj-Napoca, Editura Mega.

Gramsch, A. (2011) Theory in Central European Archaeology: dead or alive? In J. Bintliff & M. Pearce (eds), *The Death of Archaeological Theory?*, 48–71. Oxford, Oxbow Books.

Harding, A. (2009) Towards a European archaeology. *World Archaeology* 41, 629–640.

Heyd, V. (2017) Kossinna's smile. *Antiquity* 91, 348–359.

Jaeger, M. (2016) *Bronze Age Fortified Settlements in Central Europe.* Bonn/Poznań, Wydawnictwo Nauka i Innowacje/ Habelt.

Jaeger, M. (2018) Open communities – enclosed spaces. Kakucs-Turján settlement in the context of local tradition and inter-regional relations. In M. Jaeger, G. Kulcsár, N. Taylor & R. Staniuk (eds), *Kakucs-Turján. A Middle Bronze Age multi-layered fortified settlement in Central Hungary*, 191–211. Bonn, Habelt.

Jaeger, M. & Czebreszuk, J. (2010) Does a Periphery Look Like That? The Cultural Landscape of the Unetice Culture's Kościan Group. In Kiel Graduate School 'Human Development in Landscapes' (eds), *Landscapes and Human Development. The Contribution of European Archaeology. Proceedings of the International Workshop 'Socio-environmental dynamics over the last 12,000 years. The creation of landscapes (1st–4th April 2009)'*, 217–236. Bonn, Habelt.

Jaeger, M., Staniuk, R., Müller, J. Kulcsár, G. & Taylor, N. (2018a) History of Bronze Age Habitation. In M. Jaeger, G. Kulcsár, N. Taylor & R. Staniuk (eds), *Kakucs-Turján. A Middle Bronze Age multi-layered fortified settlement in Central Hungary*, 97–118. Bonn, Habelt.

Jaeger, M., Kirleis, W., Kiss, V., Kulcsár, G., Müller, J., Staniuk, R. & Taylor, N. (2018b) 'Kakucs Archaeological Expedition'. In M. Jaeger, G. Kulcsár, N. Taylor & R. Staniuk (eds), *Kakucs-Turján. A Middle Bronze Age multi-layered fortified settlement in Central Hungary*, 13–21. Bonn, Habelt.

Jones, S. (1997) *The Archaeology of Ethnicity. Constructing identities in the past and present.* London/New York, NY, Routledge.

Kadrow, S. (2011) The German Influence on Polish Archaeology. In A. Gramsch & U. Sommer (eds), *A History of Central*

European Archaeology. Theory, Methods and Politics, 125–141. Budapest: Archeolingua.

Kadrow, S. (2017) What Happened in Iwanowice at the End of the 3rd Millennium BC? Did a Rebellion Break Out? In S. Hansen & J. Müller (eds), *Rebellion and Inequality in Archaeology*, 172–185. Bonn, Habelt.

Kalicz, N. (1968) *Die Frühbronzezeit in Nordost-Ungarn*. Budapest, Akadémiai Kiadó.

Kienlin, T.L. (2010) *Traditions and Transformations: Approaches to Eneolithic (Copper Age) and Bronze Age Metalworking and Society in Eastern Central Europe and the Carpathian Basin*. Oxford, Archaeopress.

Kienlin, T.L. (2012) Patterns of Change, or: Perceptions Deceived? Comments on the Interpretation of Late Neolithic and Bronze Age Tell Settlement in the Carpathian Basin. In T.L. Kienlin & A. Zimmermann (eds), *Beyond Elites. Alternatives to Hierarchical Systems in Modelling Social Formations*, 251–310. Bonn, Habelt.

Kienlin, T.L., Fischl, K.P. & Pusztai, T. (2018) *Borsod Region Bronze Age Settlement (BORBAS). Catalogue of the Early to Middle Bronze Age Tell Sites Covered by Magnetometry and Surface Survey*. Bonn, Habelt.

Kiss, C.G. (2013) National Identity and Collective Memory. In C.G. Kiss (ed.), *Understanding Central Europe: Nations and Stereotypes*, 19–30. Budapest, Nap Kiadó.

Kiss, V. (2011) The Role of the Danube in the Early and Middle Bronze Age of the Carpathian Basin. In G. Kovács & G. Kulcsár (eds), *Ten Thousand Years Along the Danube*, 211–239. Budapest, Archaeolingua.

Kreiter, A. (2007) *Technological Choices and Material Meanings in Early and Middle Bronze Age Hungary. Understanding the active role of material culture through ceramic analysis*. Oxford, Archaeopress.

Kristiansen, K. (1998) *Europe before History*. Cambridge, Cambridge University Press.

Kristiansen, K. & Larsson, T.B. (2005) *The Rise of the Bronze Age Society. Travels, Transmissions and Transformations*. Cambridge, Cambridge University Press.

Kulcsár, G. (2011) Untangling the Early Bronze Age in the Middle Danube Valley. In G. Kovacs & G. Kulcsár (eds), *Ten Thousand Years Along the Danube*, 179–210. Budapest, Archaeolingua.

Kulcsár, G. (2013) Glimpses of the Third Millennium BC in the Carpathian Basin. In A. Anders, G. Kulcsár, G. Kalla, V. Kiss & G.V. Szabó (eds), *Moments in Time. Papers Presented to Pál Raczky on His 60th Birthday*, 643–659. Budapest, L'Harmattan.

Kulcsár, G., Jaeger, M., Kiss, V., Márkus, G., Müller, J., Pető, Á., Serlegi, G., Szeverényi, V. & Taylor, N. (2014) The Beginnings of a New Research Program – Kakucs Archaeological Expedition – KEX 1. *Hungarian Archaeology*, 1–7.

Laszlovsky, J. & Siklódi, C. (1991) Archaeological Theory in Hungary Since 1960. Theories Without Theoretical Archaeology. In I. Hodder (ed.), *Archaeological Theory in Europe. The last three decades*, 272–298. London/New York, NY, Routledge.

Lie, M.A., Cordoș, C., Găvan, A., Fazecaș, G., Kienlin, T.L. & Gogâltan, F. (2018) An Overview of the Bronze Age Tell-Settlement in Toboliu (Bihor County, Romania). *Gesta* 18, 63–76.

Ling, J., Stos-Gale, Z., Grandin, L., Billström, K., Hjärthner-Holdar, E. & Persson, P.-O. (2014) Moving metals II: Provenancing Scandinavian Bronze Age artefacts by lead isotope and elemental analyses. *Journal of Archaeological Science* 41, 106–132.

Macartney, C.A. (1937) *Hungary and Her Successors: The Treaty of Trianon and Its Consequences 1919–1937*. London, Oxford University Press.

von Márton, L. (1912) Die wichtigsten Resultate vor- und früh-geschichtlicher Forschung in Ungarn (1911). *Prähistorische Zeitschrift* 4, 175–191.

Medović, P. & Medović, I. (2011) *Gradina na Bosutu*. Novi Sad, Platoneum.

Milisauskas, S. (1990) People's revolutions of 1989 and archaeology in Eastern Europe. *Antiquity* 64, 283–285.

Minta-Tworzowska, D. (2011) Zmienność kulturowa i społeczna w ujęciu archeologii. *Przegląd Archeologiczny* 59, 5–26.

Molnár, M. (2001) *A Concise History of Hungary*. Cambridge, Cambridge University Press.

Müller, J. (2015) Eight million Neolithic Europeans: social demography and social archaeology on the scope of change – from the Near East to Scandinavia. In K. Kristiansen, L. Šmejda & J. Turek (eds), *Paradigm Found – Archaeological Theory: Present, Past And Future. Essays in Honour of Evžen Neustupný*, 200–214. Oxford, Oxbow Books.

Neustupný, E. (1991) Recent Theoretical Achievements in Prehistoric Archaeology in Czechoslovakia. In I. Hodder (ed.), *Archaeological Theory in Europe. The last three decades*, 248–271. London/New York, NY, Routledge.

Niebieszczański, J., Pető, Á., Serlegi, G., Hildebrandt-Radke, I., Galas, J., Sipos, G., Páll, D.G., Onaca, A., Spychalski, W., Jaeger, M., Kulcsár, G., Taylor, N. & Márkus, G. (2018) Geoarchaeological and non-invasive investigations of the site and its surroundings. In M. Jaeger, G. Kulcsár, N. Taylor & R. Staniuk (eds), *Kakucs-Turján. A Middle Bronze Age multi-layered fortified settlement in Central Hungary*, 43–71. Bonn, Habelt.

Niebieszczański, J., Jaeger, M., Pető, Á., Hildebrandt–Radke, I., Kulcsár, G., Staniuk, R., Taylor, N. & Czebreszuk, J. (2019) Revealing the internal organization of a Middle Bronze Age fortified settlement in Kakucs-Turján through geoarchaeological means: Magnetometric survey and sedimentological verification of a housing structure. *Journal of Archaeological Science: Reports* 25, 409–419.

Pető, Á., Serlegi, G., Krausz, E., Jaeger, M. & Kulcsár, G. (2016) Régészeti talajtani megfigyelések 'Kakucs–Turján mögött' bronzkori lelőhelyen II.: Az árokrendszer. *Agrokémia és talajtan* 65, 225–242.

Pető, Á., Niebieszczański, J., Serlegi, G., Jaeger, M. & Kulcsár, G. (2019) The site mapping of Kakucs-Turján by the means of horizontal and vertical proxies: Combining field and basic laboratory methods of geoarchaeology and archaeological prospection. *Journal of Archaeological Science: Reports* 27, 101999.

Pető, Á., Serlegi, G., Niebieszczański, J., Molnár, M., Jaeger, M., Kulcsár, G. & Taylor, N. (2018) Report on the geoarchaeological survey of Kakucs-Turján site. In M. Jaeger, G. Kulcsár, N. Taylor & R. Staniuk (eds), *Kakucs-Turján. A Middle Bronze Age multi-layered fortified settlement in Central Hungary*, 25–40. Bonn, Habelt.

Rączkowski, W. (2011) The 'German School of Archaeology' in its Central European Context: Sinful Thoughts. In A. Gramsch & U. Sommer (eds), *A History of Central European Archaeology. Theory, Methods and Politics*, 197–214. Budapest, Archeolingua.

Rassmann, K., Bátora, J., Müller-Scheeßel, N., Reiter, S., Ivanova, M., Behrens, A., Radloff, K. & Bača, M. (2018) Tracing taphonomic processes. Multiple Layer Analysis of Ceramic Distribution from Surface Collection and Excavation at the Early Bronze Age Settlement of Vráble-Fidvár. *Slovenská archeológia* 64, 219–234.

Sofaer, J. (2015) *Clay in the Age of Bronze. Essays in the Archaeology of Prehistoric Creativity*. Cambridge, Cambridge University Press.

Sommer, U. & Gramsch, A. (2011) German Archaeology in Context: An Introduction to History and Present of Central European Archaeology. In A. Gramsch & U. Sommer (eds), *A History of Central European Archaeology. Theory, Methods and Politics*, 7–39. Budapest, Archeolingua.

Sørensen, M.L.S. (1997) Reading Dress: The Construction of Social Categories and Identities in Bronze Age Europe. *Journal of European Archaeology* 5, 93–114.

Sørensen, M.L.S. & Vicze, M. (2013) Locating Household Activities on a Bronze Age Tell. In B. Berzsenyi, I. Briz I Godino, G. Kovacs & M. Madella (eds), *The Archaeology of Household*, 159–178. Oxford, Oxbow Books.

Staniuk, R. (2018a) Preliminary results of pottery analysis from Kakucs-Turján. In M. Jaeger, G. Kulcsár, N. Taylor & R. Staniuk (eds), *Kakucs-Turján. A Middle Bronze Age multi-layered fortified settlement in Central Hungary*, 137–155. Bonn, Habelt.

Staniuk, R. (2018b) The World Within a Household – Kakucs-Turján mögött Case Study and the Interrelatedness of Middle Bronze Age pottery. In B. Rezi & R.E. Németh (eds), *Bronze Age Connectivity in the Carpathian Basin. Proceedings of the International Colloquium from Târgu Mureș, 13–15 October 2016*, 55–74. Târgu Mureș, Editura Mega.

Staniuk, R. (in press) *Tradition and Practice. Study on Pottery, Chronology and Social Dynamic of the Hungarian Bronze Age*. Bonn, Habelt.

Szeverényi, V. & Kulcsár, G. (2012) Middle Bronze Age Settlement and Society in Central Hungary. In M. Jaeger, J. Czebreszuk & K.P. Fischl (eds), *Enclosed Space – Open Society. Contact and Exchange in the Context of Bronze Age Fortified Settlements in Central Europe*, 287–351. Poznań/Bonn, Bogucki Wydawnictwo Naukowe/Habelt.

Thomas, M. (2008) *Studien zu Chronologie und Totenritual der Otomani-Füzesabony-Kultur*. Bonn, Habelt.

Tompa, F. (1937) 25 Jahre Urgeschichtsforschung in Ungarn 1912–1936. *Bericht der Römisch-Germanischen* Kommission 24–25, 27–127.

Trigger, B.G. (2008) *A History of Archaeological Thought*. Second Edition. Cambridge, Cambridge University Press.

Vékony, G. (2003) The history of archaeological fieldwork in Hungary. In Z. Visy (ed.), *Hungarian Archaeology at the Turn of the Millennium*, 15–22. Budapest, Ministry of National Cultural Heritage.

Vicze, M. (2011) *Bronze Age Cemetery at Dunaújváros-Duna-dűlő*. Budapest, Eötvös Loránd University, Institute of Archaeological Sciences.

Vicze, M. (2013) Koszider: break or continuity? In M. Vicze, I. Poroszlai & P. Sümegi (eds), *Hoard, Phase, Period? Round table conference on the Koszider problem*, 15–29. Százhalombatta, Matrica Museum.

6

Exploring the Bronze Age Tells and Tell-like Settlements from the Eastern Carpathian Basin. Results of a Research Project

Florin Gogâltan, Alexandra Găvan, Marian A. Lie, Gruia Fazecaș, Cristina Cordoș and Tobias L. Kienlin

Introduction

This contribution summarises the results of a research project entitled *Living in the Bronze Age Tell Settlements: A Study of Settlement Archaeology at the Eastern Frontier of the Carpathian Basin* financed by the Romanian Ministry of National Education between 2013 and 2016. The main objective of this project was to collect and reassess all the archaeological data related to the Bronze Age tell settlements located in western Romania, and to conduct excavations and non-invasive investigations in selected tells from this region.

The Bronze Age tells are visible landmarks even today in the Carpathian Basin, a lowland area surrounded by the Carpathian, Alpine and Dinaric mountain ranges. Tell settlements were established especially in the Great Hungarian Plain, mostly located along the Danube and the Tisza Rivers and their tributaries. The development of these sites covers the late Early Bronze Age (EBA) and the Middle Bronze Age (MBA) in Hungarian-Transylvanian chronology, or broadly the EBA and incipient MBA in central European chronology, a period that is currently dated to around 2300/2200–1500/1450 BC (Gogâltan 2005; 2015; 2017; Fischl *et al.* 2015a). These artificial mounds have a long history of research and investigation dating back to the second half of the 19th century (Kovács 1988; Gogâltan 2005; Kienlin 2012; 2015). However, research carried out in various areas within the Carpathian Basin has shown that new fieldwork still has the potential to significantly change our image of Bronze Age tells by revealing settlement activity beyond the mounds themselves, mostly through non-invasive investigations. It is now clear that the Bronze Age tells were part of much more complex settlement systems than previously thought. Hence, our current interpretation of these sites, as well as our research design, should be modified to incorporate these new findings.

As mentioned above, several research projects conducted in the Carpathian Basin in recent decades have focused on non-invasive investigations, as well as excavations of tells and open sites in their vicinity (Fig. 6.1). In Slovakia such projects targeted the regions around the Hron and Nitra Rivers, with prominent sites investigated, like Vráble *Fidvár* (Bátora *et al.* 2012; Nowaczinski *et al.* 2012; Gauss *et al.* 2013; Müller-Scheeßel *et al.* 2016; Rassmann *et al.* 2017; 2018), Santovka *Nad Búrom* (Bátora & Tóth 2014; Bátora *et al.* 2015) and Vesele *Hradisko* (Marková & Staššíková-Štukovská 2015). In Hungary we have the Százhalombatta Archaeological Expedition (SAX) and the Benta Valley Project (Poroszlai & Vicze 2005; Earle & Kristiansen 2010; Earle *et al.* 2011; 2012; 2014; Sørensen & Vicze 2013; Klehm & Nyíri 2016), the Bronze Age Körös Off-Tell Archaeology or BAKOTA project (Duffy 2014; Duffy *et al.* 2019), the Kakucs archaeological expedition or KEX (Jaeger & Kulcsár 2013; Kulcsár *et al.* 2014; Pető *et al.* 2015; Jaeger *et al.* 2018; Niebieszczański *et al.* 2019) and the BORBAS – Borsod Region Bronze Age Settlement – project (Fischl 2012; Fischl *et al.* 2015b; Kienlin *et al.* 2018), with work being also done along the Berettyó Valley (Dani & Fischl 2009; Dani 2012). What these projects brought to light is that tells within the aforementioned regions followed different trajectories of development and that there are differences from region to region in terms of settlement patterns, site structure and internal organisation.

In western Romania, there were only a small number of recent field projects focusing on the investigation of

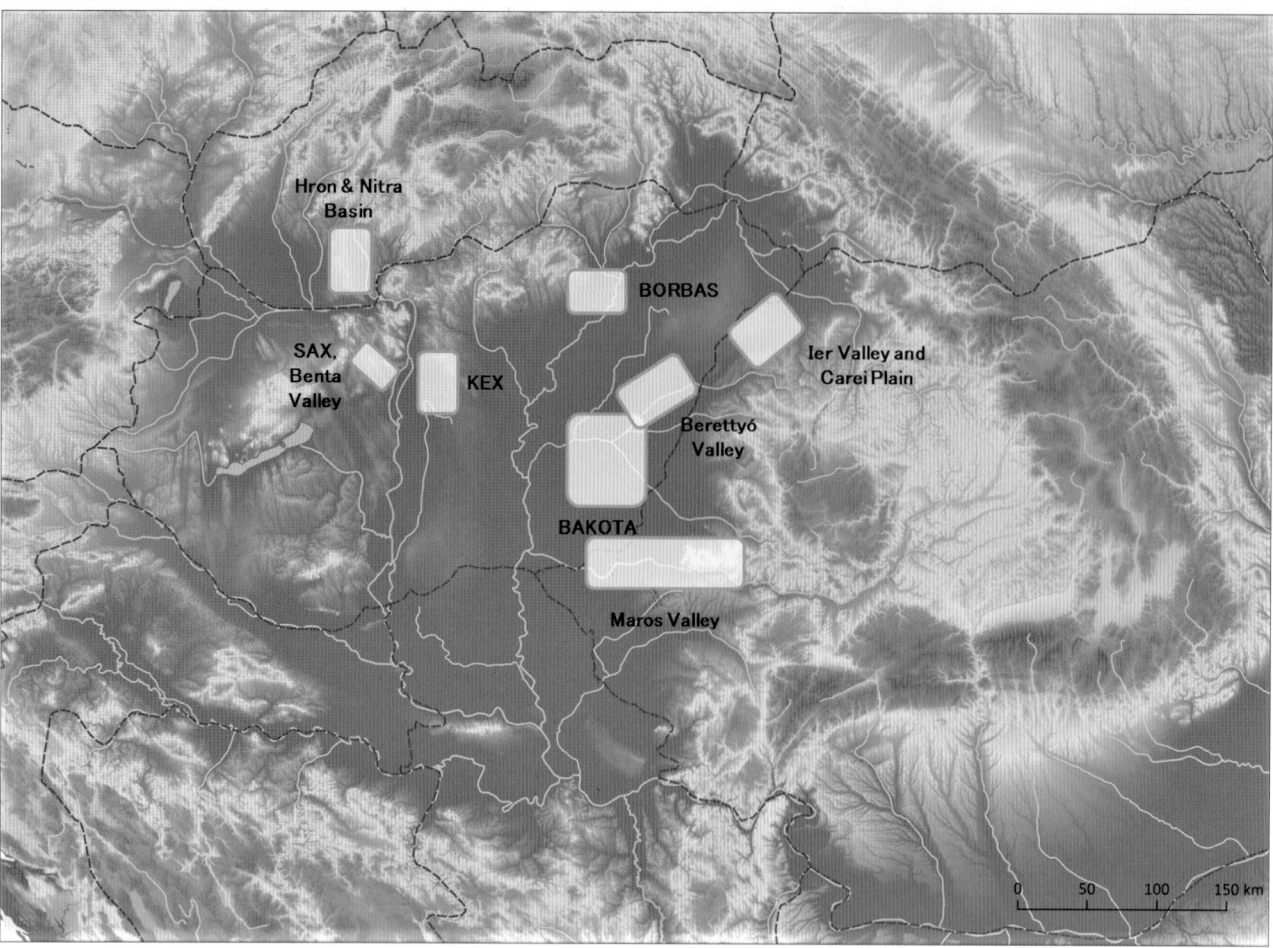

Figure 6.1 Recent research projects focusing on Bronze Age multi-layered settlements in the Carpathian Basin.

Bronze Age tell settlements (see also Fig. 6.1), two within the region encompassing the Carei Plain and the Ier/Eriu River Valley (Marta *et al.* 2010; Németi & Molnár 2012; Molnár & Nagy 2013; Kienlin *et al.* 2017), and one centred around the tell from Pecica Șanțul Mare (O'Shea *et al.* 2005; 2006; 2011; Nicodemus *et al.* 2015; O'Shea & Nicodemus 2019). Our project also targeted western Romania, focusing on two distinct regions: the lower Maros/Mureș River Valley and the Criș Rivers catchment system (Gogâltan *et al.* 2014; Gogâltan 2015; see also Figs 6.2 and 6.3). Due to limited space, and the fact that overviews of our investigations on the lower Mureș River were previously reported (see, for example, Gogâltan 2016; Sava & Gogâltan 2017), we will mainly discuss the results obtained in the latter region, while briefly summarising our research in the former.

Previous work on the Bronze Age tell and tell-like settlements in the eastern Carpathian Basin

Our project started with the collection of all available data on the Bronze Age multi-layered settlements located in western Romania, information which was summarised in an earlier volume (Gogâltan *et al.* 2014). This volume was designed as a standardised catalogue, with each multi-layered settlement from the study region presented separately. In preparing the catalogue, we used the term 'tells' as defined by Florin Gogâltan in 2002: 'multi-layered settlements that appeared in a specific geographical area as a consequence of a favourable environment ..., created through the successive accumulation of debris from large surface constructions made of clay and having a wooden structure' (Gogâltan 2002, 23). By applying this definition, Gogâltan identified 188 such Bronze Age settlements in the Carpathian Basin, 46 of which were located in western Romania. He further distinguished three categories among these multi-layered sites, depending on the thickness of their archaeological deposits and the number of layers they contained (Gogâltan 2002, 24; 2008, 40): a) proper tell sites, with at least three archaeological layers and a thickness of settlement deposits over 1 m; b) tell-like settlements, with a thickness of deposits less than 1 m and/or at least two layers; and c) mound-like settlements – sites with limited or no archaeological investigation, classified as tells due to their mound-shaped appearance and surface

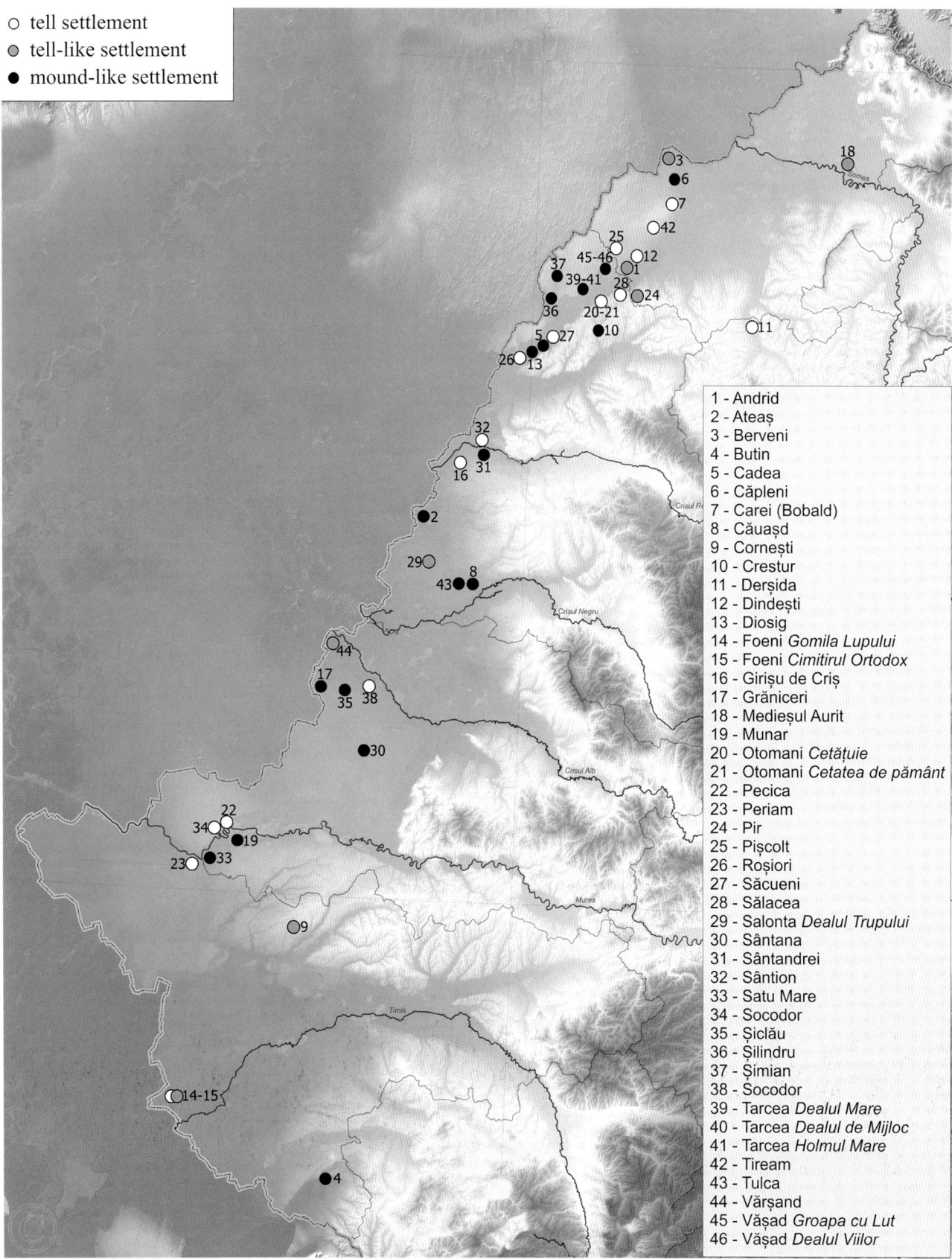

Figure 6.2 Bronze Age multi-layered settlements in Western Romania (state of research: 2014).

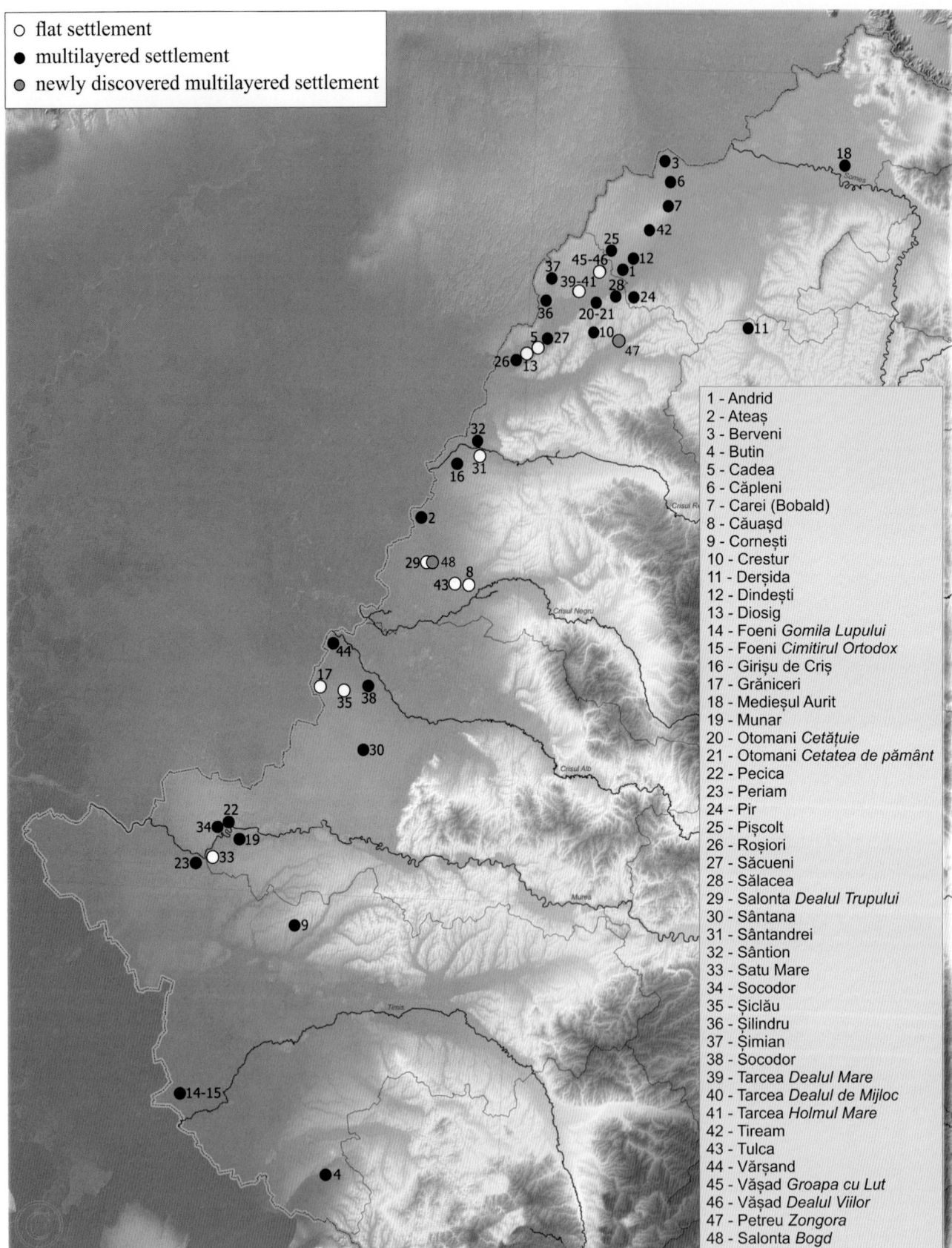

Figure 6.3 Bronze Age multi-layered settlements in Western Romania (state of research: 2019).

finds that point to continuity in occupation; the latter type also includes sites that have been excavated and referred to as tells, although the publications do not contain information regarding number of layers and thickness of deposits. Following these distinctions, out of the 46 multi-layered sites in western Romania, 17 sites could be attributed to the category of tell settlements, eight were characterised as tell-like settlements, while 21 were included in the category of 'mound-like' settlements (Gogâltan 2014a, 15; see also Fig. 6.2).

After compiling the collected data, we observed that the investigation of these settlements varied significantly. Systematic excavations conducted over the course of several campaigns were undertaken on only 17 of the 46 multi-layered sites recorded in our catalogue. In most cases, however, the investigated areas were limited in size, with the main goal being to expose the stratigraphic sequence and collect artefacts that would enrich the collections of local museums. With few exceptions, almost no data has been provided on the inner layout of the settlements; information on the structure and characteristics of the houses found within has only been reported for a couple of sites.[1] Furthermore, the results of some of these investigations have not been fully published. Another 11 of the multi-layered settlements located in western Romania have been investigated only through test trenches, which provided little information on the overall structure of these sites besides their stratigraphy. Lastly, 18 sites have only been explored by means of surface surveys and have been included in the category of multi-layered sites due to their mound-like shapes and the presence of diagnostic pottery that pointed towards continuity in their occupation throughout subsequent phases of the Early and/or Middle Bronze Age.

As for non-invasive investigations, aerial photographs and geophysical surveys were undertaken for only eight sites. Furthermore, in terms of absolute chronology, radiocarbon dates at the time of the catalogue were only published from Pecica *Șanțul Mare* (Nicodemus & O'Shea 2015), while the dates collected from Semlac still awaited publication.[2] In summary, our comprehensive overview has shown the dire need for renewed fieldwork in order to obtain up-to-date information on the Bronze Age multi-layered settlements located in western Romania, especially in regards to settlement location, chronology, internal organisation and architecture. We decided to focus specifically on the collection of radiocarbon dates for the establishment of absolute chronologies and non-invasive investigations in order to determine the inner layout and structure of these sites. Furthermore, renewed excavations in selected tells were also considered necessary for the purpose of obtaining more details regarding the architecture and building materials used in the Bronze Age multi-layered settlements.

Fieldwork done within the project
Non-invasive investigations

After all the available data on each multi-layered site in western Romania was collected, the information obtained from the published reports and museum archives was verified in the field. In some cases there was contradicting information in the literature regarding the precise location of the multi-layered sites. To clarify these issues, we designed a series of field surveys to locate them and accurately record their position and state of preservation. Due to time constraints, however, the investigations were limited to the Maros/Mureș River Valley and the Criș Rivers catchment system, areas where 36 out of the 46 multi-layered sites recorded in our volume (Gogâltan *et al.* 2014) were located.

Let us first consider the Criș Rivers catchment system, where 31 of the 46 sites in western Romania (*c.* 67%) are located. After conducting field surveys, it became clear that 13 sites (Cadea *Dealul chel/Koposz domb*, Căuașd *La Islaz*, Diosig *Colonie*, Grăniceri, Salonta *Dealul trupului/Testhalom*, Sântandrei *Fosta grădină C.A.P.*, Șiclău *Vatra satului*, Tarcea *Dealul de mijloc/Közép hegy*, Tarcea *Holmul Mare/Nagy halom*, Tarcea *Dealul Mare/Nagy domb*, Tulca *Holumb*, Vășad *Cartierul țiganilor/Cigány tanya* and Vășad *Dealul Viilor*) did not present the defining features of multi-layered settlements (as described above) and could therefore be excluded from this category. However, two new mound-like settlements could be identified in this area through the means of surface survey, one of them at Petreu *Zongora,* and the other at Salonta *Bogd* (Fazecaș & Gogâltan 2018, 119). As for the Maros/Mureș River Valley, only five Bronze Age multi-layered settlements have been registered in our catalogue (Gogâltan *et al.* 2014). Our field investigations conducted in 2014 revealed that one of them, Satu Mare *Weingarten,* is actually a flat settlement and not multi-layered as previously thought, reducing the number of Bronze Age tells in the lower Maros Valley to four. As a direct result of our field surveys and non-invasive investigations carried out in the Criș Rivers catchment system and the lower Maros/Mureș River Valley between 2014 and 2016, 14 sites were excluded from the list of tell, tell-like and mound-like settlements, while two others were added, changing the number of multi-layered settlements in these two regions from 36 to 24, and the overall number of Bronze Age multi-layered sites in western Romania from 46 to 34 (Fig. 6.3).

Another unexpected result of our unsystematic field surveys in the Criș Rivers Basin was the discovery of Early and/or Middle Bronze Age pottery sherds outside the core tell or tell-like area, indicating the practice of various activities in the immediate vicinity of some of these multi-layered sites. In some cases, these took the form of distinct outer settlements. This was the case at Ateaș *Holumbu Voghiului*, where a dense distribution of Middle Bronze Age (Otomani culture) sherds could be identified south of the mound, on a higher ground. Concentrations of Otomani pottery sherds, along with small fragments of burnt daub with twig impressions (most likely from collapsed walls of houses built in the wattle and daub technique), could also be found up to c. 280 m south and 300 m east of the central tell-like settlement in Crestur *Cetățuie*. Subsequent geophysical surveys of the site undertaken in 2016 and 2017, within the frame of a new research project developed by the University of Cologne,[3] have also confirmed the existence of an outer settlement to the south and east of the mound. The match between the distribution of surface finds and that of anomalies in the magnetometer data (mostly pits and surface houses) is remarkable. Scattered pottery fragments belonging to the Otomani cultural group have also been noted on the entire terrace south of the fortified mound from Otomani *Cetățuie*. At the newly identified multi-layered site from Petreu *Zongora*, pottery sherds dating to the second phase of the Otomani group were found up to 300 m north and northwest of the mound (Fazecaș & Gogâltan 2018, 115).

The existence of an outer settlement to the east and southeast of the multi-layered site at Roșiori *La sere* could also be confirmed by means of surface survey and later geophysical investigations, which exposed several magnetic anomalies outside of the fortified area. Unfortunately, the construction of greenhouses during recent decades led to the destruction of significant parts of the outer settlement, making an estimation of its original size impossible. Settlement activity extending south of the enclosing ditch was also detected at Sălacea *Dealul Vida*. Here, the distribution of surface finds (consisting mostly of MBA pottery sherds) corresponded to several pit anomalies. However, no house remains could be identified in the small area investigated. Evidence of occupation or some other kind of settlement activity extending outside of the fortified central mounds has also been uncovered, by means of geophysical and surface surveys, in the Ier/Eriu River Valley and Carei Plain at Andrid *Dealul Taurilor* (Marta et al. 2010, 126–130, fig. 7), Berveni *Holmoș* (Kienlin et al. 2017, 111–113, fig. 17), Carei *Bobald* (Németi & Molnár 2012, 69–72, figs 84–98), Căpleni *Drumul Căminului* (Kienlin et al. 2017, 114, fig. 19), Medieșul Aurit *Potău* (Marta & Ștefan 2011) and Pișcolt *Ógát* (Marta 2014, 186). On the other hand, in the Mureș Valley, traces of an occupation outside of the central mound are only known from Pecica *Șanțul Mare* (O'Shea & Nicodemus 2019).

Since very little was known in the previous publications about the existence of outer settlements surrounding the Bronze Age tells in western Romania, it is in this respect that recent fieldwork conducted within this larger region has brought the most important insights. This is in line with the newest results coming from other areas of the Carpathian Basin, where off-tell houses have also been uncovered through non-invasive investigations (see, for example, Kienlin et al. 2018; Rassmann et al. 2018). However, the lack of excavations or of available radiocarbon dates means that the precise chronological relation of the outer settlements with the mounds and their enclosure(s), as well as their dynamics relative to each other through time, cannot be properly reconstructed in the current state of research. Future fieldwork should therefore focus on unveiling the size, structure and precise chronology of these outer settlements, as well as their relation to the central mounds in social, economic and functional terms.

Non-invasive investigations conducted within our project also included low and medium altitude aerial survey performed by remote controlled flying platforms, also known as unmanned aerial vehicles (UAVs). The processing of the aerial images obtained using Structure from Motion algorithms allowed us to obtain ortophotographs and digital terrain models at high resolution. These investigations confirmed the existence of fortification systems consisting of deep and wide ditches at Munar, Pecica, Periam, Semlac and Toboliu. The first four sites are all located on the high terrace of the Mureș River and their fortification systems made extensive use of the natural topographic features, with the ditches connecting to deep ravines that cut into the high river terrace (Figs 6.4–6.6). The ditches were also used to delineate these multi-layered sites from the rest of the terrace. At Toboliu, a site lying in the plains, the two ditches fully enclosed the central mound, having a circular shape (Fig. 6.6). On the other hand, aerial photography undertaken at Ateaș, and the resulting digital terrain model, supported the earlier assumption that the multi-layered site was naturally protected by a former water channel that surrounded the mound. From the knowledge gained so far, the fortification systems of these sites depended on and were adapted to the natural topographic features. This was also the case for the layout of their outer settlements. There is a clear diversity between our multi-layered settlements in terms of site location, topography, and thickness of archaeological deposits, size of the mound, presence or absence of an outer settlement as well as type and size of fortification features.

Other non-invasive investigations undertaken within our project consisted of geophysical surveys carried out using a fluxgate magnetometer (Bartington GRAD 601-2).[4] The first site to be surveyed by this method was Munar *Weingarten/ Wolfsberg*. This site is located on a high terrace cut in the north by the Aranca water channel. Besides the Middle Bronze Age multi-layered site located in the northwest, close to the small river, a Late Bronze Age (LBA) fortification is also present, which extends to the south of the former settlement. Due to these considerations, the overall size of the site is considerable. A surface of 8.7 ha (covering roughly 60% of the entire site area) has been investigated through geophysical measurements in spring 2014. As the main results have been presented in detail elsewhere (Sava & Gogâltan 2017), here only a brief outline of the MBA multi-layered site will be described.

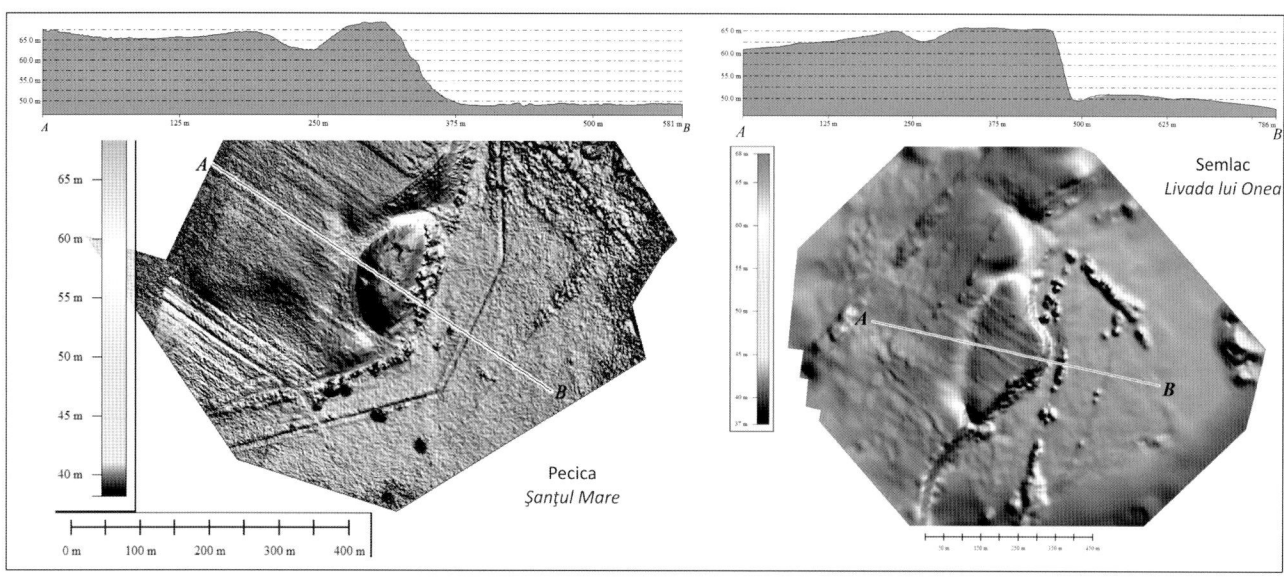

Figure 6.4 Digital terrain models of the sites from Pecica Șanțul Mare *and Semlac* Livada lui Onea.

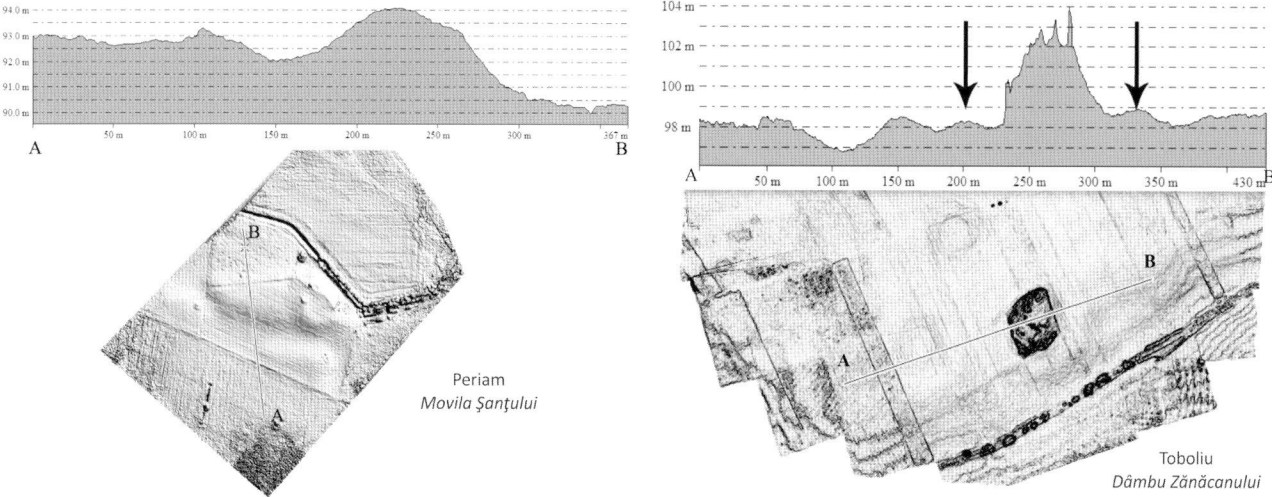

Figure 6.5 Digital terrain models of the sites from Periam Movila Șanțului *and Toboliu* Dâmbu Zănăcanului.

The magnetometer survey revealed the existence of a complex fortification system with two semi-circular ditches surrounding the mound (Fig. 6.6). These had a width of *c*. 3–4 m and were situated 20–22 m apart. The first enclosed an area of about 0.28 ha, while the area delineated by the second ditch was about 0.66 ha. Surprisingly, no anomalies could be detected within the region enclosed by the first ditch. Both ditches have a *c*. 5 m opening to the southwest, which could possibly be interpreted as entrances. A systematic surface survey was also undertaken at the site. The 40 × 40 m grids used for the geophysical survey were divided in smaller 5 × 5 m grids for the collection of archaeological finds (a method applied also in other areas of the Carpathian Basin – see, for example, Fischl *et al.* 2015b, 118–119). Pro-forma record sheets were used for recording the topographic conditions of every grid, along with additional information. The results of this survey confirmed the initial interpretation: while in the north-western part of the investigated area we only found pottery sherds dating to the MBA (Cornești-Crvenka group), in the western and southwestern parts sherds belonging to the LBA were prevalent.

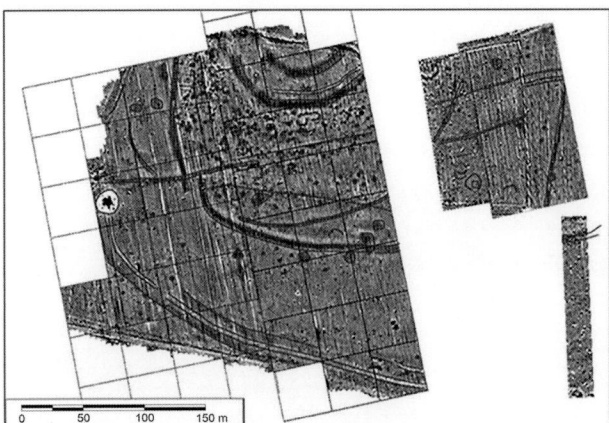

Figure 6.6 Results of the magnetometer survey at Munar Weingarten/Wolfsberg.

Geophysical measurements were also made at Sântion *Dealul Mănăstirii* in 2014 (Fig. 6.7). Unfortunately, the site has been severely damaged in the last decades by construction activities, with various metal fragments remaining from these activities seriously affecting the geomagnetic data. Geomagnetic measurements undertaken northeast of the mound did not reveal any trace of settlement activity extending beyond the tell. No features belonging to a fortification system could be observed either. In fact, there are hardly any anomalies in the magnetometer data that could be interpreted as archaeological remains. On the mound itself, an early medieval period monastery, along with graves dating to the 11th–15th centuries AD, have been identified (Fazecaș *et al.* 2016a, 183).

By far, the best results of the geomagnetic investigations were obtained at Toboliu *Dâmbu Zănăcanului* (also known as Girișu de Criș *Alceu* in the older literature). Here the geophysical survey was conducted on an area encompassing 2.56 ha (Fig. 6.8) and has revealed two concentric ditches that fully enclose the mound, along with a possible palisade (rampart) in the eastern part of the mound, located right behind the first enclosing ditch. Moreover, there is evidence of fairly well-preserved burnt houses located between the two ditches, especially on the eastern side, and extending beyond them. The burnt houses between the two ditches seem to be arranged in a concentric order, parallel to both the inner and outer ditches. Some of these houses reached a length of up to 18 m and a width of 11 m. The two ditches are situated *c.* 20 m apart and have a width of *c.* 10–15 m (with the outer ditch slightly wider than the inner). The outer ditch encloses an area of about 1.8 ha. There are two potential entrances (diametrically opposed) *c.* 10–13 m wide across the outer ditch, on its northwestern and southeastern parts (Fig. 6.8). The geophysical survey also revealed several pit anomalies located both within and outside of the fortified area. The presence of pit and house anomalies outside of the mound itself suggests the existence of an outer settlement surrounding the tell at Toboliu.

This conclusion was also reached following an intensive surface survey undertaken at the site in the following year. The survey encompassed an area of 211.19 ha and was conducted along transect lines situated 10 m apart (Fazecaș & Lie 2018). Due to time and budget constraints, the finds from the survey were not collected; instead, they were recorded using a handheld GPS (Magellane Xplorist 610) along with a brief description of their chronological attribution. The position of all MBA pottery sherds and daub fragments encountered on the predefined parallel paths was then measured and registered with different coding for single finds of pottery sherds, small finds made of clay, clusters of potsherds, clusters of potsherds and daub fragments, *etc.* The finds were then left on site at their original place of discovery without being collected, with the exception of a few small finds (fragments of miniature wheels, spindle whorls). Using this method, a total of 3476 points were recorded. Pottery sherds that could be securely assigned to the MBA, as well as occasional fragments of burnt daub, were found on a surface encompassing about 158 ha. However, the highest density of finds with clear clusters of pottery sherds and frequent fragments of daub with twig impressions (most likely coming from the collapsed walls of burnt houses built in the wattle and daub technique) come from an area of *c.* 84 ha (Fazecaș & Lie 2018, 31, fig. 3). These findings give a more accurate estimation of the actual size of the outer settlement or area densely settled at one stage. Moreover, these results make the outer settlement in Toboliu the largest open settlement surrounding a Bronze Age tell in the Carpathian Basin documented so far. As a comparison, the outer settlement surrounding the tell from Jászdózsa *Kápolnahalom* was estimated to cover an area of about 40 ha (500 × 800 m – Stanczik & Tárnoki 1992, 120); the outer settlement surrounding Vráble *Fidvár* is thought to have been around 12 ha at its maximum expansion (Rassmann *et al.* 2018, 219–220); the size of the flat settlement located in the immediate vicinity of the tell from Százhalombatta *Földvár* was approximated to 3 ha (Artursson 2010, 107); and the size of the outer settlement outside of the central fortified mound from Mošorin *Feudvar* is thought to have ranged from *c.* 1 ha to 6 ha during its various phases of existence (Falkenstein 1998, 266–268).

Additional information about the size of the areas with settlement activity outside of Bronze Age multi-layered sites in the Carpathian Basin comes from the Borsod region. Based on magnetometer surveys and fieldwalks, the outer settlements surrounding the mounds in this region have been estimated to cover an area ranging from 2.4 ha to *c.* 8 ha (Kienlin *et al.* 2018, 81, table I-5), with the exception of Emőd *Karola szőlők*, where occupation outside the core multi-layered part of the site may have extended over an area up to 25 ha (Kienlin *et al.* 2018, 80).

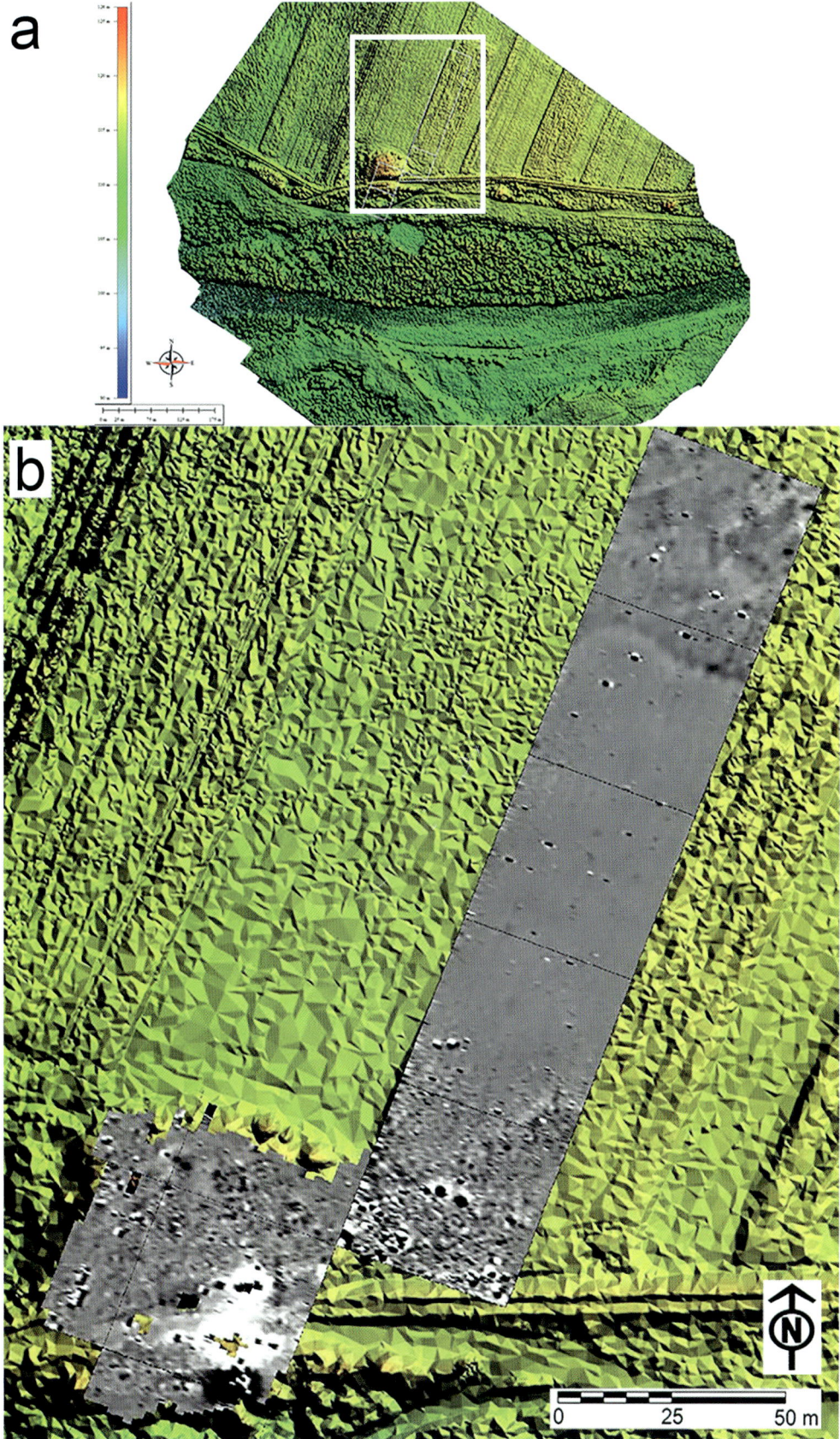

Figure 6.7 Results of the magnetometer survey at Sântion Dealul Mănăstirii. a) Location of the surveyed area, and b) magnetometric transect.

Figure 6.8 Results of the magnetometer survey at Toboliu Dâmbu Zănăcanului.

Excavations at Sântion and Toboliu

Apart from non-invasive investigations, fieldwork undertaken within our project also consisted of targeted excavations. The main objectives of these excavations were to collect samples for radiocarbon dating (given the limited number of absolute dates available for multi-layered sites in western Romania – see above) and gather data about site formation processes and architecture at tell sites. Two neighbouring tell settlements, located approximately 7 km apart, were chosen for excavation: Sântion *Dealul Mănăstirii* and Toboliu *Dâmbu Zănăcanului*. The two tells were previously believed to have developed contemporaneously, an assertion that was unfounded after evaluating the results of the radiocarbon samples collected during our investigations. The sample collected from the upper Bronze Age layers at Sântion yielded a result similar to the sample coming from the lower levels at Toboliu (Fig. 6.9), thus proving that the tell from Sântion was established earlier than the one from Toboliu. After several campaigns, it became clear that both sites follow the general pattern of Bronze Age tell site formation (multi-layered settlements with several phases of construction and reconstruction of surface houses built in the wattle-and-daub technique),

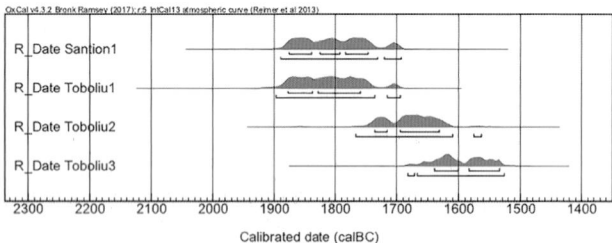

Figure 6.9 Calibrated dates and two-sigma ranges for the Sântion and Toboliu tell samples.

though each site also has specific characteristics that make it unique. In the following paragraphs a brief overview of the main results of these investigations will be presented.

Sântion *Dealul Mănăstirii* is a tell settlement located on the right bank of the Crișul Repede/Sebes-Körös River, close to the state border separating Romania and Hungary. The site was affected by a flood in 1932 when the Crișul Repede River overspilled its banks, exposing a large amount of pottery, along with other archaeological finds (Fazecaș 2014a, 236). The first excavations at the site were conducted in 1954 by a team led by A. Alexandrescu and consisted of three small test trenches (Alexandrescu 1955, 487). These investigations discovered that the Bronze Age site was superimposed by a settlement and cemetery dating to the Middle Ages, with medieval graves cutting deep into the Bronze Age deposits. The Bronze Age sequence was divided into four main levels, with the earliest dated to the beginning of the Otomani culture (Alexandrescu 1955, 491). Apart from acknowledging the existence of four successive Bronze Age layers, the brief report of the 1954 campaign does not contain any other stratigraphic information. Unfortunately, no profile drawings were made available in this report either. In the decades following these investigations, the site was partially destroyed by the construction of a road that cut through its middle part, as clearly visible on recent aerial images (Fig. 6.10). Further destructions at the site occurred in 2009, when a sand extraction company widened the above-mentioned road.

Renewed excavations at Sântion undertaken within the frame of our project started in August 2015, with two trenches located 24 m apart (Fazecaş *et al.* 2016a, 183). The first trench (S I) measured 6 × 3 m and was located roughly in the centre of the mound. Excavations in this area revealed architectural debris from a medieval monastery, along with two medieval graves placed within a stone cist, a style of burial dating between the 12th and 15th centuries (Fazecaş *et al.* 2017a, 118). Due to time constraints, excavations in this trench were stopped above the Bronze Age deposits. The second trench (S II), also measuring 6 × 3 m, was located on the southern side of the tell, overlooking the Crişul Repede River. In this trench no medieval structure or grave was identified; however, the upper Bronze Age deposits were cut by a medieval ditch. The first intact Bronze Age layer (labelled Cx 7) was reached at a depth of about 0.95 m beneath the ground level; it had a yellow colour and a clay consistency and was interpreted as the remains of a house floor (Fazecaş *et al.* 2016a, 183). Separating this phase from the next containing house remains (Cx 11) was a dark grey fill with an ashy consistency. A bone sample collected from underneath Cx 11 yielded a result around 1889–1693 cal BC at 2σ (Fazecaş *et al.* 2016a, 183; DeA-7115 3475±34 BP); this find was associated with ceramic sherds specific to the second phase of the Otomani style. In the next occupation phase, a floor containing imprints of wooden planks could be excavated on an area measuring 2.29 × 1.28 m (Cx 12). Similar house floors made of wooden planks have also been

Figure 6.10 Oblique aerial image of the tell from Sântion Dealul Mânăstirii.

uncovered at other multi-layered sites in the Carpathian Basin, for example at Bakonszeg *Kádárdomb* (Máthé 1988, 29, fig. 7), Békés *Várdomb* (Banner & Bóna 1974, 20–29, 31–41, figs 8a–d, 12–15), Gáborján *Csapszékpart* (Máthé 1988, 38, fig. 19), Töröszenmiklós *Terehalom* (Tárnoki 1992, 129, fig. 87) and Túrkeve *Terehalom* (Csányi & Tárnoki 2013, 712, fig. 2). In Vráble *Fidvár*, wooden planks have been discovered in the alleys separating the individual houses (Skorna *et al.* 2018, 105, figs 5–6).

Another wooden floor was uncovered underneath this layer in the 2016 campaign. The planks had a width of up to 30 cm and a similar orientation with those from the layer above. The following house structures uncovered at Sântion had clay floors, on top of which simple fire hearths were built (Fazecaş *et al.* 2017a, 118–119). Hearths built on a bed of stones have also been uncovered (Fig. 6.11). Although investigations at Sântion are still in progress, so far we have unveiled a complex Bronze Age sequence consisting of superimposed anthropogenic layers, notably including house floors made of clay or wooden planks and ash layers. Despite the fact that no complete structure could be exposed in the limited area excavated, stratigraphic observations confirmed that domestic structures have been built and reconstructed on the same spot for generations, leading ultimately to the development of a settlement mound.

The multi-layered settlement from Toboliu *Dâmbu Zănăcanului* lays 7.2 km southwest from Sântion, at the boundary between the Crişul Repede floodplain and the high plain of Miersig. Prior to 2007, the site was located within the administrative territory of the Girişu de Criş municipality and was designated in previous publications as Girişu de Criş *Alceu* (Ordentlich 1970, 621; 1974, 143, 145–146; Fazecaş 2014b, 113). Since 2007, however, the tell settlement belongs to the Toboliu administrative unit, therefore the name of the site was changed to Toboliu *Dâmbu Zănăcanului* (Lie *et al.* 2018, 65). The tell, which

Figure 6.11 Fire hearth built on a bed of stones from Sântion Dealul Mânăstirii.

rises approximately 4 m above the surrounding floodplain, has a round shape and a diameter of *c.* 90 m. During the 20th century several excavation campaigns took place at the site: in 1960 (led by N. Chidioşan), in 1965–1966 (under the supervision of S. Dumitraşcu), and in 1968 and 1972 (led by N. Chidioşan and D. Ignat). However, little is known about the results of all these investigations, with only some artefacts and two drawings of the stratigraphic sequence published (Chidioşan 1974; Dumitraşcu 1989). The accounts of these campaigns do not detail observations regarding potential features uncovered, or the architecture at the site, and only mention the existence of six individual Bronze Age layers, and one enclosure encircling the tell. There is also no mention of settlement activity extending beyond the mound. Our recent research has shown that the tell was only a small component of a much larger settlement complex and that the fortification system consisted of not one, but two, enclosing ditches (see above).

In order to collect samples for radiocarbon dating and obtain more data on domestic architecture at the site, new excavations were started at Toboliu in 2014 (Fazecaş *et al.* 2015; 2016b; 2017b).[5] Three main excavation units were opened (Lie *et al.* 2018, fig. 3). The first trench (No. 1), located roughly in the central section of the tell, was started in 2014 and completed in 2017. This excavation unit measured 7 × 5 m and its longer axis was oriented northwest–southeast. One of the old excavation trenches was still visible on the northeastern margin of the mound. Since the only published profiles from this site were difficult to interpret and evaluate, we reopened the unit to clean and properly document the profile, as well as to verify the stratigraphic sequence in this part of the tell. This unit, measuring 4 m in length and 2 m in width, was designated as trench 2; its excavation started in 2014 and was completed the following year. Trench 3, measuring 7 × 5 m, was located south of the second unit, at the eastern margin of the tell settlement.

Although no traces of an older archaeological trench could be observed at the surface, after the removal of the topsoil we identified an older excavation unit *c.* 1.5 m wide, which cut our trench on the long axis, being oriented north-northeast–south-southwest. Due to this reason, the stratigraphic connections between the intact Bronze Age deposits located south and north of the old trench could no longer be established on a secure basis. Underneath the topsoil, burnt debris from the collapsed walls of a house constructed in the wattle-and-daub technique was unearthed in both the southern and northern parts of this trench. The surface debris extended beyond the limits of the trench at the southern, northern and eastern profiles (Fig. 6.12). Following its removal, a yellow clay floor was uncovered in the northwestern part of the trench on an area measuring *c.* 1.5 × 3 m. No inner partition could be observed within the limited exposed area of the house. Two oval hearths were unearthed on top of the floor: a smaller one measuring 0.55 × 0.3 m and having an east–west orientation, and a larger one measuring 1.3 × 0.8 m and oriented south-south-west–north-northeast. Both hearths were plastered, had an oval shape and were seated on a bed of pottery sherds. The larger hearth showed traces of several renewal episodes and was probably used for a longer period. The inventory of the house consisted of ceramics typical for the third phase of the Otomani pottery style.

The entire tell stratigraphy was exposed only in the first and second trenches. No break in the successive occupation levels could be observed in either trench, suggesting a continuity in the development of the tell. Furthermore, no major changes in the inner layout of the houses could be documented either. Excavation in trench 2 indicated that the thickness of Bronze Age deposits at the north-eastern margin of the mound was about 3.2 m (Lie *et al.* 2018, 69, fig. 5; 2019, fig. 7), while in the centre of the mound the thickness of the tell sequence covered 4 m. This gradual reduction in the tell stratum towards the margins is most likely the result of erosion. The 3.2 m thick stratigraphic sequence exposed in trench 2 consists of a complex sequence of subsequent house floors, settlement and construction debris (Fig. 6.13). This confirms that the accumulation of the deposits was a direct result of residential practices such as the construction and renewal of houses on the same spot for several generations. Some houses have been reconstructed several times, resulting in a thicker accumulation for their respective phase. Five individual house phases, each corresponding to a distinctive residential structure, could be identified in trench 2. Every phase consisted of the construction, use, renewal and destruction of surface houses. Separating the different architectural phases is a deposition layer containing extensive domestic debris, as well as various fragmented archaeological finds. A radiocarbon sample collected from the oldest occupation phase identified in trench 2 yielded the result of 1898–1695 cal BC at 2σ (DeA-7116 3487±34 BP). A two-piece stone mould for casting socketed chisels was found within the upper Bronze Age house destruction layer of this trench (Fazecaş *et al.* 2015, 235). Along with the two clay tuyères uncovered during former investigations at the site (Dumitraşcu 1989, 119–120, pl. 1,1–2; Găvan 2015, 192–193), this find proves that metal casting activities were undertaken at the site.

A better picture of the residential structures from the tell (*i.e.* their inner layout and construction techniques) could be obtained following the excavation of the first trench. These observations, however, were limited to the lower levels of the tell, as the upper layers were partially destroyed by a modern cemetery dating to the 19th century, which cut through the Bronze Age deposits up to a depth of 1.9 m. Thirteen graves, arranged in three parallel rows oriented west–east, could be identified at a depth ranging from 0.2 m to 0.4 m below the current ground level (Lie

Figure 6.12 Toboliu Dâmbu Zănăcanului. *Remains of a burnt house in trench 3.*

Figure 6.13 Toboliu Dâmbu Zănăcanului. *Clay floor of a residential structure in trench 2.*

et al. 2015). Due to the disturbances caused by these later graves, architectural features belonging to the Bronze Age sequence were only infrequently observed in these layers. The uppermost Bronze Age layer was cut by the modern graves; A concentration of a large number of pottery fragments could be identified between the graves. This concentration most probably belonged to a house whose initial measurements can no longer be reconstructed due to the mentioned disturbances. The ceramic assemblage recovered from the house has a style different from the so-called 'classical' Otomani pottery and resembles the early finds of the so-called 'Cehăluţ-Hajdubagos' group (for a recent overview of this group see Németi 2009). It became clear, based on stratigraphic observations, as well as the analysis of the find assemblage, that the uppermost Bronze Age layer identified in this trench was later than that identified in trench 2. As mentioned above, this was most probably the result of erosion, which was more intense towards the margins of the mound where the second trench was located. An *in situ* bone fragment found underneath the pottery concentration in trench 1 was sampled for radiocarbon analysis; the result yielded a date of 1683–1528 cal BC (2σ) (DeA-5092 3323±26 BP).

In the northwestern part of the trench, fragments from a yellow clay floor belonging to the Bronze Age sequence were exposed in between the 19th century graves. After removing this layer, the southeastern part of the trench revealed an unusual feature, measuring 3.2 × 2.4 m that was clearly delineated from the surrounding cultural layer by colour and consistency. Upon excavation, this feature turned out to be a dugout structure reaching a depth of 2.1 m. As of this writing, this is a unique find, with no similar features being published from other tells in the Carpathian Basin. A hearth that bore traces of several periods of reconstruction was uncovered in the area undisturbed by the graves. Also belonging to the second occupation phase of the tell were fragments from a floor with imprints of wooden planks.

The first clear residential structure undamaged by the 19th century graves was unearthed within the third occupation phase of the tell. The house had a rectangular floor plan with an east–west orientation and was made of wattle and daub on a light framework of upright posts. An exceptional find was the well-preserved floor made of wooden planks ranging in width from 10 cm to 20 cm. The initial width and length of the house remain unknown, since only a part of the wooden floor was exposed within the limits of the trench, while the rest extended in the northern and western profiles. The exposed surface of the wooden floor measured 5.8 × 4.8 m (Lie *et al.* 2018, 70, fig. 8). Two episodes of renewal could be distinguished for this house. Close to the western profile there was a hearth which was built directly on the floor; the hearth also showed episodes of renewal.[6] Forming the base of the hearth was a mosaic of sherds, a typical feature for most of the hearths uncovered at Toboliu (Fig. 6.14). The underlying layer consisted of burnt debris coming from the collapsed walls of the subsequent house, also built in the wattle-and-daub technique. A large number of pottery vessels were associated with this layer. After removing the debris, the clay floor of the house belonging to the 4th occupation phase at Toboliu became visible. Once again, the house extended beyond the margins of the trench, the area exposed within the excavation unit measuring 5.8 × 8 m. The initial extent of the house, however, remains unclear. In its southern part was a row of postholes that were interpreted as an inner partition wall. A hearth was uncovered within the northern room of the house. Unlike the residential structure uncovered within the 3rd layer, the house from the 4th layer was oriented along a north–south axis.

The next occupation phase (no. 5) at Toboliu was characterised by the presence of unburnt clay debris. The debris, most likely coming from the collapsed walls of a house, consisted of chunks of yellow and dark clay bearing twig impressions (Fig. 6.15). The floor belonging to this house was also made of clay. Traces of two inner partition walls, clearly distinguished by rows of postholes along with beam impressions, indicated that the house had three separate rooms. Only the southern and northern rooms had a hearth, no fireplace being found in the central partition (Lie *et al.* 2018, fig. 9). The house extended once again beyond the limits of the trench into the southern, northern and western profiles. The exposed area of the house covered a surface of 4.2 × 7.6 m and had a north–south orientation. The residential structure from the following occupation phase was also unburnt and its outline could be easily distinguished from the surrounding cultural layer by its colour and consistency. The debris covering the house floor was similar to that from the 5th phase, indicating that similar construction materials and techniques have been used for both houses. However, the orientation of this house was different, with its long side roughly following an east–west axis.

Figure 6.14 Toboliu Dâmbu Zănăcanului. *Base of a hearth found within a house belonging to the 5th occupation phase.*

Figure 6.15 Toboliu Dâmbu Zănăcanului. *Unburnt debris from the 5th occupation phase.*

The floor of the house was made of clay; the part exposed within the limits of the excavation unit covered an area of 6.6 × 5 m. Its original size was bigger, since its outline could not be entirely exposed, clearly extending into the southern and western profiles. A row of small diameter postholes indicated that the house had at least two rooms. Only one hearth with a diameter of about 1.12 m was found within the western compartment of the house. A further residential structure was located in the northern part of the trench, at a distance of approximately 1.6 m from the previous house and had a roughly similar orientation. Unlike the house in its vicinity, this structure had been burnt, indicating the coexistence of burnt and unburnt houses within the same layer. Due to the fact that only a small corner of the burnt house could be exposed within the excavation unit, its original size and extent can no longer be reconstructed.

The lowermost layer was only exposed in trench 1 and could not be identified in trench 2. As a result, the horizontal extent of this early phase of the settlement remains unknown; however, clearly it did not extend to the north-eastern margin where trench 2 was located. The house corresponding to the oldest occupation phase at Toboliu was also unburnt and its outline was delineated by its debris, which covered a surface of about 4.6 × 8 m. However, the original length of the house was larger, as, again, its western and southern parts continued outside the limits of the trench. Two rows of small diameter postholes identified on the clay floor along a north–south axis indicated that the house was divided into three rooms. A hearth with a diameter of about 1.2 m and a construction technique following the general pattern identified at the site was found in the southern room. Another hearth with an unusual shape could be documented in the middle room (Lie *et al.* 2019, fig. 10). Both orientation and construction materials of this structure were like the structure from the layer above; the only differences between the two houses were the number of partitions and hearths. Following the removal of this house, a colluvial soil was uncovered, which contained no traces of anthropogenic impact (Röpke *et al.* 2019).

Macroscopic examinations of the profiles in trenches 1 and 2 indicate differences of thickness between the upper and lower layers of the tell (Fig. 6.16; see also Lie *et al.* 2018, fig. 5, 7). The upper layers are generally thicker, which might indicate that the houses from these phases

Figure 6.16 Toboliu Dâmbu Zănăcanului. *Northern profile of trench 1.*

were in use for a longer period. This interpretation is further supported by the detection of several renewal and rebuilding episodes for the residential structures belonging to the upper layers. The lower part of the sequence is characterised by thin, well-executed, superimposing clay floors that seldom show evidence of renewal. Regarding (tell) site formation processes, in Toboliu these consist of several phases, each characterised by the construction, use, renewal and destruction of surface houses with a wooden frame and wattle-and-daub walls; the postholes varied in diameter from *c*. 5 cm to max. 20 cm. All houses excavated on the tell had a rectangular floor plan. So far, there are no indications for the existence of two-storey houses in the area exposed. Although the orientation of the houses changes slightly from phase to phase, the main elements (including construction techniques and materials) are preserved. The houses comprised one, two or three rooms. This is in line with discoveries made in other tells in the Carpathian Basin such as Békés *Várdomb* (Banner & Bóna 1974, 31–34, figs 10–11), Füzesabony *Öregdomb* (Szathmári 1992, 135–136), Jászdózsa *Kápolnahalom* (Csányi *et al.* 2000, 150–151, fig. 2), Százhalombatta *Földvár* (Vicze 2013, 759–760), Tiszaálpar *Várdomb* (Bóna & Nováki 1982, 115), Tószeg *Laposhalom* (Bóna 1992, 107) and Túrkeve *Terehalom* (Csányi & Tárnoki 1992, 162–163, figs 115, 117). Fixed installations within the residential structures at Toboliu included hearths and storage pits. Most of the hearths were seated on a layer of crushed pottery sherds and had been renewed several times. There were few finds on the floors, indicating that the houses had been deliberately cleaned and emptied before their destruction. Furthermore, there is little construction debris left behind, a fact that points towards cleaning and levelling activities.

The artefact assemblage in Toboliu is dominated by pottery sherds and restorable vessels, most of them typical for the 2nd and 3rd phases of the Otomani ceramic style. In addition, sherds with different stylistic elements from other Bronze Age units in the Carpathian Basin (*i.e.*, Wietenberg, Suciu de Sus, Hatvan, Mureș and Vatina) were found. Numerous small finds such as spindle whorls, loom weights, miniature wheels from clay wagon models, ornaments of shells, boar tusks, bone and antler, along with an impressive collection of bone and antler implements were unearthed at the tell. The recovered assemblage suggests that several activities related to food production and consumption, as well as bone and antler working, took place within the houses on the tell. Besides the typical household assemblage, bronze items were also found at the tell, although in smaller proportions: a bronze knife and small bronze fragments from unidentifiable artefacts. Metal casting has also been attested at the mound by the discovery of two clay tuyères and a casting mould made of stone (see above). The presence of bronze artefacts suggests that the tell at Toboliu was taking part in long-distance exchange networks, an interpretation reinforced by the discovery of beads made of *dentalium* shell.

Concluding remarks

The analysis and processing of the finds and features from both Sântion and Toboliu are still in progress, therefore only some preliminary results were presented above. Based on the radiocarbon dates available, it seems that these tell settlements did not develop at the same time, with occupation at Sântion starting earlier than at Toboliu, and ending around the time Toboliu was established (see also Fig. 6.9). Considering the potential limitations of radiocarbon dating, and the limited number of radiocarbon dates available from Sântion, the two sites were, at best, contemporaneous for only a part of their existence. Both tell sequences evolved as the result of the gradual accumulation of building debris and other materials from residential activities. No evidence of deliberate sediment deposition to enhance the height of the mounds was detected on either of the sites. While settlement in Toboliu expanded beyond the mound to form a complex site consisting of a central tell surrounded by two enclosing ditches and a large outer settlement covering an area of about 84 ha, the entire settlement in Sântion appears to have been confined to the mound itself. Furthermore, there is no evidence of defensive works having been constructed at Sântion either. The comparison of the two neighboring sites confirms once again the assertion that tell settlements in the Carpathian Basin followed different trajectories of development (Kienlin *et al.* 2017).

Investigations carried out within our project have shown that the inner layout and structure of Bronze Age multi-layered sites in western Romania are highly diverse, and that not all these settlements evolved simultaneously. Furthermore, the detection of settlement activity outside the fortified tells for some sites implies that the multi-layered sites were just one part of a complex settlement system whose dynamics and evolution through time remains unknown. It is our hope that future research will focus on determining the chronological, functional, economic and social relations between the different parts of these systems. Open outer settlements surrounding Bronze Age tells are often assumed to have played a subordinate role in social and economic terms: they are thought of as providing the economic base of tell sites, with their economy focused on agricultural production (Artursson 2010, 102; Fischl & Reményi 2013, 729). This is, however, a theoretical model, which has not (so far) been supported by archaeological evidence. The extent and inner layout of these sites should also be explored by means of non-invasive investigations, which so far have yielded important results (see above). As shown by our overview of the state of research on multi-layered settlements in western Romania, there is a dire need for absolute dates that could help establish the chronological evolution of these sites on a secure basis. Since not all tells appear to have developed simultaneously, the chronological aspect would have deep implications for interpreting current settlement patterns, as well as reconstructing their social and economic background.

Acknowledgements

We would like to thank Antonio Blanco-González and Tobias Kienlin for inviting us to give a talk in the session 'Current approaches to tells and tell-like sites in the prehistoric Old World' organized within the 24th Annual Meeting of the EAA, and to publish in this volume. The project *Living in the Bronze Age Tell Settlements. A Study of Settlement Archaeology at the Eastern Frontier of the Carpathian Basin* was financed by the Romanian Ministry of National EducationI, grant PN-II-ID-PCE–2012-4-020. After the end of this project, excavations in Toboliu were continued in 2017 with the financial support of the Chair for the Archaeology of the Metal Ages, Department of Prehistoric Archaeology at the University of Cologne. We are extremely grateful to Raluca Burlacu-Timofte, Ashley Cercone, Alexandru Cojocaru, Andrea Demjén, Andreea Drăgan, Călin Ghemiş, Ana Ignat (Deac), Maximilian Krämer, Doru Marta, Gian-Luca Paul, Cristian Ioan Popa, Paul Petric, Vlad Roman, Astrid Röpke, Natalie Roski, Victor Sava and Mihaela Savu for their valuable assistance with conducting the necessary fieldwork. We also want to extend our gratitude to all the volunteers that participated at the excavations conducted at Toboliu between 2014 and 2016 within the program of the Association for Promoting Transylvanian Archaeological Heritage. Special thanks go to Stephen Basenfelder for proof-reading the manuscript. All the remaining errors are, of course, our own.

Notes

1. Some mentions of houses and their construction techniques have only been made for the sites of Carei *Bobald* (Molnár & Németi 2014), Derşida *Dealul lui Balotă* (Chidioşan 1980, 17–21), Foeni *Cimitirul Ortodox* (Gogâltan 2014b), Otomani *Cetăţuie* and *Cetatea de pământ* (Ordentlich 1968), Pecica *Şanţul Mare* (O'Shea *et al.* 2011), Sălacea *Dealul Vida* (Ordentlich 1968; 1972) and Tiream *Holmul cânepii* (Németi & Molnár 2014).
2. See Gogâltan (2014a, 21); meanwhile these dates have been published (O'Shea *et al.* 2019, tab. 1, fig. 6).
3. The results of these surveys will be published in a separate volume dedicated to the non-invasive investigations

conducted on multi-layered sites in western Romania undertaken within the frame of this project (Kienlin & Găvan in prep.).
4   The aerial and geophysical surveys were undertaken as part of a contract between the Romanian Academy of Sciences, Cluj-Napoca branch (represented by Dr. Florin Gogâltan) and SC Vector Studio SRL (represented by Dr Dan Ștefan).
5   Following the end of our project in 2016, excavations in Toboliu continued in 2017 in collaboration with the Chair for the Archaeology of the Metal Ages, Department of Prehistoric Archaeology at the University of Cologne.
6   In 2016 excavations within this project stopped on the wooden floor of the house in trench 1. The investigation of this trench continued in 2017 with financial support from the Chair for the Archaeology of the Metal Ages, Department of Prehistoric Archaeology at the University of Cologne (Tobias L. Kienlin, Alexandra Găvan and Marian Adrian Lie), thus securing the continuity of the Toboliu Project.

References

Alexandrescu, A. (1955) Săpăturile de salvare de la Sântion. *Studii și Cercetări de Istorie Veche* 6 (3–4), 487–495.

Artursson, M. (2010) Settlement structure and organisation. In T. Earle & K. Kristiansen (eds), *Organizing Bronze Age Societies. The Mediterranean, Central Europe and Scandinavia Compared*, 87–121. Cambridge, Cambridge University Press.

Banner, J. & Bóna, I. (1974) *Mittelbronzezeitliche Tell-Siedlung bei Békés*. Budapest, Akadémiai Kiadó.

Bátora, J. & Tóth, P. (2014) Settlement strategies in the Early Bronze Age in south-western Slovakia. In T.L. Kienlin, P. Valde-Nowak, M. Korczyńska, K. Cappenberg & J. Ociepka (eds), *Settlement, Communication and Exchange around the Western Carpathians. International Workshop Held at the Institute of Archaeology, Jagiellonian University, Kraków October 27–28, 2012*, 325–340. Oxford, Archaeopress.

Bátora, J., Tóth, P. & Bača, M. (2015) Výskumy opevnených sídlisk zo staršej doby bronzovej vo východnej časti Podunajskej nížiny. In J. Bátora & P. Tóth (eds), *Keď bronz vystriedal meď. Zborník príspevkov z XXIII. medzinárodného sympozia 'Staršia doba bronzová v Čechách, na Morave a na Slovensku' Levice 8.–11. októbra 2013*, 139–156. Bratislava, Archeologický ústav SAV.

Bátora, J., Behrens, A., Gresky, J., Ivanova, M., Rassmann, K., Tóth, P. & Winkelmann, K. (2012) The rise and decline of the Early Bronze Age settlement, Fidvár near Vráble, Slovakia. In J. Kneisel, W. Kirleis, M. Dal Corso, N. Taylor & V. Tiedtke (eds), *Collapse or Continuity? Environment and Development of Bronze Age Human Landscapes, Proceedings of the International Workshop 'Socio-Environmental Dynamics over the Last 12,000 Years: The Creation of Landscapes II (14th–18th March 2011)' in Kiel*, 111–130. Bonn, Habelt.

Bóna, I. (1992) Tószeg-Laposhalom. In W. Meier-Arendt (ed.), *Bronzezeit in Ungarn. Forschungen in Tell-Siedlungen an Donau und Theiss*, 101–114. Frankfurt, Museum für Vor- und Frühgeschichte.

Bóna, I. & Nováki, G. (1982) Alpár bronzkori és Árpád-kori vára. *Cumania* 7, 17–118.

Chidioșan, N. (1974) Sincronismele apusene ale culturii Wietenberg stabilite pe baza importurilor ceramice. *Crisia* 4, 153–176.

Chidioșan, N. (1980) *Contribuții la istoria tracilor din nord-vestul României. Așezarea Wietenberg de la Derșida*. Oradea, Muzeul Țării Crișurilor.

Csányi, M. & Tárnoki, J. (1992) Túrkeve-Terehalom. In W. Meier-Arendt (ed.), *Bronzezeit in Ungarn. Forschungen in Tell-Siedlungen an Donau und Theiss*, 159–165. Frankfurt, Museum für Vor- und Frühgeschichte.

Csányi, M. & Tárnoki, J. (2013) A dinner set from a Bronze Age house in Level 2 of the Túrkeve-Terehalom settlement. In A. Anders & G. Kulcsár (eds), *Moments in Time. Papers Presented to Pál Raczky on His 60th Birthday*, 707–723. Budapest, L'Harmattan.

Csányi, M., Stanczik, I. & Tárnoki, J. (2000) Der bronzezeitliche Schatzfund von Jászdósza-Kápolnahalom. *Acta Archaeologica Academiae Scientiarum Hungaricae* 51, 147–167.

Dani, J. (2012) Fortified tell settlements from the Middle Bronze Age in the Hungarian reach of the Berettyó Valley. In M. Jaeger, J. Czebreszuk & K.P. Fischl (eds), *Enclosed Space – Open Society. Contact and Exchange in the Context of Bronze Age Fortified Settlements in Central Europe*, 27–38. Poznán, Bogucki Wydawnictwo Naukowe.

Dani, J. & Fischl, K.P. (2009) A Berettyó-vidék középső bronzkori telljei. (Topográfiai megközelítés) – Die mittelbronzezeitlichen Tellsiedlungen des Berettyó-Gebiets. Eine topographische Übersicht. *Tisicum* 19, 103–118.

Duffy, P. (2014) *Complexity and Autonomy in Bronze Age Europe. Assessing Cultural Developments in Eastern Hungary*. Budapest, Archaeolingua.

Duffy, P., Giblin, J., Parditka, G. & Paja, L. (2019) The problem with tells: Lessons learned from absolute dating of Bronze Age mortuary ceramics in Hungary. *Antiquity* 367, 63–79.

Dumitrașcu, S. (1989) Contribuții la cunoașterea tehnologiei metalurgiei din epoca bronzului în județul Bihor. *Crisia* 19, 119–168.

Earle, T. & Kristiansen, K. (2010) *Organizing Bronze Age Societies. The Mediterranean, Central Europe and Scandinavia compared*. Cambridge, Cambridge University Press.

Earle, T., Artursson, M., Polányi, T. & Vicze, M. (2012) Rapid assessment of Bronze Age settlement studies in the Benta Valley, Hungary: A micro-regional approach – Bronzkori települési kutatások gyors és hatékony kiértékelése a Benta-völgyben: Mikro-regionális szemlélet. *Ősrégészeti Levelek* 12, 84–93.

Earle, T., Kreiter, A., Klehm, C., Ferguson, J. & Vicze, M. (2011) Bronze Age ceramic economy: The Benta Valley, Hungary. *European Journal of Archaeology* 14, 419–440.

Earle, T., Kulcsár, G. Kiss, V. Serlegi, G. & Szeverényi, V. (2014) Recent results from the Bronze Age research into Benta Valley. *Hungarian Archaeology. E-Journal*, 1–5.

Falkenstein, F. (1998) *Feudvar II. Die Siedlungsgeschichte des Titeler Plateaus*. Prähistorische Archäologie in Südosteuropa 14. Kiel, Oetker/Voges.

Fazecaș, G. (2014a) Sântion 'Dealul Mănăstirii = Klastrom domb', Bihor County. In F. Gogâltan, C. Cordoș & A. Ignat (eds), *Bronze Age Tell, Tell-Like and Mound-Like Settlements at the Eastern Frontier of the Carpathian Basin. History of Research*, 235–241. Cluj-Napoca, Mega Publishing House.

Fazecaş, G. (2014b) Girişu de Criş Alceu, Bihor County. In F. Gogâltan, C. Cordoş & A. Ignat (eds), *Bronze Age Tell, Tell-Like and Mound-Like Settlements at the Eastern Frontier of the Carpathian Basin. History of Research*, 111–116. Cluj-Napoca, Mega Publishing House.

Fazecaş, G. & Gogâltan, F. (2018) Evaluarea aşezărilor multistratificate ale epocii bronzului din Bazinul Crişurilor. In N. Rişcuţa & I.V. Ferencz (eds), *Studii şi articole de arheologie. In memoriam Ioan Andriţoiu*, 111–136. Cluj-Napoca, Mega Publishing House.

Fazecaş, G. & Lie, M. (2018) Determinarea suprafeţei sitului arheologic de epoca bronzului de la Toboliu *Dâmbu Zănăcanului* – area delineation of the Bronze Age site from Toboliu *Dâmbu Zănăcanului*. *Crisia* 47, 29–38.

Fazecaş, G., Ignat, A., Demjén, A. & Gogâltan, F. (2016a) Sat Sântion, com. Borş, jud. Bihor, Punct: Dealul Mănăstirii = Klastrom domb. *Cronica Cercetărilor Arheologice din România, Campania 2015*, 183–184.

Fazecaş, G., Lie, M., Cordoş C. & Gogâltan, F. (2015) Toboliu-Dâmbul Zănăcanului, campania 2014. *Cronica Cercetărilor Arheologice din România, Campania 2014*, 235–236.

Fazecaş, G., Lie, M., Cordoş C. & Gogâltan, F. (2016b) Toboliu, com. Toboliu, jud. Bihor, Punct: Dâmbu Zănăcanului. *Cronica Cercetărilor Arheologice din România, Campania 2015*, 101–102.

Fazecaş, G., Ignat, A. & Gogâltan, F. (2017a) Sântion, com. Borş, jud. Bihor, Punct: Dealul Mănăstirii = Klastrom domb. *Cronica Cercetărilor Arheologice din România, Campania 2016*, 118–119.

Fazecaş, G., Lie, M., Cordoş C., Drăgan, A. & Gogâltan, F. (2017b) Toboliu, com. Toboliu, jud. Bihor, Punct: Dâmbu Zănăcanului. *Cronica Cercetărilor Arheologice din România, Campania 2016*, 146–147.

Fischl, K.P. (2012) The role of the Hernad Valley in the settlement structure of the Füzesabony culture. In M. Jaeger, J. Czebreszuk & K.P. Fischl (eds), *Enclosed Space – Open Society. Contact and Exchange in the Context of Bronze Age Fortified Settlements in Central Europe*, 39–51. Poznán, Bogucki Wydawnictwo Naukowe.

Fischl, K.P. & Reményi, L. (2013) Interpretation Possibilities of the Bronze Age Tell Sites in the Carpathian Basin. In A. Anders, G. Kulcsár, G. Kalla, V. Kiss & G. Szabó (eds), *Moments in Time. Papers presented to Pál Raczky on his 60th Birthday*, 725–738. Budapest, L'Harmattan.

Fischl, K.P., Kiss, V., Kulcsar, G. & Szeverenyi, V. (2015a) Old and new narratives for Hungary around 2200 BC. In H. Meller, H.W. Arz, R. Jung, R. Risch (eds), *2200 BC – Ein Klimasturz als Ursache für den Zerfall der alten Welt? 7. Mitteldeutscher Archäologentag vom 23. bis 26. Oktober 2014 in Halle (Saale)*, 503–523. Halle (Saale), Landesamt für Denkmalpflege und Archäologie Sachsen-Anhalt.

Fischl, K.P., Kienlin, T.L., Tugya, B. (2015b) Bronze Age Settlement Research in North-Eastern Hungary. *Archeometriai Műhely* 12(2), 117–134.

Gauss, R.K., Bátora, J., Nowaczinski, E., Rassmann, K. & Schukraft, G. (2013) The Early Bronze Age settlement of Fidvár, Vráble (Slovakia): Reconstructing prehistoric settlement patterns using portable XRF. *Journal of Archaeological Science* 40, 2942–2960.

Găvan, A. (2015) *Metals and Metalworking in the Bronze Age Tell Settlements from the Carpathian Basin*. Cluj-Napoca, Mega Publishing House.

Gogâltan, F. (2002) Zur Terminologie der bronzezeitliche Tellsiedlungen im Karpatenbecken. In A. Rustoiu & A. Ursuţiu (eds), *Interregionale und Kulturelle Beziehungen im Karpatenraum (2.Jht. v.Chr.–1. Jht. n.Chr.)*, 11–45. Cluj-Napoca, Nereamia Napocae.

Gogâltan, F. (2005) Der Beginn der bronzezeitlichen Tellsiedlungen im Karpatenbecken: Chronologische Probleme. In B. Horejs, R. Jung, E. Kaiser & B. Teržan (eds), *Interpretationsraum Bronzezeit. Bernhard Hänsel von seinen Schülern gewidmet*, 161–179. Bonn, Habelt.

Gogâltan, F. (2008) Fortified Bronze Age tell settlements in the Carpathian Basin. A general overview. In J. Czebreszuk, S. Kadrow & J. Müller (eds), *Defensive Structures from Central Europe to the Aegean in the 3rd and 2nd millennia BC*, 39–56. Poznán, Bogucki Wydawnictwo Naukowe.

Gogâltan, F. (2014a) Bronze Age tell, tell-like and mound-like settlements on the eastern frontier of the Carpathian Basin. History of research. In F. Gogâltan, C. Cordoş & A. Ignat (eds), *Bronze Age Tell, Tell-Like and Mound-Like Settlements on the Eastern Frontier of the Carpathian Basin. History of Research*, 13–24. Cluj-Napoca, Mega Publishing House.

Gogâltan, F. (2014b) Foeni 'Cimitirul Ortodox', Timiş County. In F. Gogâltan, C. Cordoş & A. Ignat (eds), *Bronze Age Tell, Tell-Like and Mound-Like Settlements on the Eastern Frontier of the Carpathian Basin. History of Research*, 98–103. Cluj-Napoca, Mega Publishing House.

Gogâltan, F. (2015) The Early and Middle Bronze Age chronology on the eastern frontier of the Carpathian Basin. Revisited after 15 years. In R.E. Németh & B. Rezi (eds), *Bronze Age Chronology in the Carpathian Basin. Proceedings of the International Colloquium from Targu Mureş 2–4 October 2014*, 53–95. Târgu Mureş, Mega Publishing House.

Gogâltan, F. (2016) Building power without power? Bronze Age fortified settlements on the lower Mureş Basin. In F. Gogâltan & C. Cordoş (eds), *Prehistoric Settlements: Social, Economic and Cultural Aspects. Seven Studies in the Carpathian Area*, 87–113. Cluj-Napoca, Mega Publishing House.

Gogâltan, F. (2017) The Bronze Age multilayered settlements in the Carpathian Basin (ca. 2500–1600/1500 BC). An old catalogue and some chronological problems. *Journal of Ancient History and Archaeology* 4, 28–63.

Gogâltan, F., Cordoş, C. & Ignat, A. (2014) *Bronze Age Tell, Tell-Like and Mound-Like Settlements on the Eastern Frontier of the Carpathian Basin. History of Research*. Cluj-Napoca, Mega Publishing House.

Jaeger, M. & Kulcsar, G. (2013) Kakucs-Balla-Domb. A case study in the absolute and relative chronology of the Vatya culture. *Acta Archaeologica Academiae Scientiarum Hungaricae* 64, 289–320.

Jaeger, M., Kulcsár, G. Taylor, N. & Staniuk, R. (2018) *Kakucs-Turján: a Middle Bronze Age Multi-layered Fortified Settlement in Central Hungary*. Bonn, Habelt.

Kienlin, T.L. (2012) Patterns of change, or: Perceptions deceived? Comments on the interpretation of Late Neolithic and Bronze Age Tell settlement in the Carpathian Basin. In T.L. Kienlin & A. Zimmermann (eds), *Beyond Elites. Alternatives to Hierarchical Systems in Modelling Social Formations. International Conference at the Ruhr-Universität Bochum, Germany (October 22–24, 2009)*, 251–310. Bonn, Habelt.

Kienlin, T.L. (2015) *Bronze Age Tell Communities in Context-An Exploration Into Culture, Society, and the Study of European Prehistory. Part 1: Critique. Europe and the Mediterranean.* Oxford, Archaeopress.

Kienlin, T.L., Fischl, K.P. & Marta, L. (2017) Exploring divergent trajectories in Bronze Age landscapes: Tell settlement in the Hungarian Borsod Plain and the Romanian Ier Valley. *Ziridava. Studia Archaeologica* 31, 93–128.

Kienlin, T.L., Fischl, K.P. & Pusztai, T. (2018*) Borsod Region Bronze Age Settlement (BORBAS). Catalogue of the Early to Middle Bronze Age Tell Sites Covered by Magnetometry and Surface Survey.* Bonn, Habelt.

Klehm, C.E. & Nyíri, B. (2016) Exploring socioeconomic relationships from surface survey ceramics. New methodologies from Bronze-Age Benta Valley, Hungary. *Journal of Field Archaeology*, 41(4), 486–499.

Kovács, T. (1988) Review of the Bronze Age settlement research during the past one and half centuries in Hungary. In T. Kovács & I. Stanczik (eds), *Bronze Age Tell Settlements on the Great Hungarian Plain 1*, 17–25. Budapest, Magyar Nemzeti Múzeum.

Kulcsár, G., Jaeger, M., Kiss, V., Márkus, G., Müller, J., Pető, Á., Serlegi, G., Szeverenyi, V. & Taylor, N. (2014) The beginnings of a new research program. Kakucs archaeological expedition – KEX1. *Hungarian Archaeology, E-Journal*, 1–7.

Lie, M., Radu, C. & Fazecas, G. (2015) Cimitirul de secol XIX de la Toboliu – Dâmbul Zănăcanului (jud. Bihor). *Terra Sebus. Acta Musei Sabesiensis* 7, 261–282.

Lie, M., Cordoș, C., Găvan, A., Fazecaș, G., Kienlin, T.L. & Gogâltan, F. (2018) An overview of the Bronze Age tell-settlement in Toboliu (Bihor County, Romania). *Gesta* 17, 63–76.

Lie, M., Găvan, A., Cordoș, C., Kienlin, T.L., Fazecaș, G. & Gogâltan, F. (2019) The Bronze Age tell settlement at Toboliu (Bihor County, Romania). A brief outline of recent investigations. In K.P. Fischl & T.L. Kienlin (eds), *Beyond Divides – The Otomani-Füzesabony Phenomenon. Current Approaches to Settlement and Burial in the North-eastern Carpathian Basin and Adjacent Areas*, 351–368. Bonn, Habelt.

Marková, K. & Staššíková-Štukovská, D. (2015) Nové poznatky o opevnenom sídlisku staršej doby bronzovej vo Veselom, okr. Piešťany – New data on the Bronze Age defensive at Vesele, Okres District of Piešťany. In J. Gancarski (ed.), *Pradziejowe osady obronne w Karpatach*, 131–144. Krosno, Muzeum Podkarpackie.

Marta, L. (2014) Pișcolt 'Ógát', Satu Mare County. In F. Gogâltan, C. Cordoș & A. Ignat (eds), *Bronze Age Tell, Tell-Like and Mound-Like Settlements on the Eastern Frontier of the Carpathian Basin. History of Research*, 186–188. Cluj-Napoca, Mega Publishing House.

Marta, L. & Ștefan, D. (2011) Geophysical survey in the Bronze Age settlement from Medieșu Aurit-'Ciuncaș', Satu Mare County. In D. Măgureanu, D. Măndescu & S. Matei (eds), *Archaeology: Making of and Practice. Studies in Honor of Mircea Babeș at his 70th Anniver*sary, 363–371. Pitești, Ordessos.

Marta, L., Kienlin, T., Rung, E. & Schramm, P. (2010) Recent archaeological research on the Bronze Age fortified settlements of the Ier Valley, north-western Romania. In B. Horejs & T. Kienlin (eds), *Siedlung und Handwerk. Studien zu sozialen Kontexten in der Bronzezeit. Beiträge zu den Sitzungen der Arbeitsgemeinschaft Bronzezeit auf der Jahrestagung des Nordwestdeutschen Verbandes für Altertumsforschung in Schleswig 2007 und auf dem Deutschen Archäologenkongress in Mannheim 2008*, 121–138. Bonn, Habelt.

Máthé, M. Sz. (1988) Bronze Age tells in the Berettyó Valley. In T. Kovács & I. Stanczik (eds), *Bronze Age Tell Settlements of the Great Hungarian Plain* 1, 27–122. Budapest, Magyar Nemzeti Múzeum.

Molnár, Zs. & Nagy, J.G. (2013) Habitat models and social systems in Middle Bronze Age central north-western Transylvania. State of research. *Acta Archeologica Carpathica* 48, 5–85.

Molnár, Zs. & Németi, J. (2014) Carei 'Bobald = Bobáld', Satu Mare County. In F. Gogâltan, C. Cordoș & A. Ignat (eds), *Bronze Age Tell, Tell-Like and Mound-Like Settlements on the Eastern Frontier of the Carpathian Basin. History of Research*, 43–60. Cluj-Napoca, Mega Publishing House.

Müller-Scheeßel, N. Bátora, J., Reiter, S., Radloff, K. & Tóth, P. (2016) Prospection results in the Žitava Valley. *Študijné zvesti Archeologického ústavu SAV Nitra* 60, 79–96.

Németi, J. (2009) The Hajdubagos/Pișcolt-Cehăluț group. In S. Berecki, R. Németh & B. Rezi (eds), *Bronze Age Communities in Carpathian Basin: Proceedings of the International Colloquium from Târgu Mureș, 24–26 October 2008*, 203–221. Cluj-Napoca, Mega Publishing House.

Németi, J. & Molnár, Zs. (2012) *Bronzkori hatalmi központok Északnyugat- Erdélyben: A Nagykároly-Bobáld-tell – Bronzezeitliche Machtzentren in Nordwest-Siebenbürgen: der Tell von Carei-Bobáld.* Szeged, Szegedi Tudományegyetem Régészeti Tanszék.

Németi, J. & Molnár, Zs. (2014) Tiream 'Holmul cânepii = Kendereshalom', Satu Mare County. In F. Gogâltan, C. Cordoș & A. Ignat (eds), *Bronze Age Tell, Tell-Like and Mound-Like Settlements on the Eastern Frontier of the Carpathian Basin. History of Research*, 268–271. Cluj-Napoca, Mega Publishing House.

Nicodemus, A. & O'Shea, J.M. (2015) From relative to absolute: the radiometric dating of Mureș Culture ceramics at Pecica-Șanțul Mare. In S. Forțiu & A. Stavilă (eds), *ArheoVest, Nr. III. In Memoriam Florin Medeleț. Interdisciplinaritate în Arheologie și Istorie, Timișoara, 28 noiembrie 2015*, 691–702. Szeged, JatePress.

Nicodemus, A., Motta, L. & O'Shea, J.M. (2015) Archaeological Investigations at Pecica 'Șanțul Mare' 2013–2014. *Ziridava. Studia Arheologica* 29, 105–118.

Niebieszczański, J., Jaeger, M., Pető, Á., Hildebrandt–Radke, I., Kulcsár, G., Staniuk, R., Taylor, N. & Czebreszuk, J. (2019) Revealing the internal organization of a Middle Bronze Age fortified settlement in Kakucs-Turján through geoarchaeological means: Magnetometric survey and sedimentological verification of a housing structure. *Journal of Archaeological Science: Reports* 25, 409–419.

Nowaczinski, E., Schukraft, G., Hecht, S., Rassmann, K., Bubenzer, O. & Eitel, B. (2012) A Multimethodological Approach for the Investigation of Archaeological Ditches – Exemplified by the Early Bronze Age Settlement of Fidvár near Vráble (Slovakia). *Archaeological Prospection* 19, 281–295.

O'Shea, J.M. &. Nicodemus, A. (2019) '… The nearest run thing …'. The genesis and collapse of a Bronze Age polity in the Maros Valley of southeastern Europe. In A. Gyucha (ed.), *Coming Together: Comparative Approaches to Population Aggregation and Early Urbanization*, 61–80. Albany NY, State University of New York Press.

O'Shea, J.M., Barker, A.W. & Motta, L. (2011) Archaeological investigations at Pecica 'Şanţul Mare' 2006–2009. *Analele Banatului* 19, 67–78.

O'Shea, J.M., Barker, A.W., Sherwood, S. & Szentmiklosi, A. (2005) New archaeological investigations at Pecica-Şanţul Mare. *Analele Banatului* 12–13, 81–109.

O'Shea, J.M., Barker, A.W., Nicodemus, A., Sherwood, S. & Szentmiklosi, A. (2006) Archaeological investigations at Pecica-Şanţul Mare: The 2006 campaign. *Analele Banatului* 14(1), 211–228.

O'Shea, J.M., Parditka, G., Nicodemus, A. Kristiansen, K. Sjögren, K.-G. Paja, L. Pálfi, G. & Milašinović, L. (2019) Social formation and collapse in the Tisza-Maros region: Dating the Maros Group and its Late Bronze Age successors. *Antiquity* 93(369), 604–623.

Ordentlich, I. (1968) Anordnung und Bau der Wohnungen im Rahmen der Otomanikultur in Rumänien. *Dacia Nouvelle Série* 12, 141–153.

Ordentlich, I. (1970) Die innere Periodeneinteilung der Otomanikultur in Rumänien. In J. Filip (ed.), *Actes du VIIe Congres International des Sciences Préhistoriques et Protohistoriques. Prague 21–27 août 1966*, I, 619–622. Prague, Academia.

Ordentlich, I. (1972) Contribuţia săpăturilor arheologice de pe 'Dealul Vida' (com. Sălacea, jud. Bihor) la cunoaşterea culturii Otomani. *Studii şi Comunicări Satu Mare* 2, 63–84.

Ordentlich, I. (1974) Aspecte privind cultura Otomani. *Crisia* 4, 135–151.

Pető, Á., Serlegi, G., Krausz, E., Jaeger, M. & Kulcsár, G. (2015) Geoarchaeological survey of Bronze Age fortified settlements. Kakucs Achaeological Expedition – KEX 2. *Hungarian Archaeology, E-Journal*, 1–10.

Poroszlai, I. & Vicze, M. (2005) *Százhalombatta Archaeological Expedition. SAX. Report 2 – Field Season 2000–2003*. Százhalombatta, Matrica Museum.

Rassmann, K., Reiter, S., Bátora, J. & Müller-Scheeßel, N. (2017) The Vráble toolbox: A multidisciplinary investigation of settlement change. In B. Heeb, A. Szentmiklosi, R. Krause & M. Wemhoff (eds), *Fortifications: the Rise and Fall of Defended Sites in Late Bronze and Early Iron Age of South-East Europe: International Conference in Timişoara, Romania from November 11th to 13th, 2015*, 79–90. Berlin, Staatliche Museen zu Berlin – Preußischer Kulturbesitz.

Rassmann, K., Bátora, J., Müller-Scheeßel, N., Reiter, S., Ivanova, M., Behrens, A., Radloff, K. & Bača, M. (2018) Tracing taphonomic processes. Multiple layer analysis of ceramic distribution from surface collection and excavation at the Early Bronze Age settlement of Vráble-Fidvár. *Slovenská Archeológia* 66(2), 219–234.

Röpke, A., Zerl, T., Găvan, A., Lie, M. & Kienlin, T.L. (2019) Preliminary archaeobotanical and micromorphological investigations on the Bronze Age tell of Toboliu (Romania). Poster presentation at the International Workshop on Archaeological Soil Micromorphology. Basel, Switzerland, 2nd to 4th September 2019.

Sava, V. & Gogâltan, F. (2017) The Bronze Age fortifications in Munar 'Wolfsberg', Arad County. The 2014 and 2017 archaeological researches. *Analecta Archaeologica Ressoviensia* 12, 75–100.

Skorna, H., Kalmbach, J. & Bátora, J. (2018) Vráble, Slowakei. Herausbildung und Niedergang des frühbronzezeitlichen Siedlungszentrums – Untersuchungen zu Wirtschaft, Sozialstruktur und politischer Organisation eines Sozialverbandes und seines Umfeldes. Überblick und die Arbeiten in der Siedlung 2017. *DAI e-Forschungsberichte* 1, 101–108.

Sørensen, M.L.S. & Vicze, M. (2013) Locating household activities on a Bronze Age tell. In M. Madella, G. Kovacs, B. Kulcsarne-Berzsenyi & I. Brizi Godino (eds), *The Archaeology of Household*, 159–178. Oxford, Oxbow Books.

Stanczik, I. & Tárnoki, J. (1992) Jászdózsa-Kápolnahalom. In W. Meier-Arendt (ed.), *Bronzezeit in Ungarn. Forschungen in Tell-Siedlungen an Donau und Theiss*, 120–127. Frankfurt, Museum für Vor- und Frühgeschichte.

Szathmári, I. (1992) Füzesabony-Öregdomb. In W. Meier-Arendt (ed.), *Bronzezeit in Ungarn. Forschungen in Tell-Siedlungen an Donau und Theiss*, 134–140. Frankfurt, Museum für Vor- und Frühgeschichte.

Tárnoki, J. (1992) Törökszentmiklós-Terehalom. In W. Meier-Arendt (ed.), *Bronzezeit in Ungarn. Forschungen in Tell-Siedlungen an Donau und Theiss*, 128–130. Frankfurt, Museum für Vor- und Frühgeschichte.

Vicze, M. (2013) Middle Bronze Age Households at Százhalombatta-Földvár. In A. Anders & G. Kulcsár (eds), *Moments in Time. Papers Presented to Pál Raczky on His 60th Birthday*, 757–769. Budapest, L'Harmattan.

7

Talking Trash. Reconstructing Activities, Discard and Abandonment at Late Bronze Age Tell Sabi Abyad (Syria)

Victor Klinkenberg

History, deposits and chronologies at Tell Sabi Abyad

Reconstructing activities in ancient buildings is one of the principal tasks of archaeologists. Processes which alter, deplete or enrich archaeological deposits strongly affect their interpretation, and so in part determine which activities are ascribed to these populations. Equally so, the manner in which artefacts are deposited, through discard for instance, strongly determines how representative they are for the activities which took place. Unless objects were left behind in a Pompeii-like context (Schiffer 1972; 1985; Binford 1981), it is likely that the artefacts were introduced to the context from elsewhere as refuse. This paper describes the method which was used at Late Bronze Age (henceforth LBA) Tell Sabi Abyad to determine the mode of deposition of artefact-rich contexts. The method is illustrated with contexts which yielded cuneiform tablets. Their depositional sequence is revealed to be more complex than previously assumed.

The Assyrian conquest of Hanigalbat

Around the year 1225 BC an army of Assyrian horse-drawn chariots and foot soldiers marched into the Balikh Valley of what is today northern Syria. Under the reign of Salmaneser I, these troops expanded Assyrian territory towards the Euphrates River, taking over the former lands of Hanigalbat, until they met the borders of the Hittite Empire. After this wave of destruction, still visible in surveys as a sharp settlement decline (Lyon 2000; Kolinski 2015), the conquerors established new settlements in order to profit from, and consolidate imperial power within, the newly acquired lands. Typically, the Assyrian empire offered a fortunate and powerful few the opportunity to control part of this territory through the establishment of a centralized agricultural centre, a so-called *dunnu*. These settlements controlled surrounding agricultural land, unfree as well as free workers on it, and the local administration (Wiggermann 2000; Kolinski 2001; Düring 2015a; 2015b). Profits in agricultural surplus and taxation served both the state as well as the private owner of a *dunnu*. At Tell Sabi Abyad such a *dunnu* was founded by a particularly high-ranking individual, the viceroy of the Assyrian Empire, who ruled the western part of the empire (Jakob 2003, 59; Akkermans & Wiggermann 2015).

The settlement consisted of two central buildings and multiple, continually redeveloped surrounding structures, all surrounded by a four-metre-high wall and a three-metre-wide dry moat (Fig. 7.1). The central buildings were a tower-like structure, probably used as a stronghold or storage facility (Klinkenberg & Lanjouw 2015), and a monumental residential structure with a tripartite plan containing a central courtyard and two separate apartments with attached bathrooms. The surrounding structures varied from multi-storied apartments to purpose-built temporary pottery workshops and courtyards filled with grinding stones used for grain processing. Evidence from excavation indicated that these surrounding structures were continually remodelled. Based on evidence from cuneiform tablets from the site, the LBA architectural remains were divided into three main phases, corresponding to major political events in the capital (Akkermans & Wiggermann 2015). According to this historical perspective, the settlement was inhabited for only 100 years and then abandoned.

Excavations of the LBA remains under the direction of Prof. P.M.M.G. Akkermans, between 1991 and 2009, exposed an area of 12,000 m² and, as such, it is by far the best archaeologically documented *dunnu* (Akkermans 1987; 1999; 2006; Akkermans & Rossmeisl 1990; Akkermans *et al.* 1993; Akkermans & Wiggermann 2015). Most knowledge of the *dunnu*-system derives from historical sources in the form

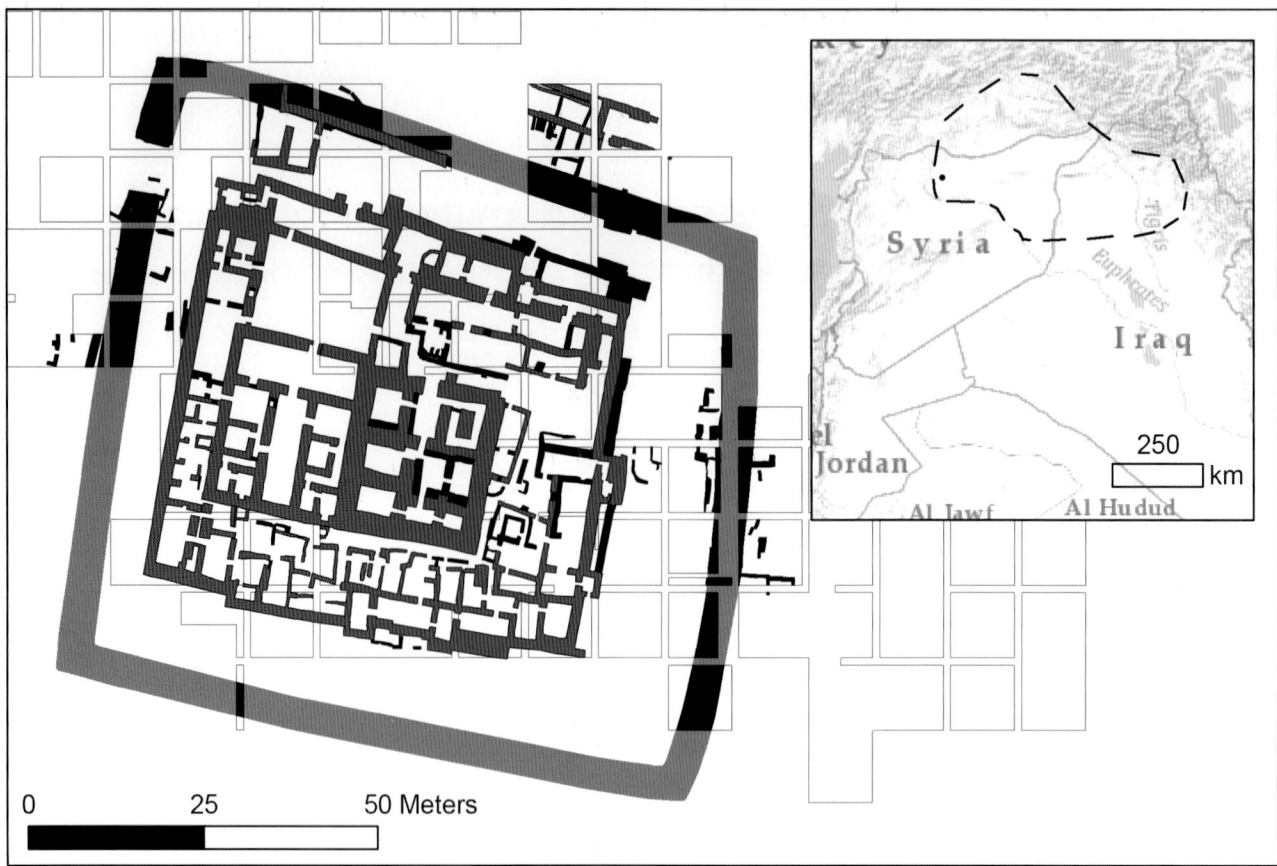

Figure 7.1 Generalised plan of the architecture of the dunnu *of Tell Sabi Abyad. The settlement is surrounded by a wide dry moat. The inset shows the location of the site and the approximate extent of the Middle Assyrian Empire during the inhabitation of the* dunnu.

of cuneiform tablets (Kolinsky 2001; Jakob 2003; Radner & Schachner 2004). The excavation at Tell Sabi Abyad therefore yielded an exciting first opportunity to investigate this settlement type from an archaeological perspective. As part of a larger European Research Council-funded project on (Assyrian) imperialism led by Dr B.S. Düring (Düring 2020), the finds from the settlement were studied to provide insight into daily life in the *dunnu* (Klinkenberg 2016a). As with every excavated context anywhere, it was vital to understand the relationship between the finds and the rooms and open spaces they were found in, and not to consider all floor level finds as unproblematic *in situ* contexts. For this study, a method was designed to characterize the deposits in which objects were found. With this, a formal relationship between objects and the space where they were found in could be established. A critical analysis of deposition in the *dunnu* indicated that the various objects were deposited at different moments in time. This allowed for the reconstruction of a detailed micro-history or 'sequence of events' for each space. Especially for the contexts which contained cuneiform tablets, this had considerable ramifications as many of these can no longer be considered *in situ*. Additionally, the improved chronological resolution does not agree with the earlier three-phase interpretation or with the absolute dating provided by these historical documents.

A necessary digital approach

Due to the outbreak of war in Syria, it was not possible to revisit the site or to access the find material, which was stored locally. In effect, the study was limited to the documentation that had been returned to Leiden. Apart from field diaries, plan drawings and sections, this comprised the detailed drawings and descriptions of 'objects' that are commonly termed 'small finds'. Unlike ceramic sherds within soil layers, 'objects' were not collected in bulk, but individually. The decision to document a find as 'object' was taken when an artefact was located seemingly *in situ*, relatively complete, or notable in some way. The location and find context were described on object forms, which also included a hand-drawn sketch of the object. Information on other parameters like sherd density or other briefly documented objects were not available for study. No additional assessments of the objects could be performed, and analysis of their function was solely based on their shape and the excavator's interpretation.

To assemble all excavation data, the entire archive was digitised by scanning all paper documents and by georeferencing and digitising in a Geographic Information System (GIS) all plans, sections and find locations. A database was set up to connect the scanned documents with all other digital data on finds and contexts. This enabled viewing all excavation data in a 3D GIS environment with the scanned documents available as hyperlinks. In effect, clicking on a find in the 3D representation immediately yielded the related excavation documents. The 3D system helped to intuitively view spatial relationships for finds and contexts and expedited queries (Klinkenberg 2014; 2016b).

Contested contexts
Investigating daily life at archaeological sites finds its theoretical and methodological home in *household archaeology*. Rooted in the assumption that archaeological investigation of domestic behaviour augments and improves our understanding of cultures otherwise known through historical or ethnographic records, household archaeology yields a bottom-up perspective of (pre)historic life (Wilk & Rathje 1982; Allison 1999; Müller 2015). This perspective also has its shortcomings, principally from pre- and post-depositional processes which remove, alter and add material to the archaeological record (Ascher 1961; Schiffer 1983; 1987; LaMotta & Schiffer 1999). Despite heated debate on the value of household perspectives and their postulated shortcomings (Schiffer 1972; 1985; Binford 1981), the majority of archaeologists still use archaeological remains to infer aspects of ancient daily life. Thorough understanding of the processes that influence the archaeological record therefore remains vital in archaeology.

Especially in Near Eastern tell sites, the abundance of find material and seemingly perfect *in situ* contexts may lead the researcher to disregard or undervalue these issues in favour of a tidy interpretation. In the case of contexts rich in cuneiform tablets, this may lead to a false assumption that these tablet groups are 'archives'. Especially with these 'special contexts' care must be given to understand how and why these were deposited.

Tablets have the added benefit that they were occasionally refitted with other fragments, and that they contain valuable information about administration, economy and aspects of daily life. Many of the correspondence letters among the tablets of Tell Sabi Abyad also provide precise dating evidence by the inscription of the day, month and year of writing in the Assyrian calendar system. The special nature of this artefact type lends itself perfectly for the systematic reconstruction of depositional processes at Tell Sabi Abyad.

Deposit characterisation and sequence of events
The relationship between excavated artefacts and the location of their discovery is best expressed in terms of the depositional history. The mode of deposition for objects allows us to determine how artefacts can be used in the reconstruction of past activities. Below follows an account of the methodology produced for and employed at Tell Sabi Abyad. Subsequently, the separate deposits in spaces in the *dunnu* are modelled in a chronological schema, to identify the changing use of spaces. The formalised analysis of the mode of deposition and the schematic representation of each sequence of events warrants a critical interpretation of contexts at this site.

Modes of deposition
Are objects left behind on the floor of a building during a major catastrophe and rapidly covered with sediments or debris? If so, then we can safely assume that these were originally used at this location, which allows functional interpretation of that space. Unfortunately for archaeologists, catastrophic fires, volcanic eruptions and devastating earthquakes were not the most common reason for the abandonment of houses and settlements. Most artefacts discovered in archaeological sites are left behind as refuse. To determine the type of deposits, following Schiffer (1987), a distinction is made between intentional and unintentional deposition, with a subsequent subdivision of unintentional deposition in catastrophe and loss, and intentional deposition in discard, caching and burial (Fig. 7.2).

Unintentional deposition occurs through loss of often small objects and through catastrophic events such as the volcanic eruption that buried Pompeii. These are obviously uncommon processes, and most archaeological remains ended in the ground as intentional deposits, through discard, caching or burials. Caches are deliberate deposits of material as ritual offerings (ritual cache) or valuables intended for later retrieval (banking cache). Burials could be considered a cache, as they are deliberate deposits of 'valuables' but have a decidedly different motivation for 'deposition'.

By far most material found its way into the ground through intentional discard. Following Schiffer's (1987) work, four types of discard are recognised. Primary refuse is waste discarded at the location of use, such as production waste next to a kiln. If waste material is collected in a pile or bin to be discarded at a later stage, it is termed provisional refuse. The material discarded away from the location of use is known as secondary refuse. The latter occurs in great quantities as middens or garbage heaps, and in small amounts amongst building rubble for instance. The last category of refuse is known as abandonment stage refuse or *de facto* refuse (Rathje & Schiffer 1982). This label is given to material left behind in a building at abandonment, but which otherwise would have been curated or used. During abandonment, small valuable items are brought along to a new location. Large heavy objects with relatively low value are often left behind, even if they could be easily (re)used. Abandonment can be rapid or gradual, sudden or planned, and will differ according to the planned distance of movement, such as within the settlement or further away.

The character of the resulting abandonment deposit will change accordingly.

Deposit characterisation and probability index

There are major differences between what materials end up in a waste dump and what is retrieved from a floor in a house struck by a sudden catastrophe. In consequence, the above described deposit types can be characterised by their artefact content (variety, structuring, size, replacement cost, damage and use-life stage of objects) by their context (in a pit, a container, on a floor, or mixed in a soil layer) and how the objects functionally relate to their context (Fig. 7.3). By identifying these elements in archaeological deposits it is possible to determine the most likely mode of deposition. For the current study, the signature characteristics for each deposit were determined in a simplified scale of high-to-low. These are briefly discussed below.

Four different 'contexts' are recognised for artefacts: in a pit, a container, on a floor or in a soil layer. These major categories of find contexts, although strongly generalised, indicate a distinction between types of depositional practices. The variety of physical materials (pottery, stone, clay, metal, *etc.*) helps identify how well organised a deposit is. Whether the objects were possibly part of the same or similar processes is indicated by the degree of structuring.

The physical characteristics of size (large, medium, small), replacement cost (high, low), damage (fragmented, damaged, complete) and use-life stage (raw material, half product, waste product, end product) help to ascertain how likely it is for these objects to be discarded as refuse. Finally, if objects have a strong link with the room they were found in, such as kiln wasters in a pottery workshop, they are likely deposited as primary or provisional refuse. When there is no obvious relation between artefacts and the context, such as a heap of burnt grain in a toilet area, the mode of deposition is more likely secondary discard.

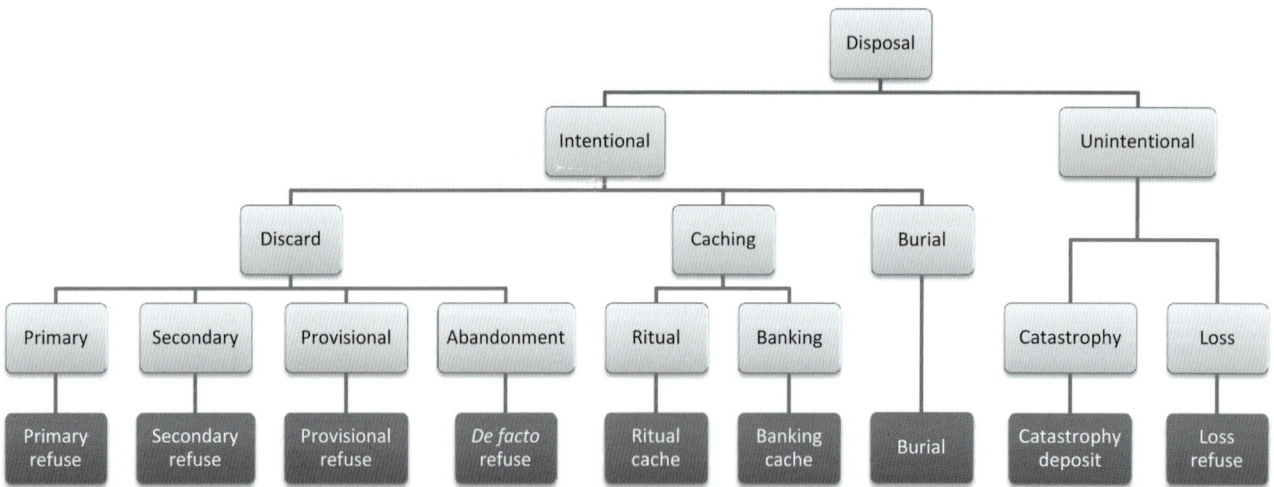

Figure 7.2 The nine modes of deposition and resulting deposit types.

	context				variety			structuring			size			uselife				damage			cost			space	
	floor	pit	dump/pile	container	high	med	low	high	med	low	large	med	small	raw material	waste product	by product	New product	whole	damaged	fragmentary	high	med	low	logical	unlogical
Primary refuse	3	0	1	0	1	2	3	4	2	0	2	2	2	3	3	3	0	0	2	2	1	1	3	2	1
Secondary refuse	1	3	3	1	2	2	2	3	2	1	2	3	3	3	3	3	0	0	3	3	1	2	3	1	3
Provisional refuse	3	1	1	3	0	2	3	4	2	1	0	2	3	3	3	3	0	0	3	3	0	1	3	3	1
De facto refuse	3	1	1	0	2	3	3	2	3	2	3	3	3	2	2	2	3	3	3	2	2	3	3	2	0
Ritual cache	1	2	1	3	1	2	3	3	3	2	1	2	3	1	0	0	3	3	2	1	3	2	1	0	3
Banking cache	1	2	1	3	0	1	3	3	3	2	0	2	3	1	0	0	3	3	1	0	3	2	0	2	3
Catastrophe deposit	3	0	0	0	2	2	3	2	2	2	2	2	2	2	2	2	3	2	2	0	2	2	2	2	0
Loss refuse	2	0	0	0	2	2	2	2	2	2	0	0	4	0	0	0	3	2	2	0	2	2	0	2	0

Legend: 0 impossible, 1 improbable, 2 possible, 3 probable, 4 required

Figure 7.3 Likely characteristics of deposit types at Tell Sabi Abyad.

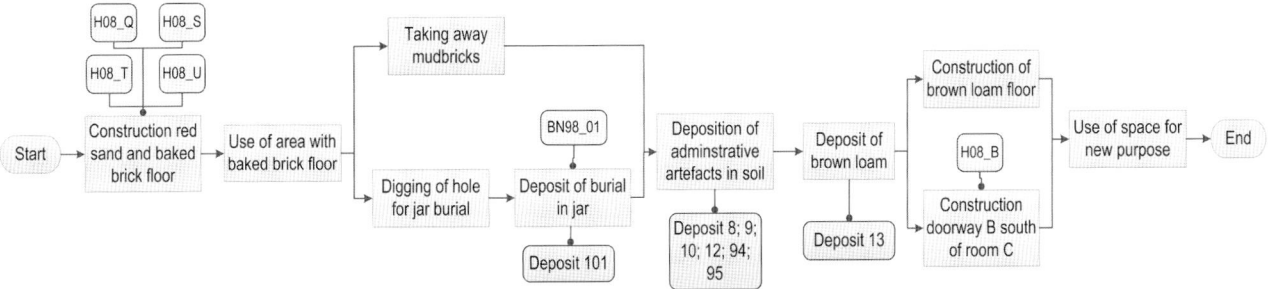

Figure 7.4 The sequence of events of the 'Office of Tammitte'. The feature names ('H08_Q') and deposit numbers relate to the excavation documentation system.

Sequence of events for each space

To chart all activities and deposits in the rooms of the Tell Sabi Abyad buildings, every event that could be reconstructed was charted in a sequence of events. Figure 7.4 illustrates the sequence of events in the 'Office of Tammitte', discussed in more detail below. The chart indicates the sequential progress of events in a certain space, similar to a Harris matrix. Rather than specifying the duration of processes, it emphasises the chronological succession of these. The chart illustrates which deposits and architectural features relate to the process. In general, a sequence of events of a single room commences with its construction, indicates the different uses, which occurred simultaneously or sequentially, and ends with the final collapse and soil layers or renovation phases which cover the structure. This formal notation of each event that can be reconstructed helps in determining the changing function of a space, and how these relate chronologically with the use-phases of the surrounding spaces. The provided resolution helps to go beyond the notion of a *main* use for any space and illustrates their complex changing nature. Below follows a discussion for the mode of deposition and sequence of events for several tablet-bearing contexts at Tell Sabi Abyad. These indicate major differences between these deposits, despite their similar nature.

The character of tablet-rich contexts at Tell Sabi Abyad

The excavations at Tell Sabi Ayad yielded nearly 400 cuneiform tablets or fragments in 15 separate contexts (Fig. 7.5). Three of these are discussed below. The largest concentration of tablets was discovered in rooms that were termed the 'Office of Tammitte', after the main dignitary mentioned in the tablets found here. It was assumed that these tablets were left behind on the floor of these rooms during a panicked flight (Wiggermann 2010). The tablets therefore would have been left behind as a catastrophe deposit, exactly where they were used. Similarly, many receipts for grain and flour discovered in the south of the settlement, in two separate contexts, were interpreted in this manner.

The 'Office of Tammitte'

In the northwest of the settlement, an apartment consisting of four connected rooms was excavated. The apartment was entered from the central courtyard of the *dunnu*. Upon entering the hallway, a doorway to the right led to a room fitted with a baked mudbrick floor, which could be used for domestic activities such as eating, sleeping or entertaining guests. Like many doorways in the *dunnu*, the entrance into the domestic room was only 60 cm high, so people were forced to enter the room by squatting or crawling. At the end of the corridor lay a double-room bathroom, which was coated with waterproof plaster and equipped with a toilet, consisting of two mudbrick footrests with a gutter between which ran outside through the wall.

Inside these rooms a total of 135 cuneiform tablets was discovered (Fig. 7.6). It was assumed that these were left behind in great haste and that they were therefore used in this apartment. The philologist Dr F.A.M. Wiggermann anecdotally described the deposit to be the result of a hurried departure out of the *dunnu*, probably in relation to advancing enemy troops; while Tammitte's staff was carrying chests with administration tablets from his office, one fell to the floor, broke apart, and caused all the tablets inside to fly over the ground (Wiggermann 2010, 22). The remains of clay sealings with impressions of wooden pegs in the same deposit were considered additional evidence for this scenario.

The character of the deposit in which the tablets were found, as well as the sequence of deposits in these rooms point to another interpretation. The following discussion describes the sequence of events which could be reconstructed for this apartment. After the construction of the walls and floors of the apartment, it is likely that the rooms were used for domestic or official purposes. The layout with a double-room bathroom follows the standard from other apartments in the *dunnu* (Klinkenberg 2016a, 212). Whether it was built solely for personal or official use is unknown, but the presence of such elaborate toilet facilities indicate that this was purpose-built for personal comfort and perhaps display of status. There are no direct signs of use during

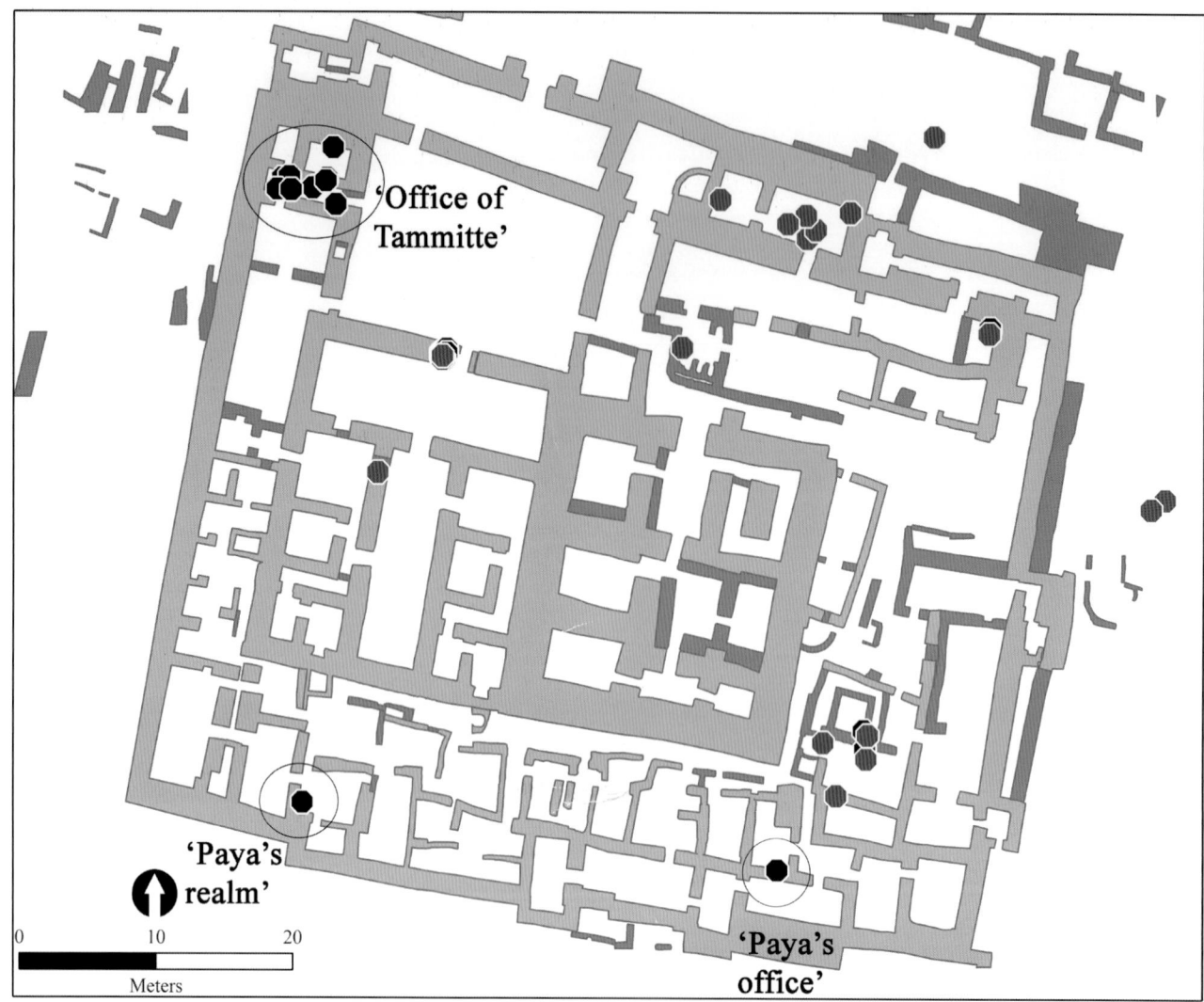

Figure 7.5 Tablet contexts in the dunnu. *The concentration in the 'Office of Tammitte' is by far the largest with 135 tablets, the other two discussed concentrations are located in the south of the* dunnu.

this habitation phase, but after the rooms were out of use, a large part of the toilet floor was demolished by removing the baked mudbricks, and a pit was dug through the floor in the 'bedroom'. In this pit a large jar was deposited, with the cremated remains of two individuals inside (Akkermans & Smits 2008). Accompanying grave gifts included stone and golden beads and pendants. Hardly any cremated burials are known from Middle Assyrian contexts and they are therefore considered non-Assyrian in identity (Tenu 2005; Pedde 2015). The wealth of the burial and its non-Assyrian style indicates that the interred individuals were of high standing but of non-Assyrian descent. It has been suggested that the manager Tammitte, with his atypical name, was the deceased (Düring *et al.* 2015, 44).

After the rooms were out of use and the burial jar was sunk into the pit of the 'bedroom', a 40 cm thick soil layer was deposited, with abundant charcoal, pottery fragments, as well as 153 registered objects. The objects included 93 clay tablets and envelopes, 21 clay sealings, 23 tokens and weights, as well as 16 other objects such as stone tools, ceramic fragments and a bronze needle. If the objects were deposited on a ground surface in some hurried event they would likely be deposited unbroken and horizontally on one level. From the object description it becomes clear that only 28% of them were unbroken. Additionally, the objects were found in a 40 cm thick soil layer and photographs of their excavation show that they were not oriented along a level plane (Fig. 7.7). Rather, the items appear to be deposited with the soil. These aspects of the deposit indicate that they were likely deposited as secondary refuse rather than as abandonment stage or catastrophe deposits. A floor was constructed on top of the tablet-rich deposit, on

7. Talking Trash. Reconstructing Activities, Discard and Abandonment at Late Bronze Age Tell Sabi Abyad

Figure 7.6 Plan of the rooms belonging to the 'Office of Tammitte'. The space indicated with D is the corridor leading into the apartment, room B is the domestic space. Rooms A and C are the bathroom structure. Doorway B was created after the tablets were deposited and the apartment was no longer in use as such. The large circles indicate the location of fragments of Tablet T98_045 discussed below.

top of which a small hearth and some complete ceramics were found. This marks a new use-phase for these rooms (see Fig. 7.4).

The spatial distribution of tablet T98-045 further emphasises the disturbed nature of the deposit. Thirteen fragments of this tablet were found in the corridor of the apartment, dispersed in an area 2.5 m wide (Fig. 7.6). In addition, the vertical distribution of these refitted fragments shows that they were deposited both on the bottom and top of the 40 cm thick layer. Another refit was found between fragments T98-040 and T99-005. The first was found amongst the discussed layer, the latter on the bottom of a cesspit some 20 m to the south. Clearly, the tablets were fragmented before deposition, a known practise for dealing with administrative documents (Taylor & Cartwright 2012).

The tablet-rich deposit in the 'Office of Tammitte' can convincingly be interpreted as a secondary refuse deposit. This means that the objects were not necessarily used in their location of discovery, and, strictly speaking, do not provide direct evidence for the function of these rooms. That these objects are concentrated in one dense assemblage, at

Figure 7.7 Tablets are carefully uncovered by workmen at Tell Sabi Abyad (photograph: P.M.M.G. Akkermans).

a location that appears suitable for official business does, however, suggest that there is a connection between them. The tablets of baker Paya, discussed below, help to understand this functional and spatial relationship.

The realm of Paya

Two contexts in the south of the *dunnu* yielded tablets and tablet fragments related to baker Paya. The southwestern area of the *dunnu* can, on the basis of many ovens and grinding installations, be considered a continuously used food production area. Several parallel grinding stations could be used for the preparation of large amounts of flour for local consumption, and these could also be used by dependent workers who did not privately own grinding equipment (Wiggermann 2000). Connected to these grinding stations was an area packed with bins and bread ovens, along the southern side of the *dunnu*. On the floor of one of the rooms in this area, numerous storage jars were left behind. On top of these remains, a layer of soil with many grinding stone fragments and cuneiform tablets was found (Fig. 7.8). The documents comprise small receipts of flour or bread for daily use. It is assumed that hundreds of these documents must have existed and that only a small subset survive among the archaeological remains.

Most small tablets from these deposits are unbroken, perhaps due to their small size, as these are less easily fragmented. In fact, since these are unbaked clay objects, if someone meant to destroy the tablet, simply submerging them in water would have sufficed. Probably, if only to provide the administrator with levigated clay for new tablets, this was done to most used tablets. Similar to the Tammitte context, the bread and flour receipts were deposited in a soil layer covered by a new floor. It appears that the tablets were deliberately purged from daily use through discard in construction layers. Again, the tablets were secondary refuse, discarded on top of the objects and installations of an earlier abandoned room. Formally, the objects should not be considered to relate directly to the use of that space. That the tablets appear to describe exactly what was archaeologically attested as the function of these spaces could be considered problematic. Luckily, yet another context with some of Paya's documents provides clarification.

Figure 7.8 Plan of the southwestern corner of the dunnu *with numerous finds amongst building debris.*

Figure 7.9 Plan of the heavily burnt rooms at 'Paya's office'. The niche where tablets were discovered is in the lower right corner of the figure.

Roughly 20 m east of the main food processing installations, two adjoining rooms were discovered that were consumed by fire (Fig. 7.9). One of the rooms was fitted with a grinding installation, at least four ovens, and several mudbrick bins. The second room contained fewer finds and was fitted with only one bin and a large mudbrick platform. Charred barley grains found inside the bins highlight that these features were all used for food storage and were used in conjunction with the other installations. The conflagration here caused the roof to collapse, trapping the materials on the floors. Considering that over half of the objects were in complete condition, and that there was grain left in the bins, indicates that this was not a controlled or deliberate fire or abandonment. Rather, this appears to be a rare catastrophe deposit. Although the finds in the second room are sparse, the continuation of the fire damage suggests that this space was also lost in a catastrophe. It is likely that the room contained more objects or installations of perishable (and flammable) materials such as cloth or wicker. Interestingly, in the south side of this room, next to the mudbrick bin, a small niche was created inside the wall. Within this niche excavators discovered six complete cuneiform tablets.

Again, these tablets were directed to, or written by, baker Paya. Their location in a wall niche could indicate a banking cache, but it is unclear whether the tablets were stored in a concealed location. Instead, the characteristics of the larger deposit, as well as its context and depositional sequence, suggest that a catastrophe deposit is a better fit. These objects therefore were most likely used in this space, and the room's role as an office or domicile is fully justified.

Discussion and conclusion

The remains of Paya's administration at Tell Sabi Abyad illustrate well how these documents were handled after use. Although many of these were deposited as refuse in construction layers, a few were discovered in more favourable circumstances. The sudden fire, and consequential collapse of the rooms in the south of the *dunnu* sealed the contexts in which the tablets were discovered. Their location in a small niche suggests they were stored there and meant to be used again or discarded elsewhere later. It is safe to assume therefore that this space was used by Paya or his administrative assistant for the administration of bread and flour distribution. His realm clearly extended beyond this room, into the extensive bread-making areas to the west. That a large collection of his private archive was discarded in that same area in a construction layer indicates that he indeed managed these rooms and installations. The location of that secondary refuse was not necessarily his administrative workplace, but simply part of his overall working environment. Perhaps the construction of a new floor offered a convenient location for Paya to impulsively discard some of the documents of finalised transactions.

The tablet-rich deposits in the rooms that were known as the 'Office of Tammitte' can probably also be interpreted in this manner. The sequence of events for this apartment clearly shows that the tablet context post-dates the destruction of parts of the floor in these rooms, and even the interment of two cremated individuals. A likely workplace for Tammitte was the central courtyard from which the apartment was entered. He may have dealt with business in the shade of the high surrounding wall, and after the apartment was no longer in use, he or his successor discarded a selection of his archive in a construction layer inside.

That the tablet contexts are problematic in nature is also illustrated by the dating evidence that is available through the attestations of the writing year, the so-called *limu* (year name). All tablets date between 1230 and 1184 BC with the majority from the period 1197–1187 BC (F. Wiggermann, pers. comm.; Klinkenberg 2016a, 226). The events described in the tablets, as well as major political events in the imperial capital, were originally considered to be the turning points for architectural modifications and were used as markers for the separate phases of the settlement (Akkermans & Wiggermann 2015). The stratigraphic location of tablets and their *limu* do not agree with this, however. Surprisingly, the oldest *limu* were attested on tablets in the youngest layers. The youngest *limu* in turn, were in fact found in some of the oldest layers (Klinkenberg 2016a, 229). In the case of Sabi Abyad, the chronological mismatch between the stratigraphy and the tablet dates reveals that the renovation phases of the *dunnu* cannot be correlated with the historical events described in tablets, underscoring the complexity of depositional practices in archaeological sites.

The methodology presented here was successful in identifying the mode of deposition for the tablet-rich contexts from the 'Office of Tammitte' and the baker's workshop. By systematically analysing the physical and functional characteristics of finds and their contexts, it is possible to formally distinguish between deposit types. In this manner the tantalising tablet contexts were transformed to secondary refuse deposits. The resulting pattern of deliberate discard of cuneiform tablets has major ramifications for their interpretation. These documents were the deliberately discarded elements of an archive, not the archive itself. The precise dating evidence offered by the *limu* attestations on many of the documents was once used to produce a chronology for the architectural development of the *dunnu*. Critical comparison of the documents with their stratigraphic position illustrates artefacts were not only discarded away from their place of use, yielding a *spatial* bias, but that they were also deposited (much) later than their use, yielding a *temporal* bias.

The tablet-rich contexts illustrate the broader phenomenon of complex discard practices. The administrative documents yield detailed information that help determine their chronological and spatial relationship to the architecture and stratigraphy. That other artefact types seldom offer such specifics does not mean that these had less complex depositional histories. Although constant mixing of artefact-rich soils and re-deposition events cannot be reconstructed in every detail, the context analyses presented here offer a handhold for understanding the nature of at least the *final* deposition of artefacts.

Acknowledgements

The research presented here was part of the project *Consolidating Empire: Reconstructing Hegemonic Practices of the Middle Assyrian Empire at the Late Bronze Age Fortified Estate of Tell Sabi Abyad, Syria, ca. 1230–1180 BC* conducted at Leiden University, directed by Dr B.S. Düring, and funded through an ERC Starting Grant (nr. 282785). I am grateful for helpful comments on an earlier draft of this paper by Bleda Düring and Daniel Turner.

References

Akkermans, P.M.M.G. (1987) Tell Sabi Abyad: Preliminary report on the 1986 excavations. *Akkadica* 52, 10–28.

Akkermans, P.M.M.G. (1999) La Forteresse de Tell Sabi Abyad. *Archéologia* 358, 56–65.

Akkermans, P.M.M.G. (2006) The fortress of Ili-Pada – Middle Assyrian architecture at Tell Sabi Abyad, Syria. In P. Butterlin, M. Lebeau, J.Y. Monchambert, J. Montero & B. Müller (eds), *Les Espaces Syro-Mésopotamiens. Dimensions de L'expérience Humaine Au Proche-Orient Ancien*, 201–211. Turnhout, Brepols.

Akkermans, P.M.M.G. & Rossmeisl, I. (1990) Excavations at Tell Sabi Abyad, northern Syria: A regional centre on the Assyrian frontier. *Akkadica* 66, 13–60.

Akkermans P.M.M.G. & Smits, E. (2008) A sealed double cremation at Middle Assyrian tell Sabi Abyad, Syria. In D. Bonatz, R.M. Czichon & F.J. Kreppner (eds), *Fundstellen – Gesammelte Schriften zur Archäologie und Geschichte Altvorderasiens ad honorem Hartmut Kühne*, 251–261. Wiesbaden, Harrassowitz.

Akkermans, P.M.M.G. & Wiggermann, F.A.M. (2015) West of Aššur: The life and times of the Middle Assyrian Dunnu at Tell Sabi Abyad. In B.S. Düring (ed.), *Understanding Hegemonic Practices of the Early Assyrian Empire. Essays Dedicated to Frans Wiggermann*, 89–124. Leiden, Nederlands Instituut voor het Nabije Oosten.

Akkermans, P.M.M.G., Limpens, J. & Spoor, R.H. (1993) On the frontier of Assyria: Excavations at Tell Sabi Abyad, 1991. *Akkadica* 84/85, 1–52.

Allison, P.M. (1999) *The Archaeology of Household Activities*. London, Routledge.

Ascher, R. (1961) Analogy in archaeological interpretation. *Southwestern Journal of Anthropology* 17(4), 317–325.

Binford, L.R. (1981) Behavioral archaeology and the 'Pompeii Premise.' *Journal of Anthropological Research* 37(3), 195–208.

Düring, B.S. (2015a) Reassessing the Dunnu institution in the context of the Middle Assyrian Empire. *Ancient Near Eastern Studies* 52, 47–68.

Düring, B.S. (2015b) *Understanding Hegemonic Practices of the Early Assyrian Empire. Essays Dedicated to Frans Wiggermann. Consolidating Empire Project I*. Leiden, Nederlands Instituut voor het Nabije Oosten.

Düring, B.S. (2020) *The Imperialisation of Assyria. An Archaeological Approach*. Cambridge, Cambridge University Press.

Düring, B.S., Visser, E. & Akkermans, P.M.M.G. (2015) Skeletons in the fortress: The Late Bronze Age burials of Tell Sabi Abyad, Syria. *Levant* 47(1), 30–50.

Jakob, S. (2003) *Mittelassyrische Verwaltung und Sozialstruktur: Untersuchungen*. Leiden, Brill.

Klinkenberg, V. (2014). Het Opwerken van Het Tell Sabi Abyad Archief Naar de 21ste Eeuw. *Tijdschrift Voor Mediterrane Archeologie* 52, 46–50.

Klinkenberg, V. (2016a) *Reading Rubbish: Using Object Assemblages to Reconstruct Activities, Modes of Deposition and Abandonment at the Late Bronze Age Dunnu of Tell Sabi Abyad, Syria*. Leiden, Nederlands Instituut voor het Nabije Oosten.

Klinkenberg, V (2016b). Are we there yet? 3D GIS in archaeological research, the case of Tell Sabi Abyad, Syria. In H. Kamermans, W. de Neef, C. Piccoli, A.G. Posluschny & R. Scopigno (eds), *The Three Dimensions of Archaeology*, 39–48. Oxford, Archaeopress.

Klinkenberg, V. & Lanjouw, T. (2015) Reconstructing the Tell Sabi Abyad Dunnu: A bottom-up perspective of the Middle Assyrian Empire. In B.S. Düring (ed.), *Understanding Hegemonic Practices of the Early Assyrian Empire. Essays Dedicated to Frans Wiggermann*, 143–165. Leiden, Nederlands Instituut voor het Nabije Oosten.

Kolinski, R. (2001) *Mesopotamian Dimatu of the Second Millennium BC*. Oxford, British Archaeological Report S1004.

Kolinski, R. (2015) Making Mittani Assyrian. In B.S. Düring (ed.), *Understanding Hegemonic Practices of the Early Assyrian Empire. Essays Dedicated to Frans Wiggermann*, 9–32. Leiden, Nederlands Instituut voor het Nabije Oosten.

LaMotta, V.M. & Schiffer, M.B. (1999) Formation processes of house floor assemblages. In P.M. Allison (ed.), *The Archaeology of Household Activities*, 19–29. London, Routledge.

Lyon, J.D. (2000) Middle Assyrian expansion and settlement development in the Syrian Jezira; The view from the Balikh Valley. In R.M. Jas (ed.), *Rainfall and Agriculture in Northern Mesopotamia: Proceedings of the 3rd MOS Symposium, Leiden, May 21–22, 1999*, 89–126. Leiden, Nederlands Instituut voor het Nabije Oosten.

Müller, M. (2015) *Household Studies in Complex Societies. (Micro) Archaeological and Textual Approaches*. Chicago IL, University of Chicago Press.

Pedde, F. (2015) *Gräber und Grüfte in Assur II: Die mittelassyrische Zeit*. Wiesbaden, Harrassowitz.

Radner, K. & Schachner, K. (2004) *Das mittelassyrische Tontafelarchiv von Giricano/Dunnu-Sa-Uzibi: Ausgrabungen in Giricano 1*. Turnhout, Brepols.

Rathje, W.L. & Schiffer, M.B. (1982) *Archaeology*. New York, Harcourt Brace Jovanovich.

Schiffer, M.B. (1972) Archaeological context and systemic context. *American Antiquity* 37(2), 156–165.

Schiffer, M.B. (1983) Toward the identification of formation processes. *American Antiquity* 48(4), 675–706.

Schiffer, M.B. (1985) Is there a 'Pompeii Premise' in archaeology? *Journal of Anthropological Research* 41(1), 18–41.

Schiffer, M.B. (1987) *Formation Processes of the Archaeological Record. Advances*. Albuquerque NM, University of New Mexico Press.

Taylor, J. & Cartwright, C. (2012) The making and re-making of clay tablets. *Scienze Dell'Antichità* 17, 297–324.

Tenu, A. (2005) La pratique de la crémation en Syrie: un usage marginal? *Ktema* 30, 37–46.

Wiggermann, F.A.M. (2000) Agriculture in the northern Balikh Valley: The case of Middle Assyrian Tell Sabi Abyad. In R.M. Jas (ed.), *Rainfall and Agriculture in Northern Mesopotamia: Proceedings of the 3rd MOS Symposium, Leiden, May 21–22, 1999*, 171–231. Leiden, Nederlands Historisch Archeologisch Instituut te Istanbul.

Wiggermann, F.A.M. (2010) Wein, Weib und Gesang in een Midden-Assyrische Nederzetting aan de Balikh. *Phoenix* 56(1–2), 17–60.

Wilk, R.R. & Rathje, W.L. (1982) *Archaeology of the Household: Building a Prehistory of Domestic Life*. Beverly Hills CA, SAGE Publications.

PART 2

THE SOCIAL LIVES OF TELLS

8

Domestication of Tells: Settlements of the First Farmers in Pelagonia (Macedonia)

Goce Naumov

Tells are a social phenomenon that occurred in the Neolithic period of the Middle East and then spread through Central Asia and the Balkan Peninsula all the way to Central Europe (Fig. 8.1). These artificially formed hills are intrinsically linked to the onset of agriculture and the continued life in particular places. This lifestyle was based on easy access to food resources and the possibility of long-term accumulation. Such economic benefits caused social changes that formed the first farming communities, and which, with smaller or larger local modifications, remained stable for several hundreds or thousands of years. In addition to their effect on the economy, these changes also affected the ideology of the first farmers, which were evident in the material culture.

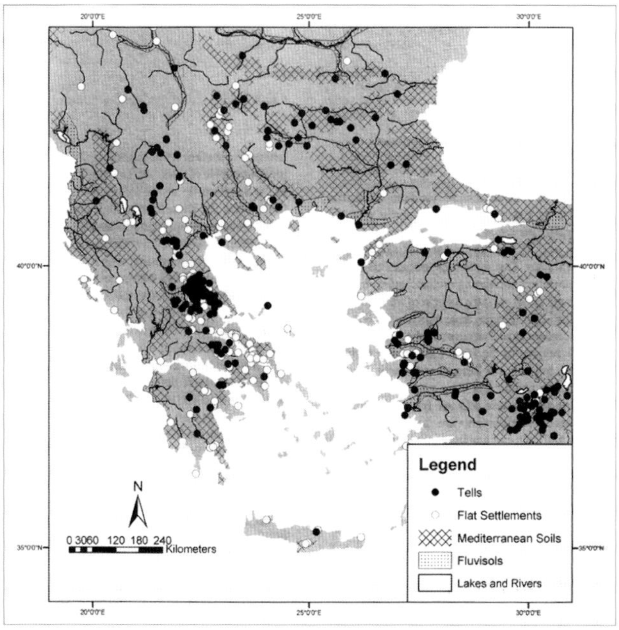

Due to their complex nature and social dynamics, tells have been approached from diverse perspectives: formation processes, demographic dynamics, architecture, inhabitation, economic practices, craftsmanship or ideology; all factors that played a key role in their development and continuity (Kotsakis 1999; Perlès 1999; Bailey 2002; Evans 2005; Gheorghiu 2007; Rosenstock 2009; Hofmann *et al.* 2012; Naumov 2016a). As a result of this extensive research, a variety of interpretations have been offered that aim to explain tells. Of course, such findings cannot generally be applied to all tells ranging from the Middle East to Anatolia, as it is more than obvious that there are numerous causes that led to local variations in this settlement phenomenon. However, there are some phenomena characteristic of tells in Anatolia that can also be traced to the Balkans and especially to Pelagonia, a region that will be elaborated in detail in this chapter.

Balkan tells at the dawn of agriculture

The Balkans are one of the regions that can provide exceptional insights into the emergence of tells as socio-architectural phenomena. The formation of these settlements in the Balkans was preceded by a process already developing in Anatolia, with demographic changes and migrations in the Early Neolithic being transposed into Thessaly. Numerous tells in this region are known to indicate rapid settlement formation and the use of large areas of the valley for agricultural activities (Perlès 1999; Rosenstock 2006). Of course, this phenomenon is also recorded in Bulgaria, Macedonia and Albania, but is almost completely

Figure 8.1 Location of Neolithic tells in the Balkans and Anatolia (Rosenstock 2006, fig. 1).

absent in Serbia, Montenegro, Croatia and Slovenia. This shows that the farmers inhabiting these settlements preferred the plains to the hilly and mountainous regions. But even in this case, it is again surprising that such sites, with rare exceptions, are absent from the plains of Serbia, Croatia and Slovenia.

This spatial distribution of tells in Southeast Europe is particularly striking given the later occurrences of this type of settlement in the Neolithic period of Romania and Hungary. Therefore, certain natural and economic factors that influenced the selection of the area of tell implementation should be considered. These factors played an exceptionally important role in the emergence of these types of settlements on the Balkan Peninsula, resulting in their high concentration in certain regions of Greece, Macedonia, Bulgaria, Albania and Romania.

In particular, the farming communities that established the tells, in addition to preferring plains, had in mind the presence of wetlands near their settlements. Such a pattern was based on economic motives for the foundation of agricultural villages in valleys, *i.e.* easy access to fertile soils on which they could grow cereals, also involving the availability of pasture and water. Indeed, the proximity of wetlands formed by the outflow of rivers or small lakes had a significant economic impact and provided fertile soils for cereal cultivation and high-quality resources for livestock breeding. Such factors also had an impact on the social structure of settlements, in turn reflected in architecture and representative objects.

The preference for the agricultural landscapes of valleys and wetlands occurred in Anatolia before being introduced to the Balkans. Such is the case with Çatalhöyük (Turkey), a site located adjacent to the marshy terrain formed by the Çarşambra River in the Konya Valley (Fig, 8.2) (Ayala *et al.* 2017). On the slopes of Mount Karadağ, which is one that forms this valley, was a smaller lake (dried in the 20th century), with Pinarbaşi site in its vicinity (Assouti & Hather 2001). Apparently, the rivers and lakes in the Konya Valley were flooded at certain periods of the year, and the presence of wetlands contributed to field cultivation. Such valleys with small lakes and rivers were also favoured by the agricultural communities that inhabited Thessaly. Based on genetic evidence, several scholars (Di Giacomo *et al.* 2004; King *et al.* 2008; Balaresque *et al.* 2010) argue that some of these communities were Anatolian migrants bearing the so-called Neolithic package and valley lifestyles similar to those from Konya. On the other hand, the local population might also have accepted the Anatolian influence resulting in the formation of tells. Regardless of the demographic character of the Thessalian Neolithic population, these communities founded their tells around Lake Karla, also drained in the 20th century (Grundmann 1937; Caputo *et al.* 1994; Perlès 2001; Alexakis *et al.* 2011). There are hundreds of tells in the vicinity of this lake that until recently have been considered the earliest Neolithic sites in Greece (Fig. 8.3). However, more recent research in Mavropigi and Paliambella confirms dates earlier than those from Thessaly (Karamitrou-Mentessidi *et al.* 2013; Kotsakis 2018). Thus, tells were not the earliest form of Neolithic settlements, inasmuch as they were preceded by villages on the slopes of mountains and hills, and only subsequently did they appear in valleys.

The phenomenon of tells spread from Thessaly to the Thessaloniki Plain and Amindeon (Greece), Korça (Albania), Pelagonia, Polog and Skopje Valley (Macedonia), Struma and Sliven (Bulgaria), Mačva (Serbia) and Visoko

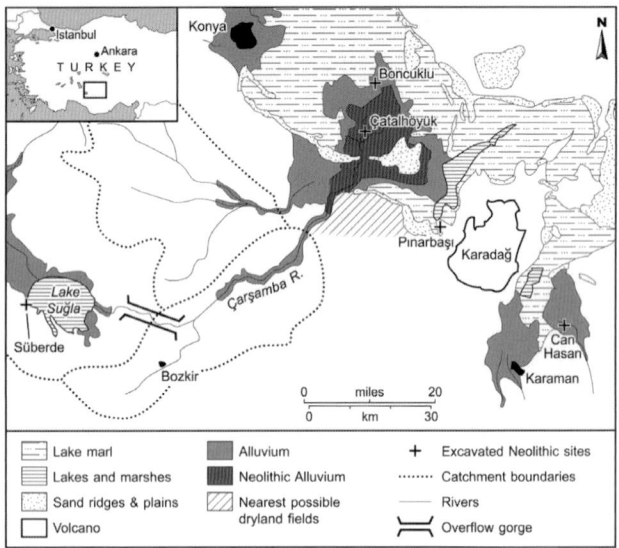

Figure 8.2 Neolithic sites, soils and wetlands in Konya plain (Turkey) (Baird et al. 2018, fig. 1).

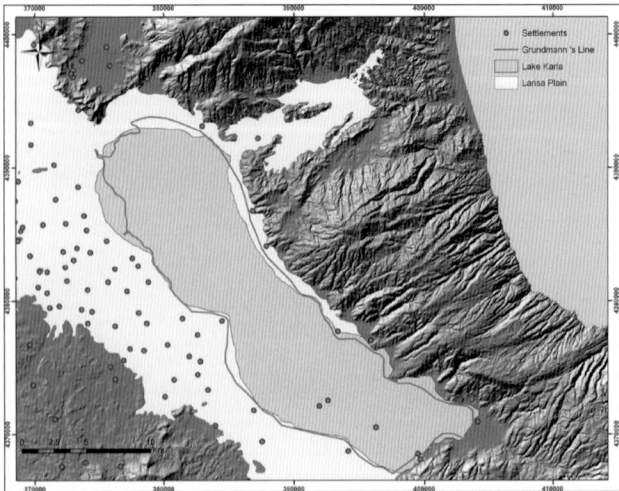

Figure 8.3 Location of now drained Lake Karla in Thessaly and the location of tells (Alexakis et al. 2011, fig. 4).

(Bosnia). The situation in Korça region is like that in Thessaly, namely, it contains the recently dried Lake Maliq, around which several Neolithic tells were established, such as Vashtëmi, Podgori and Sovian (Lera *et al.* 2002; Fouache *et al.* 2010). This is also the case with the Katlanovo Lake in the Skopje Valley (also dried up), in whose vicinity the tells of Madjari, Čair, Stajkovci, Aračinovo and Mrševci among others thrived (Tolevski & Stančevski 2017). Over time, variations in lake location and extension impacted the distribution of tells.

In the regions of Thessaly, Amindeon, Korça and the Skopje Valley, dried or active lakes have been confirmed. However, in other regions more variable wetland areas have been recorded, also dried up in the 20th century as part of melioration processes. This is especially evident in Pelagonia, with hundreds of tells immediate to wetlands (Simoska & Sanev 1976; Naumov 2016a). This region will be considered in detail in the remainder of this chapter to account for the natural, economic, social and symbolic processes associated with the formation of tells in such valleys. Settling the marshy areas was a practice in the Mačva region, where approximately 50 smaller tells (known as *obrovci*) are found (Tripković *et al.* 2013). Unlike other Balkan tells, *obrovci* consist of one or several buildings, so the question arises whether these are settlements or places of exclusively economic function. A large number of tells are also recorded in the region of Visoko, near the River Bosna, which flowed and formed smaller wetlands (Furholt 2012; Müller 2012). As far as Bulgaria and Romania are concerned, apart from the above-mentioned regions, the Danube area should be emphasised in particular. Due to the numerous tributaries and the frequent outflow of this massive river, wetlands have emerged which have been the motivation for numerous communities to establish tells in their vicinity (Benecke *et al.* 2013).

The last point in the dispersal of this tell phenomenon from the Middle East to Europe was the Körös region in the Carpathian Basin (Parkinson & Gyucha 2012). In this case tells are also often near rivers that frequently flood the surrounding area and form fertile soil. But as in the case with tells in southeastern Romania and northeastern Bulgaria, those in the Great Hungarian Plain were established later. The first tells in these regions occurred at the end of the Middle Neolithic and the Late Neolithic and they were particularly frequent in the Chalcolithic (Hansen 2015). This is probably due to the fact that the tell formation process was gradually slowing down and was not related to the establishment of the first pioneer settlements, but to agricultural communities that had a more developed social and economic structure. As mentioned above, it similarly manifested itself in the regions of Thessaly, Korça, Pelagonia, Struma and Skopje Valley, although these tells appeared at the end of the Early Neolithic.

Pelagonian tells

The Balkan Peninsula abounds in regions with high concentrations of tells, but in this case a special emphasis is to be placed on those recorded in Pelagonia (Macedonia). Pelagonia is an elongated valley surrounded by the Mountains of Baba, Buševa, Selečka, Dautica, Babuna, Nidje and Neredska, through which the River Crna flows with several smaller tributaries (Fig. 8.4). Due to this Neogene geographical structure, this valley contained a lake that flowed into the Aegean Sea during the Pliocene through the Crna and Vardar Rivers. This led to the formation of alluvial soils which would later play a key role in the formation of the first agricultural communities in this valley. In addition to such convenient geographical features, the Crna River frequently outflows and groundwater is aided by the melting of snow from the surrounding high mountains. Thus, massive seasonal wetlands were formed that flooded these soils and improved their agronomic quality. In sum, wetlands were suitable niches, offering numerous resources such as fish, birds, frogs, snakes, reeds and mud, all necessary for the nutrition and architecture of the first Neolithic communities in Pelagonia.

The important role of wetlands in Neolithic Pelagonia is confirmed by the very distribution of tells in their vicinity. The Bitolsko Pole area, located in central Pelagonia, has the largest number of tells and most of them are located around former wetlands dried up by land melioration processes in the 1960s (Simoska & Sanev 1976; Naumov 2016a; 2018). Although additional geo-archaeological research is needed for this region, such a distributional

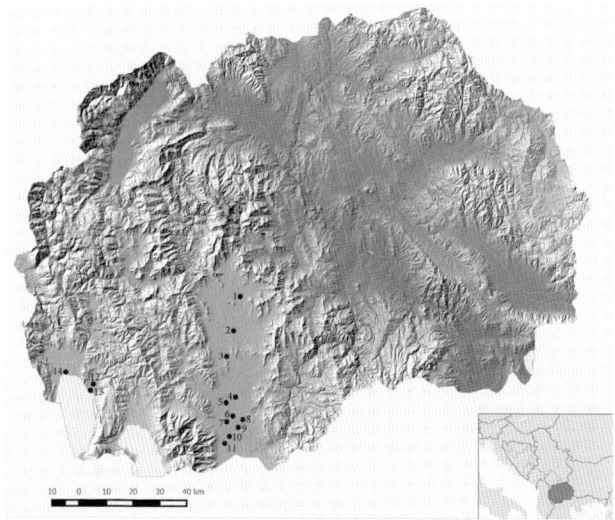

Figure 8.4 Map of Pelagonia with indication of excavated sites: 1. Ali Čair; 2. Vrbjanska Čuka; 3. Topolčani; 4. Radobor; 5. Mogila; 6. Trn; 7. Gurgur; 8. Optičari; 9. Kravari; 10. Tumba Porodin; 11. Veluška Tumba.

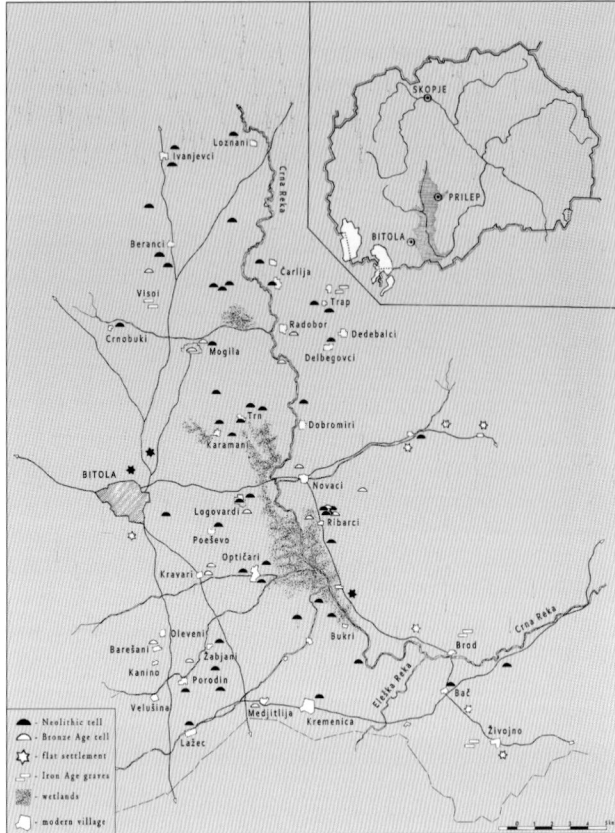

Figure 8.5 The position of tells in relation to wetlands in Pelagonia (Naumov 2016a, fig. 4; after Simoska & Sanev 1976).

layout of tells indicates that wetlands attracted Neolithic groups. Moreover, the geological research in the Prilepsko Pole area, in northern Pelagonia, confirms the existence of marshes with many tells in their surroundings (Naumov *et al.* 2018b). This clearly demonstrates that the present landscape is somewhat different from the prehistoric one, but the latest geological and archaeobotanical research, including GIS analysis, offer important insights into the Neolithic natural environment.

It is therefore apparent that one of the reasons for the rapid settling of Pelagonia in the Neolithic was the fertile soil near the wetlands. It should be noted that Mesolithic settlements are not yet recorded in this valley, although there is some scanty information on Palaeolithic tools (Kuzman 1995). Certainly, given the limited knowledge on sites from earlier prehistoric periods, the possible existence of Mesolithic sites in the valley or slopes cannot be rejected, but it is more than evident that the abrupt settling in this region occurred in the Neolithic. So far there are about 130 tells in Pelagonia and most of them date to the Early Neolithic (Fig. 8.5). This is confirmed by the archaeological excavations and surveys of the tells at Porodin, Optičari, Egri, Dobromiri, Kravari, Gurgur, Trn, Mogila, Karamani, Topolčani, Pašino Ruvci, Slavej, Vrbjani and others. In some areas, tells grouped next to each other (from two to six), indicate that these regions were particularly attractive and enabled a stable agricultural economy (Grbić *et al.* 1960; Simoska & Sanev 1975; 1976; 1977; Kitanoski 1977; 1989; Simoska *et al.* 1979; Simoska & Kuzman 1990; Naumov *et al.* 2018a).

As for the absolute chronology of these tells, it should be noted that some of them were established around 6000 BC, that is, between 6200 and 5800 cal BC (Naumov 2016b). This group of dates deviates from that of Topolčani, which can be placed in the mid-7th millennium BC, but its reliability is questionable. Namely, it is only one date, with a wide standard deviation, likely derived from a piece of wood older than its time of use. Such dates from the mid-7th millennium are known in Greece, so it should come as no surprise that such an early date also appears in Pelagonia. However, considering that it is only one sample, it is necessary to obtain further samples from this site in the future in order to verify this point. Unlike Topolčani, the dates from Vrbjanska Čuka, Veluška Tumba, Tumba Porodin, Tumba Sredselo and Tumba Optičari are based on multiple samples and are more reliable. They fall within the stated time span of several centuries *c.* 6000 cal BC, which can also be taken as the period of massive settling of Pelagonia by the first agricultural communities.

Apart from the Early Neolithic dates, the absolute chronology in Pelagonia also offers dates from the middle and second half of the 6th millennium BC, the whole of the 5th millennium BC, and *c.* 2000 BC, from sites near Mogila, Porodin, Markovi Kuli, Trn, Crnobuki and Karamani (Naumov 2016b). This means that tells were also occupied at the end of the Neolithic, as well as in the Chalcolithic and Bronze Age. Thus, this wetland area was attractive during most stages of later prehistory, except for the Iron Age, which is missing this kind of settlements.

Until recently it was considered that the tells in Pelagonia were of uniform character, *i.e.* they contained Neolithic villages with similar spatial organisation. However, in the last few years on dozens of tells geomagnetic scanning was intensively performed, giving new insights into the interior disposition of buildings and the appearance of Neolithic and Chalcolithic villages in general. The results of these studies demonstrate that not all tells are similarly organised (Fig. 8.5). Specifically, some of them are surrounded by ditches, others have linear or concentric layouts of buildings, and some have almost no buildings, as evidenced by the lack of burning of dwellings that actually provides the magnetic signals during this type of research (Naumov *et al.* 2016; 2017). This indicates that the social structure in the Neolithic settlements was not identical, which led to different settlement organisations. Although the tells are thought to be based on an ideological proposition that highlights the links between ancestors and subsequent building onto their houses (Kotsakis 1999; Nanoglou 2008), this symbolic and social principle was further developed and varied in relation to internal social conditions in each settlement separately.

This is partly reflected in the architecture and material culture recorded on Pelagonian tells. Although the Neolithic architecture contains many similarities, the building features are not the same everywhere. Current knowledge about the architecture in these tells is still modest, but it can be confirmed that their state of preservation and internal organisation are distinctive. Remains of buildings in the tells of Mogila, Optičari, Dobromiri, Gurgur and Topolčani are scanty (Simoska & Sanev 1976; Kitanoski et al. 1978; Simoska et al. 1979; Simoska & Kuzman 1990) as a result of their insubstantial construction techniques. Among these Pelagonian tells mud walls or structures are lacking. In addtion, the practice of accidental or intentional burning of Neolithic houses, especially characteristic of the Balkans (Tringham 1991; Stefanović 1997; Chapman 2000; Gheorghiu 2007), cannot be confirmed at these sites.

In contrast, on the tells at Porodin and Slavej, several buildings with clearly formed walls and internal clay installations have been recorded (Grbić et al. 1960; Kitanoski et al. 1990; Naumov et al. 2018b). These remains are certainly the result of the burning of walls, but it cannot be proven whether they were burned intentionally or accidentally. In any case, this has led to very well-preserved massive walls by which the structure is easily recognisable, i.e. the use of wooden poles and rods. But on the other hand, regardless of the presence of fire, the clay installations were solid and compact, so they were well preserved. In some of the buildings there are more such structures for processing and storing cereals, i.e. bread preparation and baking, which also speaks to the different social structure of the communities in these settlements. Compared to these settlements, no such installations were registered at the aforementioned sites without preserved building walls. This state of affairs is not due to the fact that these buildings were not burned, but to the general absence of this type of massive installation used for economic activities. This may partly be a consequence of the modest amount of research on these sites but it is also due to the fact that communities from these Neolithic villages stored and processed grain differently and also baked the bread in diverse ways.

Such differences in architecture are also reflected in the material culture of the Pelagonian agricultural communities. Pelagonia is traditionally considered as part of the Velušina-Porodin group (Garašanin 1979; Sanev 1994), primarily due to similar features in the typology and decoration of the vessels, anthropomorphic house models, altars, figurines, etc. (Fig. 8.6). However, despite the unified character and the impressive nature of these artefacts, local particularities can be observed in the design of these objects or in the prevalence of certain finds in some sites and their rarity in others. This is especially true in the domain of pottery and house models. In the central part of Pelagonia, white decorated vessels and models with prominent anthropomorphic and architectural elements dominated, while in the northern region the reduced anthropomorphic features and black pale painted decoration were more common. But in any case, the sites throughout the valley yield magnificent vessels, altars and figurines, which attest to the social and artistic achievements of the first farmers in the region.

These regional features indicate that the Neolithic communities in Pelagonia had a prominent identity that, except in relation to the Lake Ohrid region, was not equal to those living north and east of this valley (Naumov 2015; 2018). Although significant changes in material culture occurred in the first half of the 6th millennium BC within the Amzabegovo-Vršnik cultural group common for the upper half of Macedonia (Sanev 1995), the elements of visual identity in Pelagonia did not change. White painted pottery, vessel shapes, house models with anthropomorphic cylinders, and further artefacts remained unchanged until the Late Neolithic, when most items within the Trn cultural group significantly transformed and some of them disappeared. Such was the case with anthropomorphic house models and altar-tablets with architectural features, which were not produced in Late Neolithic Pelagonia. These artefacts were particularly common for the Early Neolithic in this valley, when communities focused their ideology on houses by massively producing clay models that depicted their habitats or other buildings (Simoska & Sanev 1976; Naumov 2013). The anthropomorphic equivalents of this category of objects emphasise the strong connection between particular individuals and structures by identifying them within the symbolic hybrid relationship of the human body with the buildings (Sanev 2006; Chausidis 2010; Naumov 2014). In this way the important role of certain members of the community was probably emphasised, so these items were also used as commemorative resources. The practice of burying the dead under or near buildings in many Neolithic sites in the Balkans can also be mentioned in the context of such an identification between houses and individuals (Bacvarov 2003; Naumov 2013). However, this practice was not present at all in the tells in Pelagonia, where no Neolithic burial has been uncovered so far. Unlike the Neolithic, these tells were often used as necropolises for the medieval population living in their vicinity (Simoska et al. 1979; Simoska & Kuzman 1990; Mitkoski 2005; Naumov et al. 2018b).

Vrbjanska Čuka as a case study

Perhaps one of the best explored tells in Pelagonia that provides in-depth knowledge of the first agricultural communities in the region is Vrbjanska Čuka. The site was discovered in the late 1970s and was excavated in the following

Figure 8.6 Early Neolithic pottery, figurines and house models from 'Tumba' and 'Veluška Tumba' at Porodin in Pelagonia: 1. h – 48 cm (Fidanoski 2009, pl. 66, 7); 2. w – 23 cm (Fidanoski 2009, pl. 66, 5); 3. h – 17 cm (Fidanoski 2009, pl. 67, 3); 4. h – 7 cm (Kolištrkoska-Nasteva 2005, fig. 7); 5. h – 12 cm (Kolištrkoska-Nasteva 2005, fig. 26); 6. h – 6 cm (Kolištrkoska-Nasteva 2005, fig. 5); 7. no scale (Vasileva 2005, 40); 8. h – 25 cm (Kolištrkoska-Nasteva 2005, fig. 43); 9. no scale (Vasileva 2005, 40).

decade, when initial and important information regarding the Neolithic settlement was obtained (Kitanoski 1989; Kitanoski *et al.* 1990; Mitkoski 2005). Over the last five years, this site has been studied by international teams applying multidisciplinary methods, providing more thorough insights into its chronology, architecture, material culture, economy, social structure and rituals (Naumov *et al.* 2016; 2018a; 2018a). The results of research conducted at Vrbjanska Čuka provide a better understanding of Pelagonian agricultural societies in the 6th millennium BC (Fig. 8.7).

This site is in northern Pelagonia, on the plain between Selečka and Buševa Mountain, near the villages of Slavej and Vrbjani (Fig. 8.8). It is placed on a natural sand elevation formed by a Neogene lake, whose leakage resulted in alluvial soil. In the Neolithic this fertile soil attracted the settling of first farmers. An additional factor in the choice of this location was the presence of marshy land, a few kilometres southeast of the tell, in line with the settlement pattern of tells in the Balkans (Naumov *et al.* 2018b). Apart from Blato, there are no other rivers near the tell today, but channels can be seen in the area that probably belonged to tributaries or larger streams.

In 2016 and 2019, digital topography of the tell precisely determined its volume and height (Naumov *et al.* 2016), after initial information from the 1980s on its occupation area (Kitanoski 1989; Mitkoski 2005). According to recent measurements, the tell is 4 m high and has a diameter of 130 m, making it one of the largest of such sites in northern Pelagonia. However, its size and height are smaller than Thessalian and Anatolian tells, partly due to its relatively short Neolithic occupation and the absence of further prehistoric inhabitation. It was reused in Late Antiquity and the Middle Ages, when the tell lost its settlement character and hosted economic and ritual purposes. This is also confirmed by the tell stratigraphy, studied more thoroughly in recent archaeological campaigns. Unlike research in the 1980s, when it was thought to have housed only one Neolithic layer

Figure 8.7 View on Vrbjanska Čuka tell (photo: G. Naumov).

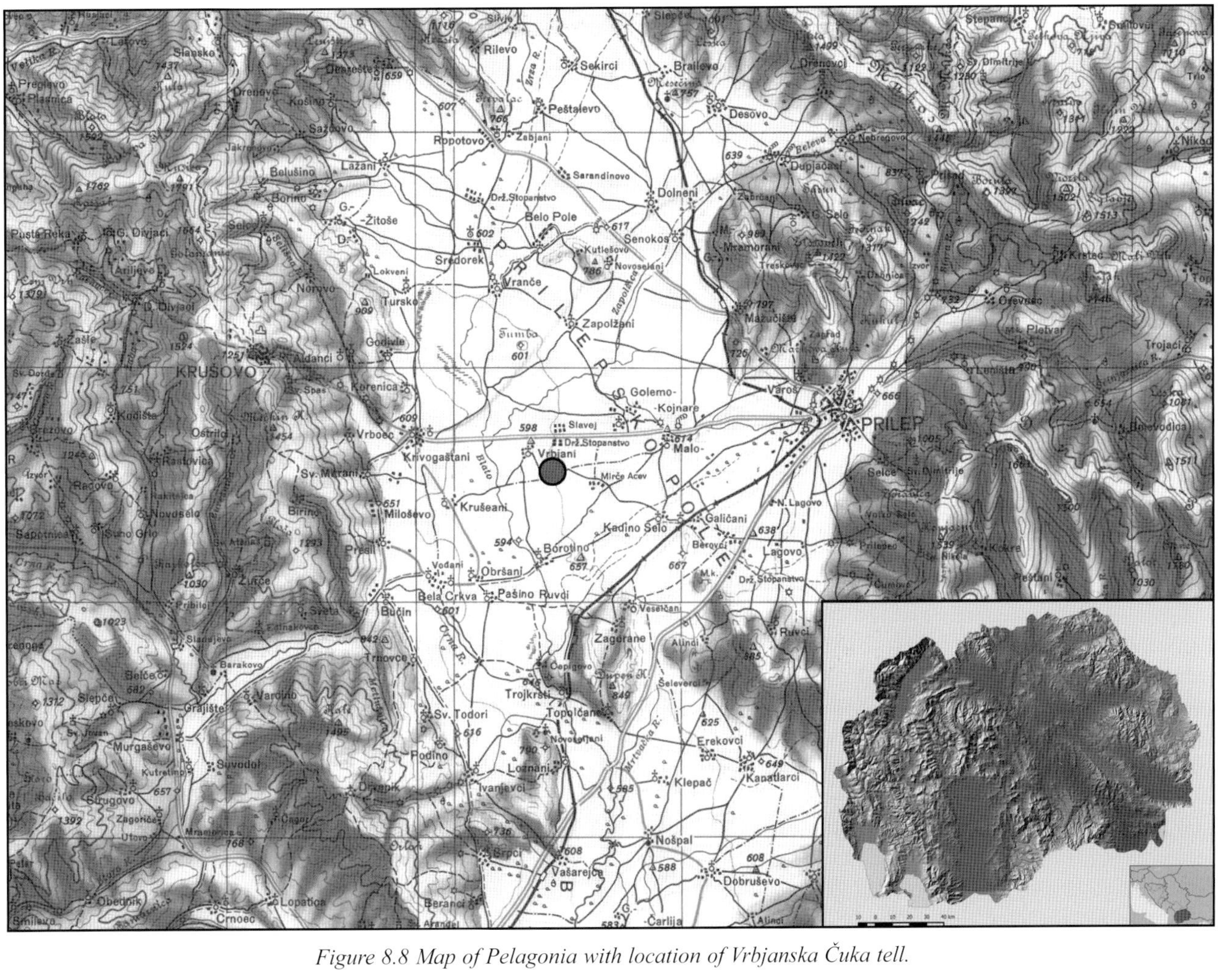

Figure 8.8 Map of Pelagonia with location of Vrbjanska Čuka tell.

and classical and medieval phases (Kitanoski 1989), recent studies have established a much more complex stratigraphy at this site (Naumov *et al.* 2018b). Indeed, the Neolithic period consists of three architectural horizons, with several layers of building and activities within them. In the earliest Neolithic horizon, there are two phases of sun-dried (*i.e.* unburnt) daub buildings. The superimposed horizon features massive burnt-daub buildings, which may be the result of accidental conflagration or deliberate burning of the walls. Above them is the latest Neolithic horizon, with several layers that combine dry daub and non-intensely burnt daub techniques. After a hiatus of five and a half millennia, a Late Antiquity horizon was formed on the tell with economic-residential buildings (*villa rustica*) and storage pits. Above them a medieval horizon is more complex than previously thought: the tell was used as a necropolis and storage area, whose deeply dug pit silos significantly damaged the Neolithic horizons.

The rich organic remains discovered during excavations in recent years have allowed intensive sampling for radiocarbon-dating, analyses of seeds, lipids and isotopes in animal bones. Thus, the abundance of radiocarbon dates enable an accurate determination of the site's chronology, whose origin can be set *c.* 6000 BC and its end *c.* 5700 BC (Naumov *et al.* 2018b). These dates demonstrate that the settlement was active in the later stages of the Early Neolithic, before the appearance of the great hiatus until Late Antiquity. This is also confirmed by Early Neolithic material culture, such as white painted pottery, clay altars with stair like legs, anthropomorphic models and figurines with belts and prominent thighs (Fig. 8.9). This dating of Vrbjanska Čuka largely coincides with that of several tells in Central Pelagonia (Naumov 2016b), indicating that almost the entire valley was originally inhabited by the first farmers from about 6000 BC. The close chronology between these settlements may also explain the likelihood of mutual communication, which also explains the similarities among their objects. Nonetheless, the first agricultural communities in Pelagonia also exhibited remarkable differences, especially in the domain of architecture. This is confirmed by the excavations of several buildings on this site, but also by the geomagnetic scanning that took place in 2016. The results of this research, which was also carried out at several other tells near Vrbjanska Čuka, show that there was a ditch around the settlement (Naumov *et al.* 2016). In the southeastern part of this ditch there was an entrance to the Neolithic village, after which a wider empty area without buildings can be seen (Fig. 8.10). The buildings are in the southwestern and central part of the tell, orientated in east–west and southeast to northwest directions. In the central part of the settlement they are particularly densely built, and some of them are larger in size than others. Together with the excavated buildings, geomagnetic surveys point to the presence of about 25 features whose chronology remains uncertain. In any case, given the radiocarbon dates, most of them might belong to the Early Neolithic unless some of the magnetic signals actually refer to Late Antiquity and medieval buildings.

Regarding the Neolithic architecture of Vrbjanska Čuka, detailed information has been obtained in recent campaigns, both on the technical character of the buildings and their layering. Approximately 17 buildings have been registered so far, three of which have been studied in detail while the others will be excavated in the coming years (Naumov *et al.* 2018b). As mentioned above, the buildings contain different technological features, characteristic of various phases of the settlement, including unburnt daub, burned walls, dug-in structures and pit-houses paved with clay mortar. In addition to their construction techniques, some of these buildings have complex interiors consisting of several clay structures, which point to the apparent differences in relation to those of other tells in Pelagonia. In this context, it is worth emphasising Building 2 as one of the more specific buildings and at the same time one of those fully exposed (Fig. 8.11). It is a 10 × 13 m building and is by far the largest and most complex Neolithic building in Macedonia (Naumov *et al.* 2018a). Its walls are made up of small and large piles with applied daub subsequently burned. Next to the north wall there is another compact whitish smeared clay, so it is unclear whether it is part of Building 2 or of any other structure fastened to it (an unprecedented one-off case in Macedonia). Next to the south wall there is a row of larger pits, probably for pillars that held the eaves or a floor at the top, for which no data is available. In the middle of the building, there are several massive pits, arranged along its length, which were used to insert the pillars holding the roof. Inside Building 2, 11 clay structures (ovens, bins, circular structures and grain milling platforms) have been recorded, making it particularly complex and unique in terms of its interior (Naumov *et al.* 2018a). There were also *c.* 30 grinding querns in its interior, all upside down, indicating a likely abandonment ritual. In addition to this is the incredibly small number of finds detected inside the building and the effects of fire. The absence of whole pots and the small number of fragments indicate the cleaning of the building prior to its abandonment, followed by its deliberate conflagration, also documented at several Neolithic sites in the Balkans (Tringham 1991; Chapman 2000).

Apart from Building 2, also Building 1, Building 4, Building 6 and Building 9 are composed of walls made of daub. Varied clay installations are also recorded in Building 4, while Building 1 has one of the most impressive interior structures in the Balkans. It is a massive granary consisting of one large and eight smaller bins attached to it, half of which were destroyed by building activities (Fig. 8.12). The large bin is decorated with stair-like applications identical to those on the altars (one of those found in its interior), giving the exceptional symbolic character to this large structure,

Figure 8.9 Pottery, figurines, tablets and house models from Vrbjanska Čuka (photo: A. Mitkoski).

with a length of 4 m (Kitanoski *et al.* 1990; Mitkoski 2005). This further emphasises the unique character of the Neolithic architecture of Vrbjanska Čuka and sets this site apart from others in Pelagonia and beyond. It also indicates the complex social structure of the community that lived in this neighbourhood.

In addition to the high technical and aesthetic capabilities of the Neolithic population in this tell, the material culture is equally impressive in its appearance and craftsmanship. It has the characteristics of Velušina-Porodina group, but it also stands out with more unique features that are present only at Vrbjanska Čuka. This mostly refers to vessels that follow the typology common to the Pelagonian Valley, yet feature distinctive decorations. These vessels include fine fabrics, especially plates, bowls and jars, which, unlike other sites in Macedonia, were made in large number. Although some of them have rare white painting, they are still dominated by thin painted lines, bent and straight

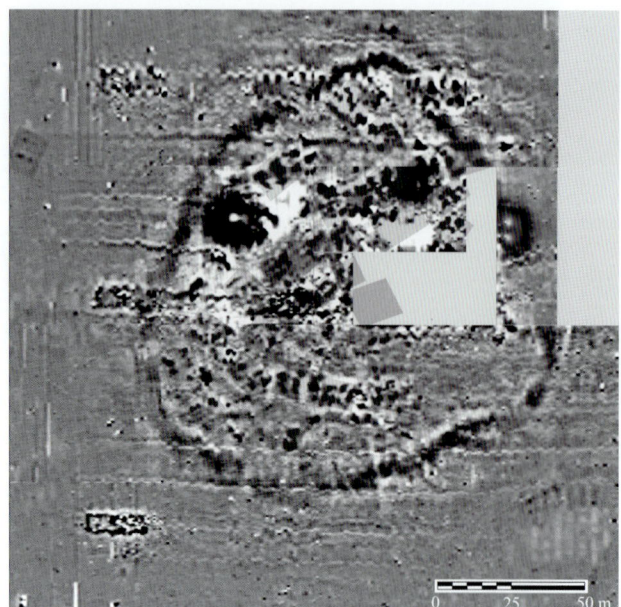

Figure 8.10 Plan from geomagnetic scanning of Vrbjanska Čuka (Naumov et al. 2016, fig. 19).

strips in black diluted colour. Except in very rare cases, they are not present in Pelagonia, so they are highlighted as features typical of Vrbjanska Čuka only. Of course, pottery with a coarser fabric, used for cooking and storage, is also present, but it has the usual general typology and rarely bears distinguished individual characteristics (Naumov *et al.* 2016; 2018b).

Further artefacts exhibit a highly symbolic character, including house models, altars, figurines, *etc*. Unlike anthropomorphic models in Central Pelagonia, those discovered at Vrbjanska Čuka are stylised and rarely feature elements that display human and architectural motifs. The cylinders have almost no anthropomorphic features, and the house representation is particularly stylised. But in any case, they follow the symbolic component common to this kind of object in Pelagonia and correspond to the commemorative ideology and their purpose as lamps. Numerous altars in the form of tablets with serrated legs, which have traces of burning and most likely served predominantly ritual functions, should also be considered. Figurines are also distinguished by their local specificity, though they contain some elements

Figure 8.11 Excavation area of Vrbjanska Čuka (20 × 20 m) with indication of Building 2 (red), Building 4 (green), Building 9 (blue) and Building 11 (yellow) (photo: H. Talevski).

Figure 8.12 3D model of granary from Vrbjanska Čuka (4 m wide) (Naumov et al. 2018b, fig. 15).

present in their equivalents from Central Pelagonia. They are mostly stylised, with cylindrical bodies, short arms, wide thighs and faces with only eyes present, albeit in rare cases (Naumov *et al.* 2016).

The round or ellipsoid projectiles made of clay could be included among the items for manual use, which are found in very large numbers, an occurrence common for sites in Pelagonia, but rare on others in Macedonia. As far as the tools are concerned, they contain the usual repertoire of Neolithic sites. The axes are relatively common and of medium and smaller size, while larger ones are rare. The flint tools are also present in large numbers and have been subjected to use wear analysis. This research demonstrates that most of them were used for harvesting, which corresponds with the major activities of the population living on this tell (Naumov *et al.* 2018b). In this vein, grinding stones have been discovered in large numbers from all phases and buildings, such as the abovementioned Building 2. The starch analysis performed on some of the querns indicates that they were used for grinding cereals and acorns (Beneš *et al.* 2018; Naumov *et al.* 2018b).

Regarding organic remains and the economy, it should be emphasized that archaeobotanical analyses were also carried out at Vrbjanska Čuka, which gave a thorough insight into the diet of the population and the vegetation around the site. The most common foods are cereals (wheat and barley), lentils and peas, and wild plants such as blackberries, elder, sloe, white orache, pigweed and knotgrass. Organic remains within buildings demonstrate the processing and use of herbs in the diet and economy, while others, especially the wild plants and snails, indicate wetlands in the vicinity of the settlement (Naumov *et al.* 2018b). As for meat consumption, zooarchaeological analyses also emphasise the high representation of cattle over sheep, goats and pigs, a picture different from the patterns from other Balkan sites where goats were preferred. The diet also included deer meat, doe, wild boar and foxes, although further raw materials (tools, tendons or fur) were also obtained from these animals. It should also be highlighted that lipid analyses on vessels indicate residues of dairy products, oils, ruminant fats and plants (Naumov *et al.* 2018b, Stojanovski *et al.* in prep.). All the aforementioned analyses point to the nutritional diversity of the Neolithic population of Vrbjanska Čuka, but also to the complex economy and rich flora and fauna in the surroundings of the tell.

Conclusion

Vrbjanska Čuka is a good example of why and how tells appeared in Pelagonia. It is a site that has no pre-Neolithic developmental phases, but immediately, from the earliest stages, it was established as an economic center focused on agriculture. Although Vrbjanska Čuka stands out from the other Pelagonia tells, especially in the domain of architecture, other settlements of this kind have similar formation processes. None of the tells explored so far has an initial phase in which the settlement adapted to the surroundings and gradually developed itself into a stable Neolithic village. On the contrary, all Early Neolithic tells established themselves as settlements with an impressive material culture that exhibited extremely high technical and aesthetic qualities from their very beginning and was not the result of experimentation. This demonstrates that those who used these objects and lived in these settlements arrived as already determined communities with a very clear purpose – the discovery of fertile soil and access to rich resources.

Where these communities came from and how they arrived is a topic that cannot be discussed here, although the similarities with the material culture and settlement concept present earlier in Thessaly are evident. The similarity in the early chronology among the Pelagonian tells again indicates that this process occurred relatively quickly, at a certain period *c.* 6000 cal BC. This means that the farming communities were looking for a specific space in which they could realize their own economic and subsistence goals, a process that probably followed the pioneering examination of the new environment. It should be noted here that so far none of the tells in Pelagonia features Mesolithic or Early Neolithic aceramic phases. Therefore, the so-called camps of the Neolithic scouts should be expected at different locations from where the agricultural population was called upon or attracted to settle in the valley's marshy areas. This process may have been rapid, but it could also have been gradual, so that Pelagonia became attractive to more communities. This is also confirmed by the already established pattern of tell formation present in Thessaly and Anatolia, which was apparently applied in Pelagonia as well. The first agricultural communities were focused on the exploitation of new areas, especially wetland valleys around which was an abundance of fertile soil. It was there that they formed smaller settlements which were intensely renewed and layered. Instead of expanding their villages, these communities built new buildings onto the older ones, so that they occupied a small spot, while also establishing strong bonds with their ancestors. So far, no intramural burials have been detected on the Pelagonian Neolithic tells, which would reinforce this intergenerational symbolic relationship. Most of them, however, have an abundance of anthropomorphic house models, and hybridized depictions of human-like architecture used as commemorative lamps. In this way, respect for the ancestors was emphasized and the relationship with them ritually strengthened. Consequently, these tells became symbolic entities that not only encompassed the essence of the agricultural economy, but also asserted the relationship between the generations that created and renewed these settlements.

Therefore, these settlements can unequivocally be referred to as tells of domestication and ancestry, since they finalise the long process of domestication of plants and animals and affirm themselves as an already formed economic and symbolic entity that disperses from the Middle East to Southeastern Europe. The primary motive for their establishment and continuous renewal was agriculture, an economic concept that was intended to locate and exploit a fertile area. The symbolic perception of this architectural space was immediately or gradually upgraded to it as a basis for establishing symbolic links between the first and subsequent inhabitants of the tells. In that sense, the study area represents a remarkable encirclement of this economic and symbolic concept manifested through anthropomorphic house models and the multitude of tells distributed around the wetland areas of the valley.

Vrbjanska Čuka, which follows this process, stands out as a separate center in which technological investment in the field of architecture was made. The massive buildings and granaries, as well as the multitude of clay installations in their interiors, emphasize the distinctiveness of this settlement and the population living there. Not only did they build these fascinating structures, but they also had an outstanding material culture consisting of fine pottery, anthropomorphic models, figurines, altars, and so on. These technical and aesthetic achievements are not only the result of the cognitive and manual abilities of the inhabitants of Vrbjanska Čuka, but also of the economic power they possessed over the hitherto known Neolithic settlements in Pelagonia. It stood out from the rest of the regions as an economic hub focused on the accumulation and processing of cereals. Of course, this economic act should not be understood solely through the prism of the economy, since the massive and numerous clay installations (granaries and bins) for storing and processing wheat and barley were decorated with identical applied motifs as those of small clay altars. It shows that the tells of domestication, at least in Pelagonia, were an economic and semantic entity that integrated the cultivation of agricultural crops, as well as their symbolic protection and reproduction.

References

Alexakis, D., Sarris, A., Astaras, T. & Albanakis, K. (2011) Integrated GIS, remote sensing and geomorphologic approaches for the reconstruction of the landscape habitation of Thessaly during the Neolithic period. *Journal of Archaeological Science* 38, 89–100.

Assouti, E. & Hather, J. (2001) Charcoal analysis and the reconstruction of ancient woodland vegetation in the Konya Basin, south-central Anatolia, Turkey: Results from the Neolithic site of Çatalhöyük East. *Vegetation History and Archaeobotany* 10, 23–32.

Ayala, G., Wainwright, J., Walker, J., Hodara, R., Lloyd, J.M., Lend, M. & Doherthy, C. (2017) Paleoenvironmental reconstruction of the alluvial landscape of the Neolithic Çatalhöyük, central southern Turkey: The implications for early agriculture and responses to environmental changes. *Journal of Archaeological Science* 87, 30–43.

Baćvarov, K. (2003) *Neolitni pogrebalni obredi*. Sofia, Bard.

Bailey, D. (2002) What is a tell? Settlement in fifth millennium Bulgaria. In J. Brück, & M. Goodman (eds), *Making Places in the Prehistoric World: Themes in Settlement Archaeology*, 94–111. Cambridge, University of Cambridge.

Baird, D., Fairbairn, A., Jenkins, E., Martin, L., Middleton, L., Pearson, J., Asouti, E., Edwards, Y., Kabukcu, C., Mustafaoğlu, G., Russell, N., Bar-Yosef, O., Jacobsen, G., Wu, X., Baker, A. & Elliott, S. (2018) Agricultural origins of Anatolian plateau. *Proceedings of the National Academy of Sciences* 115(14), 3077–3086.

Balaresque, P., Bowden, G.R., Adams, S., Leung, H., King, T., Roser, Z.T., Goodwin, J., Moisan, J., Richard, C., Millward, A., Demaine, A.G., Barbujani, G., Previdere, C., Wilson, I.J, Tyler-Smith, C. & Jobling, M.A. (2010) A predominantly Neolithic origin of European paternal lineages. *PLoS Biology* 8(1), 1–9.

Benecke, N., Hansen, S., Nowacki, D., Reingruber, A., Ritchie, K. & Wunderlich, J. (2013) Pietrele in the lower Danube region. *Documenta Praehistorica* 40, 175–193.

Beneš, J., Naumov, G., Majerovičová, T., Budilová, K., Bumerl, J., Komárková, V., Kovárník, J., Vychronová, M. & Juřičková, L. (2018) An archaeobotanical onsite approach to the Neolithic settlements in southern regions of the Balkans: The case of Vrbjanska Čuka, a tell site in Pelagonia, Republic of Macedonia. *Interdisciplinaria Archaeologica* 9, 121–145.

Caputo, R., Bravard, J.P. & Helly, B. (1994) The Pliocene-Quaternary tectosedimentary evolution of the Larissa Plain (eastern Thessaly, Greece). *Geodinamica Acta* 7(4), 219–231.

Chapman, J. (2000) *Fragmentation in Archaeology: People, Places and Broken Objects in the Prehistory of South-eastern Europe*. London, Routledge.

Chausidis, N. (2010) Neolithic ceramic figurines in the shape of a woman – house from the Republic of Macedonia. In D. Gheorghiu & A. Cyphers (eds), *Anthropomorphic and Zoomorphic Miniature Figures in Eurasia, Africa and Meso-America: Morphology, Materiality, Technology, Function and Context*, 25–35. Oxford, British Archaeological Report Ss 2138.

Di Giacomo, F., Luca, F., Popa, L.O., Akar, N., Anagnou, N., Banyko, J., Brdicka, R., Barbujani, G., Papola, F., Ciavarella,

G., Cucci, F., Di Stasi, L., Gavrila, L., Kerimova, M.G., Kovatchev, D., Kozlov, A.I., Loutradis, A., Mandarino, V., Mammi, C., Michalodimitrakis, E.N., Paoli, G., Pappa, K.I., Pedicini, G., Terrenato, G., Toffaneli, S., Malaspina, P. & Novelletto, A. (2004) Y Cheomosomal haplogroup J as a signature of the post-Neolithic colonization of Europe. *Human Genetics* 115, 357–371.

Evans, J.G. (2005) Memory and ordination: environmental archaeology in tells. In D. Bailey, A. Whittle & V. Cummings (eds), *(Un)settling the Neolithic*, 112–125. Oxford, Oxbow Books.

Fidanoski, L. (2009) Pottery production. In G. Naumov, L. Fidanoski, I. Tolevski & A. Ivkovska (eds), *Neolithic Communities in the Republic of Macedonia*, 65–80. Skopje, Dante.

Fouache, E., Desruelles, S., Magny, M., Bordon, A., Oberweiler, C., Coussot, C., Touchais, G., Lera, P., Lezine, A.M., Fanin, L. & Roger, R. (2010) Paleogeographical reconstruction of Lake Maliq (Korca Basin, Albania) between 14,000 BP and 2000 BP. *Journal of Archaeological Science* 37, 525–535.

Furholt, M. (2012) Kundurci: Developement of social space in a Late Neolithic Tell-settlement in central Bosnia. In R. Hofmann, F.K. Moetz & J. Müller (eds), *Tells: Social and Environmental Space*, 203–220. Bonn, Habelt.

Garašanin, M. (1979) Centralnobalkanska zona. In A. Benac (ed.), *Praistorija Jugoslavenskih Zemalja II – Neolitsko doba*, 79–212. Sarajevo, Akademija nauke i umetnosti Bosne i Hercegovine.

Gheorghiu, D. (2007) *Fire as An Instrument: The Archaeology of Pyrotechnologies*. Oxford, British Archaeological Report S1619.

Grbić, M., Mačkić, P., Nad, Š., Simoska, D. & Stalio, B. (1960) *Porodin: kasno-neolitsko naselje na Tumbi kod Bitolja*. Bitolj, Narodni muzej.

Grundmann, K. (1937) Magula Hadzimissiotiki. Eine steinzeitlichen Siedlung im Karla-See. *Athenische Mitteilungen* 62, 56–62.

Hansen, S. (2015) Pietrele: A Lakeside Settlement, 5200–4250. In S. Hansen, P. Raczky, A. Anders & A. Reingruber (eds), *Neolithic and Copper Age Between the Carpathians and the Aegean Sea: Chronologies and Technologies from the 6th to the 4th Millennium BCE*, 273–293. Bonn, Habelt.

Hofmann, R., Moetz, F.K. & Müller, J. (2012) *Tells: Social and Environmental Space*. Bonn, Habelt.

Karamitrou-Mentessidi, G., Efstratiou, N., Kozłowski, N., Kaczanowska, M., Maniatis, Y., Curci, A., Michalopoulou, S., Papathanasiou, A. & Valamoti, S.M. (2013) New evidence on the beginning of farming in Greece. The Early Neolithic settlement of Mavropigi in western Macedonia (Greece). *Antiquity* 87(336), Project Gallery. http://www.antiquity.ac.uk/projgall/mentessidi336/.

King, R.J., Özcan S.S., Carter, T., Kalfoglu, E., Atasoy, S., Triantaphyllidis, C., Kouvatsi, A., Lin, A.A., Chow, C.-E.T., Zhivotovsky, L.A., Michalodimitrakis, M. & Underhill, P.A. (2008) Differential Y-chromosome Anatolian influences on the Greek and Cretan Neolithic. *Annals of Human Genetics* 72(2), 205–214.

Kitanoski, B. (1977) Neolitskata naselba Čuka kaj selo Topolčani. *Macedoniae Acta Archaeologica* 3, 27–42.

Kitanoski, B. (1989) Vrbjanska Čuka. *Arheološki Pregled* 28, 47–48.

Kitanoski, B., Simoska, D. & Todorović, J. (1978) Novi arheološki istražuvanja na naselbata Čuka vo Topolčani kaj Prilep. *Macedonia Acta Archaeologica* 4, 9–32.

Kitanoski, B., Simoska, D. & Jovanović, B. (1990) Der Kultplatz auf der Fundstätte Vrbjanska Cuka bei Prilep. In D. Srejović & N. Tasić (eds), *Vinča and its World. International Symposium. The Danubian Region from 6000 to 3000 BC*, 107–112. Beograd, Serbian Academy of Science and Arts, Centre for Archaeological Research, Faculty of Philosophy.

Kolištrkoska-Nasteva, I. (2005) *Praistoriskite dami od Makedonija*. Skopje, Muzej na Makedonija.

Kotsakis, K. (1999) What tells can tell: Social space and settlement in the Greek Neolithic. In P. Halstead (ed.), *Neolithic Society in Greece*, 66–76. Sheffield, Sheffield Academic Press.

Kotsakis, K. (2018) Eating out: Food and social context in Early Neolithic of Greece. In M. Ivanova, B. Athanassov, V. Petrova, D. Tokorova & P.W. Stockhammer (eds), *Social Dimensions of Food in the Prehistoric Balkans*, 31–46. Oxford, Oxbow Books.

Kuzman, P. (1995) Podatoci za paleolitskite kulturi vo Makedonija. In G. Stardelov, C. Grozdanov & M. Mitevski (eds), *Civilizacii na počvata na Makedonija*, 11–20. Skopje, Makedonska akademija na nauite i umetnostite.

Lera, P., Touchais, G., Gardeisen, A., Renard, J. & Szepertyski, B. (2002) Sovjan (Albanie). *Bulletin de correspondance hellénique* 126(2), 627–645.

Mitkoski, A. (2005) Vrbjanska Čuka kaj seloto Slavej, Prilepsko. *Zbornik na Muzejot na Makedonija* 2, 33–46.

Müller, J. (2012) Tells, fire and copper as social technologies. In R. Hofmann, F.K. Moetz & J. Müller (eds), *Tells: Social and Environmental Space*, 47–52. Bonn, Habelt.

Nanoglou, S. (2008) Building biographies and households: Aspects of community life in the Neolithic of northern Greece. *Journal of Social Archaeology* 8, 139–160.

Naumov, G. (2013) Embodied houses: Social and symbolic agency of Neolithic architecture in the Republic of Macedonia. In D. Hoffman & J. Smyth (eds), *Tracking the Neolithic House in Europe – Sedentism, Architecture and Practice*, 65–94. New York, Springer.

Naumov, G. (2014) Neolithic privileges: The selection within burials and corporeality in the Balkans. *European Journal of Archaeology* 17(2), 184–207.

Naumov, G. (2015) Early Neolithic communities in the Republic of Macedonia. *Archeologické Rozhledy* LXVII(3), 331–355.

Naumov, G. (2016a) Tell communities and wetlands in the Neolithic Pelagonia, Republic of Macedonia. *Documenta Praehistorica* 43, 327–342.

Naumov, G. (2016b) Kalibrirana hronologija na neolitskite tumbi vo Pelagonija. In G. Naumov & L. Fidanoski (eds), *Neolit vo Makedonija: novi soznanija i perspektivi*. Centar za istražuvanje na predistorijata, 67–96. Skopje, Centar za istražuvanje na predistorijata.

Naumov, G. (2018) Formation of Wetland Identities in the Neolithic Balkans. In P. Shydlovskyi (ed.) *Prehistoric Networks in Southern and Eastern Europe*, 48–60. Kiev, Vita Antiqua Series 10.

Naumov, G., John, J. & Chvojka, O. (2017) Geophysical scanning of prehistoric tells in Central Pelagonia. In L. Fidanoski & G.

Naumov (eds), *Neolithic in Macedonia II: Step Forward in the Study of the First Farming Societies*, 161–180. Skopje, Center for Prehistoric Research.

Naumov, G., Mitkoski, A., Murgoski, A., Beneš, J., Przybila, M., Milevski, Đ., Komarkova, V., Vychronova, M. & Stoimanovski, I. (2016) Istražuvanje na Vrbjanska Čuka kaj Slavej – 2016. *Patrimonium* 14, 13–42.

Naumov, G., Mitkoski, A., Talevski, K. (2018a) Excavation Season in 2018 at Vrbjanska Čuka tell in Pelagonia. In L. Fidanoski & G. Naumov (eds), *Neolithic in Macedonia: Challenges for New Discoveries*, 35–55. Skopje, Center for Prehistoric Research.

Naumov, G., Mitkoski, A., Talevski, K., Murgoski, A., Beneš, J., Živaljević, I., Pendić, J., Stojanoski, D., Gibaja, F.J., Nicollo M., Hafner, A., Szidat, S., Dimitrijević, V., Stefanović, S., Budilova, K., Vychronova, M., Majerovičova, T., Bumerl, J. (2018ba) Research on the Vrbjanska Čuka site in 2017. *Balcanoslavica* 47(1), 253–285.

Parkinson, W. & Gyucha, A. (2012) Tells in perspective: Long-term patterns of settlement nucleation and dispersal in Central and Southeast Europe. In R. Hofmann, F.K. Moetz & J. Müller (eds), *Tells: Social and Environmental Space*, 105–116. Bonn, Habelt.

Perlès, C. (1999) The distribution of magoules in eastern Thessaly. In P. Halstead (ed.), *Neolithic Society in Greece*, 42–56. Sheffield, Sheffield Academic Press.

Perlès, C. (2001) *The Early Neolithic in Greece. The First Farming Communities in Europe*. Cambridge, Cambridge University Press.

Rosenstock, E. (2006) Early Neolithic tells settlements of Southeast Europe in their natural setting: A study in distribution and architecture. In I. Gatsov & H. Schwarzberg (eds), *Aegean – Marmara – Black Sea: The Present State of Research on the Early Neolithic*, 115–125. Langenweissbach, Beier and Beran.

Rosenstock, E. (2009) *Tells in Südwestasien und Südosteuropa. Verbreitung, Entstehung und Definition eines Siedlungsphänomens*. Remshalden, Urgeschichtliche Studien 2.

Sanev, M. (1994) Mlado kameno vreme. The neolithic period. In C. Grozdanov & D. Koco (eds), *Arheolośka karta na Repblika Makedonija 1 – Archaeological map of the Republic of Macedonia 1*, 26–42. Skopjem, Makedonska akademija na nauite i umetnostite.

Sanev, V. (1995) Neolitot i neolitskite culturi vo Makedonija. In G. Stardelov, M. Matevski & C. Grozdanov (eds), *Civilizacii na poćvata na Makedonija 2*, 21–46. Skopje, Makedonska akademija na nauite i umetnostite.

Sanev, D. (2006) Anthropomorphic cult plastic of Anzabegovo-Vršnik cultural groups of the Republic of Macedonia. In N. Tasić & C. Grozdanov (eds), *Homage to Milutin Garašanin*, 171–192. Belgrade, Serbian Academy of Sciences and Arts.

Simoska, D. & Kuzman, P. (1990) Tumba Optičari. *Arheološki Pregled* 1988, 63–66.

Simoska, D. & Sanev, V. (1975) Neolitska naselba Veluśka Tumba kaj Bitola. *Macedoniae Acta Archaeologica* 1, 25–85.

Simoska, D. & Sanev, V. (1976) *Praistorija vo Centralna Pelagonija*. Bitola, Naroden Muzej.

Simoska, D. & Sanev, V. (1977) Neolitska naselba na Mala Tumba kaj selo Trn, Bitola. *Macedonia Acta Archaeologica* 3, 215–237.

Simoska, D., Kitanoski, B. & Todorović, J. (1979) Neolitska naselba vo selo Mogila kaj Bitola. *Macedonia Acta Archaeologica* 5, 9–30.

Stefanović, M. (1997) The age of clay: The social dynamics of house destruction. *Journal of Anthropological Archaeology* 16, 334–395.

Tolevski, I. & Stančevski, I. (2017) Katlanovsko ezero-Blato i negovata okolina: kulturni impulsi od neolitskiot period. In L. Fidanoski & G. Naumov (eds), *Neolithic in Macedonia II: step forward in the study of the first farming societies*, 43–56. Skopje, Center for Prehistoric Research.

Tringham, R.E. (1991) Households with faces: The challenge of gender in prehistoric architectural remains. In J.M. Gero & M. Conkey (eds), *Engendering Archaeology. Women and Prehistory*, 93–131. Oxford, Blackwell.

Tripković, B., Cerović, M. & Bulić, D. (2013) Kulturno nasleđe Severozapadne Srbije: lokalitetit tipa 'Obrovac' četrdeset godina kasnije. In V. Filipović, R. Arsić & D. Anonović (eds), *Rezultati novih arheoloških istraživanja u Severozapadnoj Srbiji i susednih teritorijama*, 45–56. Belgrade, Srpsko arheološko društvo.

Vasileva, M. (2005) *Kade e našeto minato. Voved kon praistorijata na Pelagonija*. Bitola, Visoi.

9

Tells (and Flat Sites) as Social Agents: A View from Neolithic Greece

Stella Souvatzi

Introduction

This chapter argues for a multi-faceted approach to tells as the material expression of social relations and of time and history, and as fluid and only relatively immobile places. A major obstacle to approaching tells as social agents and as historical constructs is our tendency to contemplate a stylised view of them that is thoroughly static. Despite several alternative redefinitions and social interpretations of tells over the years concerned with context and history (*e.g.* Chapman 1997; in press; Bailey 1999; Evans 2005; Parkinson *et al.* 2018a; see also Chapman & Gaydarska 2018, 153–156 for a recent review), the prevailing image in the literature is still of a stable tell settlement, more or less firmly rooted in durable architecture, land and tradition, maintaining an unchanged space and developing, as a result, increasingly inflexible social relationships. Another problem relates to the continuing functionalist and adaptationist thinking, which views tells as passive responses to longer-term and larger-scale processes, environmental conditions and economic considerations, such as, for example, the idea that the spatial restriction, longevity and vertical rather than horizontal development of tell settlements resulted primarily from their location on fertile lands and a concern with the intensification of agricultural production. Finally, tells are also often treated as decontextualised or supra-contextual constructs and as spatially, economically and socially autonomous units. However, such views and images not only disregard agency, but also separate tells from the wider physical, social and cultural landscape in which they exist and with which they interact (*cf.* Gheorghiu 2008, 167). I suggest that we need to look instead into tells as loci of social action that incorporate dynamics, historicity, dialectics and all the complexity of life. To this end, it is essential to acknowledge and attempt to consider the interplay of multiple scales of space and time (*cf.* Souvatzi *et al.* 2018). Tells exist within a number of different spatialities and temporalities, from the intra- to the inter-site level, and from the 'long, slow form of temporality' of the growth of a mound (Chapman & Gaydarska 2018, 155) to the constant fluctuations at the small scale of everyday life.

A final note concerns the long discussion about the distinction of settlement types into tells and non-tells or flat sites. Much of this discussion has revolved around their differences, usually in terms of economy, land tenure, continuity and memory. However, the traditional over-emphasis

Table 9.1 Chronology and phases for the Greek Neolithic and the sites mentioned in the text (in alphabetical order).

Period	Date (cal BC)	Sites
Early Neolithic	6600/6500–6000	Argissa; Dikili Tash; Makrychori; Mavropigi; Nea Makri; Sesklo; Soufli Magoula
Middle Neolithic	6000/5980–5500	Argissa; Dikili Tash; Imvrou Pigadi; Koutroulou Magoula; Makri; Nea Makri; Platia Magoula Zarkou; Servia; Sesklo; Soufli Magoula; Visviki Magoula
Late Neolithic I	5500–5000	Argissa; Dikili Tash; Makri; Makrychori; Mandra; Nea Makri; Orgozinos; Platia Magoula Zarkou; Servia
Late Neolithic II	5000–4600	Argissa; Dikili Tash; Dimini; Mandra; Nea Makri; Palioskala; Servia; Sesklo
Final Neolithic	4600–3200	Argissa; Dikili Tash; Dimini; Mandra; Nea Makri; Palioskala

on the contrasts between tells and non-tells impedes the recognition of variation *within* either type of site as well as of similarities *between* the two types of site. Besides, tells themselves are not unitary or monolithic constructions. There can be considerable differences in their form, size, location, visibility, continuity and internal organisation, as well as considerable changes over time. We therefore need to look deeper into how social groups and communities formed their settlements and how they might have been connected with, or disconnected from, each other and with or from larger socio-economic groupings. In what follows, I attempt to explore what social practices, cultural understandings and ideological structures might have resulted in the creation and maintenance of tells (and of flat sites) in Neolithic Greece (7th–4th millennia BC) (Table 9.1). Special attention is directed to variation and flexibility, land uses, modes of social cohesion, history-making and the role of kinship.

Significant characteristics of Greek Neolithic tells (and flat sites)

All the Greek Neolithic tells (or *magoulas* in Greek) are anthropogenic habitation mounds. They result from the vertical superimposition of orderly arranged houses and compacted settlement layouts and the accumulation of habitation layers over hundreds or thousands of years.

Tells abound in the large plains and lowlands of central and northern Greece. In Thessaly alone (Fig. 9.1), the best-researched landscape in Neolithic Greece, the corpus of registered Neolithic tells amounts at present to more than to 440 (http://igean.ims.forth.gr/). But whether these regions could be characterised as 'landscapes of tells' (*cf.* Parkinson *et al.* 2018b) is questionable. Tell is no longer the only settlement type in the plains, as was believed until recently. Apart from the well-known example of Sesklo (Fig. 9.2), which combines a tell and flat settlement below, other previously unknown site combinations or multi-component sites are continuously

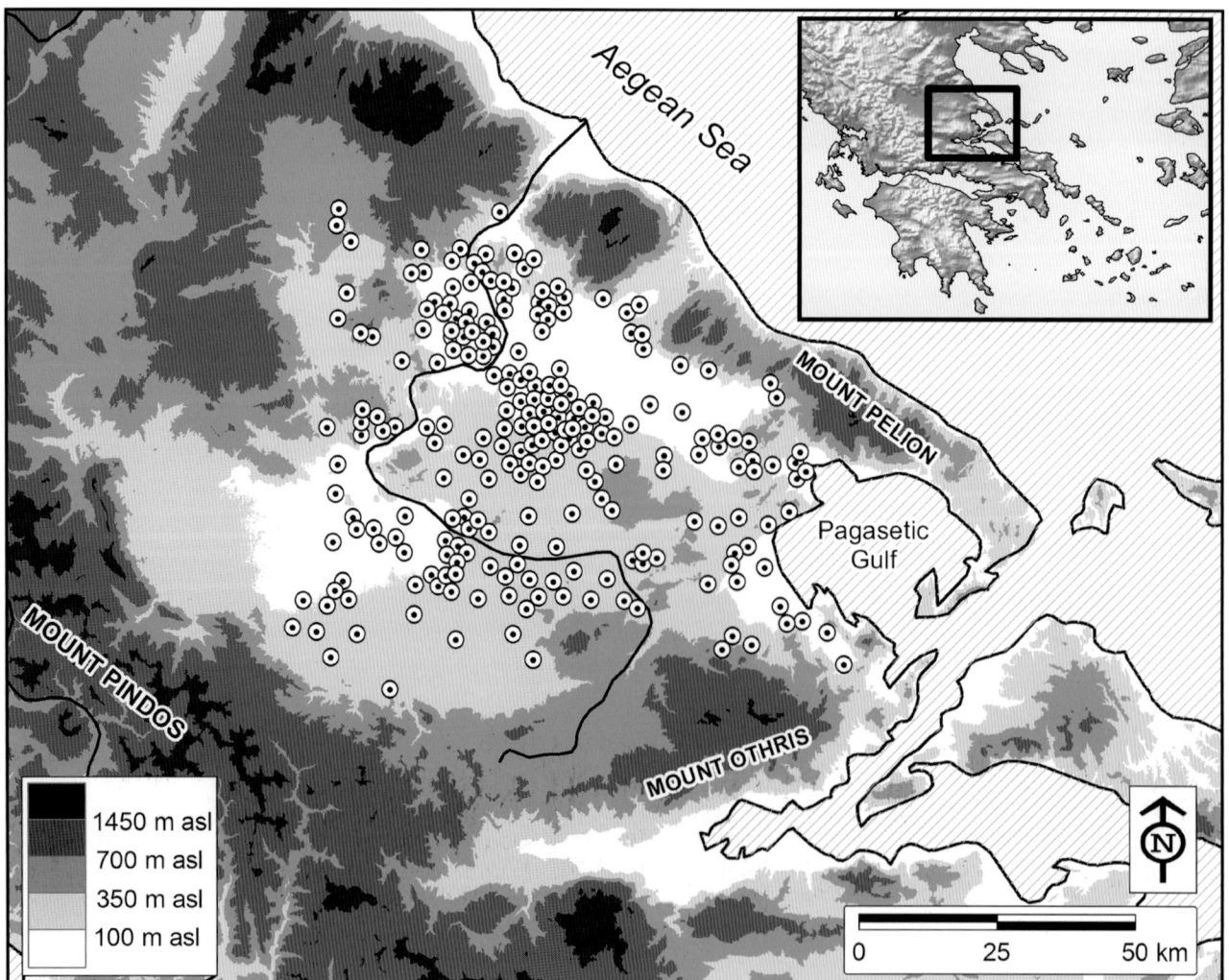

Figure 9.1 Map of Neolithic sites in Thessaly (redrawn from the map at Diachronic Museum of Larissa by Antonio Blanco González).

Figure 9.2 The tell of Sesklo at the beginning of excavation in the 1950s (Sesklo archive).

brought to light by recent research (see below). Besides, Greek Neolithic settlements overall show such a diversity of patterns, types, locations, principles of organisation, house forms, and building techniques and materials (see Souvatzi 2008, 161–175 for detailed discussion) that renders any generalisation simplistic. Tells and tell-like sites exist also in southern mainland Greece and the Aegean islands, along with flat sites, while other settlement types include nucleated hamlets, small rural sites, horizontal but non-shifting sites on prominent landscape settings (see Dietz *et al.* 2018; Sarris *et al.* 2017a; 2017b; Souvatzi 2008, 161–175 for overviews).

The substantial mudbrick, sometimes on stone foundations, or post-framed tell houses were free-standing and had rectangular or rectilinear plans, 1–3 rooms and sometimes also two-storeys, internal lofts, and basements. Together with their courtyards, the houses contain a rich inventory of facilities and finds, often found in place, indicating a wide range of activities, from subsistence to ritual. These include food processing, cooking and consumption, storage, cerami-, ornament, stone tool and textile production, domestic rituals (*e.g.* foundation offerings and symbolic sealing of house floors) and frequently human burials – primary or secondary – usually of children.

One important characteristic of Greek Neolithic tell architecture and design that usually goes unnoticed is the vital importance of open space. No matter how compacted a tell settlement layout may be (and there certainly existed tells with loosely spaced buildings – see below), none of the tell houses failed to be associated with some kind of open space, from the more private yards, sometimes in the form of porches or porticos, to the more shared and public lanes, passageways, and 'squares' or 'plazas' between clusters of houses or in the centre of tells. These important external spaces, with their carefully made floors, often stone-paved or pebbled, and built features, can contain hearths, ovens, storage, cooking and ritual structures or facilities, workshops, often specialised, including pottery 'kilns', food remains and complete pots. They apparently constituted an organic part of household space, of community space and of social life. This shows that 'domestic' and 'public' were not opposed but closely intertwined and that tells, despite their high-density housing, may not represent such an extremely packed way of living as we often believe. The range of practices within and outside households created more or less public kinds of interactions and brought people into a variety of social relations with each other.

This last point is further strengthened by another significant feature, the presence of large-scale architectural works, including spatial demarcation, segmentation and boundaries, common to both tells and flat sites alike. They range from concentric stone enclosures to perimeter ditches, single or multiple, and from habitation terraces to retaining walls. Such constructions are very widespread across Greece and throughout the Neolithic (see Souvatzi 2008, 175–178 and Toufexis 2017, 387–428 for syntheses). They connected different households into a larger corporate group, through exchange of labour and resources at different times. I return to these points later.

Extra-mural cemeteries are very rare in Neolithic Greece overall, in marked contrast to the abundance of settlements, and very few of them have been associated with tells thus far, two known examples being the cremation cemeteries at Platia Magoula Zarkou and at Soufli Magoula (Gallis 1982; 1996; Souvatzi in press). It seems that funerary rituals outside the settlement, whether tell or flat site, were not a particularly important means of ancestor veneration or of social identification, integration or distinction.

We know less about other off-tell activities as well as about flat sites, partly because for a long time research focused exclusively on the obtrusive tells (see also Krahtopoulou *et al.*, this volume, Chapter 3) and partly because the large plains of Thessaly and Macedonia have undergone important alluvial, lake, marshy and anthropogenic sedimentation, as well as agricultural modernisation (*e.g.* Orengo *et al.* 2015; Lespez *et al.* 2017; Caputo *et al.* in press; Krahtopoulou *et al.*, Chapter 3). Nevertheless, recent large-scale excavations, intensive surveys and geophysical investigations reveal that flat or low-elevated settlements of an extended and shifting habitation pattern, extensive open spaces and rather short-term occupation were a significant alternative to tells (see Krahtopoulou 2019 for a recent review). They exist along with habitation on mounds and were found buried under alluvia. A key characteristic is their large size, in some cases as much as 50–100 ha. However, this size results from the horizontal replacement of buildings and the important hiatuses observed at many of these sites. It has been suggested that in reality the population of tells and flat sites was largely comparable (Isaakidou & Halstead 2018, 66–81). This, in addition to the shared presence of boundaries, would be one more reason not to exaggerate the contrasts between flat and tell villages.

Tell biographies and fixity vs. flexibility

Similarly, there is no reason *a priori* to assume that tells remained static and stable or that they retained the same internal organisation over time. The persistent view of tell settlements as representing spatial fixity and social inflexibility or at best as 'immobile places within a landscape in flux' (Gheorghiu 2008, 172) denies agency to tells and their inhabitants. It also risks both disregarding the flexibility of spatial boundaries of social groups and collapsing the multiple time scales embedded in a tell.

First of all, as Chapman & Gaydarska (2018, 155), citing Barrett (1994), point out, the final form of a site should not be equated with its initial form, and no tell began as a fully-formed monument; it began as a 'flat' site. Indeed, completed site formations represent the *gradual* and *collective* result of a number of people over *considerable spans of time*. It is likely that at an early stage of the Neolithic all sites were more-or-less flat. While no tell in Neolithic Greece has been completely excavated, the complex tell stratigraphies and life histories of individual buildings are suggestive. Recent deep probes into the tell of Dikili Tash in Macedonia, rising today 15 m above the surrounding surface, suggest that the settlement, established in 6400/6300 cal BC, remained a large flat, and probably shifting site, for a long time, taking its tell form only from 5400 BC onwards (Lespez *et al.* 2017, 51–52). At Visviki Magoula in Thessaly an earlier more dispersed habitation pattern to the east of the mound was followed by a more compact one concentrated on the central part of the mound (Alram-Stern *et al.* 2017, 145). At Perdika 2 the geomagnetic data indicate a complex site layout with at least three settlement cores, two spatially overlapping in part and one spatially separate, all of which were surrounded by ditches (Kalaycı *et al.* 2017). One important implication from the new evidence is that spatially shifting or more dispersed habitation is not exclusively associated with flat sites but can also apply to tells.

Secondly, tells are variable, not unitary constructions. In Thessaly tell size ranges from 2 m to over 8 m in height and 30–300 m in diameter (http://igean.ims.forth.gr/). Even tells which are close to each other can present a picture of intersite contrasts, including differences in economic specialisations. For example, the mounds of Orgozinos, Koutroulou, Imvrou Pigadi and Rizava are all located in the Western Thessalian Plain. At Orgozinos the buildings were probably wattle-and-daub huts rather than over-ground rectangular structures, the site had a short life which lasted only during the LN1 (Table 9.1), and on the basis of certain particularities in its material culture, it has been interpreted as mostly an agricultural unit (Nikolaou *et al.* 2008), while it is also argued that it belonged to the flat rather than the tell settlement type (Krahtopoulou 2019, 77). Koutroulou Magoula, on the other hand, is a large tell (*c.* 3.7 ha and 6.6 m high) typically characterised by a compacted layout and intense building activity on the same spot (Hamilakis *et al.* 2017). At Magoula Imvrou Pigadi and Magoula Rizava domed kilns, concentrations of pottery and other spatial arrangements suggest the presence

Figure 9.3 The tell of Argissa (Neolithic and Bronze Age).

of specialised pottery workshops (Kyparissi-Apostolika 2012; Krahtopoulou *et al.* 2018).

There is also interesting variation in the degree of continuity of tell settlements. Some of the earliest sites, such as Argissa (Fig. 9.3) and Sesklo, two of the earliest settlements in Neolithic Europe (Table 9.1), continued into the subsequent Neolithic phases to become impressive tells, others were abandoned for good, while yet others were reinhabited but only after a gap. For example, Sesklo, which forms a tell 8.5 m high (Fig. 9.2), was abandoned for about 500 years before reoccupation in the Late Neolithic. Several other settlements were also reoccupied after a hiatus, often following fire destruction. Fire destruction is widely reported from all over Neolithic Greece, but it is not clear whether it was deliberate or accidental or how it occurred and why. The aforementioned probes into Dikili Tash show levels of occupation, abandonment and some thin layers of colluvial deposits prior to the archeologically excavated succession of occupation levels dated from 5400 BC until the end of the 5th millennium BC, when it was abandoned for a few centuries (Lespez *et al.* 2017, 52–53). At Makrychori the excavated deposits date to the Early and Late Neolithic and the lack of evidence of occupation during the Middle Neolithic may suggest that the site was abandoned in between (Toufexis 2017). At the same time, new radiocarbon dates, even though they are far apart stratigraphically, show that several large and continuous tells were rather short-lived within the time frame of the Neolithic. For example, at Platia Magoula Zarkou (Fig. 9.4) the 6 m thick deposits were accumulated within only 400 years (G. Toufexis, pers. comm.), while in Koutroulou Magoula the close clustering of dates for deposits 5 m thick suggests a rapid accumulation within just 150–170 years (Hamilakis *et al.* 2017, 87). Meanwhile, open or flat settlements continued to be established. They were not necessarily less continuous or less complex. They just had different notions of continuity. For example, Nea Makri in central Greece, with its 12 successive habitation layers, spanning 2000 years (Pantelidou-Gofa 1991), and

Figure 9.4 The tell of Platia Magoula Zarkou and surrounding cultivated land.

Mavropigi in Macedonia, with its three building phases, spanning 700 years (Karamitrou-Mentessedi *et al.* 2015), verify the fact that flat villages can be as long-lived as tells (*cf.* Bayliss & Whittle 2018).

Shifts in intrasite organisation at the house/household level over time also are standard for many tells. Of the more sufficiently exposed settlements Sesklo offers the best example of a constant process of structuring and restructuring domestic space over the different building phases, suggesting that important reorganisation of internal areas was played out against the long-term stability of the village (see Souvatzi 2008, 98–101 for details). At Makri in Thrace micromorphology analysis of successive house floors indicates constant alteration of flooring techniques and of types of deposits on the floor (Karkanas & Efstratiou 2003; 2009). Houses at Servia over the seven successive Neolithic phases were either relocated and the old plots left temporarily vacant, or the old structural debris was levelled and new building programmes on the same plots were undertaken (Mould & Wardle 2000). At Platia Magoula Zarkou interior and exterior space often changed location, alternating with one another over the different building phases, and levelling programmes seem to have taken place regularly (Toufexis & Batzelas in press).

The demographics of tell communities must have also been flexible due at least to geographical mobility and an often rapid economic development. Indeed, a remarkable feature of Neolithic Greece is the development of craft specialisation and of multiple and long-distance exchange networks at a very early stage. In Thessaly alone a minimum of ten ceramic (Pentedeka 2017) and two major lithic (Karimali 2009) exchange networks operated simultaneously. The development of such networks suggests mobility of people, travel and possibly also seasonal relocation for certain traders or specialists. Residential mobility and seasonal or permanent relocation can also result from numerous other reasons – for example, to ensure the reproductive viability of local populations through marriage patterns (exogamy) and to exchange labour, goods, and visits. Deliberate social fissioning may have also been at a work as a means of dealing with intra-community tensions or conflict situations in order to remain within the limits of co-operative social order. I return to this point later.

In short, tells were not simply a source of stability, continuity and representation of an unchanging past. They were also vehicles for change. This diversity in space and time is a first step towards addressing the agency involved in the different decisions made by Neolithic tell communities and the different tell occupation strategies.

Landscape, land uses and territoriality

When approaching tells in terms of their links to land and landscape, a central issue regards the identification of modes of land tenure and ownership. A common view is that tells were territorially-based communities aiming at high agricultural productivity, intensively exploiting fixed fields around them, appropriating and 'banking' vital economic resources and objectifying the relationship between land, time and resources (*e.g.* Halstead 1989; 1999; Bailey 1999, 107; *cf.* Alušik 2017). This is supposed to have created a degree of control over the surrounding countryside and a sense of private land ownership of both house and field plots. Such views may embrace a narrow conception of the associations of people with land. As I have argued elsewhere (Souvatzi 2013), land and notions of territoriality are better seen in terms of social relations between people rather than just a series of formalistic or technical matters focusing upon resources, restrictions and competition. They are part of a much larger package that also includes wider social relationships and dependencies. In addition, land resources and values are not only narrowly economic in their character; they are also non-material, ideal and symbolical.

In Thessaly the mean distance between neighbouring sites is often less than 5 km, with some settlements even located only 2–3 km apart (Gallis 1992; Perlès 2001, 121–151; Johnson & Perlès 2004). This exceptional intersite density may have indeed posed 'a demanding subsistence challenge' (Isaakidou & Halstead 2018, 73) for each village, but this does not necessarily bring about conflicts, exclusion and competition. Instead, it is more prone to contributing to balanced interaction by providing a density necessary for the creation and maintenance of social networks throughout the plains. Many of these mounds were found at the junction of radial road networks (Orengo *et al.* 2015, 307). Anthropological studies demonstrate that pre-capitalist non-hierarchical societies tend to break in order to prevent internal conflicts and to remain within the limits of an egalitarian society, estimated at around 200–300 individuals maximum (see Bintliff in press for a recent discussion). Incidentally, estimated population sizes for tells throughout Greece rarely exceed 300 inhabitants (*e.g.* Halstead 1999;

Perlès 2001). As mentioned earlier, closely comparable population sizes (*i.e.* from around 60 to 200–300 inhabitants) are also suggested for flat sites. This may represent a deliberate social strategy. Analysis of tell patterns in eastern Thessaly indicate a long history of powerful social constraints on demographic expansion and site territories, *i.e.* their number and spacing in the landscape, implying regular fission and possibly also conscious relocation of whole villages (Perlès 2001, 121–151; Johnson & Perlès 2004; *cf.* Peltenburg 1993 for Neolithic and Chalcolithic Cyprus).

Likewise, territorial borders can differ considerably, depending on the social dimensions of different groups, the contemporaneity or dis-contemporaneity of sites and the local topographic particularities. For instance, several Greek Neolithic tells were located in active floodplains and during flooding episodes water level reached their foot (*e.g.* Kalaycı & Sarris 2016, 12; Sarris *et al.* 2017a, 46; Lespez *et al.* 2017; also Krahtopoulou *et al.*, this volume, Chapter 3). Neolithic settlements built on floodplains are also fairly common across the Balkans (*e.g.* Bailey *et al.* 2002; Andreescu & Mirea 2008; Parkinson *et al.* 2018b). In these tells the local hydrology may suggest a cyclical pattern of the extent of land availability (*cf.* Bailey *et al.* 1998, 392), as well as a periodic re-location of off-tell activities. A well-researched example in Greece is Platia Magoula Zarkou (Fig. 9.4). It was established in a lacustrine-to-marshy environment and its surroundings were subject to frequent flooding for much of the Neolithic life of the site (van Andel *et al.* 1995; Caputo *et al.* in press; Sarris *et al.* in press). Parenthetically, this site has been taken by earlier research as a prime example for illustrating the possibility of seasonal occupation of tells (*e.g.* van Andel & Runnels 1995; Whittle 1996; Bailey 1997). This assumption is not confirmed by the recent analysis of the stratigraphy and archaeological data, all categories of which attest instead to an uninterrupted year-round occupation throughout the Neolithic sequence (Alram-Stern *et al.* in press). In turn, this reflects social choice and a dynamic human–landscape interaction that calls for greater awareness of human agency and knowledge concerning changing local geographies and their impact. Across the large plains of northern and central Greece villages tend to show a general preference for lowland rather than upland regions, thus having an unlimited amount of arable land at their disposal and spread in all directions with little concern for their boundaries. As Alušik (2017, 193–194) points out, in flat regions, such as Thessaly, territorial borders do not need to be clearly visible or set, but their disruption or crossing can be easily recognisable. In addition, mobility between and within settlements and house or settlement discontinuity, abandonment or fragmentation into others are all present in Neolithic Greece, as we have already seen, in parallel to the longer-term social stability, and say much about the nature and duration of land ownership and territoriality.

The traditional explanation of boundaries, either built or ditched, in terms of defence, fortification and territoriality (*e.g.* Runnels *et al.* 2009; Alušik 2017) cannot be retained either. It presupposes hostility, warfare or social hierarchy of which there is little evidence (*cf.* Kienlin & Fischl forthcoming). Besides, a spatial demarcation primarily controls access to a site itself, physically or symbolically, rather than within the surrounding lands. Detailed consideration of the process and effect of such large-scale collective constructions emphasises their central importance in providing a framework for human agency and social interaction. Scepticism should also be directed at the idea of land ownership by individual tell households. While house rebuilding on the same spot may suggest a form of ownership of domestic space, this does not necessarily mean that individual households can exclude others from the use of community land. A hypothesis of communal or collective ownership of land and resources may be far more likely for Neolithic tells (*cf.* Chapman 1989; Tankosić & Katsianis 2017; see also Wilk 1983; Segalen 1986, 14–20 and White & Schweitzer 1998 for ethnographic examples), whose formation and maintenance over time anyway represents a large-scale collective enterprise requiring co-operation at supra-household level (*cf.* Drașovean & Schier 2010).

Flat extended settlements might be viewed as having a more fluid use of space and land, involving more limited use of, or attachment to, specific places and landscapes and perhaps regular movement of the cultivation plots within these extensive sites, interspersed with non-fixed habitation structures. Although tells and flat sites represent alternative modes of land use, environmental and economic factors alone fail to explain the co-occurrence of these two settlement types in the same geographical region. The long duration of some flat sites such as Mavropigi and Nea Makri discussed earlier and other expressions of continuity, including the constant digging of pits and ditches, should not be overlooked either. They may reflect different ways to express spatial relations or land connections. It is therefore more likely that the differences between tells and flat sites derive from other factors such as different modes of social integration and kinship patterns rather than from fixed systems of territorial rights and ownership.

Kinship and social relations

Kinship is the most heavily neglected and under-theorised aspect in the archaeology of tells, and in social archaeology in general. Despite abstract references to family, lineage, ancestry, genealogy and so on, social explanations of tell creation and living or of the distinction into tells and flat sites do not actually show how exactly kinship can actually play a role in connections, distinctions and transformations, nor do they make suggestions regarding specific ways of detecting such aspects.

Many tells in Neolithic Greece – and broadly in the Balkans and the Near East – with their ordered, and often segmented, layouts, their central focal spaces and their abundance of agricultural surplus, point to unilineal descent groups (see Souvatzi 2017 for detailed analysis). One cross-cultural pattern for those groups is segmentation and another consists of residential areas surrounding a focal open space and/or ceremonial building. One more pattern that is relevant and widespread cross-culturally and which is very common in Neolithic Greece is that of concentricity or circular boundaries. Circular, concentric or more generally 'ring-shaped' settlements have attracted the attention of anthropology since the 19th century and have been shown to spatially configure a range of social groups (see Means 2007 for an overview and analysis; *cf.* Souvatzi & Skafida 2003, 430–434; Gheorgiu 2008, 174). In Thessaly, the well-known mound of Dimini with its multiple stone enclosures shows both circular organisation and consistent spatial segmentation, as well as a central space which remained unbuilt and unaltered throughout the lifetime of the settlement. The lakeside tell of Palioskala (6 m high, exposed for 3500 m^2) is also surrounded and internally divided by multiple stone-built concentric enclosures, with the dwellings limited to the central parts of the mound and habitation extending also outside the mound (Toufexis 2016). Complete geophysical plans of Neolithic tells, now widespread in Thessaly, provide further evidence. Many of these tells (*e.g.* Rizomylos 2, Almyros 2, Almyriotiki, Karatsandagli and Perdika 1 and 2) were both surrounded and internally divided by a series of concentric ditches and built enclosures of various sizes, functions and distances from each other and in various combinations (Kalaycı & Sarris 2016; Kalaycı *et al.* 2017; Sarris *et al.* 2017a; 2017b). In each tell some of these enclosures apparently served mainly as boundaries, whereas others seem to have created habitation zones either with tightly packed or with more loosely arranged buildings. In some cases, the dwellings were further separated by open zones in between. At Rizomylos 2 four main radial entrances or passages aligned more or less on a straight line, like those at Dimini, across both ditch and built enclosures suggest that all enclosures coexisted at some stage at least. In short, the layout of many tell villages suggests a descent group, most likely one lineage for the smaller tells and multiple lineages for larger tells showing multiple rings of dwellings and/or clustering of houses in distinct zones or areas. The recursive relationship of architecture with unilineal descent organisation may well be a reason for the creation and maintenance of a specific and consistent settlement plan which formed over the years the social landmarks that are now known as 'tells'. Furthermore, in non-hierarchical societies, the construction of enclosures can also be seen as the material representation of lines of descent.

Within tells, long sequences of rectilinear and freestanding houses of a more or less uniform size and analogous contents seem to indicate conjugal (not to be equated with 'nuclear') family households, although with variations regarding patrilocality and matrilocality (Souvatzi 2017, 177–178). In any case, the day-to-day interaction over substantial spans of time in production, storage and ritual areas in tells would have strengthened 'relatedness' (Carsten 2000), resting on biological, fictional, or ritual kinship bonds.

Flat and extended settlements, on the other hand, raise the possibility of a different organisational ideal. Their generally scattered habitation, the lack of obvious planning, the sparsely arranged or informal clustering of dwellings, the possible mixing of habitation and cultivation plots and the lack of clear spatial distinction between household and communal areas may suggest bilateral societies. In these shorter-term villages, a primary concern might be to achieve and maintain social integration. The evidence for intra-mural communal rituals here, including large-scale feasting, is stronger than in the tells. For example, at the newly excavated site of Mavropigi, one of the earliest settlements in Macedonia (6600–5900 BC), a large circular pit in the centre of the site which was used as such throughout the three phases of the settlement and which later developed into a substantial above-ground building, yet retaining its circular form, indicates the importance of a repeated ritual function (Karamitrou-Mendessi *et al.* 2015; see also Bonga 2017).

We now also have a better idea of tells found within larger, horizontal sites (Orengo *et al.* 2015; Sarris *et al.* 2015, 291–292; Kalayci *et al.* 2017; Toufexis 2017), although we do not yet know enough about the relationship between the two settlement components. At Sesklo the distinction between the tell and the flat sector suggests the co-functioning of two levels of identity, one with patrilineal descent group and another with more emphasis on bilateral descent, respectively (Souvatzi 2017, 177–178).

Equally interesting is the co-occurrence of tell and flat sites in the same region. As mentioned earlier, in the large plains of Macedonia and Thessaly flat sites were often situated among the numerous contemporary tells. Apart from different spatial connections and notions of memory, the two types may just as well be due to kinship systems, including fissioning caused by a realignment in kinship and marriage patterns. This is not least because these flat sites often date to later stages of the Neolithic than the tells. Some of these newer, flat villages may have been daughter settlements of tells, while others may have been founded by a relocation of an older village. Incidentally, this can explain the inhabitation of previously uninhabited or sparsely inhabited areas over the course of the Neolithic. These new settlements would require exogamous marital networks to maintain viability. The same could apply to the smaller tells. Bintliff (in press), drawing on Wobst's (1974) calculations of (inter)breeding networks (*i.e.* 500–600 people to safely maintain endogamy), argues convincingly that the typically face-to-face societies (*i.e.* lower than 300 people), such as those which form the majority in Neolithic Greece, need to engage in regular exchange of marriage partners with several neighbouring settlements. Kinship, spouse mobility and post-marital relocation may also more fully explain certain socio-economic patterns observed in Neolithic Greece, for example the early development of craft specialisation and networks of exchange, which connected sites through the circulation of people, materials and ideas. The political economic dynamics of kinship and marriage would have provided the framework behind ownership, production, exchange, and interaction on local and regional scales. The labour necessary for a number of other important activities, such as harvesting and threshing (*cf.* Gurova 2018, 209–210), also required a particular kinship organisation.

Time and history

An approach to tells as historical constructs entails recognition of tell as an ever-emergent social institution, as the physical venue for repeated, meaningful interaction within a particular span of time. In this way, we can move beyond the assumption that tells are static and the equation of social stability with static society, which only strengthen the stereotype of the *a-historic* tell. Studies that privilege continuity and ancestry in social reproduction and the construction of social memory also often place too much emphasis on stability. Chapman (1997) rightly argues that the tell is a powerful ancestral space, achieved through commitment to a long-term supra-household place-value. There has also been a plethora of important new insights into tells as social landmarks that generated memory and history through the repeated reconstructions of buildings, the daily repetition of practices and the inter-generational transmission of ritual, social and material knowledge (*e.g.* Bayliss & Whittle 2018; Chapman & Gaydarska 2018; Hodder 2018; Chapman in press), in alignment with the wider reconceptualisation of social memory in prehistoric archaeology as a material and historical process (*e.g.* Hendon 2010; Watkins 2014). But perhaps it is time to direct similar attention to the social dynamics of mobility between and within settlements and to house or settlement discontinuity, fragmentation or abandonment as has been devoted to continuity and stability. It is also essential to account for the interplay between the long and the short term (Souvatzi *et al.* 2018). Real-life practices and relationships have a variety of time scales. Although the relatively slow degree of social transformation during the Neolithic may explain the search for mechanisms that ensure stability, these mechanisms become successful only through small-scale agency. In this way, stability is tested through everyday agency, including acts of resistance to the dominant social structures as well as to social change.

The Greek Neolithic tells and their households provide a good illustration of these observations, as we have already seen through many examples so far. For instance, underneath the bigger picture of structure and consistency, there is nothing to suggest that households within a community remained stable in social, material and compositional terms over time (see Souvatzi 2008 for further details). The restlessness at the household level prevents social relations from being objectified and allows social structures to be contested.

Tell settlement space, architecture and layouts also incorporate temporality, transition and histories of action. For instance, the process of large-scale construction of stone enclosures and ditches can be understood as a record of social relations and thus, as a social history, given also that the evidence suggests that these works constituted a continuous process of construction, maintenance and modification events. During the lifetime of a tell, the addition of new enclosures or ditches, the abandonment or adaptation of old ones, the levelling of entire areas, the undertaking of new building programmes and the successive accumulation of deposits on a mound would have created a frame for the negotiation of power relations and social differences, as people's understanding and motives changed in the course of their lives. In the context of Southeast Europe, Chapman & Gaydarska (2018) examine settlements through a series of 'timemarks', particularly through intentional tell forming and house burning, showing that people could be conscious agents in the construction of social time as well as having a perception of a medium term.

Changes in entire village layouts reflect the development of new, or the modification of existing, social institutions. At some sites, the small sparsely arranged huts of the initial phases were replaced in the subsequent phases by more solid, overground rectangular buildings. For example, the tell of Mandra in the three earlier phases consisted mostly of pits surrounded by ditches, while in the two later phases a new building programme took place: the settlement area was levelled, the ditches and pits were filled with debris and were replaced by a large stone-built enclosure and the buildings became more substantial, square or rectangular structures constructed with mud brick on stone foundations (Toufexis 2017). This suggests a growing commitment to space and consensus to community control. Some villages must have resulted from a small number of families that left their village and founded a new one, while others may have been founded by a relocation of an older village. The reasons for break-ups and changes in communities of this kind are varied and multi-causal. They can collapse for economic, social, and cultural reasons arising from developments in wider society, but also for internal reasons such as the disagreements inherent in life in a densely-packed community.

Contradictions in the relationships between household and community should not be overlooked either. As I have argued elsewhere (Souvatzi 2012), they may be a better cause of tension and transformation within a social system rather than other, external factors outside of it. Such contradictions appear together with the first farming communities in Greece, continue until the end of the Neolithic and leave little space for fixity and rigidity in social relationships. They can be identified in largely similar processes, revolving around architecture, economy, ritual and burial – for example, in contrasts between settlement uniformity and structured layout on the one hand, and house/household variability on the other, between domestic rituals and public rituals, between children and adult burials, and between specialised, thus restricted, material production and yet even distribution of craft-specialized products (see Souvatzi 2012 for detailed analysis). Thus, the same material and spatial means can retain a double meaning of both individual differentiation and collective identification through different manipulation at different scales, contexts and times.

Regarding the longer term, mainstream models of Neolithic social 'evolution' tend to see things in terms of a contrast between two main stages: Early–Middle Neolithic, viewed as relatively simple and the repository of real communal values and interdependence, and Late–Final Neolithic, viewed as more complex and characterised by a sense of new awareness of household, the erosion of communal ideals and a progression towards political centralisation (*e.g.* Halstead 1995; 1999; Kotsakis 2018; see also discussion in Chapman in press). Such a simplistic contrast, paralleled by a teleological view of social change and of complexity as equated with hierarchy, cannot stand up to any in-depth analysis (Souvatzi 2007). Greek Neolithic tell (and flat) communities as a whole continually confront us with a picture of flux and ambiguity and with trajectories and social choices that do not fit into such typologies. They underline the fact that human history is much more than just a linear narrative of 'progress' and that time was not necessarily experienced in the past according to its Eurocentric conceptualisation as linear progression (Souvatzi *et al.* 2018). For example, the inhabitants of the floodplains tells, who regularly witnessed alternating phases of dry and wet environmental conditions and related climatic fluctuations, would have most likely formed a seasonal or cyclical rather than strictly linear perception of time and history, at least a sense of repetitiveness and periodicity. In the tell lands of Thessaly and Macedonia there is a remarkable absence, even in later prehistory, of any clear evidence for settlement hierarchy or a centralised socio-political formation comparable to the proto-urban centres and later the palatial economies that were developed in southern mainland Greece and Crete. Instead, Neolithic tell communities had a long and successful history of resistance to changes defined as linear, cumulative processes towards hierarchisation (Souvatzi 2007; 2008, 216–240). Nor did overall site size and structural complexity in Neolithic Greece exhibit a stepwise progression from smaller to larger or less complex to more complex settlements. Many of the earlier communities disappeared in the Final Neolithic, when, apparently, the mechanisms of social interaction identified above were no longer in use. Incidentally, this might help explain why the Final Neolithic is neither observed everywhere in Greece nor well known (see Dietz *et. al.* 2018). Renfrew (2018, 10) argues that the Greek Final Neolithic is characterised by the decline of the tell settlement type and a general shift from the large plains of central and northern Greece to coastal locations in southern Greece and the Aegean islands. In any case, the nature of the transition between the later Neolithic and the Early Bronze Age was so multi-faceted and diverse, and its duration so long, lasting for almost 1500 years, that it requires the rewriting of prehistoric narratives from fresh perspectives.

Conclusions

In this study I have sought to contribute to a multi-faceted analysis and understanding of tells (and flat sites) as dynamic, flexible and ever-emergent social formations that incorporate dialectics and historical process, along with geomorphological and physical conditions. The theoretical arguments and the Greek Neolithic archaeological evidence discussed indicate that tells (and flat sites) are not static, monolithic, uniform or supra-contextual constructs. Rather, they are a combination of habitual social practices and associated material, domestic architecture remains, conscious decision and communal effort to live within a restricted and ordered space, specific social relations, specific perceptions of history-making and attachment to place and the multiple scales of space and time at which all this happened. As such they allow us to examine a range of relationships, as well as to consider the interplays between the macro- and micro-levels. Indeed, as with other important analytical candidates for a multi-faceted and multi-scalar analysis (see Souvatzi *et al.* 2018, 13–17), tells can also be seen as loci for multiple networks and different structuring principles as well as agency at different levels, *e.g.* household, community, landscape, region and intra- and inter-regional connections. Such an approach may also change our views and interpretations of the contrasts between tells and flat sites. As the Greek Neolithic examples suggest, differences in social and kinship relationships, in degrees and modes of social integration and in manifestations of social identity may be a more important distinction between tells and non-tells than fixed notions of continuity, stability, permanence. Seen as analytical tools for examining the dialectics between action and structure, between variation and uniformity, and between stability and change, tells (but also, flat sites) can provide a unifying framework for the various bodies of local archaeological perspectives and for cross-cultural comparison.

Acknowledgements

Many thanks to Antonio Blanco-González and Tobias Kienlin for inviting me to the 'Current approaches to tells and tell-like sites in the prehistoric Old World' session on the 24th Annual Meeting of the EAA in Barcelona and to contributing to this volume. It all has been a very fruitful experience.

References

Alram-Stern, E., Gallis, K., Toufexis, G. & Pentedeka, A. (in press) *Platia Magoula Zarkou Volume 1: The Neolithic Period: Environment, Stratigraphy and Architecture, Small Finds*. Vienna, Austrian Academy of Sciences Press.

Alram-Stern, E., Sarris, A., Vouzaxakis, K., Almatzi, K, Arxachoviti, P., Rondiri, V., Efstathiou, D., Stamelou, E., Simon, F.X., Cantoro, G., Donati J. & Manataki M. (2017) Visviki Magoula revisited. Comparing past excavations' data to recent geophysical research. In A. Sarris, E. Kalogiropoulou, T. Kalayci & L. Karimali (eds), *Communities, Landscapes, and Interaction in Neolithic Greece*, 137–148. Ann Arbor MI, International Monographs in Prehistory.

Alušik, T. (2017) Communities, interaction and (intended) land use in Neolithic Greece: The testimony of the defensive architecture. In A. Sarris, E. Kalogiropoulou, T. Kalayci & L. Karimali (eds), *Communities, Landscapes, and Interaction in Neolithic Greece*, 187–198. Ann Arbor MI, International Monographs in Prehistory.

Andreescu, R.-R. & Mirea, P. (2008) Tell settlements: A pattern of landscape occupation in the lower Danube. In D.W. Bailey, A. Whittle & D. Hofmann (eds), *Living Well Together: Settlement and Materiality in the Neolithic of South-East and Central Europe*, 28–34. Oxford, Oxbow Books.

Bailey, D.W. (1997) Impermanence and flux in the landscape of early agricultural South Eastern Europe. In J. Chapman & P. Dolukhanov (eds), *Landscapes in Flux: Central and Eastern Europe in Antiquity*, 41–58. Oxford, Oxbow Books.

Bailey, D.W. (1999) What is a tell? Settlement in the fifth millennium bc Bulgaria. In J. Bruck & M. Goodman (eds), *Making Places in the Prehistoric World: Themes in Settlement Archaeology*, 87–110. London, University College of London Press.

Bailey, D., Andreescu, R.-R., Howard, A., Macklin, M. & Mills, S. (2002) Alluvial landscapes in the temperate Balkan Neolithic: transition to tells. *Antiquity* 76, 349–355.

Bailey, D.W., Tringham, R., Bass, J., Stevanovic, M., Hamilton, M., Neumann, H., Angelova, I. & Raduncheva, A. (1998) Expanding the dimensions of early agricultural tells: the Podgoritsa archaeological project, Bulgaria. *Journal of Field Archaeology* 25, 373–396.

Barrett, J.C. (1994) *Fragments from Antiquity: An Archaeology of Social Life in Britain, 2900–1200 BC*. Oxford, Blackwell.

Bayliss, A. & Whittle, A. (2018) What kind of history in prehistory? In S. Souvatzi, A. Baysal & E.L. Baysal (eds), *Time and History in Prehistory*, 123–146. London/New York, Routledge.

Bintliff, J. (in press) *The Complete Archaeology of Greece* (2nd revised edition). London/New York, Routledge.

Bonga, L. (2017) Thoughts on the preliminary study of Early Neolithic decorated pottery from the central Origma at Mavropigi-Filotsairi. In A. Sarris, E. Kalogiropoulou, T. Kalayci & L. Karimali (eds), *Communities, Landscapes, and Interaction in Neolithic Greece*, 374–387. Ann Arbor MI, International Monographs in Prehistory.

Caputo, R., Helly, B., Bravard, J.P., Rapti D. & Valkaniotis S. (in press) Latest Quaternary evolution of the Piniada Valley, Central Greece, and its effects on Neolithic and Historical settlements distribution. In E. Alram-Stern, K. Gallis, G. Toufexis & A. Pentedeka (eds), *Platia Magoula Zarkou Volume 1: The Neolithic Period: Environment, Stratigraphy and Architecture, Small Finds*. Vienna, Austrian Academy of Sciences Press.

Carsten, J. (2000) Introduction: Cultures of relatedness. In J. Carsten (ed.), *Cultures of Relatedness: New Approaches to the Study of Kinship*, 1–36. Cambridge, Cambridge University Press.

Chapman, J. (1989) The early Balkan village. *Varia Archaeologica Hungarica* 2, 33–53.

Chapman, J. (1997) Places as timemarks – the social construction of landscapes in Eastern Hungary. In J. Chapman & P. Dolukhanov (eds), *Landscapes in Flux: Central and Eastern Europe in Antiquity*, 137–162. Oxford, Oxbow Books.

Chapman, J. (in press) *Forging Identities in Balkan Prehistory: Dividuals, Individuals and Communities, 7000–3000 BC*. Leiden, Sidestone Press.

Chapman, J. & Gaydarska, B. (2018) Concepts of time and history on Chalcolithic tell settlements and Trypillia mega-sites. In S. Souvatzi, A. Baysal & E.L. Baysal (eds), *Time and History in Prehistory*, 145–171. London/New York, Routledge.

Dietz, S., Mavridis, F., Tankosić Ž. & Takaoğlu, T. (2018) *Communities in Transition: The Circum-Aegean Area in the 5th and 4th Millennia BC*. Oxford, Oxbow Books.

Draşovean, F. & Schier, W. (2010) The Neolithic tells of Parţa and Uivar (Romanian Banat) A comparison of their architectural sequence and organization of social space. In S. Hansen (ed.), *Leben auf dem Tell als soziale Praxis*, 165–187. Bonn, Kolloquien zur Vor- und Frühgeschichte 14.

Evans, J. (2005) Memory and ordination: Environmental archaeology in tells. In D. Bailey, A. Whittle & V. Cummings (eds), *(Un)settling the Neolithic*, 112–125. Oxford, Oxbow Books.

Gallis, K. (1982) *Kafseis Nekron apo ti Neolithiki Epochi sti Thessalia*. Athens, Tameio Archaeologikon Poron kai Apallotrioseon.

Gallis, K. (1992) *Atlas Proïstorikon Oikismon tis Anatolikis Thessalikis Pediadas*. Larissa, Etaireia Istorikon Erevnon Thessalias.

Gallis, K. (1996) Burial customs. In G.A. Papathanassopoulos (ed.), *Neolithic Culture in Greece*, 171–174. Athens, Goulandris Foundation.

Gheorghiu, D. (2008) Cultural landscapes in the lower Danube area: experimenting tell settlements. *Documenta Praehistorica* 35, 167–178.

Gurova, M. (2018) Prehistoric agricultural toolkits in diachronic perspective: a case study from Bulgaria. In M. Ivanova, B. Athanassov, V. Petrova, D. Takorova & P.W. Stockhammer (eds), *Social Dimensions of Food in the Prehistoric Balkans*, 190–214. Oxford, Oxbow Books.

Halstead, P. (1989) The economy has a normal surplus: economic stability and social change among early farming communities of Thessaly, Greece. In P. Halstead & J. O'Shea (eds), *Bad Year Economics: Cultural Responses to Risk and Uncertainty*, 68–80. Cambridge, Cambridge University Press.

Halstead, P. (1995) From sharing to hoarding: The Neolithic foundations of Bronze Age society. In R. Laffineur & W.-D. Niemeier (eds), *POLITEIA. Society and State in the Aegean Bronze Age. Proceedings of the 5th International Aegean Conference University of Heidelberg, Archäologisches Institut, 10–13 April 1994*, 11–22. Liège/Austin, TX, Aegaeum 12.

Halstead, P. (1999) Neighbours from hell? The household in Neolithic Greece. In P. Halstead (ed.), *Neolithic Society in Greece*, 77–95. Sheffield, Sheffield Studies in Aegean Archaeology 2.

Hamilakis, Y., Kyparissi-Apostolika, N., Loughlin, T., Carter, T. Cole, J. Fakorellis, Y., Katsarou, S., Kaznesi, A., Pentedeka, A., Tsamis V. & Zorzin, N. (2017) Koutroulou Magoula in Phthiotida, Central Greece: a Middle Neolithic tell in context. In *A. Sarris, E. Kalogiropoulou, T. Kalayci & L. Karimali (eds), Communities, Landscapes, and Interaction in Neolithic Greece*, 81–96. Ann Arbor MI, International Monographs in Prehistory.

Hendon, J.A. (2010) *Houses in a Landscape: Memory and Everyday Life In Mesoamerica*. Durham NC, Duke University Press.

Hodder, I. (2018) Contested history-making as part of the building of social networks at Neolithic Çatalhöyük, Turkey. In S. Souvatzi, A. Baysal & E.L. Baysal (eds), *Time and History in Prehistory*, 250–262. London/New York, Routledge.

Isaakidou, V. & Halstead, P. (2018) Carcasses, ceramics and cooking in Makriyalos I: towards an integrated approach to human diet and commensality in Late Neolithic northern Greece. In M. Ivanova, B. Athanassov, V. Petrova, D. Takorova & P.W. Stockhammer (eds), *Social Dimensions of Food in the Prehistoric Balkans*, 66–85. Oxford, Oxbow Books.

Johnson, M. & Perlès, C. (2004) An overview of Neolithic settlement patterns in eastern Thessaly. In J. Cherry, C. Scarre, & S. Shennan (eds), *Explaining Social Change: Studies in Honour of Colin Renfrew*, 65–79. Cambridge, McDonald Institute for Archaeological Research.

Kalayci, T. & Sarris, A. (2016) Multi-sensor geomagnetic prospection: A case study from Neolithic Thessaly, Greece. *Remote Sensing* 8(966), 1–14.

Kalayci, T., Simon, F.-X. & Sarris, A. (2017) A manifold approach for the investigation of Early and Middle Neolithic settlements in Thessaly, Greece. *Geosciences* 7(79), 1–24.

Karamitrou-Mentessedi, G., Efstratiou, N., Kaczanowska, M. & Kozlowski, J. (2015) Early Neolithic settlement of Mavropigi in Western Greek Macedonia. *Eurasian Prehistory* 12, 47–116.

Karimali, E. (2009) Katanomi lithinon proton ylon sti Neolithiki Thessalia: mia sygritiki exetasi. In A. Mazarakis Ainian (ed.), *Archaeological Meeting of Thessaly and central Greece 2*, 17–29. Volos, Ministry of Culture and University of Thessaly.

Karkanas, P. & Efstratiou, N. (2003) Anazitontas ton kathimerino hrono sti Neolithiki Makri: mikrodomi kai mikro-stromatographia dapedon, epifaneion hrisis kai exoterikon horon. *Archaiologiko Ergo sti Makedonias kai Thraki* 15(2001), 1–8.

Karkanas, P. & Efstratiou, N. (2009) Floor sequences in Neolithic Makri, Greece: micromorphology reveals cycles of renovation. *Antiquity* 83, 955–967.

Kienlin, T.L. & Fischl, K.P. (forthcoming) On the Interpretation of Bronze Age Tell Settlement in the Carpathian Basin: The Borsod Example. In K. Šabatová, L. Dietrich & A. Harding (eds), *Bringing Down the Iron Curtain: Paradigmatic Change in Research on the Bronze Age in Central and Eastern Europe?*

Kotsakis, K. (2018) Eating out: food and social context in the Early Neolithic of Greece. In M. Ivanova, B. Athanassov, V. Petrova, D. Takorova & P.W. Stockhammer (eds), *Social Dimensions of Food in the Prehistoric Balkans*, 31–46. Oxford, Oxbow Books.

Krahtopoulou, A. (2019) Archaeology in Greece 2018–2019: Current approaches to the Neolithic of Thessaly. *Archaeological Reports* 65, 73–85.

Krahtopoulou, A., Dimoula, A., Livarda, A. and Saridaki, A. (2018) The discovery of the earliest specialised Middle Neolithic pottery workshop in western Thessaly, central Greece. *Antiquity* 92(362), e5, 1–7.

Kyparissi-Apostolika, N. (2012) Indications of the presence of Middle Neolithic pottery kilns at Magoula Imvrou Pigadi, SW Thessaly, Greece. *Documenta Praehistorica* XXXIX, 1–10.

Lespez, L., Tsirtsoni, Z., Darcque, P., Malamidou, D., Koukouli-Chryssanthaki, H. & Glais, A. (2017) Identifying the earliest Neolithic Settlements in the Southeastern Balkans. In A. Reingruber, Z. Tsirtsoni & P. Nedelcheva (eds), *Going West? The Dissemination of Neolithic Innovations Between the Bosphorus and the Carpathians*, 43–55. London/New York, Routledge.

Means, B.K. (2007) *Circular Villages of the Monongahela Tradition*. Tuscaloosa AL, University of Alabama Press.

Mould, C.A. & Wardle, K.A. (2000) The stratigraphy and phases. In C. Ridley, K.A. Wardle & C.A. Mould (eds), *Servia I. Anglo-Hellenic rescue excavations 1971–73*, 17–70. Athens, British School at Athens.

Nikolaou, E., Rondiri, V. & Karimali, L. (2008) Magoula Orgozinos: a Neolithic site in western Thessaly, Greece. In H. Erkanal, H. Hauptmann, V. Şahoğlu & R. Tuncel (eds), *The Aegean in the Neolithic, Chalcolithic and the Early Bronze Age*, 387–398. Ankara, Ankara University, Research Centre for Maritime Archaeology.

Orengo, H., A., Krahtopoulou, A., Garcia-Molsosa, A., Palaiochoritis, K. & Stamati, A. (2015) Photogrammetric re-discovery of the hidden long-term landscapes of western Thessaly, central Greece. *Journal of Archaeological Science* 64, 100–109.

Pantelidou-Gofa, M. (1991) *I Neolithiki Nea Makri: Ta Oikodomika*. Athens, Archaiologiki Etaireia.

Parkinson, W.A., Ridge, W.P. & Gyucha, A. (2018a) Village nucleation and centralisation in the Later Neolithic of South-Eastern Europe: a long-term, comparative approach. In S. Dietz, F. Mavridis, Ž. Tankosić & T. Takaoğlu (eds), *Communities in Transition: The Circum-Aegean Area in the 5th and 4th Millennia BC*, 17–26. Oxford, Oxbow Books.

Parkinson, W.A., Gyucha, A., Karkanas, P., Papadopoulos, N., Tsartsidou, G., Sarris, A., Duffy, P. & Yerkes R.W. (2018b) A landscape of tells: Geophysics and microstratigraphy at two Neolithic tell sites on the Great Hungarian Plain. *Journal of Archaeological Science Reports* 19, 903–924.

Peltenburg, E. (1993) Settlement discontinuity and resistance to complexity in Cyprus, ca. 4500–2500 BC. *Bulletin of the American Schools of Oriental Research* 292, 9–23.

Pentedeka, A. (2017) Pottery exchange networks under the microscope: the case of Neolithic Thessaly. In A. Sarris, E. Kalogiropoulou, T. Kalayci & L. Karimali (eds), *Communities, Landscapes, and Interaction in Neolithic Greece*, 339–352. Ann Arbor MI, International Monographs in Prehistory.

Perlès, C. (2001) *The Early Neolithic in Greece*. Cambridge, Cambridge University Press.

Renfrew, C. (2018) Inventing the Final Neolithic. In S. Dietz, F. Mavridis, Ž. Tankosić & T. Takaoğlu (eds), *Communities in Transition: The Circum-Aegean Area in the 5th and 4th Millennia BC*, 3–11. Oxford, Oxbow Books.

Runnels, C.N., Payne, C., Rifkind, N.V., White C., Wolff, N.P. & LeBlank, S.A. (2009) Warfare in Neolithic Thessaly: A case study. *Hesperia* 78, 165–194.

Sarris, A., Simon, F.X., Donati, J., Garcia, C.C., Manataki, M., Cantoro, G., Karampatsou, G., Kalogiropoulou, E., Argyriou, N., Dederix, S., Manzetti, C., Nikas, N., Vouzaxakis, K., Rondiri, V., Arachoviti, P., Almatzi, K., Efstathiou, D. & Stamelou, E. (2015) Cultural variations of the Neolithic landscape of Thessaly. *Archaeological Prospection* 22(4), 289–292.

Sarris, A., Kalayci, T. Donati J., Garcia, C.C., Manataki, M., Cantoro, G., Karampatsou, G., Kalogiropoulou, E., Argyriou, N., Dederix, S., Manzetti, C., Nikas, N., Vouzaxakis, K., Rondiri, V., Arachoviti, P., Almatzi, K., Efstathiou, D. & Stamelou, E. (2017a) Opening a new frontier in the Neolithic settlement patterns of eastern Thessaly, Greece. In A. Sarris, E. Kalogiropoulou, T. Kalayci & L. Karimali (eds), *Communities, Landscapes, and Interaction in Neolithic Greece*, 27–48. Ann Arbor MI, International Monographs in Prehistory.

Sarris, A., Kalogiropoulou, E., Kalayci T. & Karimali L. (2017b) *Communities, Landscapes, and Interaction in Neolithic Greece*. Ann Arbor MI, International Monographs in Prehistory.

Sarris, A., Kalayci T. & Donati J. (in press) Geophysical investigations at Platia Magoula Zarkou. In E. Alram-Stern, K. Gallis, G. Toufexis & A. Pentedeka (eds), *Platia Magoula Zarkou Volume 1: The Neolithic Period: Environment, Stratigraphy and Architecture, Small Finds*. Vienna, Austrian Academy of Sciences Press.

Segalen, M. (1986) *Historical Anthropology of the Family*. Cambridge, Cambridge University Press.

Souvatzi, S. & Skafida, E. (2003) Neolithic communities and symbolic meaning: perceptions and expressions of social and symbolic structures at Dimini, Thessaly. In L. Nikolova (ed.), *Early Symbolic Systems for Communication in Southeast Europe*, 429–441. Oxford, British Archaeological Report S1139.

Souvatzi, S. (2007) Social complexity is not the same as hierarchy. In S.E. Kohring & S. Wynne-Jones (eds), *Socialising Complexity: Approaches to Power and Interaction in the Archaeological Record*, 37–59. Oxford, Oxbow Books.

Souvatzi, S. (2008) *A Social Archaeology of Households in Neolithic Greece: An Anthropological Approach*. Cambridge, Cambridge University Press.

Souvatzi, S. (2012) Between the individual and the collective: household as a social process in Neolithic Greece. In B.J.

Parker & C.P. Foster (eds), *Household Archaeology: New Perspectives from the Near East and Beyond*, 15–43. Winona Lake IN, Eisenbrauns.

Souvatzi, S. (2013) Land tenure, social relations and social landscapes. In M. Relaki & D. Catapoti (eds), *An Archaeology of Land Ownership*, 21–45. London/New York, Routledge.

Souvatzi, S. (2017) Kinship and social archaeology. *Cross-Cultural Research* 51(2), 172–195.

Souvatzi, S. (in press) The physical and social landscape of Platia Magoula Zarkou. In E. Alram-Stern, K. Gallis, G. Toufexis & A. Pentedeka (eds), *Platia Magoula Zarkou Volume 1: The Neolithic Period: Environment, Stratigraphy and Architecture, Small Finds*. Vienna, Austrian Academy of Sciences Press.

Souvatzi, S., Baysal, A. & Baysal E.L. (2018) Is there prehistory? In S. Souvatzi, A. Baysal & E.L. Baysal (eds), *Time and History in Prehistory*, 1–27. London/New York, Routledge.

Tankosić, Ž. & Katsianis, M. (2017) Cycladic or mainland? The prehistoric landscapes of southern Euboea. In A. Sarris, E. Kalogiropoulou, T. Kalayci & E. Karimali (eds), *Communities, Landscapes, and Interaction in Neolithic Greece*, 234–246. Ann Arbor MI, International Monographs in Prehistory.

Toufexis, G. (2016) Palioskala: a Late Neolithic, Final Neolithic and Early Bronze Age settlement in the eastern Thessalian plain (central Greece). In Z. Tsirtsoni (ed.), *The Human Face of Radiocarbon: Reassessing Chronology in Prehistoric Greece and Bulgaria, 5000–3000 cal BC*, 361–380. Lyon, Maison de l'Orient et de la Méditerranée.

Toufexis, G. (2017) *Oikistiki Drastiriotita kai Organosi tou Horou stous Oikismous tis Neoteris Neolithikis sti Thessalia. Paradeigmata apo tous Oikismous ston Profiti Ilia Mandras, Makrychori, Galene and Rachmani*. PhD thesis, University of Thessaly.

Toufexis, G. & Batzelas, C. (in press) Stratigraphy and Architecture. In E. Alram-Stern, K. Gallis, G. Toufexis & A. Pentedeka (eds), *Platia Magoula Zarkou Volume 1: The Neolithic Period: Environment, Stratigraphy and Architecture, Small Finds*. Vienna, Austrian Academy of Sciences Press.

van Andel, T.H. & Runnels, C.N. (1995) The earliest farmers in Europe. *Antiquity* 69, 481–500.

van Andel, T.H., Gallis, K. & Toufexis, G. (1995) Early Neolithic farming in a Thessalian river landscape, Greece. In J. Lewin, M.G. Macklin & J.C. Woodward (eds), *Mediterranean Quaternary River Environments*, 131–143. Rotterdam, Balkema.

Watkins, T. (2014) Time and place, memory, and identity in the Early Neolithic of southwest Asia. In S. Souvatzi & A. Hadji (eds), *Time and Space in Mediterranean Prehistory*, 101–119. London/New York, Routledge.

White, D.R. & Schweizer, T. (1998) Kinship, property transmission and stratification in Javanese villages. In T. Schweizer & D.R. White (eds), *Kinship, Networks and Exchange*, 36–58. Cambridge, Cambridge University Press.

Whittle, A. (1996) Houses in context: buildings as process. In T. Darvill & J. Thomas (eds), *Neolithic Houses in Northwest Europe and Beyond*, 13–26. Oxford, Neolithic Studies Group Seminar Papers 1.

Wilk, R.R. (1983) Little house in the jungle: The causes of variation in house size among modern Kekchi Maya. *Journal of Anthropological Archaeology* 2, 99–116.

Wobst, H.M. (1974) Boundary conditions for Palaeolithic social systems. *American Antiquity* 39, 147–178.

10

Human Activities on a Late Neolithic Tell-like Settlement Complex of the Hungarian Plain (Öcsöd-Kováshalom)

András Füzesi, Knut Rassmann, Eszter Bánffy and Pál Raczky

Introduction: The Late Neolithic in the Tisza region

It has since long been known that in the Southern Hungarian Plain, north of the River Maros, tell-type settlements made their appearance at the turn of the 6th and 5th millennia BC, whereby this region, together with southern Transylvania, became part of the northern periphery of the world of Balkanic tells (Bognár-Kutzián 1966; Kalicz 1970; Makkay 1982; Kalicz & Raczky 1987, 8–9; Whittle 1996, 107–113; Chapman 1997; Gogâltan 2003; Link 2006; Parkinson 2006; Rosenstock 2009; Kienlin 2015, 7–32). These tells, tell-like settlements and single-layer settlements, which can be associated with the Tisza-Herpály-Csőszhalom complex, a cultural unit distinguished on the basis of ceramic ornamentation, dotted the Tisza region.

In the 1970s and 1980s, investigations of the Neolithic tells of Hungary focused on clarifying the stratigraphic sequences of these settlements at the local scale and the settlement mounds themselves were seen as representative arenas of domestic and ritual life. An international exhibition presenting the major tell settlements of Hungary was conceived in this spirit and the catalogue accompanying the exhibition was published in English, German and French (Tálas & Raczky 1987; Meier-Arendt 1990; Jannet-Vallat & Thevenot 1991). The world of the Late Neolithic tell cultures on the Hungarian Plain was presented and set into a coherent historical narrative based on the findings of the excavations conducted at Hódmezővásárhely-Gorzsa, Szegvár-Tűzköves, Öcsöd-Kovásholom, Vésztő-Mágor and Berettyóújfalu-Herpály (Kalicz & Raczky 1987; 1990; 1991). This included the first publication of the excavations conducted at Öcsöd-Kovásholom by the Institute of Archaeological Sciences of the Eötvös Loránd University between 1980 and 1987 as part of a comprehensive overview of the Late Neolithic in Hungary (Fig. 10.1, 1).

Despite the limited information provided by the small-scale investigations of the Neolithic tell settlements of the Carpathian Basin, international archaeological scholarship strove to set these sites into the broader context of Southeast European settlement patterns and the region's overall chronological framework (Sherratt 1982; Chapman 1989; Gimbutas 1991, 71–77; Whittle 1996, 107–112; Parkinson 2006). For example, it was suggested that the early tell settlements of Southeastern Europe and the Central European enclosures could be interpreted as central places of outstanding significance in regional settlement networks (Meier-Arendt 1991; Parzinger 1992). One prominent example of the fusion of tells and palisaded enclosure systems and the creation of a coherent architectural unit was the Polgár-Csőszhalom settlement complex in the Upper Tisza region (Raczky *et al.* 2015, with the earlier literature). A similar duality, *i.e.* the fusion of a stratified settlement mound and a Lengyel-type enclosure system, was also identified at the Hajdúböszörmény-Pród site, lying some 15 km from Polgár (Raczky *et al.* 2010), indicating that the interface of the different modes of the social representation of the Southeast European and Central European Neolithic as embodied by the monuments constructed according to diverse community norms lay in the Upper Tisza region at the onset of the 5th millennium BC (Raczky 2019, 273–276). The joint British-Hungarian Upper Tisza Project (UTP) undertaken in the 1990s identified a network of nucleated Late Neolithic settlements around the Polgár-Csőszhalom tell settlement on Polgár Island in northeastern Hungary (Chapman 1994). Drawing from the survey data of the Hungarian Archaeological Topography in County Békés,

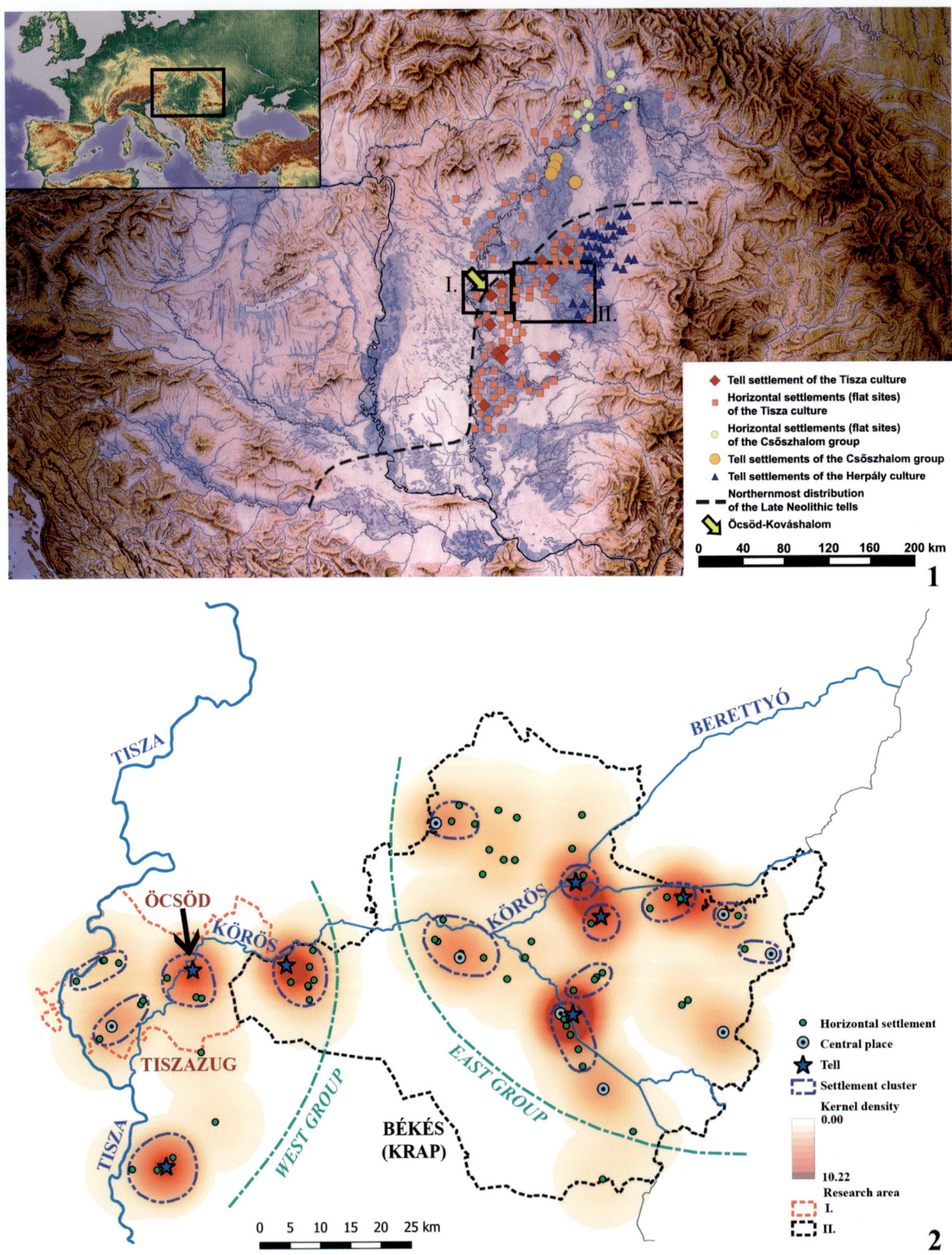

Figure 10.1 1: Late Neolithic tells, tell-like and single-layer settlements on the Hungarian Plain with the location of the Öcsöd-Kováshalom site. The map shows the northern boundary of the distribution of stratified mounds and the areas of major regional research programs: Tiszazug Micro-Regional Project (I: TMRP) and the Körös Regional Archaeological Project (II: KRAP); 2: The distribution of the Late Neolithic settlement clusters in the Körös region, showing the eastern and western regional units.

the American-Hungarian Körös Regional Archaeological Project (KRAP) reconstructed micro-regional settlement clusters along the Körös Rivers in the Late Neolithic (Gyucha & Parkinson 2008) that shared numerous similarities with the settlement network around Okolište in the Visoko basin in Bosnia (Hofmann 2015).

Even though the emergence of the Late Neolithic settlement networks and the very appearance of tell settlements on the Hungarian Plain has long since been on the research agenda of Hungarian archaeological scholarship, the main focus was initially on the macro-context and regional tendencies, on the broader geographical distribution (Raczky 1995, with the earlier literature). More recent approaches are multi-scalar in order to avoid the pitfalls of reductionism (Gyucha *et al.* 2009; Yerkes *et al.* 2009), enabling the identification of various types of interactions and their variants at various scales (Duffy *et al.* 2013). At the same time, an important caveat also relevant to the Late Neolithic on the Hungarian Plain is that the site hierarchy reconstructed for the region does not necessarily imply the existence of a social hierarchy (Duffy 2015). Much of current archaeological research is aimed at reconstructing the configurations of the social system – assumed to have been hierarchical – by 'decoding' the spatial/chronological dimensions of the finds and features of the Late Neolithic Tisza-Herpály-Csőszhalom-type settlements. We can take our cue from Ian Hodder's studies, according to which material culture and settlement patterns are not mechanic correlates of the texture of one-time social life (Hodder 1982). Martin Furholt (2017, 308–310) has argued that the early settlement communities of the European Neolithic and Early Bronze Age can be described as non-correspondence systems in which residence groups and social groups cannot be automatically correlated. Ian Kuijt (2018) came to an essentially similar conclusion in his case study on Çatalhöyük:

> Researchers have grown aware that in contemporary villages, including a wide range of cultural case studies, household members, potentially consisting of some combination of grandparents, aunts, uncles and cousins, did not always live in the same building. Instead, it is more likely that, while community members identified and recognized each other as being members of a specific multi-family household, they often lived in non-contiguous houses (Kuijt 2018, 566).

Another dimension is added by Manuel DeLanda's assemblage theory, a new philosophical approach to social complexity inspired by Gilles Deleuze, who views the social whole in the new interpretation of assemblage (*i.e.* the system of human and non-human components) as the unique combination of interacting heterogeneous components (DeLanda 2016). In this sense, we are not dealing with one social ontology that can be broadly typified, but with a multitude of ontologies (Harris 2017), which also calls for a measure of healthy scepticism regarding the unity and coherence of extended social entities.

One significant realisation in archaeological scholarship was that the Late Neolithic settlement patterns of the Tisza region provided the framework of the social arenas in another dimension too during the period between 5000 and 4500 BC (Chapman 1994, 86; Salisbury & Morris 2009). Bruno Latour's Actor Network Theory (ANT) offered a theoretical framework for a wholly new, complex approach to this problem, whose most important point relevant to this study can be summed up as follows: 'Things don't have intrinsic properties or *a priori* identities: neither are they social in themselves' (Latour 2005, 259). Instead, it is their mutual relations to other actors (human and non-human) that define them (Fahlender 2017, 74).

Based on these theoretical considerations, the possible correlations between the natural and the built environment as well as the relations between the individual and community dimensions of one-time activities were chosen as the subject of various case studies drawn from the Late Neolithic of the Tisza region (Parkinson 2006, 29–33, 123–147; Raczky 2019). Enquiries at multiple geographic scales have proven to offer the most fruitful approach to the reconstruction of one-time social interactions in relation to the Carpathian Basin (Gyucha *et al.* 2009; Duffy *et al.* 2013) and other European regions (Bickle & Whittle 2014, 2–8). The bottom-up scales employed in the Körös micro-region were as follows: (1) the tell settlement with its house and other features; (2) the tell and the outer single-layer settlement; (3) the micro-region; and (4) the region. This system was employed in the case of the Öcsöd-Kováshalom site in the Tiszazug micro-region. However, we shall follow the top-down sequence conforming to the phases of successive archaeological investigations in the discussion of the spatial organisation and the problems relating to that analytical scale, moving to increasingly higher-resolution spatial segments, similarly as in our earlier studies (Raczky & Füzesi 2016). Simultaneously, we shall highlight the specific and heterogeneous processes associated with the site that underlay the seemingly uniform and identical phenomena if viewed at the regional scale, and actually operated with different dynamics and at different scales.

The place of Öcsöd-Kováshalom in the Late Neolithic settlement network of the Körös region

The topographic surveys conducted as part of the KRAP project in the Körös-Berettyó Region demonstrated that the hubs of the Late Neolithic settlement clusters were tells, tell-like settlements or extensive single layer settlements ('supersites'), around which there were 1–6 smaller single-layer settlements. The ten settlement clusters each covered an area of 1–72 km², with 6–20 km² large unoccupied areas between them (Gyucha & Parkinson 2008, fig. 8; Gyucha *et al.* 2013, 161, fig. 2). The Tiszazug micro-region, covering some 570 km² at the confluence of the Tisza and Körös Rivers in County Szolnok, lies adjacent to the 2857 km² large KRAP study area in Békés County (Fig. 10.1, 2). The topographic data indicated the presence of three Late Neolithic settlement clusters in the Tiszazug micro-region (Raczky & Füzesi 2016, fig. 6.3). The tell-like settlement of Öcsöd-Kováshalom and its broader area with the smaller single-layer 'satellite' settlements is located in the easternmost part of this settlement system which, in the east, borders directly on the Szarvas-Kovácshalom tell and the associated six smaller settlements along the Körös River (Makkay 1982, 128–129, under the name Szarvas-Botanical garden; Gyucha & Parkinson 2008, 85, fig. 8). It appears that the three settlement clusters in the Tiszazug region and the cluster around Szarvas-Kovácshalom made up the western unit of the Körös-Tisza Region during the Late Neolithic. Neighbouring on this larger unit in the south was the cluster made up of the Szegvár-Tűzköves tell and the three smaller single-layer settlements around it (Korek 1987; Gulyás & Sümegi 2011, fig. 2; Hungarian National Museum, Ariadne Database). The western settlement unit represented by the Tiszazug Region is separated by a roughly 20 km wide empty zone from the eastern settlement unit in which William Parkinson and Attila Gyuha identified nine settlement clusters along the Körös River (Fig. 10.1, 2).

It seems possible that as the single known stratified site in the Tiszazug micro-region, Öcsöd-Kováshalom had played a central role in the Late Neolithic. Moreover, as the northernmost tell-type settlement of the Körös-Tisza region, on a larger scale, Öcsöd represents the northernmost 'frontier centre' in the regional settlement network of the Tisza culture on the southern Hungarian Plain (Raczky & Füzesi 2016).

Öcsöd-Kováshalom, the centre of a Late Neolithic settlement cluster in the Tiszazug micro-region

In the wake of previous work in the region as described above, it became clear that the Late Neolithic site of Öcsöd-Kováshalom and the associated settlement landscape could be fitted into the general process characterised by settlement concentration and nucleation from the close of the Middle Neolithic (*c.* 5250 BC). Concurrently with this structural reorganisation, we witness the appearance of tells and tell-like 'monumental architectures' on the Southern Hungarian Plain, representing novel forms of a community's self-definition.

It became clear that the tell-like settlement of Öcsöd-Kováshalom was not a solitary phenomenon (as assumed in the 1980s), but one in a chain of nucleated settlements together with other Tisza sites along the margins of the floodplains of the Tisza and the Körös Rivers. This realisation was in itself a novelty compared to our previous perception of local Late Neolithic settlement organisation, given that comprehensive data on settlement patterns in the broader area of Öcsöd-Kováshalom were unavailable in the 1980s.

The smaller settlement aggregation emerging within a radius of 5 km around the tell-like settlement of Öcsöd-Kováshalom was an independent spatial unit in the Tiszazug micro-region, made up of three smaller single-layer settlements (Kunszentmárton–Nagy-ér keleti partja, Öcsöd–Határ-út and Kunszentmárton–Gyalu-puszta II). Of the geographic elements that largely defined the palaeo-environment of the settlement cluster around Öcsöd-Kováshalom, the one-time meanders of the Körös River must be highlighted. The settlements were located directly beside a wide Körös channel, as can be seen on the map of the Second Military Ordnance Survey (1861–1864) (Fig. 10.2, 1). Given that there are two similar channels in the catchment area around the settlement, we may assume that prior to the regulation of the Tisza in the 19th century, the environment was largely defined by the one-time watercourses, which played a prominent role in the Neolithic ecological landscape.

The Late Neolithic settlement complex of Öcsöd-Kováshalom and its enclosure system

The tell-like settlement and the associated agglomerated single-layer settlement of Öcsöd-Kováshalom

As part of the preliminary intensive local investigations in the early 1980s, we examined the scatter of the surface finds, from which we estimated that the extent of the settlement was around 21 ha. This was rather striking since it was previously believed in Hungarian research that with their 10–12 ha average sizes, Szegvár-Tűzköves and Dévaványa-Sártó were the largest settlements of the Tisza culture on the Hungarian Plain. We systematically collected the surface finds in a system of circles of 50 m radius adjusted to the 100 × 100 m grid over the Öcsöd site. We generated pie charts for each circle based on the number and size of the pottery fragments, which was then projected onto the contour map of the entire settlement in order to display the spatial concentrations in the distribution of the pottery (Fig. 10.2, 2).

In order to compare the surface scatter of finds with the location of the buried features, we performed a series of corings for obtaining information on the subsurface stratification and the stratigraphic sequence of the settlement as a whole (Raczky & Füzesi 2016). The results of the corings and their assessment revealed that the Öcsöd site actually incorporated three major and five smaller settlement units that were separated by 'empty', unoccupied zones ranging between 10 m and 100 m (Fig. 10.2, 2). The size of the eight settlement nuclei ranged between 3320 m² and 8640 m², while the tell-like central settlement with its 130–160 cm thick layer sequence covered an area of 7750 m². The total area of the eight reconstructed settlement nuclei was

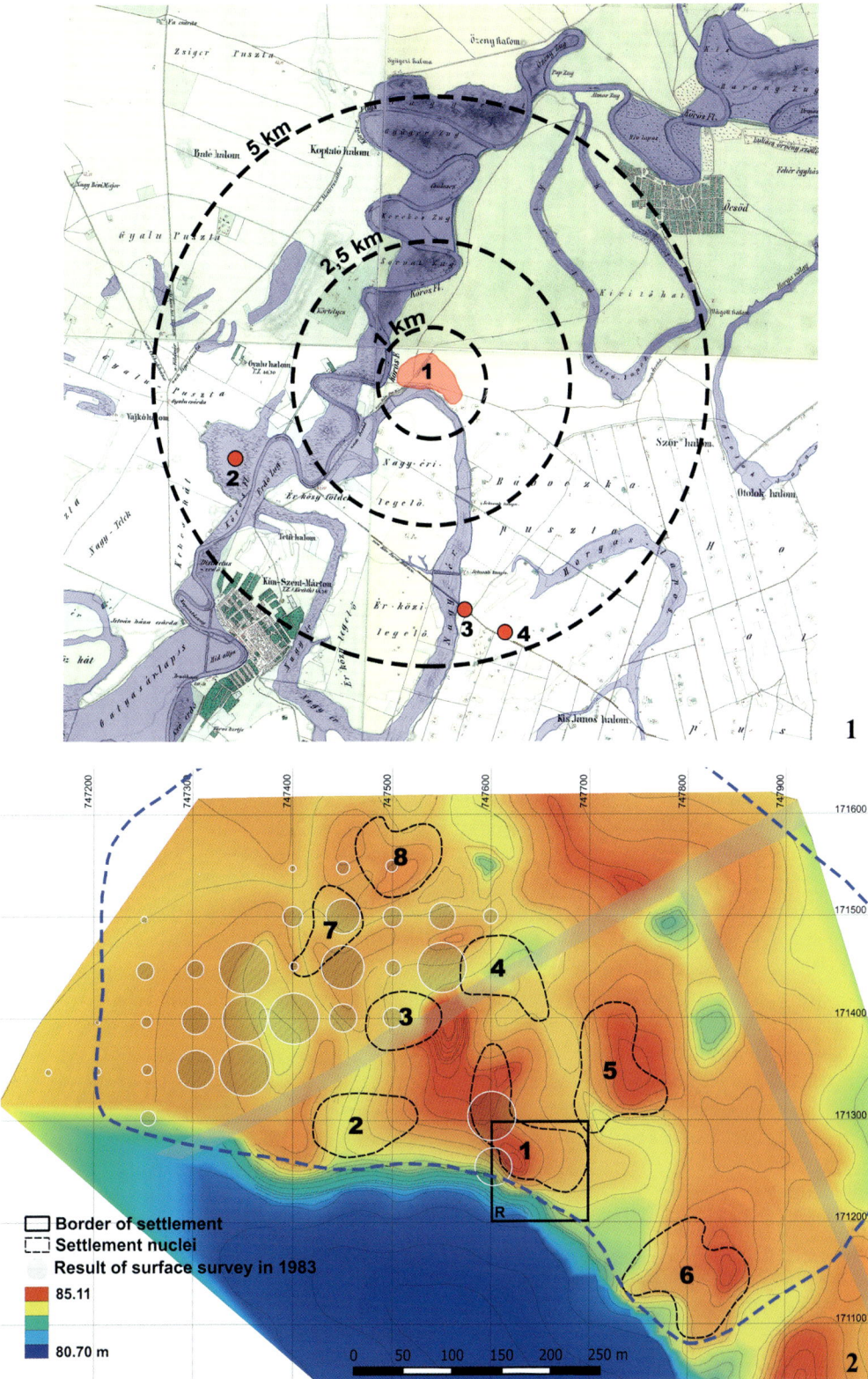

Figure 10.2 1: The one-time environment of the Öcsöd-Kováshalom site (1) and its settlement clusters (2–4) on the map of the Second Military Ordnance Survey (1881–1863), with the circles representing the potential catchment areas; 2: Boundary and internal layout of Öcsöd-Kováshalom based on the field survey in 1983 and the magnetometer prospection in 2018–2019. The density of surface finds and the results of the test corings outlined the tell-like centre (1) and the seven single-layer settlement clusters (2–8) within the 45.5 ha extent of the whole site.

calculated as 4.5 ha. In this sense, one of the greatest peculiarities of the Öcsöd settlement was that it did not form one large continuous spatial unit but was a loose network of smaller, 'islet-like' co-residential units. This realisation suggested, already in 1987, that what we had here was the outcome of a specific nucleation process in the course of which the house clusters were integrated into a single settlement space but nevertheless retained their spatial 'sovereignty'. The Late Neolithic settlement complex of Öcsöd thus represents an extraordinary agglomerative cluster in the Tiszazug micro-region, which cannot be described using the conventional and normative definitions of house, hamlet, or village formation (Chapman 2008), meaning that the settlement's vertical and horizontal segments, representing individual modules, formed a specific local settlement layout. One distinctive trait that needs to be highlighted is that the tell-like settlement mound overlooking the former watercourse played a central role in the settlement system which also incorporated seven single-layer settlement units. This assertion seems to be underpinned by the fact that the mound rising above the surrounding land was a prominent element of the viewscape of each of the five nearby single-layer settlements which encircled it. These five settlement nuclei lay at an average of 100 m from the tell-like centre. The two farther lying settlement nuclei, from which the central mound was not visible, were located 100 m from the nuclei making up the inner residential zone. The settlement complex at Öcsöd-Kováshalom can be conceptualised as a configurational space, which in Bill Hillier's (2014) interpretation simultaneously embodies both the period's general and the locally specific relations.

As a social arena, the spatial configuration of the Öcsöd settlement complex represented a social domain which acted as a centripetal force and a central reference point for the entire settlement during a specific period. The research team directed by Robert Hofmann identified similar norms of spatial organisation and the associated social forms at the Late Neolithic Tisza-Vinča site of Borđoš. At the latter settlement, the centripetal organisational norm was expressed in the spatial relation between the houses: 'In contrast, a centripetal pattern, while still highlighting house equality, most visibly emphasises the central convex space. The main difference to the house-row layout therefore points to a more important role of social negotiations, that is communality built upon bottom-up agency' (Hofmann et al. 2019). However, the identification of the exact social modules participating in the face-to-face interactions in the ecologic-economic landscape of Öcsöd is no easy task and it remains uncertain whether the generally accepted normative terms such as nuclear family, extended family group, lineage, band and tribe do justice to the colourful social diversity of the Late Neolithic on the Hungarian Plain (Parkinson 2006, table 7.10). Despite these uncertainties, we may nevertheless assume that that physical framework of the discrete settlement clusters can best be correlated with a coalescent model of several local co-resident groups (Birch 2013). It seems to us that the community settling at Öcsöd can be best described using Oliver Harris' words: 'Communities are thus assemblages of people, places, animals and things, bound together at times by co-presence, but always by particular kinds of practice and the affective fields these generated' (Harris 2014, 92). In all likelihood, the Öcsöd community can be too characterised by the most diverse interactions in a system of overlapping and nested scales, and the community thus lived in a continuous state of change, in a state of becoming. It is possible that this changing community that constantly redefined itself was moulded by the alternating systems of fission and fusion (Duffy et al. 2013) since a functioning social network is invariably embedded in a specific time/space context. Moreover, the Öcsöd social system was part of a higher-level system that followed the ebb and flow of increasing and decreasing social differences (Müller 2017, fig. 2).

The 35 AMS dates from samples collected during the excavation of the tell-like settlement at Öcsöd indicated that it was established around 5025–4960 cal BC (68.2%) and was abandoned around 4915–4840 cal BC (68.2%). In contrast to the earlier data (Raczky 2009; Raczky & Füzesi 2016), these dates suggest that the central part of the settlement was occupied for no more than 90–100 years, corresponding to the Tisza I and Tisza II ceramic style phases. It is also possible that the single-layer settlement clusters of the Öcsöd settlement complex represent a later period compared to the central one (however, radiocarbon dates are lacking for these settlement nuclei).

The 'pseudo-ditch' system enclosing the settlement complex of Öcsöd-Kováshalom

We strove to complement the investigations conducted in the 1980s with new multidisciplinary research and launched a new complex project in 2018. The magnetic prospection undertaken by Knut Rassmann and his team of the Romano-Germanic Commission of the German Archaeological Institute (RGK) in late February 2018 and 2019 set the previous research findings in an entirely new perspective. The prospection was conducted with a 14-channel magnetometer system mounted on a vehicle-towed, non-magnetic array. The gradiometers were set at 0.25 m intervals on a 3.3 m wide sensor array, itself set at right-angles with a 6 m long tow bar. With speeds of approximately 12–16 km/h and a sample rate of 200 readings per second (Hertz), the system provided 150 magnetometer readings per m^2 on average. The 14 magnetometers used were FGM-650B tension band fluxgate vertical gradiometers with 650 mm sensor separation, a ±3000 nT measurement range and 0.1 nT sensitivity. For precise georeferencing of the magnetometer data, a Leica RTK-DGPS system consisting of a base station and a rover with the DGPS were used. The accuracy of the position of the measured points is generally ±0.05 m. The size of the prospection area was around 65 ha and extended across a wide area around the central tell-like settlement.

The magnetic map shows *c.* 30,000 anomalies, of which 1500 could be of archaeological importance (Fig. 10.3, 1–2). The ditch segments with lengths of *c.* 20–30 m could be easily identified. These were presumably part of an enclosure system of three semi-circular ditches. Other clearly visible features were old field boundaries, burnt houses and around 980 pits. The close correlation between the ditch segments and the distribution pattern of Late Neolithic surface finds argues for their dating to the same period of the Tisza culture. The same holds true for the pits. Other anomalies such as the field boundaries and paths can more likely be associated with recent activities. The magnetometer prospection indicated that, in contrast to earlier estimates of 21 ha (Raczky & Füzesi 2016), the Late Neolithic settlement at Öcsöd extended over some 45.5 ha. On the testimony of the magnetic survey, the section of another enclosure system lay some 150 m from the previously already identified settlement and the triple enclosure ringing it. The line of the new enclosure could not be traced owing to the area's forest coverage. We regard this feature as representing another site.

The most striking features on the magnetogram are the ditch segments whose estimated lengths range between 20 m and 30 m. The Neolithic pits are not evenly distributed, but form clusters. One potential explanation for the distribution pattern of the pits could be the one-time existence of house groups, even though the dwellings themselves did not show up. House remains can only be detected by magnetic prospection under certain conditions, for example burnt clay from house walls or materials with a relevant magnetic contrast to the natural ground such as ovens. At Öcsöd-Kováshalom, we found some house remains in the southwestern part of the surveyed area (Fig. 10.3, 1), but none was detected in the settlement's central part or in the vicinity of the pit clusters. Other Neolithic and Eneolithic settlements in Southeastern and Eastern Europe offer an entirely different picture, where very often hundreds of burnt houses dominate the magnetic maps (Tringham 2005). The lack of living quarters at Öcsöd-Kováshalom can probably be explained because they were unburnt or their remains had been destroyed by erosion and only the pits or, more precisely, the deeper sections of the settlement pits survived. This set of circumstances suggests, at least on the testimony of the magnetic map, that the intentional destruction of houses by burning appears to have been the exception rather than the rule at Öcsöd-Kováshalom.

The results of the test corings in 2018 can be briefly summarised as follows: The multichemical analysis and susceptibility measurements provided a rough indication of the depth of the circular ditch segments. The likely depth is highlighted. Three anomalies were cored during the prospection campaign in 2018 (Fig. 10.3, 2). The goal was to determine the depth of the anomalies and to collect samples for soil chemistry. Because of the cold weather in February 2018 with temperatures around –15°C, it was impossible to extend the drilling. Nevertheless, the initial results provided valuable insights. First, the depth of the ditches could be precisely measured: the innermost (Core B1) had a depth of 290 cm from the current surface, the middle one (Core B2) a depth of 190 cm, while the outer one (Core B3) a depth of 270 cm. The coring of the enclosure section southeast of the triple enclosure indicated a depth of 290 cm (Core B4). The floor level of each ditch could be clearly identified in every core. The results of the soil chemistry analyses shed some light on the infilling process of the ditches. All cores indicated a slight shift in phosphorus values. Clearly higher phosphorus values were noted in the natural ground, too, which were measured some 20–30 cm deeper than the floor of the ditch. In Core B1, higher phosphorus values were only measured in the core's lower section between 1 and 2 m, which might indicate an accumulation of settlement debris in the ditch's deeper section. The low P-values (phosphorus) in the upper 1 m section indicate the infilling of the ditch with natural soil. A similar interpretation seems likely in the case of Core B2. Low P-values were measured in the deeper section, indicating an accumulation of natural soil, overlain by layers with soil from the settlement. Core B3 generally had higher P-values throughout. Although there are indications of two phases of infilling, there is some uncertainty in the currently available data in this respect. Soil chemistry contributed relevant information for the interpretation of the ditches. Firstly, there are differences in their depth and the proportion of the relevant elements such as phosphorus, rubidium, strontium and calcium, which sheds some light on the infilling processes. Interestingly enough, the magnetic data similarly indicated differences between the ditches. The thickness of the anomaly served as a proxy for estimating the width of the ditch, while higher nT-values were an indication of greater depth.

In sum, the archaeological results of the geomagnetic survey and the test corings conducted in 2018 and 2019 revealed that the Late Neolithic settlement complex at Öcsöd had once been ringed by a triple semi-circular enclosure (Fig. 10.3, 1–2). The diameters of the ditches of the triple enclosure were 500 m, 400 m and 250 m respectively, making it a monumental earthwork even by modern standards. At the same time, the enclosure system cuts across some of the settlement clusters. Another important aspect is that the central part of the area ringed by the enclosure was occupied by the tell-like mound of the Öcsöd settlement complex, an indication that the architecture of the enclosure system was essentially incorporated into the overall spatial organisation of the Late Neolithic settlement. It was therefore either contemporaneous with the Late Neolithic settlement at Öcsöd or was constructed shortly after life on the settlement ended, during a period when the location of

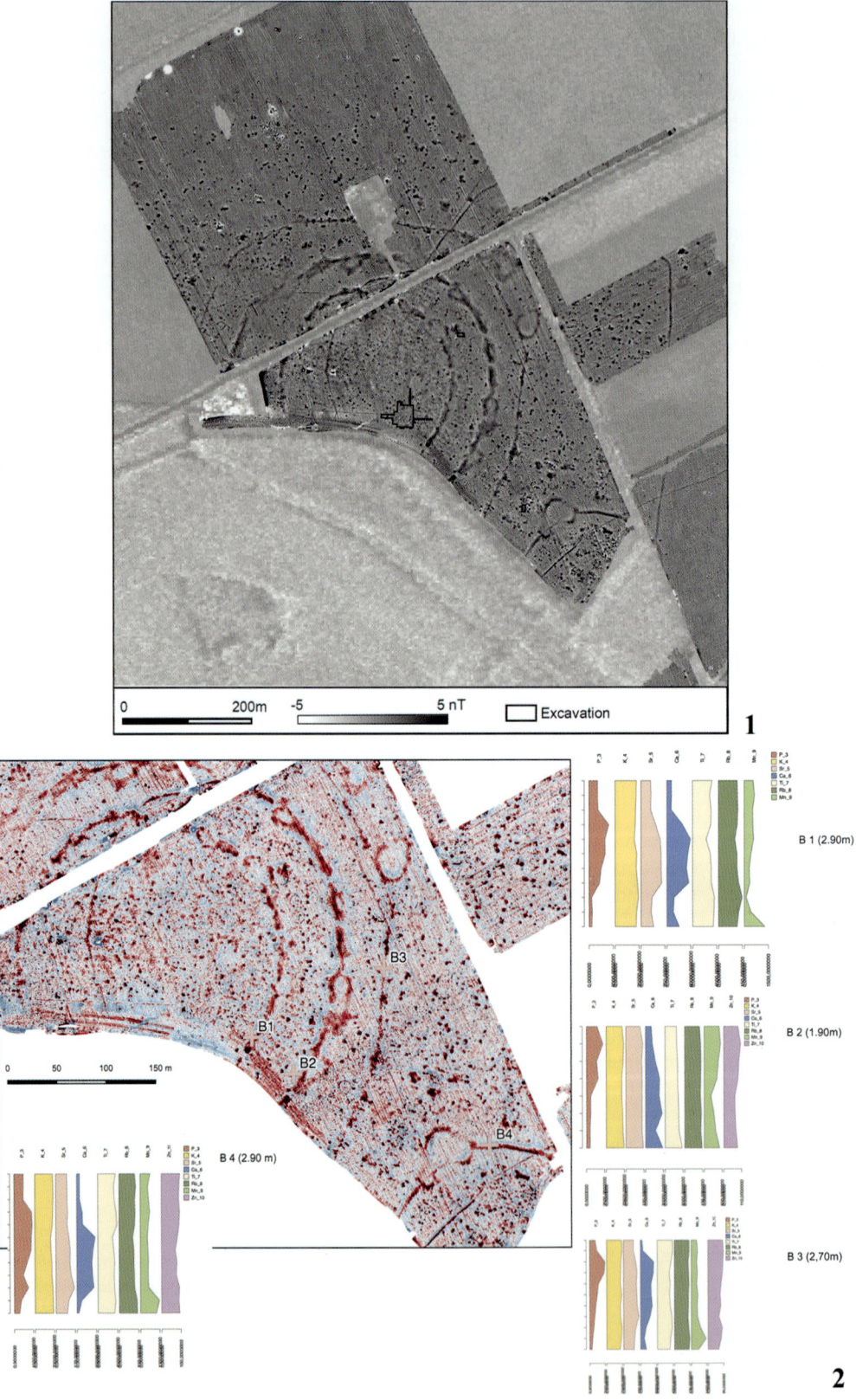

Figure 10.3 1: Magnetometer survey showing the plan of the segmented triple enclosure system ('pseudo-ditch') with circular features in the gaps between the segments ringing the settlement clusters of Öcsöd-Kováshalom; 2: Primary results of the multichemical analysis of the test corings at Öcsöd-Kováshalom (sampling locations B1–B4) in 2018.

the settlement's central part was still known and normative for the community that had built the enclosure. At present, this is no more than a tentative hypothesis – further archaeological investigations will no doubt clarify the site's exact stratigraphic and chronological relations.

There is a growing body of evidence on the norms governing the spatial organisation of the Late Neolithic tells, enclosures and single-layer settlements of the Tisza region based on large-scale and extensive geophysical surveys, which provide a firm springboard for addressing macro-regional patterns. Recent investigations allow the comparison of the specific traits of local and transregional development for larger areas of the Hungarian Plain. Moving northward along the Tisza River, the survey data for Gradište (Marić et al. 2016), Borđoš (Medović et al. 2014; Hofmann et al. 2019), Uivar (Schier & Draşovean 2004; Draşovean & Schier 2010), Hódmezővásárhely-Gorzsa (unpublished magnetometer survey by Knut Rassmann and the RGK research team in 2019), Berettyóújfalu-Szilhalom (Neumann et al. 2014), Szentpéterszeg-Kovadomb (Raczky & Anders 2014), Vésztő-Mágor (Sarris et al. 2013), Szeghalom-Kovácshalom (Papadopoulos et al. 2014), Csárdaszállás, Site 26 (Salisbury et al. 2013), Polgár-Csőszhalom (Raczky & Anders 2010), Polgár-Bosnyákdomb (Raczky & Anders 2014) and Hajdúböszörmény-Pródi halom (Raczky et al. 2010) consistently indicate that spatial configurations are strongly contingent on the elements of a particular settlement. Thus, for example, at Vésztő-Mágor and Hódmezővásárhely-Gorzsa, the tells were ringed by enclosures, but there was no single-layer settlement. In contrast, at Öcsöd-Kováshalom and Szeghalom-Kovácshalom, the tell settlement had an associated single-layer settlement but, while at Öcsöd the enclosure system ringed the entire settlement, at Szeghalom only the small central mound was enclosed by a ditch. The settlement mound, the ditched enclosures and the single-layer settlement were structured into distinctive spatial configurations amidst local socio-ecologic conditions; moreover, the spatial elements underwent formal transformations during their use-life or were recombined into new configurations.

One of the most striking traits of the circular enclosure system discovered at Öcsöd in 2018 is that the lines of the ditches are not continuous but made up of segments. This enclosure variant can be assigned to the pseudo-ditch causewayed enclosure type that was widespread in Central and Western Europe in the early 5th millennium BC, also known as the Rosheim type after its first archaeological identification (Lefranc et al. 2017). This is all the more surprising because the pseudo-ditch at Öcsöd-Kováshalom lies far from the type's core distribution in Europe and is therefore a unique phenomenon in the Carpathian Basin, as is the association of a segmented enclosure with a tell-like settlement. The magnetometer images revealed another curious trait of the Öcsöd ditches, namely traces of closed oval features in the 'gaps' between the enclosure segments (Fig. 10.3, 1–2). Traces of two particularly large circular structures with an estimated diameter of 30–40 m can be made out along the northeastern section of the outermost ditch. Similar round features were identified along the northwestern section of the enclosure lying south of the main enclosure system. These formal elements have also been reported from Late Neolithic Lengyel contexts in southern Transdanubia: Similar round structures along enclosures are known from Kaposújlak-Várdomb-dűlő (Somogyi 2007, figs 5–6, 10), Szólád-Kisaszó (Osztás et al. 2004, 61–63, pl. xx. 3), Szemely-Hegyes (Bertók & Gáti 2014, figs 58–64) and Villánykövesd-Jakabfalusi út mente (Bertók & Gáti 2014, figs 70–75). The geophysical survey of the latter site revealed that the outer ditch of the double enclosure was made up of a series of segments and that the curved horseshoe-like elements lay along these segments (Bertók & Gáti 2014, figs 74–75). The formal segmentation of the ditches and the simultaneous presence of the semi-circular connecting element embodied efforts to both separate and link the discrete parts of the earthwork. In this sense, there are many shared similarities with the formal traits of the enclosure system at Öcsöd. The Lengyel enclosures cited as parallels can most likely be linked to a later period in the Lengyel sequence, to the period characterised by a ceramic style with red and white inlaid painting (Lengyel II: Kalicz 1998). Taking this chronological position as a springboard, one might plausibly assume that the two outer ditches of the Öcsöd enclosure system and the associated circular features can be assigned to the Tisza III phase, i.e. the period after life on the central settlement (occupied during the Tisza I–II period) had ceased. Obviously, the chronological relations can only be determined once there are series of AMS measurements for the enclosure system. If our tentative hypothesis proves to be correct, it implies a general shift in how space was structured in the life of the Öcsöd settlement. The early period of the settlement's life was structured by a centripetal spatial organisation (with the tell-like central mound in the focal position), while the later occupation was characterised by a centrifugal one (the segmented enclosure system). This scenario has much in common with the transformation of the inner spatial and social reference system as observed at Polgár-Csőszhalom, conforming to the dynamics described by Edward Hall (Hall 1990, 108; Raczky 2018, 32).

We may contend that the pseudo-ditch at Öcsöd, which enclosed the clusters of the domestic settlements, was essentially unsuitable for functioning as a defensive structure owing to its many 'entrances' and it can therefore in all likelihood be regarded as a construction of symbolic significance associated with symbolic actions. Regarding the Öcsöd settlement as a whole, the areas of daily life – the intensely occupied settlement clusters – and the arenas of ceremonial activities – the ditches of the enclosure

– interacted with each other (Fig. 10.4, 1). This can be interpreted as an indication that on the scale of the entire settlement, the arenas of domestic and symbolic activities were linked or formally even enmeshed. At Öcsöd, the shifting and enmeshed networks of the systems of activities were articulated in the systems of settings (Rapoport 1990, 9). On the one hand, the formal traits of the ditched enclosure reflect a dual structural scale: the curve of the ditches, their concentric alignment reflects the continuity of a community convention that physically persisted over a longer time period, while on the other, the physical independence of the ditch sections embody the social/chronological segmentation of the process of its construction. It has been argued that the digging and backfilling of these segmented ditches can be associated with the activity of smaller groups of the community occupying the settlement. At the same time, these smaller group actions followed patterns embedded into the broader social background (Lefranc *et al.* 2017, 168–169). In this interpretation, each segment of the ditch can be seen as a metaphor of each group pooling its efforts towards a common goal. Yet, it seems problematic if the colourful and diverse social groups of the Öcsöd settlement (*e.g.* households or household clusters) were automatically equated with the groups participating in the symbolic ritual actions. Oliver Harris has convincingly argued that imagined communities were another important dimension in community formation during prehistory: Moving beyond the face-to-face groups, he highlighted how common goals were another important element in active group formation and maintenance in the arena of non-domestic relations (Harris 2014, 79).

The details of the social background to the collective actions underlying the construction of the segmented ditches at Öcsöd remain uncertain until the full assessment of the excavation results: households, diverse sodalities and non-residential allegiances as well as their combinations can all be legitimately invoked, similarly to the social configurations of the preceding Linearbandkeramik (LBK) (Bickle & Whittle 2014). Martin Furholt has extended the model of social groups to embrace the entire European Neolithic: In his view, these created 'strong translocal social relations and fluid, heterogeneous residential groups' (Furholt 2017, 315–317). Accordingly, the difficulty lies not only in securely identifying the make-up of residential groups, but also in proving that symbolic collective actions were organised on a social basis. Whichever the case, the pseudo-ditch at Öcsöd was an arena of special communal activities.

The segments of the Öcsöd ditched enclosure system were parts of an impressive collective monument, which articulated the higher-integrity unity of the larger community occupying the entire settlement or perhaps even its broader area. Underlying this claim is the possibility that the immense communal effort that went into the construction of the enclosure was possibly undertaken not only by the population of the settlement, but, periodically, by groups from the micro-region or the broader region. There are several potential interpretations of the entire Öcsöd settlement complex, and particularly of the 'great earthwork', ranging from aggregation and assembly place to ritual, congregation or pilgrimage centre, many of which have become popular catchphrases in Near Eastern and Eastern European archaeological case studies. A similar interpretative framework was also proposed for the Polgár-Csőszhalom site, given its impressive spatial extent and the complexity of its spatial components (Raczky 2018).

The study of the Central and Western European pseudo-ditches indicated that their segments were backfilled soon after they had been dug. The cores extracted from the ditches of the Öcsöd enclosure reflect a similarly rapid and homogeneous infilling. It appears that the ultimate goal of the communal action was not the creation and maintenance of a visible ditch as an enduring 'end-product', but rather participation in a communal process, in a ceremonial ritual, as part of a ritual communal action. One part of the series of communal acts was probably the digging of a ditch segment and the performance of certain symbolic actions in its area, followed by the backfilling of the ditch segment. The countless pig mandibles found in the pseudo-ditch uncovered at Duntzenheim and similar phenomena observed at other sites strongly suggest that these segmented ditches were arenas of ceremonial actions, possibly of events involving communal sacrificial feasts (Raczky 2018).

Integrating the scenarios outlined above into the overall interpretation of the archaeological features at Öcsöd, it seems likely that the choreography of the communal actions relating to the ditched enclosure system were cyclically repeated over a longer period in the local world of the Neolithic landscape. This roughly conforms to what Tim Ingold (1993, 158) described as a taskscape, 'an array of related activities', in an ongoing process of becoming. Another important point is that in the light of the above, the enclosure system did not materialise as a collective monument, as a clearly visible architectural 'whole' at Öcsöd. Yet, we agree with James Osborne that this continually changing structure in the making appeared as a monument in the mentalscape of the community/communities engaged in its construction, which also rewarded the active participants with a sense of monumentality (Osborne 2014). This would imply that the segmented enclosure system embodied a wholly novel representational system in the Neolithic world of Eastern Hungary since in contrast to the three-dimensional tokens of tells and tell-like mounds, enclosures were a space-creating intervention under the ground. Viewed from this perspective, the act of digging can be construed 'as an act of intervention into the ground in terms of the consequences of adjusting ground surface and of creating negative space. This focus raises different questions from those of conventional

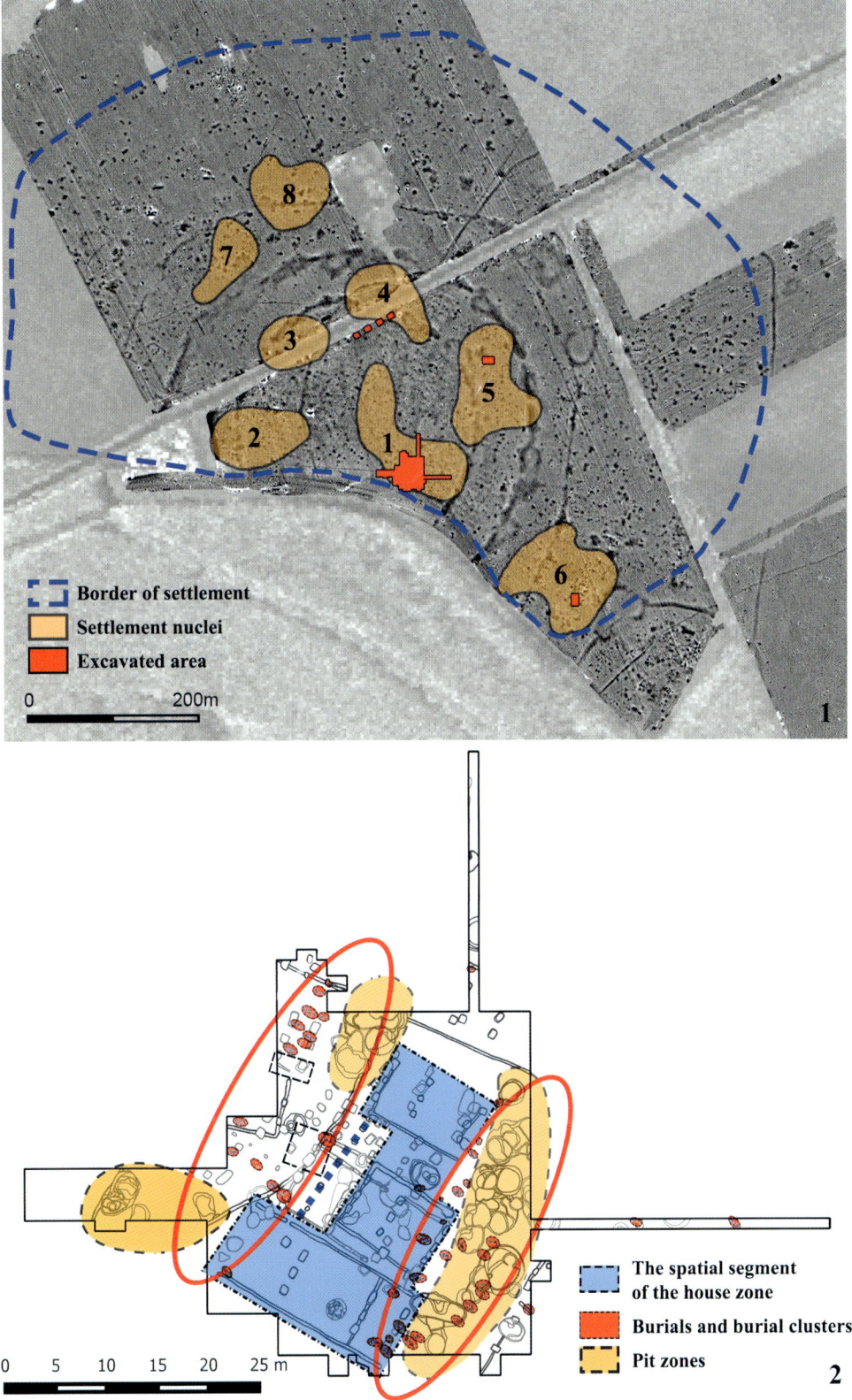

Figure 10.4 1: The seven settlement clusters around the tell-like settlement of Öcsöd-Kováshalom, the location of the excavation trenches, the triple enclosure revealed by the magnetometer survey and the probable extent of the settlement complex; 2: Main activity zones of the early occupation level (Tisza I) of the tell-like settlement of Öcsöd-Kováshalom with the central unit of the houses, the pits and burial clusters.

archaeological studies: Not 'How should we describe the material assemblages that a pit contains' or 'What can these assemblages tell us about ancient activities?', but 'What are the unintended consequences for Neolithic people of digging, using, experiencing, filling, forgetting (or remembering) such features?' (Bailey & McFayden 2010, 571). The shift in approach would be from a search for a social meaning to a consideration of the affordance that comes from digging-as-intervention.

At Öcsöd, then, the memory of group actions associated with the pseudo-ditch was not intended to create a visual and material reference for the participants, but instead preserved an enduring community experience arousing strong psychological effects. The assumed choreography of social interaction recalls the imagistic rituals which involve the psychologically enduring experience of dysphoric arousal (Whitehouse & Hodder 2010). A peculiar cognitive duality can be noted at Öcsöd-Kováshalom: the artificially raised mound in the settlement's centre was aimed at achieving a visual effect, while the actions associated with the ditch segments dug into the ground and then backfilled around settlement's central area coded permanent community messages into the non-visible, underground sphere. In our view, this ditched enclosure system incorporated certain social communal actions into the ground and can in this sense be conceptualised as a particular form of external symbolic storage, which ultimately focused on the process of the action, including acts of remembrance and long-term cultural memory (Renfrew 1998; Furholt 2012, 115–117; Gosden & Malafouris 2015).

The internal spatial patterns of the tell-like settlement at Öcsöd-Kováshalom and the associated social interactions

The excavations at Öcsöd focused on the settlement mound within the loosely agglomerated settlement complex, which seemed to be the most intensely occupied area. The main excavation was carried out between 1983 and 1987 over an approximately 1143 m^2 area. The excavated archaeological features on this tell-like central mound clearly outlined activity areas that formed concentric zones (Fig. 10.4, 2). This concentrated and well-structured settlement unit was enclosed with a rectangular fence measuring 35 × 42 m during the initial occupation period (Tisza I phase), providing clear boundaries for the habitation area (Raczky 1987, 67–68). In the earliest occupation phase, four rectangular wattle-and-daub houses formed a closed unit in the centre of the enclosed area (Fig. 10.5, 2–3). In this spatial organisation, the rectangular modules of the fence and the houses contrasted with the semi-circular alignment of the settlement clusters and the circular line of the pseudo-ditch system. Following Richard Bradley's approach, we may speak of the incorporation into one system of the circular and rectangular archetypes of the two architectural structural traditions (Bradley 2012, 7–16, 139–140).

The Tisza II occupation period had seven rectangular residential buildings, meaning that the habitation area extended beyond the earlier area bounded by the fence, making the latter superfluous (Fig. 10.5, 1–2). Another distinctive trait of the Öcsöd houses was the narrow space between the houses lacking the long pits flanking the longhouses of the earlier Middle Neolithic Alföld Linear Pottery Culture (ALPC) (Domboróczki 2009). This reflects a profound change in the local Late Neolithic treatment of space compared to the general norms of the earlier spatial organisation: the ALPC houses and the associated pits forming household clusters were supplanted by a new configuration of settlement features at Öcsöd (Raczky & Füzesi 2016): the houses and the pits formed separate, but associated, spatial zones leading to the emergence of a spatial pattern that can best be described as a community activity zone. The narrow open areas adjacent to the houses, between the buildings and the pits, were the settings of domestic activities. The dead were buried in the southeastern area before and the northwestern area behind the houses, again a break with the former ALPC tradition in which the deceased were interred separately, adjacent to the entrances of the houses (Raczky 2019). The new spatial reorganisation, the new community activity areas and the system of 'intermediate co-residential units' (Parkinson 2006, 128–129) undoubtedly emerged from the new networks of novel social interactions and their novel spatial configurations from the close of the Middle Neolithic onwards, which doubtless involved task-specific activities and artefact use in this context.

Underlying the structural physical reconfiguration of the settlement's spatial elements is the assumed social and integrative transformation of the household units of the ALPC, leading to the emergence of larger social collectives in the Late Neolithic on the Hungarian Plain (Raczky 2019, 270–272). Following the greater mobility of the early periods of the Neolithic, the Late Neolithic witnessed a general decline of mobility in Southeastern Europe, a sedentary constituted prosperity within a system of greater agglomeration, and the appearance of a social organisation with a strong internal ritual regulation (Furholt 2017). The appearance of richly diverse clay figurines and remarkable ritual paraphernalia was one accompanying feature of this process, and simultaneously its medium, for example on the settlements of the Tisza culture (Kalicz & Raczky 1987, 22–24; Whittle 1996, 112–113; Bánffy 2017, 714). The appearance of tells and agglomerated large single-layer settlements with their permanent sedentism and tokens of institutionalised ritual regulation represent variants of the correspondence system. Thus, a duality can be noted in the socio-ecologic world of the local Late Neolithic around 5000 BC, with the adaptive capabilities and resilience of the two formations differing

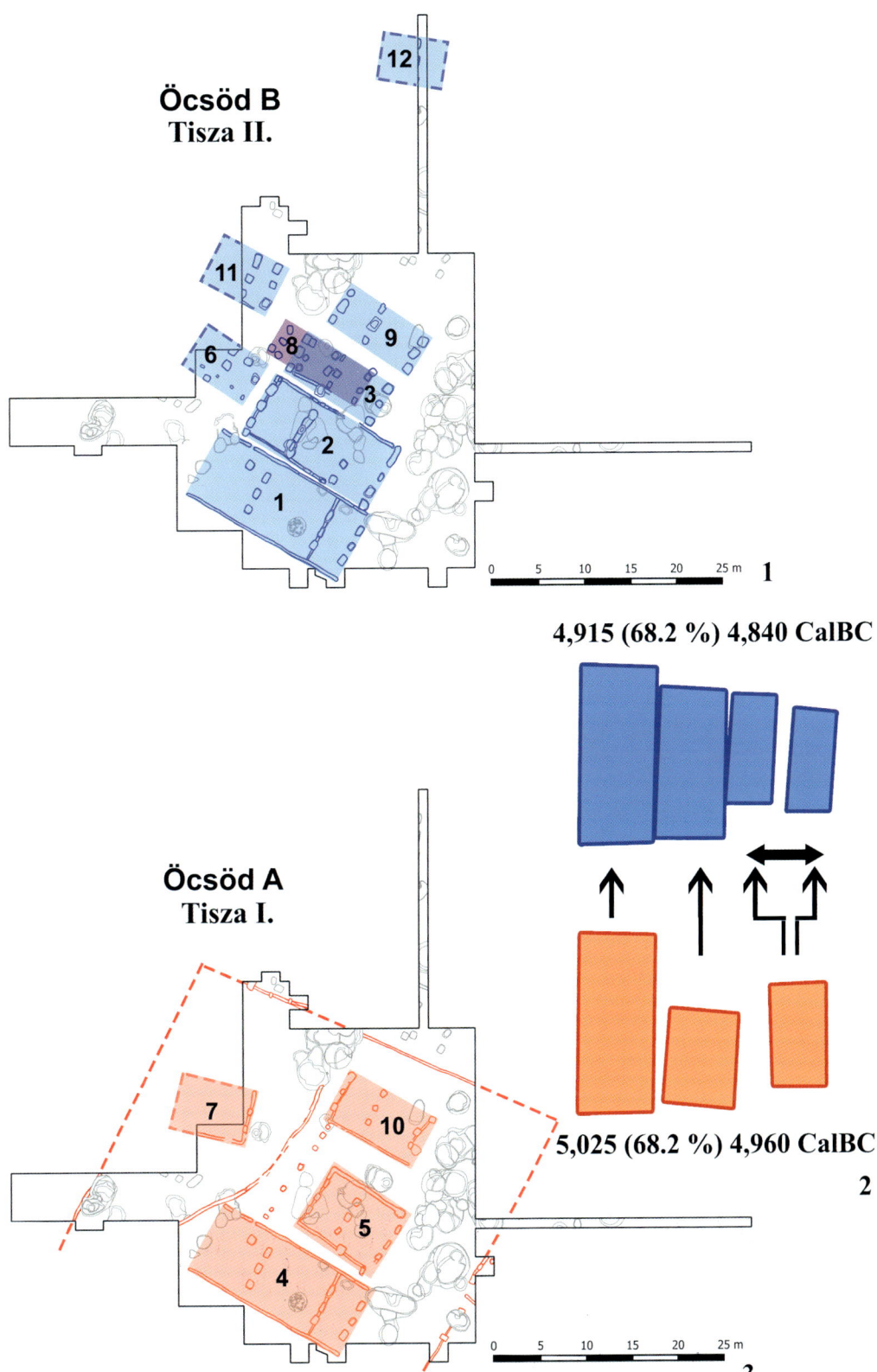

Figure 10.5 Öcsöd-Kováshalom; 1, 3: Plan of the excavated area of the central tell-like settlement with the house remains of the superimposed occupation levels (Tisza I and Tisza II); 2: The new spatial configuration of the Tisza II occupation after the reorganisation following the early occupation (Tisza I), the location of the buildings, and the changes relative to each other.

significantly. The study of this phenomenon in the broader context of the European Neolithic suggested that the initial rapid population growth accompanying the general spread of agriculture was followed by a decline on a continental scale (Downey *et al.* 2016). In this respect, it is hardly surprising that the agglomerated correspondence system was abandoned in the Copper Age for a return to a diffuse settlement network, to a non-correspondence system ensuring greater adaptive abilities (Gyucha 2015, 195–198). The immensely diverse ritual paraphernalia, the mediums of central ritual regulation, likewise disappeared at the onset of the Copper Age (Bánffy 2017, 717).

On the tell-like mound of Öcsöd, the range of social communal actions was extended into the vertical dimension with the superimposed occupation levels representing one variant of taskscapes (the Tisza I and Tisza II levels with their joint layer thickness of 130–160 cm), implying that we should study not only the horizontal configurations of one-time human activities, but also their vertical dimensions alongside their long-term chronological patterns (Hofmann 2012). Aside from the physical disposition, already mentioned in the foregoing, the demographic dimension as an independent key variable likewise played a role in the forms of social relations, as major differences can be noted between the prosperity of smaller groups and larger communities. While the stability of smaller clique-like groups is guaranteed by the low number of long-term personal relations, the survival of larger communities is ensured through the dynamic changes in their membership. In the latter case, the system's internal mechanism creates an institutionalised regulation that tends to be independent of individuals (Palla *et al.* 2007, 667). This assertion has major implications for the reconstruction of the processes underlying the changes appearing in the archaeological record. In the case of Öcsöd-Kováshalom, for example, the institutionalised community regulation emerging in the unit of the larger population can be studied in the context of two spatial segments. The first calls for a focus on the material relics and the interactions of the domestic and symbolic actions of the community occupying the tell-like mound of the agglomerated settlement, the second for the identification of the social range of the institution represented by the pseudo-ditch that both moulded and renewed the community's self-definition in the long term. The detailed micro-morphological analysis of the ditch will hopefully shed light on the scenario(s) of the actions associated with it and their chronology, as well as on the overall impact on the landscape. Our initial impression is that the appearance of community regulation and a long-term set of community norms at Öcsöd can be linked to the emergence of a communications system coded into external symbolic mediums such as carefully choreographed communal ceremonies, diverse performances and richly varied ritual paraphernalia.

The social background of the structural transformation of the central house cluster on the tell-like settlement at Öcsöd

The excavation of the central settlement mound brought to light the remains of four timber-framed houses with bedding trenches from the earlier occupation phase, of which three formed a closed unit during the Tisza I phase. House 5 was rebuilt first, creating the foundation and floor of a new house. This new building (House 2) was thus enlarged with an additional room on the eastern side (Fig. 10.5, 1 and 3). An entirely new building was erected between Houses 5 and 10 during the spatial reorganisation of the settlement, which called for a shift of the long walls of the two houses towards the north and south to ensure that the new building (House 3) would fit in breadthwise between the earlier two dwellings. This reorganisation led to the creation of the new unit of four houses (nos 1, 2, 3 and 9) above the earlier residential units at the beginning of the Tisza II phase (Fig. 10.5, 2). At the same time, the spatial organisation of the activity area, the pits and the burial area remained unchanged. It must be noted here that the construction of the houses called for well-organised corporate cooperation and collective action. Taking the minimal number of individuals participating in the communal action associated with the Öcsöd living quarters and assuming 5–6 occupants per house suggests a figure of 20–24 participants for the social unit involved, *i.e.* the size of the neighbourhood cluster among local conditions.

Deposition and the spatial manipulation of unusual ceramics in the open area of the co-residential house cluster

Two remarkable ceramic assemblages were deposited in the area bounded by Houses 4 and 10 and the fence of timber posts at the time of the reorganisation of the Tisza I settlement. The deposition locations lay near the north-eastern corner and the northern long wall of House 5, a small building (Fig. 10.6, 1–2) (Raczky *et al.* 2018, fig. 7). It is particularly noteworthy that the approximately 100 × 50 cm large deposition locations with the stratified vessel deposits remained undisturbed during the later occupation too. During the rebuilding, the house's occupants apparently took care to preserve the material relics of the earlier actions. It appears that the assemblages of burnt vessels and the community events associated with these depositions probably meant the termination of the settlement's early phase (Tisza I) and, simultaneously, the creation of the foundations for a new residential cluster (Tisza II).

Deposit 1: The most spectacular part of the deposit in Location 1 is made up of the fragments of a 72 cm high storage vessel (Raczky 2000, figs 1–4), which had broken into many pieces and bore traces of intense burning (Fig. 10.6, 5). What makes this vessel particularly

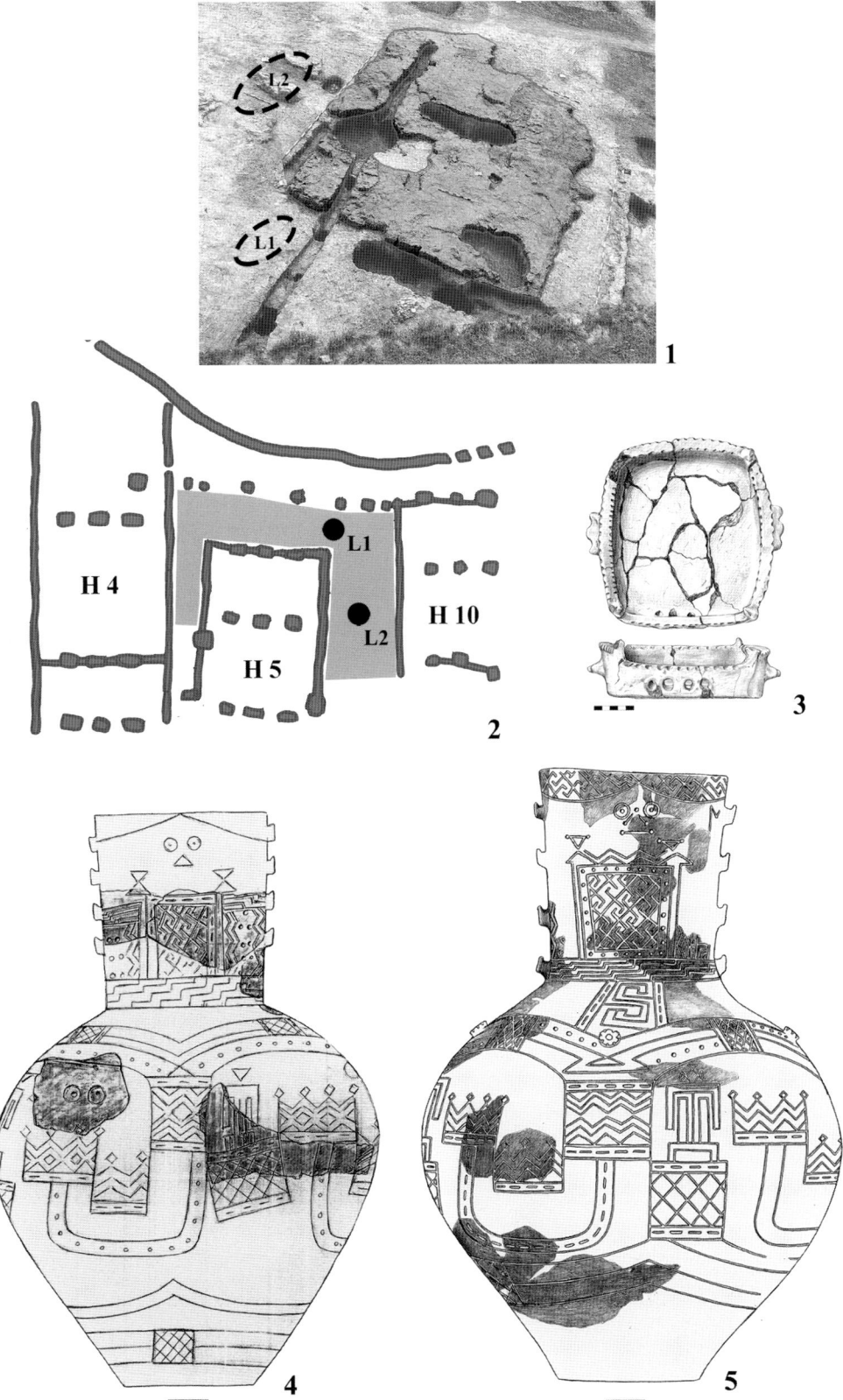

Figure 10.6 Öcsöd-Kováshalom; 1–2: Location of House 5 of the Tisza I occupation and the two deposition locations (L1 and L2) on the tell-like settlement; 3: A shallow quadrangular bowl from the ceramic deposit found in Location 1; 4: Reconstructed face pot found in Location 2; 5: Reconstructed face pot from the ceramic deposit found in Location 1.

Figure 10.7 Öcsöd-Kováshalom; Spatial distribution and number of the re-fitted fragments of the face pot found in the ceramic deposit of Location 1 of the Tisza I occupation of the tell-like settlement.

noteworthy is that it essentially represents a reinterpreted version with special ornamental motifs and elements of the face pots of the Middle Neolithic Szakálhát culture (Kalicz & Makkay 1977, 108–110; pls 152–153; Goldman 1978, 13–58; 167–171; Raczky 2015, II. 75, II. 79–88; Sebők 2018, figs 2–7). The lower part of the vessel surface is divided into distinct segments by the four differently represented human figures in the imagery encircling the vessel's belly. Four pairs of modelled upward-held hands were set on the vessel's neck, suggesting that the face and the hands were not the attributes of a single individual. In contrast, the face pots of the preceding Szakálhát period had a single pair of upheld arms or a pair of handles on either side of the face, possibly a reference to the portrayal of a single individual. In this sense, the face and body of the Öcsöd vessel could represent the collective corpus of a broader social integration articulated in the context of group relations.

Mixed up among the fragments of the face pot that remained in the ceramic deposit lay the fragment of an unusual vessel, a shallow rectangular bowl with one side shorter than the other three (Fig. 10.6, 3). The non-quotidian function of this vessel is indicated by the four round perforations on its shorter side (Raczky et al. 2018, 125–126, 128–129, fig. 11). Four stylised animal heads were set on each of the four corners on the rim. The form of the bowl suggests that it had been used for holding liquid, which had perhaps been poured out through the perforations. The cultural ancestry of vessels with perforations for pouring can be traced to the similar pieces known from ALPC contexts (Kalicz & Makkay 1977, pls 88–89; Hajdú & Nagy 2015, fig. 30.3). Comparable vessels with four or four pairs of inward-looking animal or human heads represented a standard formal canon of the long Vinča cultural development (Spacić & Crnobrnja 2014, fig. 1, pl. 1.1).

The refitting and restoration of the vessels provided several new insights. As it turned out, of the 86 fragments that survived of the face pot, only 20 larger pieces came from the deposition. The other 66, mostly smaller fragments, were dispersed over a larger area of the excavated mound. We found that the scatter of the vessel's fragments (Fig. 10.7) showed a concentration towards north and south, even though the northwest to southeast oriented houses had obviously obstructed any spontaneous dispersal in the north–south direction. The 'movement' of the pottery sherds can only be conceptualised through human agency – in other words, the horizontal dispersal of the vessel fragments can hardly be attributed to local taphonomic displacements and movements in the process of natural layer formation. The large vessel broken into so many small fragments seems likely to reflect some intentional act of the type labelled deliberate fragmentation by John Chapman (Chapman 2000; Chapman & Gaydarska 2007). The quadrangular vessel of the discussed assemblage broke into 15 pieces, of which 13 lay in the deposit. Just for the comparison: While 76% of the large face pot's fragments lay at some distance from the place of primary deposition, this proportion was 13% in the case of the rectangular vessel. This might reflect two different attitudes to the two vessels in the period following their primary use. In our narrative, the face pot and the rectangular vessel were both broken as the concluding act of an earlier action and the participants then took certain fragments of the large face pot to various parts of the settlement. With this symbolic act, the community's specific ritual act was extended from the smaller area to a wider zone of the Öcsöd settlement.

It seems to us that the two deposited vessels had been used together for the regulated manipulation of some liquid substance, perhaps an alcoholic fermented beverage that was transferred from the large face pot to the rectangular bowl and then strained through the latter into smaller vessels for consumption. This would suggest that what we have here are the remains of the community's ritual on a special occasion, of a ritual feasting (Whittle 1997, 139; Twiss 2008), which might also have involved the consumption of special beverages.

Deposit 2: Fragments of another large face pot were discovered near House 5, of which only 12 neck and shoulder fragments were preserved at Location 2 (Fig. 10.6, 4). The physical 'survival rate' of the deposition location and of the assemblage itself were less fortunate than in the previous case, in part explaining why the refitting and reconstruction of the face pot remains incomplete. Indeed, no other fragments of this vessel were found during the excavation, meaning either that the remaining fragments had been scattered in a farther-lying area of the site or that the fragments could not be identified among the roughly 200,000 vessel fragments brought to light (Füzesi & Raczky 2018, 49).

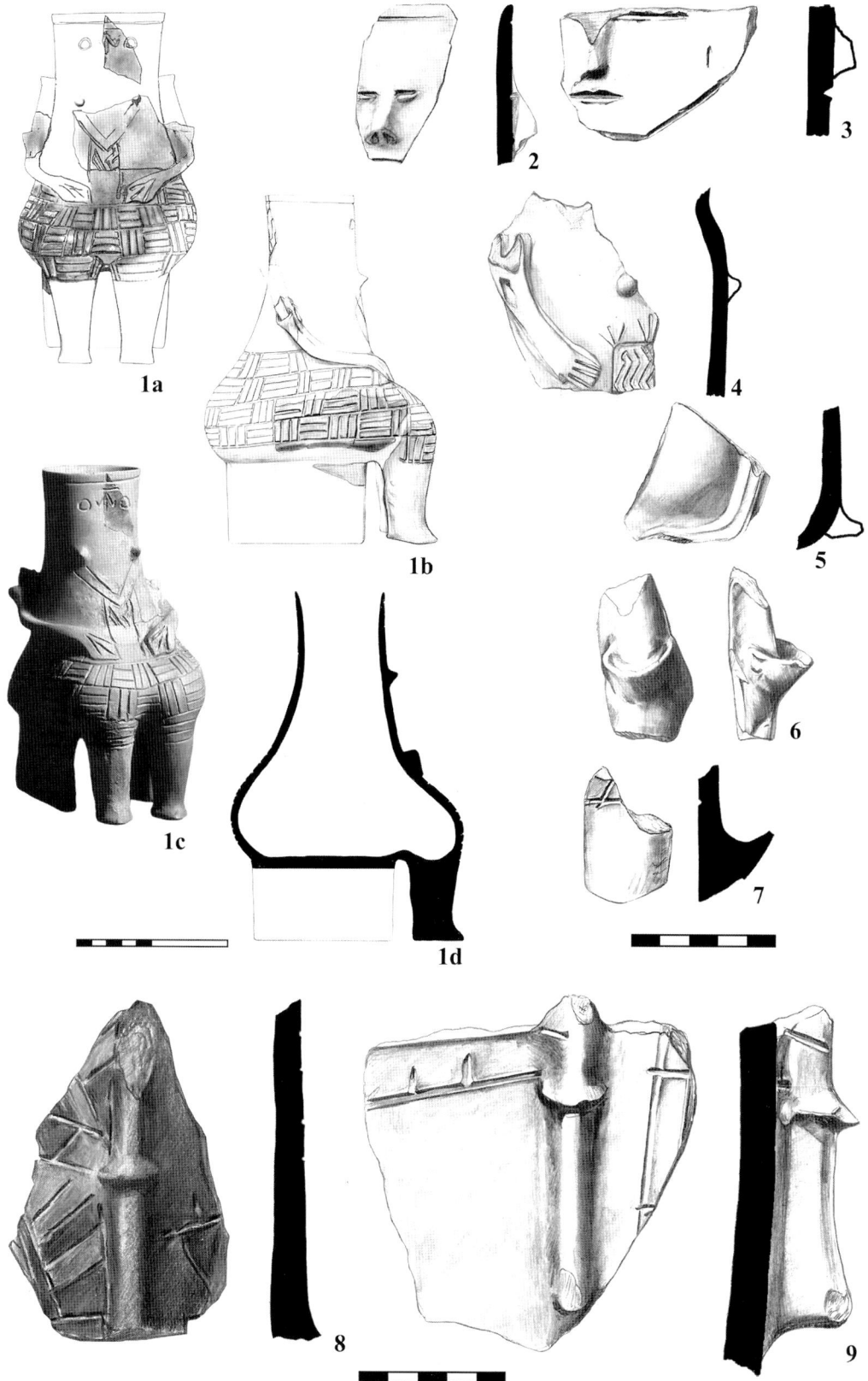

Figure 10.8 Öcsöd-Kováshalom; Finds from different features of the tell-like settlement; 1a–d: Reconstruction of an anthropomorphic vase depicting an enthroned female figurine with bracelets; 2–3: face fragments from small face pots; 4–9: body part fragments with arms and bracelets from face pots.

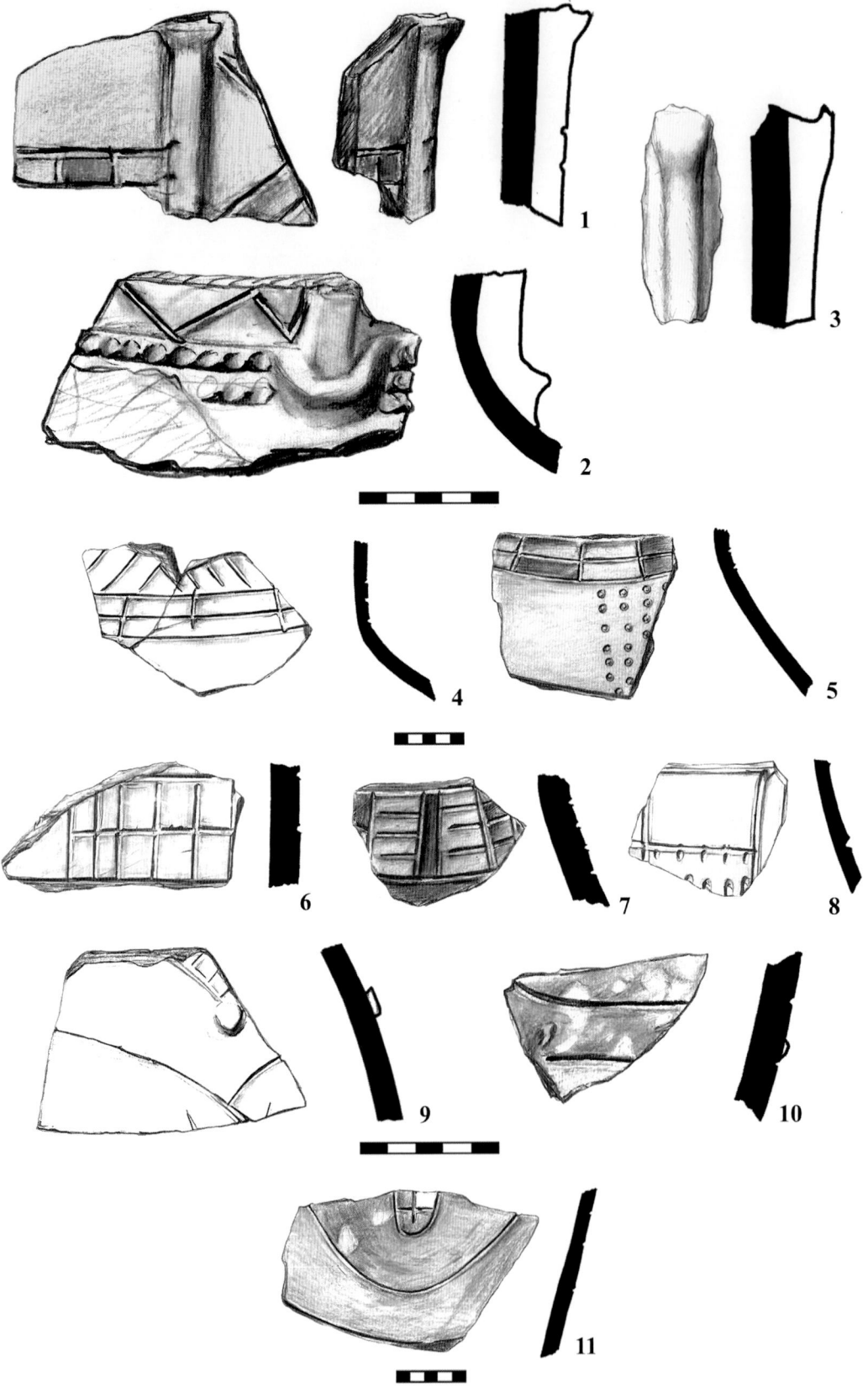

Figure 10.9 Öcsöd-Kováshalom; Finds from different features of the tell-like settlement; 1–3: body part fragments with arms and bracelets from face pots; 4–11: body part fragments with incised and painted decoration from face pots.

Nevertheless, we can assert that the size and ornamentation of this large face pot was identical to the exemplar from Deposit 1 and it seems likely that it had been used in a similar manner. The vessel's neck also bears several upward-raised hands, suggesting that this vessel functioned as a symbolic reference for group identity. Judging from the other deposit, it had probably been part of a set with one or more smaller vessels.

The locations and the contexts of the two depositions in the open-air activity area of the Öcsöd tell-like settlement were spatial segments closely allied to the economic and social milieu of daily life, clearly demonstrating the local meshing of subsistence and ritual activities. Moreover, commemorative and inter-personal as well as confirmative activities were also included in these structured settings. The distinctive traits of the large face pots were a reference to the 'collective body', embodying its metaphor in the given context. This is a relevant point because the various features of the tell-like settlement at Öcsöd yielded countless face pots and other anthropomorphic vessels which quite visibly had individual traits (Figs 10.8–10.9). One possible explanation for this duality is that the local community had embraced one specific concept of personhood. In this system, the different aspects of identity were articulated according to the role played by the individual in the community, whether he/she was an individual actor or a collective actor without a personal identity incorporated into a larger social group (Thomas 2005, 168). This mechanism can perhaps be invoked for explaining the deliberate breakage of large face pots after their use, whereby the possibility of a new social negotiation and the framework for a new social contract, a new social 'refitting' was created. The scattered individual interests could thus be united in a community that periodically renewed itself within a relational system that in the Balkans Neolithic can best be described with Douglass Bailey's (2000) words: 'Exclusion, incorporation and identity'.

Conclusion

The multidisciplinary surveys in 2018–2019 at Öcsöd-Kováshalom, a Late Neolithic site known for a long time, yielded important new information on the earlier excavated settlement. The settlement aggregation at the onset of the 5th millennium cal BC led to the appearance of a settlement complex made up of several smaller single-layer settlement clusters and a tell-like mound in the micro-region at the confluence of the Tisza and Körös Rivers. The central settlement mound acted as a spatial reference in this complex. The magnetometer survey revealed the presence of a triple ditched enclosure ringing the entire settlement, with which it constituted a formal unit. The segmented earthwork created over a longer period of time represents the European pseudo-ditch type in the Late Neolithic of the Hungarian Plain. The ditch segments that were dug out and backfilled from time to time highlight the performative nature of the one-time social actions and draw attention to one particular type of memory making, in which the emphasis was not on visual representation. The rite repeatedly performed in relation to the ditch system created a relational association between the ecological and artefactual milieus as well as time in the memory of the participating individuals and groups. In all likelihood, the ultimate goal of the construction of this 'monument' was the repeated renegotiation and confirmation of this network of social interactions and relations. The two major spatial units, the settlement and the pseudo-ditch, which encapsulated distinctive spheres of the local landscape, were meshed into a specific unit in the system of the complex landscape. The activities and actions performed at different scales, which outline archaeologically visible and often overlapping taskscapes, were conducted in social organisations of different composition within this large system. We were able to identify traces of symbolic, ritual actions in the zone of domestic activities in the archaeologically investigated part of the central tell settlement that provide a clear indication of the local intertwining of the two activities. Looking at the increasingly larger areas of communal activities, the integrated zone of houses, activity areas, pits and burials, we find that collective agents and individuals both participated in the symbolic actions within and transcending these. In the case of fortuitous find circumstances (such as deposition Location 1), we can gain an insight into the sequence of the ritual activities performed in these locations as well as an idea of the norms according to which ritual paraphernalia were treated. This process associated the humans and artefactual agents with specific chronological and spatial contexts. The Öcsöd case study presented here reflects the colourful diversity of community actions and their complex patterns as well as the dynamics of their spatio-temporal changes.

References

Bailey, D.W. (2000) *Balkan Prehistory: Exclusion, Incorporation and Identity*. New York, Routledge.

Bailey, D. & McFayden, L. (2010) Built objects. In D. Hicks & M. Beadry (eds), *The Oxford Handbook of Material Culture*, 556–581. Oxford, Oxford University Press.

Bánffy, E. (2017) Neolithic Eastern and Central Europe. In T. Insoll (ed.), *The Oxford Handbook of Prehistoric Figurines*, 705–728. Oxford, Oxford University Press.

Bertók, G. & Gáti, Cs. (2014) *Old Times – New Methods*. Budapest, Archaeolingua.

Bickle, P. & Whittle, A. (2014) Introduction: Integrated and multi-scalar approaches to early farmers in Europe. *Proceedings of the British Academy* 198, 1–19.

Birch, J. (2013) Between villages and cities: Settlement aggregation in cross-cultural perspective. In J. Birch (ed.), *From*

Prehistoric Villages to Cities: Settlement Aggregation and Community Transformation, 1–22. New York, Routledge.

Bognár-Kutzián, I. (1966) Das Neolithikum in Ungarn. *Archaeologia Austriaca. Beiträge zur Paläanthropologie, Ur- und Frühgeschichte Österreichs* 40, 249–280.

Bradley, R. (2012) *The Idea of Order: The Circular Archetype in Prehistoric Europe*. Oxford, Oxford University Press.

Chapman, J. (1989) The early Balkan village. In S. Bökönyi (ed.), *Neolithic of Southeastern Europe and its Near Eastern Connections*, 33–53. Budapest, Varia Archaeologica Hungarica 2.

Chapman, J. (1994) Social power in the early farming communities of eastern Hungary – perspectives from the Upper Tisza Project. *A nyíregyházi Jósa András Múzeum Évkönyve* 26, 79–99.

Chapman, J. (1997) The origins of tells in eastern Hungary. In P. Topping (ed.), *Neolithic Landscapes*, 139–164. Oxford, Oxbow Books.

Chapman, J. (2000) *Fragmentation in Archaeology. People, Place and Broken Objects in the Prehistory of South-eastern Europe*. New York, Routledge.

Chapman, J. (2008) Meet the ancestors: Settlement histories in the Neolithic. In D. Bailey, A. Whittle & D. Hofmann (eds), *Living Well Together? Settlement and Materiality in the Neolithic of South-East and Central Europe*, 68–80. Oxford, Oxbow Books.

Chapman, J. & Gaydarska, B. (2007) *Parts and Wholes. Fragmentation in Prehistoric Context*. Oxford, Oxbow Books.

DeLanda, M., (2016) *Assemblage Theory*. Edinburgh, Edinburgh University Press.

Domboróczki, L. (2009) Settlement structures of the Alföld Linear Pottery Culture (ALPC) in Heves County (north-eastern Hungary): Development models and historical reconstructions on micro, meso, and macro levels. In J.K. Kozłowski (ed.), *Interactions Between Different Models of Neolithization North of the Central European Agro-Ecological Barrier*, 75–127. Kraków, Polish Academy of Arts and Sciences.

Downey, S.S., Haas, W.R. & Shennan, S.J. (2016) European Neolithic societies showed early warning signals of population signals. *Proceedings of the National Academy of Sciences* 113(35), 9751–9756. www.pnas.org/lookup/suppl/doi:10.1073/pnas.1602504113/-DCSupplemental.

Draşovean, F. & Schier, W. (2010) The Neolithic tell sites of Parţa and Uivar (Romanian Banat). A comparison of their architectural sequence and organization of social space. In S. Hansen (ed.), *Leben auf dem Tell als soziale Praxis*, 143–163. Bonn, Kolloquien zur Vor- und Frühgeschichte 14.

Duffy, P. (2015) Site size hierarchy in middle-range societies. *Journal of Anthropological Archaeology* 37, 85–99.

Duffy, P., Parkinson, W.A., Gyucha, A. & Yerkes, R.W. (2013) Coming together, falling apart: A multiscalar approach to prehistoric aggregation and interaction on the Great Hungarian Plain. In J. Birch (ed.), *From Prehistoric Villages to Cities: Settlement Aggregation and Community Transformation*, 44–62. New York, Routledge.

Fahlender, F. (2017) Ontology matters in archaeology and anthropology. People, things and posthumanism. In J.D. Englehardt & I.A. Rieger (eds), *These 'Thin Partition': Bridging the Growing Divide Between Cultural Anthropology and Archaeology*, 69–86. Boulder CO, University Press of Colorado.

Furholt, M. (2012) Monuments and durable landscapes in the Neolithic of southern Scandinavia and northern Central Europe. In M. Furholt, M. Hinz & D. Mischka (eds), *'As time goes by?' Monumentality, Landscapes and the Temporal Perspective. Proceedings of the International Workshop 'Socio-Environmental Dynamics over the Last 12,000 Years: The Creation of Landscapes II (14th–18th March 2011)' in Kiel*, vol. 2, 115–131. Bonn, Universitätsforschungen zur prähistorischen Archäologie 206.

Furholt, M. (2017) Translocal communities – exploring mobility and migration in sedentary societies of the European Neolithic and Early Bronze Age. *Prähistorische Zeitschrift* 92(2), 304–321.

Füzesi, A. & Raczky, P. (2018) Öcsöd-Kováshalom. Potscape of a Late Neolithic site in the Tisza region. *Dissertationes Archaeologicae* 3(6), 43–146.

Gimbutas, M. (1991) *The Civilization of the Goddess: The World of Old Europe*. San Francisco CA, HarperCollins Publishers.

Gogâltan, F. (2003) Die neolithischen Tellsiedlungen im Karpatenbecken. Ein Überblick. In E. Jerem & P. Raczky (eds), *Morgenrot der Kulturen. Frühe Etappen der Menschheitsgeschichte in Mittel-und Südosteuropa. Festschrift für Nándor Kalicz zum 75. Geburtstag*, 223–262. Budapest, Archaeolingua.

Goldman, G. (1978) Gesichtsgefäße und andere Menschendarstellungen aus Battonya. *Békés megyei Múzeumok Közleményei* 5, 13–60.

Gosden, C. & Malafouris, L. (2015) Process archaeology (P-Arch). *World Archaeology* 47, 701–710.

Gulyás, S. & Sümegi, P. (2011) Riparian environment in shaping social and economic behavior during the first phase of the evolution of Late Neolithic tell complexes in SE Hungary (6th/5th millennia BC). *Journal of Archaeological Science* 38, 2683–2695.

Gyucha, A. (2015) *Prehistoric Village Social Dynamics. The Early Copper Age in the Körös Region. Prehistoric Research in the Körös Region*, Vol. 2. Budapest, Archaeolingua.

Gyucha, A. & Parkinson, W.A. (2008) A Körös-vidék településrendszerének változásai a Kr.e. 5. évezredben. In G. Bóka & E. Martyin (eds), *Körös-menti évezredek. Régészeti ökológiai és településtörténeti kutatások a Körös-vidéken*, Gyulai Katalógusok 13, 65–106. Gyula, Erkel Ferenc Múzeum.

Gyucha, A., Duffy, P. & Parkinson, W.A. (2013) Prehistoric human-environmental interactions on the Great Hungarian Plain. *Anthropologie* 51(2), 157–168.

Gyucha, A., Parkinson, W.A. & Yerkes, R.W. (2009) A multiscalar approach to settlement pattern analysis: The transition from the Late Neolithic to the Early Copper Age on the Great Hungarian Plain. In T.L. Thurston & R.B. Salisbury (eds), *Reimagining Regional Analysis: The Archaeology of Spatial and Social Dynamics*, 100–129. Newcastle-upon-Tyne, Cambridge Scholars.

Hajdú, Zs. & Nagy, E. G. (2015) Különleges funkciójú, középső újkőkori tál Hajdúböszörmény határából. A Middle Neolithic bowl with a unique function from Hajdúböszörmény. *Ősrégészeti Levelek – Prehistoric Newsletter* 14, 25–31.

Hall, E.T. (1990) *The Hidden Dimension*. New York, Anchor.

Harris, O.J.T. (2014) (Re)assembling communities. *Journal of Archaeological Method and Theory* 21(1), 76–97.

Harris, O.J.T. (2017) Assemblage and scale in archaeology. *Cambridge Archaeological Journal* 27(1), 127–139.

Hillier, W.R.G. (2014) Spatial analysis and cultural information: The need for theory as well as method in space syntax analysis. In E. Paliou, U. Lieberwirth & S. Polla (eds), *Spatial Analysis and Social Spaces: Interdisciplinary Approaches to the Interpretation of Prehistoric and Historic Built Environments*, 19–48. Boston MA, De Gruyter.

Hodder, I. (1982) *Symbols in Action. Ethnoarchaeological Studies of Material Culture*. Cambridge, Cambridge University Press.

Hofmann, R. (2012) Tells: Reflections of social and environmental spaces – an introduction. In R. Hofmann, F.K. Moetz & J. Müller (eds), *Tells: Social and Environmental Space. Proceedings of the International Workshop 'Socio-Environmental Dynamics over the Last 12,000 Years: The Creation of Landscapes II (14th–18th March 2011)' in Kiel*, vol. 3, 15–18. Bonn, Universitätsforschungen zur Prähistorischen Archäologie 207.

Hofmann, R. (2015) The Bosnian evidence: The new Late Neolithic and Early Copper-Age chronology and changing settlement pattern. In S. Hansen, P. Raczky, A. Anders & A. Reingruber (eds), *Neolithic and Copper Age Between the Carpathians and the Aegean Sea. Chronologies and Technologies from the 6th to the 4th Millennium BCE. International Workshop Budapest 2012*, 219–241. Bonn, Archäologie in Eurasien 31.

Hofmann R., Medović, A., Furholt, M., Medović, I., Stanković-Pešterac, T., Dreibrodt, S., Martini, S. & Hofmann, A. (2019) Late Neolithic multicomponent sites of the Tisza region and the emergence of centripetal settlement layouts. *Prähistorische Zeitschrift* https://doi.org/10.1515/pz-2019-0003.

Ingold, T. (1993) The temporality of the landscape. *World Archaeology* 25(2), 152–174.

Jannet-Vallat, M. & Thevenot, J.-P. (1991) *Les agriculteurs de la Grand Plaine Hongroise (4000–3500 av. J.-C.)*. Dijon, Musée Archéologique de Dijon.

Kalicz, N. (1970) Südliche Beziehungen im Neolithikum des südlichen Donaubeckens. In F. Schlette (ed.), *Evolution und Revolution im Alten Orient und in Europa. Das Neolithikum als historische Erscheinung*, 145–157. Berlin, Akademie Verlag.

Kalicz, N. (1998) *Figürliche Kunst und bemalte Keramik aus dem Neolithikum Westungarns*. Budapest, Archaeolingua.

Kalicz, N. & Makkay, J. (1977) *Die Linienbandkeramik in der Grossen Ungarischen Tiefebene*. Budapest, Studia Archaeologica 7.

Kalicz, N. & Raczky, P. (1987) The Late Neolithic of the Tisza region. A Survey of recent archaeological research. In L. Tálas & P. Raczky (eds), *The Late Neolithic of the Tisza Region. A Survey of Recent Excavations and their Findings: Hódmezővásárhely-Gorzsa, Szegvár-Tűzköves, Öcsöd-Kováshalom, Vésztő-Mágor, Berettyóújfalu-Herpály*, 11–30. Budapest–Szolnok, Directorate of the Szolnok County Museums.

Kalicz, N. & Raczky, P. (1990) Das Spätneolithikum im Theißgebiet: Eine Übersicht zum heutigen Forschungsstand aufgrund der neuersten Ausgrabungen. In W. Meier-Arendt (ed.), *Alltag und Religion. Jungsteinzeit in Ost-Ungarn. Ausgrabungen in Hódmezővásárhely-Gorzsa, Szegvár-Tűzköves, Öcsöd-Kováshalom, Vésztő-Mágor, Berettyóújfalu-Herpály und Funde*, 11–30. Frankfurt am Main, Museum für Vor- und Frühgeschichte.

Kalicz, N. & Raczky, P. (1991) Le Neolithique recent de la region de la Tisza. Etat de la recherche actuelle, d'après les dernières fouilles archéologiques. In M. Jannet-Vallat & J.-P. Thevenot (eds), *Les agriculteurs de la Grand Plaine Hongroise (4000–3500 av. J.-C.)*, 11–32. Dijon, Musée Archéologique de Dijon.

Kienlin, T.L. (2015) *Bronze Age Tell Communities in Context. An Exploration into Culture, Society and the Study of European Prehistory. Part 1: Critique, Europe and the Mediterranean*. Oxford, Archaeopress.

Korek, J. (1987) Szegvár-Tűzköves. In L. Tálas & P. Raczky (eds), *The Late Neolithic of the Tisza Region. A Survey of Recent Excavations and their Findings: Hódmezővásárhely-Gorzsa, Szegvár-Tűzköves, Öcsöd-Kováshalom, Vésztő-Mágor, Berettyóújfalu-Herpály*, 47–60. Budapest–Szolnok, Directorate of the Szolnok County Museums.

Kuijt, I. (2018) Material geographies of house societies: Reconsidering Neolithic Çatalhöyük, Turkey. *Cambridge Archaeological Journal* 28(4), 565–590.

Latour, B. (2005) *Reassembling the Social. An Introduction to Actor-Network-Theory*. Oxford, Oxford University Press.

Lefranc, Ph., Denaire, A. & Arbogast, R.-M. (2017) Feasts and sacrifices: Fifth millennium 'pseudo-ditch' causewayed enclosures from the southern Upper Rhine valley. In P. Bickle, V. Cummings, D. Hofmann & J. Pollard (eds), *The Neolithic of Europe. Papers in Honour of Alasdair Whittle*, 159–173. Oxford, Oxbow Books.

Link, T. (2006) *Das Ende der neolithischen Tellsiedlungen: Ein kulturgeschichtliches Phänomen des 5. Jahrtausends v. Chr. im Karpatenbecken*. Bonn, Universitätsforschungen zur prähistorischen Archäologie 134.

Makkay, J. (1982) *A magyarországi neolitikum kutatásának új eredményei: Az időrend és a népi azonosítás kérdései*. Budapest, Akadémiai Kiadó.

Marić, M., Mirkovic-Marić, M., Molloy, B., Jovanović, D., Mertl, P., Milašinović, L. & Pendić, J. (2016) New results of the archaeological excavations on the site Gradište near Iđoš: Season 2014. *Glasnik. Journal of the Serbian Archaeological Society* 32, 125–153.

Medović, A., Hofmann, R., Stanković-Pešterac, T., Dreibrodt, R., Medović, I. & Pešterac, R. (2014) The Late Neolithic settlement mound Borđoš near Novi Bečej, Serbian Banat, in a multiregional context: Preliminary results of geophysical, geoarchaeological, and archaeological research. *Rad Muzeja Vojvodine* 56, 1–33.

Meier-Arendt, W. (1990) *Alltag und Religion. Jungsteinzeit in Ost-Ungarn. Ausgrabungen in Hódmezővásárhely-Gorzsa, Szegvár-Tűzköves, Öcsöd-Kováshalom, Vésztő-Mágor, Berettyóújfalu-Herpály und Funde*. Frankfurt am Main, Museum für Vor- und Frühgeschichte.

Meier-Arendt, W. (1991) Zu Tells und tellartigen Siedlungen im Spätneolithikum Ost-Ungarns, Siebenbürgens und des Banat: Überlegungen zu Entstehung und Funktion. In F. Drașovean & S.-A. Luca (eds), *Internationales Symposion „Die Vinča Kultur – Rolle und ihre Beziehungen" Reschitza–Herkulesbad–Temeswar, 12–17. Mai 1991. Banatica* 11, 77–85. Reşița, Muzeul Banatului Montan Reşița.

Müller, J. (2017) Inheritance, population development and social identities. Southeast Europe 5200–4300 BCE. In M. Gori & M. Ivanova (eds), *Balkan Dialogues: Negotiating Identity between Prehistory and the Present*, 156–168. New York, Routledge.

Neumann, D., Siklósi, Zs., Scholz, R. & Szilágyi, M. (2014) Preliminary report on the first season of fieldwork in

Beretyóújfalu-Szilhalom. *Dissertationes Archaeologicae* 3(2), 377–403.

Osborne, J.F. (2014) Monuments and monumentality. In F. Osborne (ed.), *Approaching Monumentality in Archaeology*, 1–19. Albany NY, State University of New York Press.

Osztás, A., Marton, T. & Sófalvi, A. (2004) Szólád-Kisaszó. A tervezett M7-es autópálya Somogy megyei szakaszának megelőző régészeti feltárásai (2002–2003), *Somogyi Múzeumok Közleményei* 16, 61–63.

Palla, G., Barabási, A.-L. & Vicsek, T. (2007) Quantifying social group evolution. *Nature* 446, 664–667.

Papadopoulos, N.G., Sarris, A., Parkinson, W.A., Gyucha, A., Yerkes, R.W., Duffy, P. & Tsourlos, P. (2014) Electrical resistivity tomography for the modelling of cultural deposits and geomophological landscapes at Neolithic sites: A case study from southeastern Hungary. *Archaeological Prospection* 21(3), 169–183. DOI: 10.1002/arp.1480.

Parkinson, W.A. (2006) *The Social Organization of Early Copper Age Tribes on the Great Hungarian Plain.* Oxford, British Archaeological Report S1573.

Parzinger, H. (1992) Zentrale Orte – Siedelverband und Kultgemeinschaft im karpatenländischen Neo- und Äneolithikum. In R. Samardžić (ed.), *Homage a Nikola Tasić a l'occasion des ses soixante ans*, 221–230. Belgrade, Balcanica XXIII.

Raczky, P. (1987) Öcsöd-Kováshalom. A settlement of the Tisza culture. In L. Tálas & P. Raczky (eds), *The Late Neolithic of the Tisza Region. A Survey of Recent Excavations and their Findings: Hódmezővásárhely-Gorzsa, Szegvár-Tűzköves, Öcsöd-Kováshalom, Vésztő-Mágor, Berettyóújfalu-Herpály*, 61–83. Budapest–Szolnok, Directorate of the Szolnok County Museums.

Raczky, P. (1995) Neolithic settlement patterns in the Tisza region of Hungary. In A. Aspes (ed.), *Settlement Patterns between the Alps and the Black Sea 5th to 2nd Millennium BC. Modelli insediativi tra Alpi e Mar Nero dal 5° al 2° Millennio A.C. Atti del Simposio Internazionale. Verona-Lazise 1992*, 77–86. Verona, Museo Civico di Storia Naturale di Verona.

Raczky, P. (2000) A unique face pot from the Öcsöd-Kováshalom settlement of the Tisza culture. In D. Gábler & É. Garam (eds), *Stephano Bóna Anniversarium Septuagesimum Feliciter Agenti Gratulamur ex Animo Amici Discipulique. Acta Archaeologica Academiae Scientiarum Hungaricae* 51, 9–22.

Raczky, P. (2009) Archaeological data on space use at a tell-like settlement of the Tisza Culture (new results from Öcsöd-Kováshalom, Hungary). In F. Draşovean, D.L. Cibotaru & M. Maddison (eds), *Ten Years After: The Neolithic of the Balkans, as Uncovered by the Last Decade of Research. Proceedings of the Conference held at the Museum of Banat on November 9th–10th*, 101–136. Timişoara, Editura Marineasa.

Raczky, P. (2015) Settlements in South-east Europe. In C. Fowler, J. Harding & D. Hofmann (eds), *The Oxford Handbook of Neolithic Europe*, 235–253. Oxford, Oxford University Press.

Raczky, P. (2018) A complex monument in the making at the Late Neolithic site of Polgár-Csőszhalom (Hungary). In A.T. Bács, Á. Bollók & T. Vida (eds), *Across The Mediterranean – Along The Nile. Studies in Egyptology, Nubiology and Late Antiquity Dedicated to László Török on the Occasion of His 75th Birthday*, 15–60. Budapest, Institute of Archaeology, Research Centre for the Humanities, Hungarian Academy of Sciences.

Raczky, P. (2019) Cross-scale settlement morphologies and social formations in the Neolithic of the Great Hungarian Plain. In A. Gyucha (ed.), *Coming Together. Comparative Approaches to Population Aggregation and Early Urbanization*, 259–294. New York, State University of New York Press.

Raczky, P. & Anders, A. (2010) Activity loci and data for spatial division at a Late Neolithic site-complex (Polgár-Csőszhalom: A case study). In S. Hansen (ed.), *Leben auf dem Tell als soziale Praxis*, 143–163. Bonn, Kolloquien zur Vor- und Frühgeschichte 14.

Raczky, P. & Anders, A. (2014) Szentpéterszeg-Kovadomb. Egy késő neolitikus lelőhely tér-képei – Szentpéterszeg-Kovadomb. Image-scapes of a Late Neolithic settlement. In A. Anders, Cs. Balogh & A. Türk (eds), *Avarok pusztái. Régészeti tanulmányok Lőrinczy Gábor 60. születésnapjára – Avarum solitudines. Archaeological studies presented to Gábor Lőrinczy on his sixtieth birthday*, 23–42. Budapest, Martin Opitz Kiadó.

Raczky, P. & Füzesi, A. (2016) Öcsöd-Kováshalom. A retrospective look at the interpretations of a Late Neolithic site. *Dissertationes Archaeologicae* 3(4), 9–42.

Raczky, P., Füzesi, A. & Anders, A. (2018) Domestic and symbolic activities on a tell-like settlement at Öcsöd-Kováshalom in the Tisza region. In S.A. Luca (ed.), *Volume of the International Symposium: The Image of Divinity in the Neolithic and Eneolithic: Ways of Communication (Sibiu, Romania, 26th–28th October 2017)*, 117–140. Suceava, Editura Karl A. Romstorfer.

Raczky, P., Anders, A. Sebők, K., Csippán, P. & Tóth, Z. (2015) The times of Polgár-Csőszhalom: Chronologies of human activities on the Polgár-Csőszhalom horizontal settlement. In S. Hansen, P. Raczky, A. Anders & A. Reingruber (eds), *Neolithic and Copper Age between the Carpathians and the Aegean Sea: Chronologies and Technologies from the 6th to the 4th Millennium BCE*. Archäologie in Eurasien 31, 21–48. Bonn, Habelt.

Raczky, P., Sümegi, P., Bartosiewicz, L., Gál, E., Kaczanowska, M., Kozłowski, J.K. & Anders, A. (2010) Ecological barrier versus mental marginal zone? Problems of the northernmost Körös Culture settlements in the Great Hungarian Plain. In D. Gronenborn & J. Petrasch (eds), *Die Neolithisierung Mitteleuropas – The Spread of the Neolithic to Central Europe*, 147–173. Mainz, Römisch-Germanischen Zentralmuseums.

Rapoport, A. (1990) Systems of activities and systems of settlings. In S. Kent (ed.), *Domestic Architecture and the Use of Space: An Interdisciplinary Cross-Cultural Study*, 9–20. Cambridge, New Directions in Archaeology.

Renfrew, C. (1998) Mind and matter: Cognitive archaeology and external symbolic storage. In C. Renfrew & C. Scarre (eds), *Cognition and Material Culture: The Archaeology of Symbolic Storage*, 1–6. Cambridge, McDonald Institute for Archaeological Research.

Rosenstock, E. (2009) *Tells in Südwestasien und Südosteuropa. Verbreitung, Entstehung und Definition eines Siedlungsphänomens.* Urgeschichtliche Studien 2. Remshalden, B.A. Greiner.

Salisbury, R.B. & Morris, M.R. (2009) Social and settlement dynamics in the Hungarian Late Neolithic and Early Copper

Age – a regional inquiry. In T.L. Thurston & R.B. Salisbury (eds), *Reimagining Regional Analysis: The Archaeology of Spatial and Social Dynamics*, 130–163. Newcastle-upon-Tyne, Cambridge Scholars.

Salisbury, R.B., Bácsmegi, G. & Sümegi, P. (2013) Preliminary environmental historical results to reconstruct prehistoric human-environmental interactions in eastern Hungary. *Central European Journal of Geosciences* 5(3), 331–343.

Sarris, A., Papadopoulos, N., Agapiou, A., Salvi, M.C., Hadjimitsis, D.G. Parkinson, W.A., Yerkes, R.W., Gyucha, A. & Duffy, P. (2013) Integration of geophysical surveys, ground hyperspectral measurements, aerial and satellite imagery for archaeological prospection of prehistoric sites: the case study of Vésztő-Mágor Tell, Hungary. *Journal of Archaeological Science* 40, 1454–1470.

Schier, W. & Draşovean, F. (2004) Vorbericht über die rumänisch-deutschen Prospektionen und Ausgrabungen in der befestigten Tellsiedlung von Uivar, jud. Timişoara, Rumänien (1998–2002). *Prähistorische Zeitschrift* 79, 145–230.

Sebők, K. (2018) On the possibilities of interpreting Neolithic pottery – Az újkőkori kerámia értelmezési lehetőségeiről. *Dissertationes Archaeologicae* 3(6), 13–42.

Sherratt, A. (1982) Mobile resources: Settlement and exchange in early agricultural Europe. In C. Renfrew & S. Shennan (eds), *Ranking, Resource, and Exchange: Aspects of the Archaeology of Early European Society*, 13–26. Cambridge, Cambridge University Press.

Somogyi, K. (2007) Die besonderen Grabenanlagen der Lengyel-Kultur in Kaposújlak-Várdomb-dűlő im Komitat Somogy (SW-Ungarn). In J. Kozłowski & P. Raczky (eds), *The Lengyel, Polgár and Related Cultures in the Middle/Late Neolithic in Central Europe*, 329–344. Kraków, Polska Akademia Umiejętności.

Spacić, M. & Crnobrnja, A.N. (2014) Vinčanske zdele sa protomama. Vinča bowls with protom. *Starinar* 64, 185–203.

Tálas, L. & Raczky, P. (1987) *The Late Neolithic of the Tisza Region. A Survey of Recent Excavations and their Findings: Hódmezővásárhely-Gorzsa, Szegvár-Tűzköves, Öcsöd-Kováshalom, Vésztő-Mágor, Berettyóújfalu-Herpály*. Budapest-Szolnok, Directorate of the Szolnok County Museums.

Thomas, J. (2005) Ambiguous symbols: why there were no figurines in Neolithic Britain. *Documenta Praehistorica* XXXII, 167–175.

Tringham, R.E. (2005) Weaving house life and death into places: a blueprint for a hypermedia narrative. In D. Bailey, A. Whittle & V. Cummings (eds), *(Un)settling the Neolithic*, 98–111. Oxford, Oxbow Books

Twiss, K.C. (2008) Transformations in an early agricultural society: Feasting in the southern Levantine Pre-Pottery Neolithic. *Journal of Anthropological Archaeology* 27, 418–442.

Whitehouse, H. & Hodder, I. (2010) Modes of religiosity at Çatalhöyük. In I. Hodder (ed.), *Religion in the Emergence of Civilization: Çatalhöyük as a Case Study*, 122–145. Cambridge-New York, Cambridge University Press.

Whittle, A. (1996) *Europe in the Neolithic: The Creation of New Worlds*. Cambridge, Cambridge University Press.

Whittle, A. (1997) Fish, faces and fingers: presences and symbolic identities in the Mesolithic-Neolithic transition in the Carpathian Basin. *Documenta Praehistorica* 25, 133–150.

Yerkes, R.W., Gyucha, A. & Parkinson, W.A. (2009) A multiscalar approach to modeling the end of the Neolithic on the Great Hungarian Plain using calibrated radiocarbon dates. *Radiocarbon* 51(3), 1071–1109.

11

The Practice of Everyday Life on a European Bronze Age Tell: Reflections from Százhalombatta-Földvár (Hungary)

Joanna Sofaer, Marie Louise Stig Sørensen and Magdolna Vicze

Background and problematisation

Our understanding of life on Bronze Age tells in temperate Europe has, until recently, been directed by a generic idea of what tells are, and an assumption that this distinctive form of settlement implies a particular social organisation and way of functioning. The core descriptive characteristics of a tell are easy to agree: a particular kind of stratigraphy resulting from repeated rebuilding of houses on the same plot, a central location (often at a high point and located next to major rivers), and dense and clearly laid out habitation. However, in themselves these features reveal little about what tells are and how life within them was organised and experienced. The prevailing universalising understanding of tell living is neither helpful nor illuminating if our aim is insights rather than merely categorising sites. It puts at risk our readiness to pay attention to diversity and differentiation within this settlement form and also to whether, and how, it has distinct characteristics when encountered in particular regions, such as the Carpathian Basin during the Middle Bronze Age.

The persistence of a universal model is, in part, due to the limited data available until the last few decades and a consequent inability to reconsider factually, refine, or refute interpretations. Disagreements too easily then become a matter of theoretical position, rather than due to better insights into the characteristics of these communities. It is, therefore, important to recognise that our ideas of life on Bronze Age tells in temperate Europe have traditionally been greatly informed by evidence from tells in the Near East and by well-preserved and extensively excavated Neolithic tells in southeastern Europe. The resulting interpretations have been furthered by a gradually evolving meta-narrative of the European Bronze Age, rooted in V. Gordon Childe's understanding of the period and his assumptions about the role of tells within trade networks (Childe 1929, 269). Rather than investigating the data, the tell narrative has further consolidated assumptions about hierarchical societies in which leaders and their followers exercised control. On the basis of such narratives, tells in temperate Bronze Age Europe have most commonly been understood through their assigned socio-political and economic roles within extensive regional networks (*e.g.* Bóna 1975; Kovács 1994a, among others). In recent years, this interpretation has even been used to sustain interpretations of a specific Bronze Age economy (Earle 2002). However, although this interpretation has provided an apparently coherent explanation for a striking social phenomenon – as is the way of meta-narrative – the interpretation has become an all-consuming self-referential imposition that has left the evidence provided by excavations and surveys outside the discourse and neglected to engage critically with its own assumptions.

The meta-narrative has persevered partly because most earlier excavations focused on fixed points of chronology and paid limited attention to the evidence of life suspended between horizons of floors, so little data existed with which to test or challenge the arguments about central socio-economic and political roles. Thus, there has been a tendency to privilege the interpretation of site stratigraphy over the detailed analysis of the material of which tells are composed. In other words, there has been a focus on identifying chronological sequences rather than activities. While this has contributed useful knowledge, it has also resulted in somewhat abstract accounts in which sites are conceptualised and presented as neatly compartmentalised into a series of horizons. Tells are without doubt important resources for understanding diachronic change (*e.g.* Bóna 1992; Kovács 1994b; O'Shea *et al.* 2019) and comprehending change over time is vital to understanding the nature of tells. However, a focus on chronology alone without an accompanying grasp of sociality and how tells were created as a product of people living on them, risks turning tells into archaeological concepts used to establish general frameworks, rather than investigating tells as entities in their own right with their own distinct questions and issues. Thus, whilst the analysis of tells is suited to both horizontal and vertical site description, all too often a traditional focus on vertical stratigraphy has caused horizontal understandings of space to become a blind spot; the conditions for the creation of space, and thus the processes that underpin stratigraphy – life on the tell – are forgotten. As a result, the taken for granted hierarchical model was for long left unquestioned.

Recent re-evaluations of the meta-narrative of Bronze Age temperate Europe have attempted to reduce this emphasis on hierarchical social relations and to introduce a more egalitarian slant to the interpretation of tells (*e.g.* Kienlin 2015). However, even in these attempts to recast tells there can be a risk of replacing one universal narrative with another. Here we suggest that we need to move beyond critique of former interpretations and explore how we can get closer to a more nuanced and evidence-based understanding of how specific settlements functioned on what we may refer to as an everyday level of practice. In other words, we argue that we need to take a 'bottom-up' approach to the interrogation of tells, seeing them as outcomes of people's daily lives as well as structural impositions, rather than being guided solely by a 'top-down' view of this settlement form as an essentially political phenomenon. To do this requires a series of changes in our approach to tells. The first is a shift in analysis towards the investigation of space in terms of its varied and particular expressions in order to understand the arrangements and specific nature of the varied activities that through time made up a settlement. Secondly, it requires rebalancing conceptualisations of the temporality of tells by adding understandings of short-term processes or events that are reflective of the everyday to the present emphasis on tracing long-term chronological change. We need to increase the temporal resolution at which we operate in order to explore the timing and duration of actions and their effects, and how these may be linked together within the *longue dureé* over which a site existed. Thirdly, accessing life on a tell requires a reappraisal of how to deal with archaeological data. This is a matter of exploring how Bronze Age people engaged with the material world on the most fundamental level and thus of taking an archaeological approach that is focused on analysis of the forms, distribution and use of material culture. The ensuing challenges are considerable – how do we account interpretatively for the minutia of life on a tell and yet not lose sight of larger structuring principles in order to reach coherent and comprehensible accounts? How do we learn to write more detailed stories about tell life?

This is where the insights from recent excavations and surveys can make a difference. With several on-going projects investigating Bronze Age tells through advanced methodologies we can now begin to reassess how well our pre-existing ideas match the evidence in the ground. The application of new surveying techniques and innovations in excavation methods mean that new kinds of data have been amassed, and these in turn begin to question some of the core assumptions that have been underwriting normative views of tells. In particular, whereas the long tradition of spit-digging with its aim of uncovering sequences and the layer-by-layer excavations concentrating on house-floors lent themselves to top-down narratives focused upon structures, the single-context excavation methods now pursued provide a more explicit focus on the activities and small-scale events that accumulated to make the site (for a more detailed discussion of this shift see Sørensen *et al.* 2020). This evidence does not merely provide alternatives to established meta-narratives but also enables different ways of thinking about tell communities and their ways of living. Tell excavations are costly, both in resources and time, but they are important for gaining insights into what we call the *situated milieu of human action* in a manner that is not entirely reduced to volumetric data. Without such insights, we cannot advance effectively understandings of tell communities. Furthermore, recent excavations such as at Kakucs (Jaeger *et al.* 2018) or at Pecica (Nicodemous 2014); survey projects, such as the Benta (Earle *et al.* 2012), the BORBAS project (Kienlin *et al.* 2018) or BAKOTA (Duffy 2014); catalogues (Gogâltan *et al.* 2014) and analyses such as Alexandra Găvan's (2015) study of metal and metal working evidence from tells and other Middle Bronze Age sites in the Carpathian Basin hint at potential differences between tells. We are thus at a point where we have the methodological tools to develop a new level of insight regarding tell life but we lack appropriate interpretative structures for this level of engagement and, at times, we even miss a useful terminology. Compared to our familiarity with models for Bronze Age political organisation, the everyday retains a certain strangeness and unfamiliarity.

In response to such challenges, this paper aims to reflect on how we may engage with the nature of life on a Bronze Age tell through consideration of the Middle Bronze Age tell at Százhalombatta-Földvár, Hungary.

The Százhalombatta-Földvár tell

Százhalombatta-Földvár lies on the west bank of the River Danube 30 km south of Budapest. Due to the systematic and detailed recording conducted, the results from the on-going excavation can be used to engage critically with questions about the character of tells. In the following we therefore use the experience of excavating and analysing the data from Százhalombatta-Földvár as our reflexive foundation. We aim to think through the kind of issues that the site and its data force upon us. We are not arguing for an inductive approach to the site but, nonetheless, find that data must play a more central role in interpretation, and that we must engage reflexively with the dynamic between the site, data and interpretative propositions. To understand the site, we must enter into dialogue with its data.

The history of the excavation of Százhalombatta-Földvár, including its aims and methodology, has been provided elsewhere (Poroszlai & Vicze 2000; 2004; Vicze *et al.* 2017). Suffice to say that the core aims of the excavation are to investigate the settlement structure and architecture, as well as daily life, technology, and material culture. Within this broad remit we are particularly concerned with understanding the spatial organisation of the settlement in a manner that both includes and yet moves beyond houses, including the layout of streets, areas between houses and working areas. We want to understand how different kinds of spaces were generated, how people created and inhabited spaces on the tell, and how the production and consumption of material culture and other matters were linked to social lives, and the consequential generation of a settlement.

Two points about the site need to be made. First, the site is important due to the size of its excavation. The current excavation trench is 20 × 20 m (see Vicze & Sørensen in press for the history of earlier interventions on the site). This represents only a part of the original site but it is, nonetheless, the largest Bronze Age tell excavation in the Carpathian Basin in recent decades and it provides us with a uniquely detailed data set. It is becoming obvious, for instance, that various kinds of surfaces such as paths, yards or working areas – not just floors – were used regularly as part of daily life on the tell. Although there was little formality to their construction, as they resulted from usage and practices, they were important aspects of community life as most of the productive activities took place on such areas outside the houses (the houses are relatively clean). It seems obvious that the human and temporal dimension of these features should be appreciated; indeed, the dynamic nature of living spaces has been pointed to in many different contexts (*e.g.* Boivin 2000). However, interpretations of tells have traditionally paid little attention to such surfaces other than recognising that they might exist. In their informal character (*i.e.* outside of the architectural elements of the houses), they often have very different lifecycles to 'normal' floors, and we are ill-equipped when attempting to excavate and analyse them. They developed as people walked on them, worked on them, sat there, conducted secondary agricultural activities and crafted objects. They are the outcome of both deliberate acts and of unintended consequences, often without clear boundaries and shifting through time. It is therefore important to recognise that various aspects of excavation recording, including both the Harris Matrix and the single-context excavation method (which we use), in their core principles are dependent on absolutes. They are concerned with classifying surfaces and events rather than identifying fluid units such as a continuously developing and changing yard surface. Thus, our recording techniques in themselves limit our insights into tell-life, and in turn challenge us about how we may nonetheless respond to important questions about how to capture everyday life beyond mere snapshots.

Secondly, the formation processes of the tell are complex. This is partly due to the number of pits, including those inside houses so typical of Vatya sites (Bóna & Nováki 1982; Poroszlai 1988; Vicze 2013a), and partly due to the considerable degree of collapse, subsidence and infill, much of this taking place during the occupation of the site. These features in themselves make recording and interpretation complicated but they also provide insights into how the inhabitants dealt with, for example, subsiding floors. They are, therefore, important aspects of behaviour that reveal people responding to the particularities of living on a potentially unstable tell surface. Recognising this complexity of site formation pushes us to rethink the site beyond the 'layer cake' model of a tell as a series of relatively simply articulated stratigraphic layers. It instils a change of focus as the matrix is different to expectation and site life far more dynamic than foreseen.

Addressing the everyday: Interpretative challenges

Archaeological interest in the everyday has been expressed since the 1990s (*e.g.* Barrett 1994). Originally strongly influenced by theoreticians such as Pierre Bourdieu (1977; 1984), Anthony Giddens (1984) and Clifford Geertz (1973), it has been gradually explored against ever more diverse archaeological situations (*e.g.* Hodder & Cessford 2004; Wilson 2008). Investigating the everyday nonetheless remains a difficult undertaking. More specifically, in terms of the applicability of such theoretical frameworks to Bronze Age tells there are problematic aspects as well as interesting potential avenues to explore. As regards the former, many approaches have been concerned with the dynamics around social rules, and many of the arguments tied to structural characteristics of modern societies in which social and political organisations are easy to identify and isolate analytically, and in which the individual and the social are seen as separate. Bourdieu's seminal concept of habitus, for instance, assumes that rules and constraints (*i.e.* the social) act on individuals, even in terms of such daily routines as eating, sitting and moving in domestic spaces, and that such rules become embodied. Evidentially this dynamic is challenging for archaeology and, in reality, many archaeologists exploring concepts of daily practices have ended up focusing on broad social dynamics, rather than the relationship between individuals and society. This turns research towards questions about power (*e.g.* Barrett 1994). In such cases the social does not just partake in everyday life practices but dominates our analysis, and daily practices/everydayness is rarely explored as a constitutive basis of the lived experiences of past communities.

Explorations of social memory, in particular the work of Paul Connerton (1989), which reconsiders Bourdieu through the lens of memory as a means of understanding repeated practices (Strathern 1996), have also been influential in archaeological approaches. This line of thought is of particular interest to tell investigations as a way of understanding repeated practices, such as the rebuilding of houses on the same plot or, in the case of Near Eastern Neolithic tells, the burials inside houses generation after generation (*e.g.* Hodder & Cessford 2004; Guerrero *et al.* 2009). The specificity of social memory construction has rightly been raised as an important question in such studies, although the 'rhetorical power' of memory as a notion has also been flagged as leading to a loss of precision in interpretation (Gillis 1994; Berliner 2005). The guarding of tradition through memory and employment of various confirmative cultural practices (for example regulatory practices, Sørensen 2019) is, indeed, a core aspect of tell communities. In addition, there can also be a loss of memory and that might lead people to do things differently. This aspect, however, remains largely unexplored, despite important questions regarding the ways that rules are set and agreed to, and especially why at times such order breaks down and why rules are not adhered to consistently. The latter concerns are particularly relevant to the later phases of tells.

One of the challenges that has arisen from the data from Százhalombatta-Földvár, as discussed below, is exactly the inconsistency in adherence to structural conventions. This leads us to consider the work of thinkers who have argued for the need to explore specific practices. For instance, de Certeau (1984, xi) argues that a focus on practice is a matter of comprehending the modes of action characteristic of people in specific settings by making explicit the combination of operations that compose culture and sense of self. These actions are not simply reducible to individuals, but necessarily require a level of analysis at which social relations determine the terms under which individuals operate. De Certeau points out that this is not accessible through descriptive or statistical methods alone since quantitative investigation grasps the material elements of practices but not their form. It 'determines the elements used, but not the "phrasing" produced by the bricolage (the artisan-like inventiveness) and the discursiveness that combine these elements' (de Certeau 1984, xviii). This suggests that we should aim to get 'under the skin' so to speak of everyday practices to reveal their 'rhythms and reasons' rather than merely their surface appearance. De Certeau's interest in everydayness is articulated as a contrast to societal instructions (strategies) imposed by the powerful with the everydayness located in how individuals traverse those structures/instructions in their own ways (tactical decisions). However, as with other theoretical frameworks, it is difficult to use such arguments straightforwardly in the analysis of our tell without inadvertently making top-down assumptions about how these societies functioned or about their regulatory mechanisms and the existence of particular kinds of power structures. In other words, while it is possible to agree with many elements of de Certeau's intellectual argument, they should be used selectively as a means of exploring issues rather than imposing modern notions on to the past, and we remain mindful that the degree of insightfulness possible when employing contemporary theoretical frameworks to investigate past societies remains a challenge.

Nonetheless, in addressing our observations at Százhalombatta-Földvár, de Certeau's argument about people engaging in deliberate actions in a creative manner that goes beyond habitus and repeated action is of help. His core considerations of strategy and tactics provide us with an awareness of the need to consider what may structure people's behaviour and what may affect the dynamics between such structures and individual tactics. They therefore challenge us to reconsider the formative elements of the tell community – those that gave it shape and consistency – reminding us that the inconsistencies we observe can only be noted against expectations of conventions and regulations. In this manner, the Százhalombatta-Földvár data confirm that the classic concern with the dynamics located between structure and action is still central to our investigations of the site, while we can also benefit from de Certeau's account of how particular divergences often arise not in the political sphere but in the actual practices of how place is used. In addition, in the case of our Bronze Age tell we propose that the nature of the structures around which individuals and groups navigate were not just explicit social instructions, but also took the more intangible form of tradition and memory. Thus, we argue that, in the apparently modestly ranked community who inhabited the tell, many daily decisions were made by individuals or small groups and were shaped through complex interplays of social instructions, tradition and memory, functional needs, material constraints, and individual tactics. Of these, traditions are the strongest conservative factor striving to impose continuity on how things were done and are thus a high profile and archaeologically accessible element but also one that at times may be subverted or deliberately rejected or altered.

To further explore these dimensions, we now turn to Százhalombatta-Földvár focusing on two everyday practices – walking and dwelling – that de Certeau (1984) calls 'the arts of doing'. These practices are not the background to social activity but constitute them in the most fundamental way; the term 'arts' is used to indicate that daily life requires day-to-day problem solving and creative responses to the world in the broadest sense. We outline two examples that reveal the 'arts of doing' within our material, illustrating how this approach provides a distinct lens on how life on the site was organised. Thus, for 'walking' we identify the tell as a place of motion in order to discuss attitudes to different kinds of spaces in terms of cleanliness and messiness.

To explore the nature of 'dwelling' we consider practice in relation to the regeneration of houses through time (or lack thereof) and the eventual abandonment of the tell in terms of order and disorder. Following de Certeau (1984), both examples also evidence the interplay of regulation and alternatives (strategy and tactics) as distinct aspects of how this particular place was produced over time.

The tell as a place of motion: Cleanliness and messiness

In order to access the practice of everyday life at Százhalombatta-Földvár we have to understand the tell as a place of motion. This is to imagine explicitly the site as a place where people walked, ran, crawled, played, made things or threw things out. The nature and direction of motion are spatial practices that both define and create space at any given point in time. This means that motion is intrinsic to site formation and people's experience of movement was defined by the spatial organisation of the settlement (*cf.* Merleau-Ponty 1962); motion and space exist in a reciprocal relationship and both are subject to strategies and tactics. The tell was a place where, as de Certeau puts it in relation to city spaces, 'bodies follow the thicks and thins of an urban "text" they write without being able to read it … The networks of these moving, intersecting writings compose a manifold story that has neither author nor spectator, shaped out of fragments of trajectories and alterations of spaces' (de Certeau 1984, 93).

To our surprise, the excavation has revealed that the expected regularity through time, which the label 'tell' suggests, does not match how people lived on the site and how it was generated through time. So, motion was complex and shifting through the history of the tell as the degree of spatial organisation and apparent regulations (*i.e.* path, open areas, road, house plots) varied, and with them the individual's tactical decisions. In particular, the locations and 'feel' of the paths between houses, rather than being permanent throughout the Middle Bronze Age, changed through time as the use of areas shifted (Vicze 2013b). In turn, movements had to adjust or be reinvented. This is particularly striking when during the Middle Bronze Age a substantial road made out of a heavily compacted grey clay was constructed on top of earlier domestic constructions of houses and pits. The road runs across the trench from south to north, presumably continuing outside the trench in both directions and was marked by deep wheel-ruts extending for several metres (Fig. 11.1). The distance between these was 120 cm, suggesting it was used for heavy wagons. Through a part of the life of the tell the road was maintained and repaired, and it was most likely a major artery for movement, but also one that could be joined or traversed in different manners. After some time it was transformed into a kind of open-air working area (for detailed analysis of this see Sørensen & Vicze 2013), again affecting the regulation of movements and use.

However, a focus on motion applies not only to paths or to the road through the settlement. It allows us to consider *all* surfaces as space and outcome of movement and this, in turn, leads us to consider *the specific practices of space* as ways of operating within them (see de Certeau 1984, 93). Throughout the Middle Bronze Age levels we see people discriminating in their use of space: house floors and external working areas are kept cleaned, but other areas, such as immediately around the house, were often dirty or messy in terms of the accumulation of bones, pot sherds and other things (Fig. 11.2). Messiness and cleanliness both imply movement, for example throwing things out or sweeping things up, that creates or impedes possibilities for movement through different parts of the site; areas that are used frequently tend to be cleared up in order to avoid obstruction (Murray 1980; Hayden & Cannon 1983) and in some cases it seems that houses may have been cleaned prior to deliberate destruction and rebuilding as part of their lifecycle. Messiness and cleanliness also imply regulations or their absence – what kinds of spaces were included in regulations about either cleanliness or rubbish? In this regard we interpret the messiness around houses not as a regulated rubbish management but rather as a kind of liminal zone lacking social regulation and therefore used by individuals (tactically) for random movements of debris. Yet even within apparently 'clean' spaces we observe differences in practice. For example, in Level 3 (belonging to the Koszider phase of the site) there are differences in sherd abrasion between the remnant of the inside of a house and the open-air working surface. In both cases the majority of sherds are small to medium size (95% and 96% of sherds respectively) and less than 5% of the total 9380 sherds examined from these contexts can be refitted. This indicates trampling and substantial dispersal, and deliberate cleaning of both these surfaces. However, there is a statistically significant difference in sherd abrasion between the house floor and the working area. There is greater and more frequent abrasion of sherds from the latter (Jones 2018), revealing more intense movement in this area and thus both very similar and very different kinds of activities in the two clean spaces.

Moreover, it is possible to identify areas of the site where pottery appears to have been deliberately redeposited, possibly in order to level out the tell and to allow creation of new kinds of surfaces on which structures or working areas could be established. For example, in Level 5 which is near to the top of the tell and should therefore be a firmly Koszider level, the chronologically and typologically mixed nature of the assemblage includes earlier Vatya and Early Bronze Age material. This, along with a lack of sherds that can be refitted (or that even belong to the same vessel), suggests that sherds were deliberately moved from the edge of the site (or at least outside the area of our trench) to create the 'foundations' of a new surface. The archaeological impression of such an assemblage is one of 'messiness' and inconsistency

Figure 11.1 Százhalombatta-Földvár. View of the road with wheel ruts from the south.

Figure 11.2 Százhalombatta-Földvár. Messiness on the side of the road.

but this is not a midden. Here the messiness that we observe is a result of deliberate and ordered decision-making that reflects attitudes to the use of space; it is a form of recycling and reuse that reintegrates material into the life of the tell, rather than an act of disposal that attempts to remove it from use. Recognising such forms of 'dynamic maintenance' of the tell by its inhabitants not only offers new insights into tell living but also asks us to re-evaluate the temporal and material complexity of site formation processes.

The tell as a place of dwelling: Order and disorder

Towards the end of *The Practice of Everyday Life* de Certeau explicitly uses archaeological terminology as a means of encapsulating the complexity of the relationship between place and practice. Thus, he talks about 'stratified places' (de Certeau 1984, 200) and argues that 'place is a palimpsest' (de Certeau 1984, 202), by which he means that places are fields for layers of multiple actions piled on to one another. He states: 'The kind of difference that defines every place is not on the order of a juxta-position but rather takes the form of imbricated strata' (de Certeau 1984, 200). In other words, differences in practice between places can be identified by sorting through a suite of actions that accumulate over time. Consideration of such 'action stratigraphy' brings us to a discussion of houses at Százhalombatta-Földvár since not only is dwelling in its various expressions a fundamental form of practice but previous work on tells has tended to promote the idea of 'the house', its repeated destruction and rebuilding as the physical stratigraphy, and by implication also the stratigraphy of action and practice, that characterises tells as a distinctive settlement form.

This focus has tended to identify tells as highly regulated and normative places where genealogies of houses were created as new buildings emerged from, and were constructed on, their predecessors. Excavators have frequently focused on the identification of house floors in order to identify sequences of assumed rebuilding and this, in turn, has reinforced perceptions of the nature of tell life. Thus, houses tend to be reported and understood as 'complete units' that are rarely questioned in terms of their integrity, even if the actual archaeological evidence for them is partial.

Although the (re)building of houses generation after generation is integral to how tells functioned, at Százhalombatta-Földvár we find that there is far more variation in how this is done than we would expect. On one hand, regularity as well as variation are expressed within the planning and construction of the individual houses. The houses follow the same alignment (this is one of the most regulated aspects through the history of the site) and their size and proportions are comparable, but whereas some houses are planned and erected as two-room buildings, others were divided at some stage during their life (Sørensen 2010; Vicze 2013b). On the other hand, there are also periods within the site history when we find that the expected accumulations composed of 'sandwiches' of floors, burnt wall rubble, levelling fills, and then the next floor is lacking – the predictable sequence of actions disappears (Vicze 2013a). In other words, the genealogy of houses by which each seems to emerge and follow from its predecessor breaks down. For example, around the Early Bronze Age/Middle Bronze Age change, the site is very dynamic, or busy, with a large amount of various kinds of general fills deposited, and piles of plant ash repeatedly being produced and dumped, at times into large shallow depressions. There are patches of house floors within this matrix, but they are not burned, they lack the distinct deposit of rubble associated with the houses higher up in the sequence, and the walls have been extensively removed. It has not been possible to discern any order or overarching structuring of activities within this sequence of the settlement's life. In this phase there seems to have been no veneration associated with houses and their regeneration: the very essence of what characterises a tell-way of living seems absent. Instead there is a kind of disorderliness: a dissolution of existing practices and norms without their obvious replacement or transformation into other similar structured behaviours.

It may be that at this time buildings in this part of the tell were utilised in a manner that did not link them to the idea of house genealogy, or that house genealogy was not consistently the primary concern affecting behaviour and that, at this particular stage, other needs and interests (overarching or individual ones) resulted in what we archaeologically see as rather chaotic levels that lack structures. Whatever the reasoning behind the breakup of the house sequences, the point to be aware of is that the trope of tells has been so closely tied to the idea of houses and their regeneration that lacking such within the sequence of the site development leaves us 'interpretatively blank'. We have no model for how to interpret the layers when the site does not behave as a tell ought to. In response we now find that the way we have been discussing tells tends to reduce the vast variability of human action to an abstraction that then becomes an archetype or trope in which the destruction and rebuilding of houses becomes the dominant narrative line. The result is a compression of the range of activities that led to the gradual development of the site, with its intricacies of order and disorder. The practice of everyday life is far more subtle and complex than the trope of the house would have us believe.

A further example of disorderliness can be seen in the final phase of the site when the tell tradition dissolves, but it takes time. In our analysis of this process we write:

> The previous careful 'sandwiches' of floors, rubble and general levelling fill is not maintained throughout [this] phase ... Overall, there seems to be a continuation of a dominant memory of the normative layout of the site affecting some aspects of how the area was used, at the same time as other elements, such as the dense layout of houses, were lost ... what we observe is more about disintegration than challenge to existing norms as we do not see the introduction of new structured behaviour – rather a certain sense of *ad-hoc* gradually comes to characterise the use of the area. This is, we believe, what abandonment was about in the case of our tell – a gradual disintegration, a leaving behind of a tradition and a lack of replacement of these practices with new ones. Through such actions the tell-way of living was not just physically moving towards its end, it was also moving in that direction psychologically – people stopped behaving according to what was required to be tell communities. (Vicze & Sørensen in press).

The tell literature contains many erroneous statements about the abandonment of the tell-way of life, including about the abandonment of Százhalombatta-Földvár (Poroszlai 1996; Earle & Kristiansen 2010). The point of stressing the story that arrives from 'close reading' of the data is that details within the archaeological record, if extracted carefully, can show us the human face of this process. In our case this reveals abandonment as a period of gradual disintegration of a way of life, taking place over some time. Disorder gradually came to characterise how people lived on the site during this phase.

Conclusion

Accounts of Bronze Age tells have tended to present such settlements in terms of unambiguous, clear stratigraphies formed through the rebuilding of houses on the same location. These stratigraphies have typically been constructed through the *a priori* classification of contexts that produces a well-defined and readable account of tells. Whilst such narratives lend themselves to chronological accounts, the tendency to privilege site stratigraphy over the detailed analysis of material from which such stratigraphy is derived is likely to under-estimate the complexity of human practice and how this relates to site formation processes. While we too engage with traditional archaeological practices of documentation, as we excavate the tell at Százhalombatta-Földvár and work with the material from the site, we are acutely aware that the site is not an image. Drawings of stratigraphy and plans are of course useful, but they are abstracted mnemonics of excavation that tend towards self-referential classification and literally flatten out the tell by confining it to paper and abstracting from it the people who lived there. They are not the reality of the tell itself. In order to understand life on the tell we need to reconceptualise it as a living place and 'let the tell speak' through a renewed focus upon the complexity of our data.

The most striking observation has been that we are encountering far greater complexity and variations within the matrix of our site than expected. This observation sits in an uneasy relationship with understandings of tells as highly regulated and normative places that resulted from the repeated destruction and rebuilding of houses. To engage with this observation, we have used some of de Certeau's ideas of the practice of the everyday life to reflect on the tell as a place of movement and of dwelling through the lens of cleanliness and messiness, order and disorder. These concepts serve as ways of discussing both how some parts of the site may appear neat and others scruffy, and also refer to stages in the site development when it seems to lack order and structures. These two sets of concepts, while at times physically overlapping and maybe even sometimes sharing causality, refer to essentially different phenomena. We have here highlighted examples that reflect such practices but which also highlight that cleanliness and messiness, and order and disorder, while appearing to be binary oppositions are actually the ends of spectrums and that there will be areas of the site which sit at different points between these; the characteristics of the site do not always fall into neat structuralist boxes.

Nonetheless, our reflection on everydayness through a focus on the 'texturology' of the tell (de Certeau 1984, 91) allows us to explore attitudes to different spaces in terms of contrasting kinds of practices, and to identify considerable variations through time. Within this fluctuation we may find some of the dynamics between the individual household and various larger social units, such as a neighbourhood, which can be addressed in terms of the relationship between individual tactics and imposed social strategies. Thus, approaching tells bottom-up, through 'thick description' (Geertz 1973) and through attention to 'the small things forgotten' (Deetz 1977) brings new nuances into our understanding of these communities. Structures and objects may be easily comprehended in terms of their roles, but we must ask what about the rest of the site – the spaces beyond floors, the general fills, the areas where we have objects but not linked to any structures – are they not part of the site history? How should we understand this material, and how do we connect it to the story of the tell and to arguments about how this community behaved?

Beneath the ideological blanket that has so far covered tells are the lives of people. Our work on Százhalombatta-Földvár has demonstrated that the rigid 'trope of the tell' does not really apply to much that took place there. To understand tells is therefore to think of variability and plurality as real and to make ways of thinking about this effectively. In order to further tell research, we must address how people inhabited the tell in everyday realities through their spatial practices rather than treat tells as abstractions. At the same time, there is also a danger of fragmentation if we now entirely replace a focus on structure with one on activities, and if a top-down insistence on tells as socio-political organisations is replaced by bottom-up details of what people did. Both scales are needed, but currently it is the latter that is still the least developed. In this paper our aim has been to argue for the need to add such nuancing to tell research.

References

Barrett, J. (1994) *Fragments from Antiquity*. Oxford, Blackwell.

Berliner, D. (2005) Social thought & commentary. The abuses of memory: Reflections on the memory boom in anthropology. *Anthropological Quarterly* 78(1), 197–211.

Boivin, N. (2000) Life rhythms and floor sequences: Excavating time in rural Rajasthan and Neolithic Catalhöyük. *World Archaeology* 31(3), 367–388.

Bóna, I. (1975) *Die mittlere Bronzezeit Ungarns und ihre Südöstlichen Beziehungen*. Budapest, Archaeologia Hungarica 49.

Bóna, I. (1992) Bronzezeitliche Tell-Kulturen in Ungarn. In W. Meier-Arendt (ed.), *Bronzezeit in Ungarn. Forschungen in Tell-Siedlungen an Donau und Theiss*, 9–39. Frankfurt am Main, Museum für Vor- und Frühgeschichte.

Bóna, I. & Nováki, Gy. (1982) Alpár bronzkori és Árpád-kori vára. *Cumania* 7, 17–117.

Bourdieu, P. (1977) *Outline of a Theory of Practice*. Cambridge, Cambridge University Press.

Bourdieu, P. (1984) *Distinction: A Social Critique of the Judgement of Taste*. Cambridge MA, Harvard University Press.

Childe, V.G. (1929) *The Danube in Prehistory*. Oxford, Clarendon Press.

Connerton, P. (1989) *How Societies Remember*. Cambridge, Cambridge University Press.

de Certeau, M. (1984) *The Practice of Everyday Life*. Berkeley CA, University of California Press.

Deetz, J. (1977) *In Small Things Forgotten: An Archaeology of Early American Life*. New York, Anchor.

Duffy, P. (2014) *Complexity and Autonomy in Bronze Age Europe. Assessing Cultural Developments in Eastern Hungary*. Budapest, Archaeolingua 31.

Earle, T. (2002) *Bronze Age Economics. The Beginnings of Political Economies*. Boulder CO, Westview Press.

Earle, T. & Kristiansen, K. (2010) *Organizing Bronze Age Societies. The Mediterranean, Central Europe, and Scandinavia Compared*. Cambridge, Cambridge University Press.

Earle, T., Kiss, V., Kulcsár, G., Szeverényi, V. & Polányi, T. (2012) Bronze Age landscapes in the Benta Valley – research on the hinterland of Bronze Age centres. *Hungarian Archaeology e-journal*, 1–4. DOI: 10.1080/00934690.2016.1199197

Găvan, A. (2015) *Metal and Metalworking in The Bronze Age Tell Settlements in the Carpathian Basin*. Cluj-Napoca, Mega Publishing House.

Geertz, C. (1973) Thick description: Toward an interpretive theory of culture. In C. Geertz, *The Interpretation of Cultures. Selected Essays*, 3–30. New York NY, Basic Books.

Giddens, A. (1984) *The Constitution of Society. Outline of a Theory of Structuration*. Cambridge, Polity.

Gillis, J. (1994) Memory and identity. The history of a relationship. In J. Gillis (ed.), *Commemorations: The Politics of National Identity*, 3–17. Princeton NJ, Princeton University Press.

Gogâltan, F., Cordoş, C. & Ignat, A. (2014) *Bronze Age Tell, Tell-Like and Mound-like Settlements on the Eastern Frontier of the Carpathian Basin. History of Research*. Cluj-Napoca, Editura Mega.

Guerrero, E., Molist, M., Kuijt, I. & Anfruns, J. (2009) Seated memory: New insights into Near Eastern Neolithic mortuary variability from Tell Halula, Syria. *Current Anthropology* 50(3), 379–391.

Hayden, B. & Cannon, A. (1983) Where the garbage goes: Refuse disposal in the Maya Highlands. *Journal of Anthropological Archaeology* 2(2), 117–163.

Hodder, I. & Cessford, C. (2004) Daily practice and social memory at Çatalhöyük. *American Antiquity* 69(1), 17–40.

Jaeger, M., Kulcsár, G., Taylor, N. & Staniuk, R. (2018) *Kakucs-Turján. A Middle Bronze Age Multi-layered Fortified Settlement in Central Hungary*. Bonn, Studien zur Archäologie in Ostmitteleuropa 18.

Jones, P. (2018) *What Can Pottery Tell Us? Using Ceramics from Százhalombatta-Földvár to Determine Site Formation*. Unpublished BA dissertation, University of Southampton.

Kienlin, T. (2015) *Bronze Age Tell Communities in Context. An Exploration into Culture, Society, and the Study of European Prehistory. Part 1: Critique. Europe and the Mediterranean*. Oxford, Archaeopress.

Kienlin, T., Fischl, K.P. & Pusztai, T. (2018) *Borsod Region Bronze Age Settlement (BORBAS). Catalogue of the Early to Middle Bronze Age Tell Sites Covered by Magnetometry and Surface Survey*. Bonn, Universitätsforschungen zur prähistorischen Archäologie 317.

Kovács, T. (1994a) *Treasures of the Hungarian Bronze Age*. Budapest, Hungarian National Museum.

Kovács, T. (1994b) Chronologische Fragen des Überganges von der mittleren- zur Spätbronzezeit in Transdanubien. *Zalai Múzeum* 5, 159–172.

Merleau-Ponty, M. (1962) *The Phenomenology of Perception*. London, Routledge & Kegan Paul.

Murray, P. (1980) Discard location: The ethnographic data. *American Antiquity* 45(3), 490–502.

Nicodemus, A.J. (2014) *Bronze Age Economies of the Carpathian Basin: Trade, Craft Production, and Agro-pastoral Intensification*. Unpublished PhD Thesis, University of Michigan.

O'Shea, J., Parditka, G., Nicodemus, A. & Kristiansen, K. (2019) Social formation and collapse in the Tisza-Maros region: Dating the Maros Group and its Late Bronze Age successors. *Antiquity* 93(369), 604–623.

Poroszlai, I. (1988) Preliminary report about the excavation at Nagykőrös-Földvár (Vatya-Culture): stratigraphical data and settlement structure. *Communicationes Archaeologicae Hungariae*, 29–39.

Poroszlai, I. (1996) Excavations in the Bronze Age earthwork in Százhalombatta between 1989 and 1993. In I. Poroszlai (ed.), *Excavations at Százhalombatta 1989–1995*, 5–15. Százhalombatta, Matrica Múzeum.

Poroszlai, I. & Vicze, M. (2000) *Százhalombatta Archaeological Expedition, Annual Report 1*. Százhalombatta, Matrica Múzeum.

Poroszlai, I. & Vicze, M. (2004) Methodological background of a modern tell excavation in Hungary. In J. Bátora, V. Furmánek & L. Veliacik (eds), *Einflüsse und Kontakte Alteuropaischer Kulturen. Festschrift für Jozef Vladár zum 70. Geburtstag*, 231–240. Nitra, Archäologisches Institut der Slowakischen Akademie der Wissenschaften.

Strathern, A. (1996) *Body Thoughts*. Ann Arbor MI, University of Michigan Press.

Sørensen, M.L.S. (2010) Households. In T. Earle & K. Kristiansen (eds), *Organizing Bronze Age Societies. The Mediterranean, Central Europe and Scandinavia Compared*, 122–154. Cambridge, Cambridge University Press.

Sørensen, M.L.S. (2019) What is gender transformation, where does it take place and why? Reflections from archaeology. In J.K. Koch & W. Kirleis (eds), *Gender Transformations in Prehistoric and Archaic Societies. Scales of Transformation in Prehistoric and Archaic Societies*. Kiel, Kiel University/Sidestone Press Academics.

Sørensen, M.L.S. & Vicze, M. (2013) Locating household activities on a Bronze Age tell. In M. Madella, G. Kovács, B. Kulcsarne-Berzsényi & I. Briz i Godino (eds), *The Archaeology of Household*, 159–178. Oxford, Oxbow Books.

Sørensen, M.L.S., Vicze, M. & Sofaer, J. (2020) Paradigm shift? Bronze Age Tell Archaeology after 1989. Reflections from the

Százhalombatta-Földvár Excavation Project. In L. Dietrich, O. Dietrich, A. Harding, V. Kiss & K. Šabatová (eds), *Bringing Down the Iron Curtain: Paradigmatic change in research on the Bronze Age in Central and Eastern Europe*, 147–156. Oxford, Archaeopress.

Vicze, M. (2013a) Expecting the unexpected: Százhalombatta-Földvár surprises once again, In S. Bergerbrant & S. Sabatini (eds), *Counterpoint: Essays in Archaeology and Heritage Studies in Honour of Professor Kristian Kristiansen*, 71–76. Oxford, British Archaeological report S2508.

Vicze, M. (2013b) Middle Bronze Age households at Százhalombatta-Földvár. In A. Anders, G. Kulcsár, G. Kalla, V. Kiss & G.V. Szabó (eds), *Moments in Time. Papers Presented to Pál Raczky on His 60th Birthday*, 757–769. Budapest, L'Harmattan.

Vicze, M. & Sørensen, M.L.S. (in press) *Living in a Tell: Memory and Abandonment. Százhalombatta-Földvár Phase I (Late Koszider)*. Százhalombatta, Matrica Museum

Vicze, M., Sørensen, M.L.S. & Sofaer, J. (2017) Advances in tell research – methodological reflections on the SAX Project. In G. Kulcsár, V.G. Szabó, V. Kiss & G. Váczi (eds), *State of the Hungarian Bronze Age Research. Proceedings of the Conference Held Between 17th and 18th of December 2014*, 487–495. Budapest, Ősrégészeti Társaság.

Wilson, G. (2008) *The Archaeology of Everyday Life at Early Moundville*. Tuscaloosa AL, University of Alabama Press.

12

Social Life on Bronze Age Tells. Outline of a Practice-oriented Approach

Tobias L. Kienlin

Introduction: Tells and Bronze Age social modelling

This is a paper that focuses on Bronze Age settlement mounds in the Carpathian Basin and beyond, on the interpretation of this fascinating way of life by means of analysis of the material remains of long-term architectural stability and references back to ancestral places. It is also a contribution on the implications that an understanding of this way of living and its specific materiality as a medium of past social action has for the study of wider European prehistory and Bronze Age research in particular.

Archaeologically speaking, we are concerned with the period *c.* 2400/2300–1500/1400 BC, the Early Bronze Age in terms of wider relative chronology, or the late Early and Middle Bronze Age in Hungarian terminology. During this time span the majority of (future) tell sites was first occupied sometime between *c.* 2300 and 1950 BC, or during horizon 3 as defined by F. Gogâltan (2017, 32–34). They are found in some numbers along the terraces accompanying the Danube south of Budapest and on the lower plains and banks along the Tisza River and its eastern tributaries; and they belong to various different archaeologically defined groups or 'cultures' such as Vatya, Hatvan, Otomani-Füzesabony or Maros/Mureş. Such tell settlement is a recurrent phenomenon in the prehistory of southeastern Europe. Accordingly, our Bronze Age tells were not the first settlement mounds in the area, but there was an earlier horizon that started – south of the Danube and along the Morava River – at the beginning of the Middle Neolithic Vinča culture (*c.* 5500/5400 BC), and subsequently expanded north along the Tisza River during the Late Neolithic Tisza culture, as well as into the neighbouring Herpály and Csőszhalom groups from broadly 5200/5000 to 4500 BC (Link 2006, 16, fig. 8; Parkinson 2006, 57, fig. 4.4). Both horizons are separated by a more dispersed settlement pattern during the local 'Eneolithic' or 'Copper Age', *i.e.* the Tiszapolgár, Bodrogkeresztúr and Baden sequence, as well as during subsequent groups like Vučedol and Makó/Kosihy-Čaka (from *c.* 2800/2600 BC) which in local terminology constitute the beginnings of the Bronze Age.

For both periods, it is important to bear in mind that none of these sites would have been founded by its first inhabitants with an impressive multi-layer settlement in mind, set apart from its surroundings by its height and qualitatively distinct from neighbouring single-layer settlements or with an intention to dominate the landscape. Rather each site was the result of countless decisions taken through time and specific practices. These may have related to the environmental background and topographic setting, to subsistence strategies and the availability of different building materials, as well as to specifically cultural notions of where and how to live which encouraged permanency in the choice of settlement location and accelerated the accumulation of settlement debris into a tell. Hence, at least initially there would not have been a marked difference between a tell-to-be and those 'normal' horizontal settlements also known in certain numbers. It is also important to recall that we are not talking about a uniform phenomenon in chronological terms, but broad horizons that were defined to describe the occurrence of Neolithic or Bronze Age tells when, in fact, each settlement followed its own trajectory in terms of settlement layout, internal dynamics and the rate – if so – at which settlement debris eventually accumulated. Finally, for both the Neolithic and the Bronze Age the reasons for the final decline of tell settlement are unclear. For both periods there are related discussions, and suggestions range from changes in climate, subsistence patterns and economy, to perceived structural limits of social life on tells.

In terms of theoretical approach, it has previously been argued at length that much Bronze Age research is dominated by a problematic top-down approach, *i.e.* by a rather narrow interest taken in the evolution of stratified society and the socio-political impact of metalworking (*cf.* Kienlin 2012a; 2015a; 2015b). In this context, Bronze Age tell sites of the Carpathian Basin are routinely interpreted as 'proto-urban' settlements that more or less successfully drew upon agricultural and other resources from their surroundings and controlled the exchange of valuable objects and raw materials from abroad. They were home, supposedly, to some kind of functionally and politically differentiated population composed of peasants, craft specialists – and those in charge of all of this (*e.g.* Hänsel 2002, 80–83; Gogâltan 2010; Earle *et al.* 2015, 641–642).

This particular modelling of Bronze Age society that is also evident in the current relapse into talk of Bronze Age 'castles', playing on the medieval analogy (Hansen & Krause 2018), Bronze Age proto-states, 'standing armies' and large-scale 'warfare' instead of mere conflict (Meller 2017; Horn & Kristiansen 2018), results in a distinctly 'political' Bronze Age, conceptualised in different terms than the preceding Neolithic. It perpetuates notions of a historically unique European Bronze Age that ultimately go back to the work of V.G. Childe (*e.g.* 1950), his 'Urban Revolution' in the Near East and the supposed effects of metal working, mobility and exchange on European societies of the Bronze Age. Childe's vision of a progressive Bronze Age Europe opposite a magic-ridden Orient, of the specifically European freedom and creativity of Bronze Age craftsmen leading right up to modern western civilisation involved a strong worldview (*cf.* Rowlands 1994). And much like in Childe's case this worldview helped him organise his profound knowledge into popular syntheses of European prehistory, what we currently see is the return of grand narratives of 'The Rise of Bronze Age Society' (Kristiansen & Larsson 2005) and various brands of 'Neo-Diffusionism' – irradiating from a strong school of Scandinavian Bronze Age archaeology across central and southeastern Europe (*e.g.* Bergerbrant & Sabatini 2013; Vandkilde 2016). Drawing on evidence of personal mobility, the exchange of amber and metal and an optimistic reconstruction of political hierarchies in the likeness of Mediterranean palaces, it is argued for dependency of European societies of the Bronze Age on the Mediterranean. Ultimately, convergence is postulated of what an unbiased observer may perceive as socially and culturally distinct societies widely set apart in space and historical circumstance (*cf.* Harding 2013). The 'Bronze Age' that emerges is one qualitatively different from the preceding Neolithic and is historically unique on a pan-European scale (*e.g.* Kristiansen & Larsson 2005; Kristiansen & Earle 2015).

Derived from either traditional diffusionist approaches or a reading of World System Theory, regional variability in both the 'core' and the 'periphery' is ignored, and at no point is attention drawn to the differential outcomes of contact and exchange depending on local valuations, specific historical trajectories and peripheral choice or agency opposite outside 'influence' (*cf.* Stein 1999; Dietler 2010; Kienlin 2017). Moreover, such modelling of Bronze Age society involves considerable extrapolation from the archaeological record, and there is often a strange misfit between the prehistoric situation being studied and the anthropological model applied – such as when 'tell society' that is characterised in particular by its long-term stability and reference back to ancestral place instead of by rapid change is conceptualised in terms of ethnographically derived 'prestige goods economies', some of which, such as the *potlatch*, are quite uniquely competitive and the direct result of modern colonial encounters between indigenous groups and the industrialised 'West'. We are still thinking and analysing, then, in terms of the same supposedly universal categories such as 'chiefs', 'redistribution', 'wealth finance' or 'prestige goods exchange' that have – for decades – been applied to so many and entirely different prehistoric societies. There is a 'centralization bias' in our approaches (Blanton *et al.* 1996, 2) and 'complexity' is wrongly equated with hierarchy and executive power (*cf.* Wynne-Jones & Kohring 2007). Undue emphasis is put on vertical political differentiation and the emergence of hierarchical systems, when rather than competition and the attempt to establish political hierarchies in the Bronze Age, as in the previous Neolithic, we also see a concern with communal values. We end up, for example, with the 'chiefly courts' of the Bronze Age tell cultures in the Carpathian Basin (*e.g.* Kristiansen & Larsson 2005, 167) modelled on broadly the same terms as the later Mycenaean palaces – which they thus come to reflect albeit in a somewhat less perfect manner and on a smaller scale.

The social, space and materiality

For an alternative approach to the mainstream modelling of Bronze Age society rejected above, it is suggested here that we turn to the field of practice theory. Among the commonalities of this body of approaches is the anti-essentialising stance of its adherents, who, one way or the other, argue that the social is in permanent flux, and 'society' or social 'structure' do not have independent or prior existence. In fact, the argument of practice theory is two-sided and takes aim at both the notion of social totalities being more than their parts, as well as at the 'individualist' attempt to build up the social directly from individual human actions (*e.g.* Schatzki 2001, 1–4; Reckwitz 2008, 106–112; Schäfer 2016a, 10–14). In opposition to both these notions, it is instead argued that sociality crucially depends on practices, that is on arrays or bundles of *organised* human activities linked by shared practical understandings. Apart from this anti-essentialising conception of the social as a field of practices as such, practice theory as it stands today is attractive because of its emphasis on the fact that practices and understandings are *embodied*, and because of the explicit interest taken in the importance of *materiality* in social life. Thus, second generation practice theorists argue for a 'flat' ontology of social life and for an understanding of social phenomena as 'slices or aspects of nexuses of practices *and* material arrangements' (Schatzki 2010, 123; italics added, TLK) that all occupy the same level of reality. In this latter aspect, of course, the 'flat' ontology of human and non-human material entities and their interactions argued for, current practice accounts are part of a broader 'material turn', and they share certain aspects, but – crucially – not others, with vaguely related so-called 'post-humanist' approaches (*cf.* Schatzki 2001, 10–11; Reckwitz 2008, 128–129; 2016, 38–40). In particular, from the perspective advocated here, it is of outmost importance to avoid the latter's blurring of human and material 'agencies', and to retain the 'unique richness' and integrity of *human* agency (Schatzki 2002, 201).

Given that in part of this debate, and with the rapid succession of 'turn' upon 'turn' ('spatial', 'material', 'corporeal', 'ontological' *etc.*), we currently see a tendency to reinvent the wheel under the permanent pressure to stress the originality of one's approach, let it be clear then from the start that the approach taken here is *not* new. Instead, it stands in a tradition of archaeological readings of the first generation of practice theorists, Anthony Giddens (1979; 1984) and Pierre Bourdieu (*e.g.* 1977; 1990), that extends back well into the late 1980s and 1990s (see also Gardner 2008; Ribeiro 2016, 233). However, unlike phenomenology, the detour at that time to hermeneutics or the effects of the linguistic turn with material culture perceived as 'text', such practice-oriented approaches attracted much less attention than one should have wished for. It is for this reason, so it seems, that for example the second generation practice theorist Th. Schatzki's reformulation of practice theory to fully acknowledge materiality – referred to at length below – between his 1996 *Social Practices* and *The Site of the Social* from 2002, stands strangely unrelated besides J. Barrett's *Fragments from Antiquity* (1994) and the broadly comparable archaeological interest initiated therein in past human actions organised into practices and invariably bound to practical understandings and manipulations of a material world. The approach taken, then, is to go back, by way of example, to one of the 'classics' first, to Anthony Giddens, in an attempt to recall to what extent space and materiality were already present in his argument, and what possibly prevented the full recognition of the essential materiality of all social life that we subsequently find in the work, for example, of Schatzki. His, arguably, is the most concise outline of materiality and social life in terms of practice theory available, which – combined with his disavowal of 'Actor-Network-Theory' (ANT) and the like's non-human material 'agencies' – is why he features as a key informant of the approach suggested in this paper.

Theory of practice and 'time-space'

The two classic studies by A. Giddens that are relevant in our context are his 1979 *Central Problems in Social Theory* and his *The Constitution of Society* from 1984 – both widely acknowledged, alongside the work of P. Bourdieu, as paradigmatic for a first generation of practice theorists. In both studies Giddens sought to overcome rigid structure/action dichotomies[1] in traditional social thought, questioning both the existence of objectified social structures and their determinant role for human action in 'structural' or 'wholist' approaches, and, vice versa, the 'individualist' notion that social order somehow is built up directly from individual actions, understandings and interaction.

In prehistoric archaeology, the consequent notion that 'the social is a field of embodied, materially interwoven practices centrally organized around shared practical understandings' (Schatzki 2001, 3) became part of the post-processual critique of previous 'checklist-type' social archaeology, albeit combined with quite diverse and partly contradictory theoretical approaches (*e.g.* Shanks & Tilley 1987; 1992; Dobres & Robb 2000). This development is unfortunate since it detracts from the importance of practice theory for our understanding of the social. Therefore, the position taken here is that there is no way back behind the essential tenets first outlined by Giddens and Bourdieu *etc.*, even though social modelling in prehistoric archaeology still leans heavily on the structural side and reified social 'types' such as the notorious Hawaiian chiefdoms (Earle 2002) or, more recently, Bronze Age 'Vikings' (Ling *et al.* 2018) still hold sway.

Apart from our notion of the social as such, ultimately current interest in 'embodiment', 'personhood', 'social space' and 'materiality' also draws on a tradition of thought that extends back to Giddens and Bourdieu, expanded, of course, by a second generation of (practice and related) theorists' attempts to break down yet another dichotomy (Kalthoff *et al.* 2016, 20–21), namely that of the social and the material world, or society and materiality (*e.g.* Schatzki 2002; 2010). This shift of interest is remarkable from the perspective of (prehistoric) archaeology and anthropology with their somewhat longer tradition of theorising material culture or 'materiality'. It is enriching and potentially brings both disciplines, and archaeology in particular, into closer contact and intellectual exchange with sociology and wider cultural studies.

However, we also see different strands of theorising 'materiality', sometimes ignorant of similar concerns elsewhere and drawing on different intellectual traditions to derive sometimes similar, sometimes quite incommensurate notions of the material (and spatial) context of the human condition and human action – some of them are thought of as problematic here, such as an interest in materiality in the guise of ANT or the like. It is worthwhile, therefore, turning back to the 'classics' first, to try to reconstruct their concerns and arguments, before pursuing subsequent developments in practice theory and beyond and their specific dealings with issues of materiality. Drawing on the above mentioned studies by A. Giddens we will try to retrace how a still rather abstract sociological interest in 'time-space intersections as essentially involved in all social existence' (Giddens 1979, 54) gradually developed into a fuller recognition of 'materiality' – including moveable objects ('artefacts' *etc.*), space and architecture – in the constitution of the self and society.

Giddens' well-known 'theory of structuration' departs from previous functionalism and structuralism in social analysis, even though the influence, in particular, of Claude Lévi-Strauss is still to be felt and eventually detracts from a full appraisal of materiality in Giddens' own dealing with the situatedness of human action and the 'social' in time and space ('time-space'). In particular, Giddens argues against the existence of objectified social 'structure' or an overarching, ahistorical societal totality determining human perception and action, or the course of history: 'social systems have no purposes, reasons or needs whatsoever; only human individuals do so. Any explanation of social reproduction which imputes teleology to social systems must be declared invalid' (Giddens 1979, 7). This critique of 'structural' approaches, drawing among others on the work of M. Heidegger and the later L. Wittgenstein, clearly stands, and in the work of Giddens entails a series of perceptive discussions and categorial shifts.[2]

Starting, once, not with the oft-quoted 'duality of structure' itself, Giddens' anthropology or his 'theory of the acting subject' (Giddens 1979, 2) is of interest, since it is here that the famous 'knowledgeable' actor enters the stage: 'every social actor knows a great deal about the conditions of reproduction of the society of which he or she is a member' (Giddens 1979, 5). This, clearly, is more flattering than P. Bourdieu's more deterministic 'habitus', and it is certainly preferable that human action or the enactment of social life be distinguished by an informed or 'reflexive' monitoring on behalf of those human agents involved. However, Giddens being a sociologist mainly concerned with modern western society, this clearly begs the question of what knowledgeability exactly means in different historical and pre-modern culture contexts. His view of the positive role of knowledge and reflexivity in the reproduction of (modern) society and potentially in bringing about change clearly is an optimistic one (*cf.* Ortner 1984, 150–157; Löw 2016, 157–158).

In Bourdieu, by contrast, habitus is embodied or incorporated history (Bourdieu 1990, 56–57), or the internalisation of 'objective structures' (Bourdieu 1977, 81), that alone allows the:

> … production of a commonsense world endowed with the *objectivity* secured by consensus on the meaning … of practices and the world, in other words the harmonization of agents' experiences and the continuous reinforcement that each of them receives from the expression, individual or collective …, improvised or programmed …, of similar or identical experiences (Bourdieu 1977, 80).

As such, crucially, habitus is acquired largely in socialisation, and Bourdieu's examples of this process often come from his early fieldwork among the Kabyle (*e.g.* Bourdieu 1977, 87–95; 1990, 66–79), whereby an emphasis clearly is on embodiment, tacit knowledge and the largely non-discursive assimilation into social life and the practices of a child's or youth's group. Even though it stands in permanent confrontation with 'reality', that is the ever changing social and material world around us, habitus, thus, systematically discourages deviance and tends to 'avoid' situations that might entail disclosure of its own naturalising effect and its fundamental arbitrariness (Bourdieu 1977, 163–164; 1990, 61). For this reason, the concept of 'habitus' has been criticised for its more 'deterministic' or constraining connotations than Giddens' account of knowledgeable actors reflexively monitoring the enactment of social life (*e.g.* Schatzki 1996, 136–144; Dünne 2006, 301; Schäfer 2016b, 139). It is surely important here to avoid essentialising distinctions between 'modern' society, more on Giddens' side of the positive role of knowledge and reflexivity in social reproduction and potentially in bringing about social change, and 'traditional' society, on Bourdieu's side favouring reproduction over change and social actors caught in the routines implied by their traditional habitus – even though this may be what we are seeing in the case of the tell communities under consideration: a measure of variability and agency that did not – over an extended period of time – erode the foundations of 'tell society' as such. Rather, both 'options' have to be understood as located on a continuum of potential trajectories open to societies on different levels of 'complexity' or 'integration', and they always have to be established by reference to the specific evidence at hand, not *a priori* presumed. Having said that, we clearly owe Giddens the important qualification that the knowledge involved in social reproduction often will not operate or normally be available on a discursive level, but we instead see what he calls practical consciousness drawing on tacit knowledge skilfully applied in the routines of daily social life (*e.g.* Giddens 1979, 40; 1984, 21–22). Interestingly, in prehistoric archaeology this conception lives on in discussions of skill, tacit knowledge and embodiment in craft production (*e.g.* Sørensen & Rebay-Salisbury 2013), rather than in general social modelling that still tends to be fascinated by the role of aggressive aggrandising alpha males in supposedly upward-bound social evolution.

Second, importantly, there is Giddens' (1979, 53–65, 198–210; 1984, 25, 110–144) emphasis on the situatedness of all social life in time and space, and his insistence that the 'social' cannot be reasonably studied in terms of static snapshots trying to define the given 'nature' of social systems, institutions or social relations and interaction. From this anti-essentialist perspective, society or the social is not a given entity exterior to or opposite the individual, but only comes into existence in its permanent (re-)production by individual agents 'organised' in social practices extending across space and time. The social, then, is a process, and it has to be studied as such; in Giddens' (1984, 2) words it is 'recursive', and as there is change to the specific practices involved, so is there also change to the respective social system(s). This clearly entails that all social activity, all social reproduction, practices and social systems are historically situated or culturally specific. Indeed, several chapters in Giddens (1979; 1984) are explicitly devoted to aspects of time and space, and 'contextuality' is listed among the basic concepts of structuration theory (Giddens 1984, 282).

This concern with the 'time-space' dimension of social life clearly is one of the reasons for the interest in Giddens' work taken in subsequent fields of cultural studies, history or the social sciences, for example in the so-called 'spatial' or 'material' turns (*e.g.* Löw 2016, 26–32; Schatzki 2010, 125–128) – the general thrust of the argument then going via 'time' to the historical situatedness of practice and human action, and via 'space' to their grounding in a specific material world. For the same reason, obviously, Giddens is discussed here, though arguably his relevant passages are much weaker than his famed foundation of a theory of structuration as such. We will return to these shortcomings below, because they are telling as regards the consequences of too narrow an 'interactionist' sociological approach to contextuality for a profound understanding of society and materiality.

Third, however, before engaging in a critique of his deficiencies in terms of theorising 'materiality', let us turn to the lasting merits of Giddens and his 'theory of structuration', that – alongside Bourdieu – was pioneering for subsequent practice theory approaches:

> The concept of structuration involves that of the *duality of structure*, which relates to the *fundamentally recursive character of social life, and expresses the mutual dependence of structure and agency*. By the duality of structure I mean that the structural properties of social systems are both the medium and the outcome of the practices that constitute those systems ... The identification of structure with constraint is also rejected: structure is both enabling and constraining (Giddens 1979, 69).

What Giddens is essentially proposing here is a radical move away from previous dualisms in social theory by allowing that 'structure' is 'virtual' and 'outside' time and space, but unlike structuralism's subconscious, timeless mental or linguistic templates (*i.e.* 'parole') putting the emphasis not on the abstract status of 'structure' (*e.g.* Giddens 1979, 3, 17, 64), but on the 'instantiations' through which it is realised in practice and 'translated' into the tangible reality of social systems (Giddens 1984, 25) by the implementation of rules and resources: '"Structural analysis" in the social sciences involves examining the structuration of social systems ... with the crucial proviso that social systems are patterned in time as well as space, through continuities of social reproduction' (Giddens 1979, 64). In this conception, 'structure'[3] is differentiated from 'system', but both are bracketed and recursively linked by their reproduction in practice through knowledgeable actors:

> The concept of agency as I advocate it here, involving 'intervention' in a potentially malleable object-world, relates directly to the more generalised notion of *Praxis*. I shall later treat regularised acts as *situated practices*, and shall regard this concept as expressing a major mode of connection between action theory and structural analysis. Second, it is a necessary feature of action that, at any point in time, the agent 'could have acted otherwise' (Giddens 1979, 55–56).

As such the outcome of the social process is fundamentally open. It is framed by the actors taking recourse to rules and resources (= 'structure' or 'structural properties') in social reproduction, but it is not determined since all human knowledgeability is 'bounded' and the unintended consequences of action feed back into the (partly unacknowledged) conditions of future action (Giddens 1979, 66, 70; 1984, 26–27).

With all the benefit of hindsight, and from the perspective of archaeology which unlike sociology has a traditional focus on the material remains of (past) social life, we may now ask how Giddens' failure to fully appreciate materiality comes about, given that his emphasis on the situatedness of social life in time and space – sometimes explicitly understood to comprise 'the sum of the cultural products of past generations' (Giddens 1979, 204) – clearly implies a corresponding interest. Arguably, we see here the combined result of his being a sociologist, with sociology from its beginnings conceptualising the social as normative order(s) arising from the interaction among individuals and collectives in spatial configurations thought given, *i.e.* either face-to-face, or in the nation states of the 19th to early 20th century,[4] the structuralist influence on his essentialising notion of 'traditional' versus 'modern' society, and his interest in the spatiality of the body (see also Schroer 2006, 127, 130–131). The problem is best illustrated by reference to the pertinent chapters on 'Time, Space and Social' and 'Time, Space and Regionalization' (Giddens 1979, 198–233; 1984, 110–144).

Apart from the problematic duality of 'hot' and 'cold' societies alluded to, we see here 'traditional' society characterised by face-to-face interaction, *i.e.* the foundations of 'society' in sociology as such, plus 'tradition and kinship', which may be read fairly as discursive in the sense of the kinship terminology studied by structural anthropology. Cities, by contrast, or 'modern society' is characterised above all by the possible 'delay' of communication in time and its expansion in space brought about by the introduction of writing. That is to say, both the 'stretching' of social systems across time and space as such, and the typology and succession of 'cold' and 'hot' societies, are closely tied to just one medium, *i.e.* speech and written language, used to define and differentiate them, when even a cursory glance at history shows that this focus on orality and writing is reductionist. Thus, for example, from a historical perspective one might argue that an emphasis on architectural monumentality, read space and materiality, as a medium of the social (*e.g.* Delitz 2010), clearly runs right through from the earliest Neolithic (*e.g.* Göbekli Tepe), via historic to modern times, and across the divide postulated by reference to the introduction of writing. Throughout history, too, from illiterate to literate society, from band to state so to speak, we see people 'relying' on the specific communicative potential of 'mundane' material culture, other than language and text (*e.g.* Miller 1985; 2005; Tilley *et al.* 2006), to express and negotiate their standing and identity *etc.* on a non-discursive level, and to provide permanence to otherwise intransient social life.

How exactly material culture 'works' in such different contexts, from more or less unknowingly shaping perception and guiding action to massive statements enforcing (bodily) compliance, is subject to an extensive discussion in anthropology and archaeology *etc.*, with concepts ranging from, say, 'external symbolic storage' in a processual tradition (*e.g.* Renfrew 1998) to late post-processual material 'entanglement' (*e.g.* Hodder 2012). This entire field – or what approaches were already available back in the late 1970s and early 1980s when he was writing – goes unnoticed by Giddens, focusing instead on how '[i]n face-to-face interaction, the presence of others is a major source of information utilised in the production of social encounters' (Giddens 1979, 203).[5] Furthermore, there is clearly more to 'organising the contextuality of action and the sustaining of ontological security' (Giddens 1984, 124) than just the corporeal modalities of face-to-face interaction, and this leads on to another point of contention, namely the status of the 'body' and phenomenological approaches in Giddens' argument. While heralding an interest in 'embodiment' and the role of the body in the human perception of the world *etc.*, in Giddens, again, this unfortunately boils down to rather simplistic and reductionist universals, such as when, drawing on T. Hägerstrand the 'indivisibility of the human body', the 'finitude of the life span of the human agent', his/her limited potential for multi-tasking ('turn-taking') or the 'limited "packing capacity" of time-space', are declared to 'express the material axes of human existence and underlie all contexts of association in conditions of co-presence' (Giddens 1984, 111–112). Similarly, while corporeal front/back orientations and distinctions are clearly an important element of some phenomenological approaches, this not only applies to the organisation of face-to-face encounters, but to a wider social and material world that the individual confronts. It is an understanding of this wider field, that we are aiming at – the physical/corporeal *and* the broader context of material possibilities as a medium of social action by past human beings and their social and cultural 'reality' thus created.

'Flat ontologies': Social life and materiality

For a comprehensive reformulation of practice theory with an explicit focus on the essential materiality of all social life we are indebted to the philosopher Theodore Schatzki. In his two major works *Social Practices* (1996) and *The Site of the Social* from 2002, drawing on insights by the later L. Wittgenstein and M. Heidegger, Schatzki outlines a 'flat' ontology of social life (see also Schatzki 2016; 2019a, 26–50), where the social, first, is understood as a dynamic field, as 'a nexus of practices and the sociality opened in this nexus as the basis, or "substance", of all sociality in human life' (Schatzki 1996, 169) – a notion that is subsequently refined and expanded to an understanding of social phenomena as 'slices or aspects of nexuses of practices *and* material arrangements' (Schatzki 2010, 123; italics added, TLK). In the tradition of practice theory, Schatzki (1996, 2–9) is critical here of both the notion of social totalities being more than their constituent parts as well as of 'individualism' that builds up the social from the individual human subject. Instead he posits practice(s) – that is arrays or bundles of organised activities linked by shared practical understandings (Schatzki 1996, 89–110; 2002, 70–80) – as the central element in the constitution of sociality and social order. This approach may be said to involve a 'flat' ontology in a two-fold way: first, on the traditional 'sociological' side, in that fields or nexuses *etc.* of practices that constitute the social are all conceived to be laid out on just one level of reality – unlike, for example, higher-level 'macro' structure and the 'micro' level of human individuals in traditional thought *etc.*; and second, in that Schatzki explicitly recognises that sociality, that is everything to do with the 'hanging-together of human lives' (Schatzki 2016, 31) is inextricably linked and not external to the material world: 'Social orders are thus the arrangements of people, artifacts, organisms, and things through and amid which social life transpires, in which these entities relate, occupy positions, and possess meanings' (Schatzki 2002, 22). In this latter aspect, Schatzki is part of a broader 'material turn' in social and cultural studies, including various brands of 'post-humanism'. Importantly, however, his approach stands for the urgently needed attempt to retain the 'intactness and unique richness' of human agency (Schatzki 2002, xxii, 105–122, 190–210) instead of, for example, ANT's blurring of human and object 'agencies'. It is worthwhile, therefore, to outline the key concepts of Schatzki's reading of practice theory and trace their development towards a full appreciation of materiality in social life.

Starting with 'practice' itself, for Schatzki this concept combines two distinct 'aspects', namely its constituent 'parts' on the one hand, and notions of how these are linked or organised on the other. Thus, we are told, practice is: 'a temporally unfolding and spatially dispersed nexus of doings and sayings', where the individual doings and sayings (= actions) are linked and oriented '(1) through understandings, for example, of what to say and do; (2) through explicit rules, principles, precepts, and instructions; and (3) through ... "teleoaffective" structures embracing ends, projects, tasks, purposes, beliefs, emotions, and moods' (Schatzki 1996, 89). As to the 'constituents' of practices mentioned, the 'doings' here carry the notion of embodiment and the role of socially produced bodies in the constitution of practices (Schatzki 1996, 19–87), while the 'sayings' are more on the discursive side without being restricted to language, such as, for example, in the bodily act of shaking the head to signal disagreement (Schatzki 2002, 72). The 'linkages', on the other hand, thought to be involved in organising bundled sets or 'nexuses' of human actions – doings and sayings – into distinct practices, carry a relatively strong normative connotation, in that apart from 'practical understandings' modelled on 'habitus' (Bourdieu) and 'practical consciousness' (Giddens; Schatzki 2002, 79), they explicitly comprise what Schatzki calls 'teleoaffective' structures, that is notions held and discursively formulated of the 'oughtness' or 'rightness' and the 'acceptability' of actions (Schatzki 1996, 100–102; 2002, 80–81). Schatzki's 'practice', then, 'governs how people act' (Schatzki 1996, 96) and 'establishes' orders (Schatzki 2002, 89–105). However, just like Giddens so Schatzki, too, explicitly grants knowledgeability to social actors (Schatzki 1996, 104, 111–112); and like both first-generation practice theorists – Bourdieu and Giddens – his notion of practice is a processual and relational one devoid of the 'givenness' of structure or the like in other schools of social thought. The social process, that is to say, is indeterminate, with certain actions being 'signified' as the ones to perform at that moment, in the current situation (Schatzki 1996, 121–122), but ultimately '[u]ntil action occurs, it is never determinate which end a person will have acted for, what project he will have carried out for that end, what emotions will have affected this, and even whether he will have acted for any end at all' (Schatzki 1996, 166).

Arguably, the most important shift pending already in his earlier study is a growing awareness of the importance of materiality as a part of social phenomena that goes back to his specific reading of Wittgenstein and Heidegger (*e.g.* Schatzki 1996, 12–13; 2002, xii, 11–13). This shift can be traced along two related avenues – namely 'world intelligibility' and the 'production' of meaning on the one hand, and how sociality is established in practices on the other. It is worthwhile looking at both aspects in the earlier version, before turning to the fully developed concept in Schatzki's (2002) subsequent *The Site of the Social*.

'World intelligibility', namely how things (the world, people, actions *etc.*) make sense and acquire meaning (Schatzki 1996, 111), in the context of his discussion of what informs and guides human action, is understood – drawing on Wittgenstein's notion of language games – as situated in and depending on practice:

> Understanding is expressed and acquired in a tightly interwoven nexus of doings and sayings in which neither the doings nor the sayings have priority. How things make sense is articulated primarily within social practices, for it is within practices that what things are understood to be is established (Schatzki 1996, 112).

As such, in the context of practice, intelligibility is not a linguistic or discursive phenomenon only, but 'understanding is acquired through exposure to and the performance of nonverbal as well as verbal behaviors' (Schatzki 1996, 111). That is to say, all meanings *qua* practice are also 'practical' meanings, and they are tied to bodily doings as well as sayings – where doings clearly are directed towards both a social and material outside world, and 'doing' is much more than mere putting things to a specific use: 'People also observe objects, examine them, measure them, admire them, draw them, and talk about them in numerous ways that do not pertain to use' (Schatzki 1996, 114). Here, clearly, is an emphasis on the specific materiality of the world that humans perceive and encounter in their actions that is mediated by and linked to practices. The 'worlds' thus constituted are irreducible to mere discourse (Schatzki 1996, 114–115, 128–130); and (social) spaces where practices are 'correctly and acceptably performed' (Schatzki 1996, 115, 189) clearly have an indispensable material side to them that prefigures practices unfolding in specific settings – be it only, as the first step towards a more comprehensive appreciation, in physically excluding certain actions while allowing others (Schatzki 1996, 163).

Partly overlapping with what has just been said, this tendency is also obvious in Schatzki's discussion of practices and sociality. Social life is understood here as a 'nexus of practices' (Schatzki 1996, 169), that is a potential multitude of practices each opening a field of sociality, or 'a tissue of coexistence among its participants that arranges them vis-à-vis one another and molds the progression of their lives (and identities) within the practice' (Schatzki 1996, 172). Other than this passage implies, among the specific forms of sociality subsequently discussed, 'commonality' (*i.e.* shared understandings and rules *etc.*), and its opposite, 'orchestration' (*i.e. different* understandings *etc.* 'nonindependently determining what different people do'; Schatzki 1996, 186–187), that govern interpersonal encounters or face-to-face interaction, are distinctly just one such medium of sociality that is considered (Schatzki 1996, 186–195). And we also find here explicit consideration of the 'settings' of action, the 'spaces of places' where practices are 'correctly and acceptably performed' (Schatzki 1996, 115, 189), and their underlying (material) places and their physical connections: 'These places are anchored in objects, which are combined into settings. A setting is thus a particular (experientially circumscribed) configuration of objects that anchors a space of places' (Schatzki 1996, 189).

The full step is taken in his 2002 *The Site of the Social* and in subsequent works (*e.g.* Schatzki 2010; 2016; 2019a), where social life, previously understood as a 'nexus of practices' only, is explicitly redefined as a nexus of practices – doings and sayings organised by understandings, rules and norms – *and* material 'arrangements' or 'orders' which are thereby accorded 'compositional significance' for human coexistence and sociality (Schatzki 2010, 132–133):

> Human coexistence is inherently tied, not just to practices, but also to material arrangements. Indeed, social life … always transpires as part of a *mesh* of practices and arrangements: practices are carried on amid and determinative of, while also dependent on and altered by, material arrangements. I call the practice-arrangement nexuses, as inherently part of which human coexistence transpires sites of the social (Schatzki 2010, 130).

In a down-to-earth sense, 'material arrangements' are conceived here as 'interconnected material entities' that comprise humans, artefacts, organisms and things of nature (Schatzki 2010, 129; also 2002, 22–23, 174–180). However, from the perspective of Heideggerian and Wittgensteinian 'site approaches' or ontology that Schatzki is referring to, there is much more to such an arrangement than mere physical coexistence in time and space, since it is only in and through their arrangement that the meaning and the identity of what is arranged come into being:

> Social things organized in configurations, where they hang together, determine one another via their connections, as combined both exert effects on other configurations of things and are transformed through the action of other configurations, and therewith constitute the setting and medium of human action, interaction, and coexistence (Schatzki 2002, xiii).

It is as such that arrangements of humans, artefacts, organisms and things are conceived as social orders 'through and amid which social life transpires, in which these entities relate, occupy positions, and possess meanings' (Schatzki 2002, 22). We should not, therefore, be expecting fixed uses and meanings of things, including objects, artefacts *etc.*, in such relational configurations – we are looking instead into the social process as unfolding in the interplay of human doings and sayings and the material world. Also, opposite, for example, M. Löw (2016) there is no dichotomy between things (objects, settings, spaces *etc.*) socially construed, and things material or natural, since any material element of an arrangement in the above sense as such is inherently social (Schatzki 2010, 133).

If materiality – alongside practice(s) – is thus conceived as (co-)constitutive of human coexistence and sociality, the nature of the interrelationship of practices and material arrangements awaits closer scrutiny, and Schatzki (2010, 139–141) offers a discussion of this matter centred on the possible relations of causality, prefiguration, constitution and intelligibility. Causality, in a straightforward sense, occurs, whenever human actions – doings (and sayings) – and practices intervene with the material world, 'altering, creating, or rearranging material entities' (Schatzki 2010, 139). Such intervention involves specific forms of practical knowledge referring to the skilful and expedient manipulation of matter or objects (Schatzki 2010, 136). It is a feature of many practices, and, more fundamentally, such doings or interventions are (co-)constitutive of human practice and sociality as such. If this already seems trivial, one has to recall traditional understandings of the social that get along largely without reference to a material world beyond human norms and interaction *etc.* More importantly, however, causality as it is here understood is a distinctly recursive relation, because non-human material entities 'act' back – in the structured context of practices – on humans, as well as on other material entities: 'both the properties of material entities and the events that occur to them lead people to perform actions and practices to take certain courses' (Schatzki 2010, 139). This point is of utter importance, since it brings into clear focus what was largely missing in the conception of Giddens above, namely that the *material* world is both fundamentally the outcome of action, and vice versa that it structures that action in the context of organised practices. Thus, for example, the specific longevity of material arrangements, 'the decades that a house stands, the centuries that a rock fence perdures' (Schatzki 2010, 137), or the lack thereof and the relative transience of other arrangements, clearly makes a difference for subsequent opportunities for action and social practices.

Material arrangements, therefore, prefigure future practices, where 'prefiguration', Schatzki's second relation between practices and material arrangements, is 'the social present shaping/influencing/affecting the social future' (Schatzki 2010, 140). Prefiguration here is distinctly understood not to involve the background operation of some abstract virtual entities or 'structure', but it is conceived as 'a product of the actual concrete state of the social site' (Schatzki 2002, 222–223). Crucially, this cautions us against any oversimplified and deterministic reconstruction of the social process based on an insufficient understanding of the current state of the social and teleological assumptions about where we are going to. Instead, we – the observer or the actual participant in social life – are confronted with or enmeshed in a complex nexus of practices *and* material arrangements that together constitute the current condition of the social site. We are consequently facing a complex array or field of possibilities for future action and how to proceed from where we stand, depending on ongoing practices *and* existing material arrangements. This cannot be reduced – for the scholarly observer or the participant – to simple ends, rational choices or obvious options; and Schatzki makes it quite clear that we have to allow for

> ... the multitudinous ways that the mesh of practices and orders makes courses of action easier, harder, simpler, more complicated, shorter, longer, ill-advised, promising of ruin, promising of gain, disruptive, facilitating, obligatory or proscribed, acceptable or unacceptable, more or less relevant [*etc.*] (Schatzki 2002, 225).

This, obviously, refers back, on the one hand, to the field of understandings, rules and teleoaffective structures that organise and guide the doings and sayings in social practices, while on the other hand pointing on towards 'constitution' and 'intelligibility', the last two sorts of relation that exist among practices and material arrangements: Constitution may be understood as an extreme form of causation and prefiguration in the down-to-earth sense that certain courses of action may be physically impossible or unfeasible, and that certain practices depend on the presence or availability of specific material arrangements (Schatzki 2010, 140). Intelligibility, on the other hand, in this context recalls that the meaning and the identity of all things arranged depend on their being arranged as such, and the specific modalities of their arrangements. Consequently, the perception of material entities, their meaning, the way they are drawn upon and their potential to guide future action crucially depend not only on their physical properties, but on their situatedness in specific material arrangements and corresponding social practices (Schatzki 2010, 141).

If the 'site of the social' is a mesh of practices and orders or arrangements, where human activity is not 'a self-contained and self-sufficient impulse that moves through the world', but rather is a 'dealing with the orders of entities that are always already there for a person' (Schatzki 2002, 106), and where these entities comprise other humans, organisms as well as artefacts and things of nature to which action is causally and constitutively bound, at first sight this bears some family resemblance with certain so-called 'post-humanist' approaches which have it that the social field be analysed in terms of networks where neither human agency nor non-human, 'material' agency can claim priority.[6] This, however, is a misconception that Schatzki (2002, 105–122, 189–210; 2019a, 36–40) goes to some length to discourage, calling for resistance against the post-humanist 'blackmail' in certain quarters of the 'ontological turn' that 'one is either a head-in-the-sand humanist or an up-to-date posthumanist' (Schatzki 2002, 193–194). Since the position taken here is broadly the same, namely that anything along the lines of ANT or the like is a poor guide to past social life and materiality, and impoverishes our understanding of a more complex ancient reality, Schatzki's critique of post-humanism deserves explicit mention here.

His argument takes two slightly different lines of approach, where the first one refers to the obvious fact, one should think, that everything we analyse as social or cultural phenomena – past or present – in fact bears witness to the 'special constitutional, causal, and prefigurational significance of human activity in both human life in general and social existence in particular' (Schatzki 2002, 116). This point is nicely made by reference to the example of post-humanist case studies from science and technology studies (Schatzki 2002, 108–116, 119–122), in which, clearly, objects and arrangements have an enabling and constraining effect and as such 'deserve' to be analysed in terms of networks – or Schatzki's own nexuses of practices and orders –, but where objects have no capacity to institute ends and meanings, and 'things contribute to what happens in and through them because humans have set matters up that way' (Schatzki 2002, 117). We are analysing, that is to say, nexuses of practices and (material) arrangements, where the setup of the arrangement side of the argument in the first instance depends on specifically human intentionality, and the ends and the meanings of actions and objects were constituted in practice – *human* doings and sayings linked and oriented through *human* understandings, rules and teleoaffective structures (see also Lindstrøm 2015, 216–217, 221–222):

> What artifacts, organisms, things, and people qua components of arrangements do is enabled and constrained by other components and features of the arrangements into which human activity inserts them ... Conversely, these entities enable and constrain the activities humans perform, including what humans do with them. Even amid, however, such apparent symmetry, activities hold the edge. For ... the enabling and constraining effects of objects and arrangements on activities are relative to actors' ends, projects, hopes, fears, and so on (Schatzki 2002, 117).

Schatzki's second line of argument is centred on a related point, namely the 'unique richness' of human agency opposite 'material' agency, and the general necessity to allow for the existence of different 'types' of agency, instead of collapsing them into one, in a vain attempt to accord intentionality to things. With agency simply understood as 'doing' (Schatzki 2002, 191), and objects and orders thought to exert a causal and prefigurational influence on activities and practices (*e.g.* Schatzki 2002, 107–108; 2010, 130, 132–135), for Schatzki, clearly, objects (material entities, artefacts, things of nature *etc.*) do have agency. They do so, however, expressly in a different way than humans do, whose doings and sayings are organised into practices by understandings, rules and teleoaffective structures, that is by specifically human 'ends, projects, tasks, purposes, beliefs, emotions, and moods' (Schatzki 1996, 89). Thus, geomagnetic storms, the example referred to by Schatzki (2002, 198), do have agency in the sense that they do bring about the breakdown or closure of electronic communication, but this amounts to hardly more than physical causality (see also Lindstrøm 2015, 221–222; Ribeiro 2016, 230–231). They cannot be said to have done so on purpose, intentionally and in consequence of deliberate planning:

> Actor-network theory's proliferation of agency does not subvert the unique richness of the intentional, deliberate, planning, and self-conscious agency humans enjoy. Attributing agency to animals, machines, storms, and social phenomena such as day trading firms only, at best, corrects a misguided humanism that proclaims people the sole agents (Schatzki 2002, 201).

Back to tells: Implications and outlook

Remarkably, in archaeology a related approach has already been outlined in John Barrett's congenial *Fragments from Antiquity* (1994), drawing his inspiration mainly from Giddens' 'theory of structuration' and to a lesser extent from Bourdieu. Underlying Barrett's approach was the endeavour to steer clear from both I. Hodder's (and others) attempt at that time to read *meaning* back into the minds and material culture of prehistoric people (*cf.* Barrett 1987, 471) – a radical example being his *Domestication of Europe* (Hodder 1990) –, as well as from the 'personal empathy' with places (*cf.* Barrett 1994, 35) as perceived and experienced through a universal human body in phenomenological approaches, a prominent example then being C. Tilley's *Phenomenology of Landscape* (1994). It is unfortunate, from the perspective advocated here, that the particular brand of post-processual archaeology proposed by Barrett did not receive similar attention (but, see, for example, Gardner 2008, 103; Ribeiro 2016, 232–233) like Hodder's fascinating but problematic mixture of structuralist and hermeneutic approaches (*cf.* Gibbon 1993), or attract numerous followers as did the phenomenologically inspired landscape archaeology heralded by Tilley (*cf.* Brück 2005; Johnson 2012). For even though Barrett's interpretation of specific aspects of the Neolithic to Bronze Age monuments and landscapes of southern Britain that *Fragments* deals with, may be controversial – or subject to modification due to the availability of new data –, the overall approach outlined and the objectives of archaeology formulated, clearly do stand. They require due consideration in any attempt at social archaeology, not least in that Barrett – adhering to central tenets of Giddens' version of practice theory – throughout assumes a specifically human agency.[7]

What Barrett proposes, then, is an archaeology that does not operate on a generalising level anymore, seeking to identify this social structure or 'type' of social organisation or that, and in doing so treats the material remains of past social life as an externalised record of some pre-existing, higher level of social reality (*e.g.* Barrett 1994, 1–6, 35–37). Historical, or for that matter archaeological knowledge, it is argued, does not involve the uncovering, by acts of methodological sophistication, of some 'transcendental truth' or fixed meanings laid out in material culture, subsequently distorted by formation processes, but in principle still available to reconstruct an ancient, static 'reality' (Barrett 1994, 32–33, 71–72; 2006, 201–207). Instead, we are always looking at a dynamic record of past human actions, organised into and oriented by practices,[8] and invariably bound to practical understandings and manipulations of a material world that was permanently constituted *and* drawn upon in the unfolding of social life and practices:

> The argument ... moves us away from dealing with the material evidence as if it were some externalized and objective record of a past process, and leads to the recognition that the material was implicated in the creation of past human subjectivities. The object of archaeological analysis should be to understand how those subjectivities could have been constituted out of a human agency which worked upon the material conditions it inhabited. People know the world they inhabit, and they rework that knowledge through their active engagement with that world ... This situates our analysis of the past in a frame of reference which is more local and particular than is normally employed, simply because we are now concerned with the day-to-day maintenance of traditional practice by people rather than with the long-term existence of some abstract 'social system' (Barrett 1994, 35–36).

This is, of course, the central message of all approaches inspired by practice theory as outlined above, with the important caveat that the interest in 'past human subjectivities' should not be mistaken for some kind of particularistic individualism (*cf.* Schatzki 1996, 6–9, 13; Schäfer 2016a, 12–13), but as the expression of the underlying anthropology that – now and in the past – allows for knowledgeable actors, or humans 'who had memories and expectations about themselves, others and the world which they inhabited' (Barrett 1994, 66). As such, however, their lives, their understandings and agencies, were historically, that is socially, situated.

They were contextualised in practices and implicated in a pre-existing material world structured – in part – by those same practices. What archaeologists should aspire to, from this perspective, is an understanding, referring to *specific* settings and materialities, 'of what the possibilities were of being human within those material and historical conditions' (Barrett 1994, 5; see also 2016a, 134). This is the call for a fine-grained reconstruction of the particular engagements with historically specific material conditions in social practices; the study of how knowledges and understandings were produced and reworked in discourse and the material world; and how material culture as a structuring medium enabled and constrained the doings and sayings of those involved:

> ... archaeologists should seek to understand how people may once have lived out their lives, and not limit themselves to the more restricted quest of interpreting the archaeological record. These are not one and the same thing. Those lives were lived as routines which were built as people engaged with the empirical realities which they recognized as being available to them. Such engagements could only have arisen from positions of informed pre-understanding. This is an archaeology of memory and of practice ... Traditions are thus enabling and they are carried forward in the action and discourse of human agency (Barrett 1994, 95).

People in the past were confronted, then, with 'empirical realities', and it is this common materiality, which is not entirely malleable, that we draw upon in our 'readings' of the past as well (Barrett 1994, 6, 170). But we should not expect, on the other hand, any single and consistent meaning and understanding to emerge in the social process – neither in the past, nor in the archaeological endeavour:

> We have not uncovered what those monuments meant, and this does not matter for they were never the expression of a single truth. Instead, we have understood how the logic of the known world could have been revealed and sustained, thought and acted through afresh, as various traditions of knowing were reworked upon the available physical resources (Barrett 1994, 71–72).

Material culture, artefacts and their arrangements, architecture and space *etc.*, that is to say, do not have an intrinsic meaning, but only obtain meaning in specific social practices and interpretative frameworks. Such meanings are permanently reworked as the things of life are drawn upon in new contexts and social practices, while at the same time contributing to the knowledges and understandings characteristically held in specific contexts and practices (*e.g.* Barrett 1994, 75–76, 95, 168–169).

This assertion, of course, is an imposition on the traditional perception of archaeologists, that we are unearthing some kind of static truth or historical reality, even though this may be delimited by the material remains which are at our disposal only. In fact, however, the situation is not that much different from any other attempt to understand the 'other' since this will always involve an act of interpretation. We can never lay claim to have exposed fixed meanings or understandings existing out there in human collectivities or held by individuals, even if we were able to talk to them as ethnographers may. However, even if it is always possible to create meaning, and in fact different meanings, from the archaeological remains (Barrett 1994, 169–170), Barrett's approach distinctly is not relativistic, but takes aim at a contextualised understanding of social practices and their material conditions that is clearly delimited by the 'empirical realities' and the specific materialities studied (Barrett 1994, 110) – by the particular settings of social practices, and the unique possibilities of perceptions and actions provided and reworked, and not others *etc*. His is an interest, that is to say, in how practices got orientated, how *dominant* or joint – not individual – understandings of the social world arose, were given material expression, *i.e.* stability, and how they were reproduced in social practices (*e.g.* Barrett 1994, 14, 18–19; 2016a, 137); an interest in these 'other interpretive regimes', past interpretations and the 'prejudices which are other than our own' (Barrett 1994, 170) that once operated upon the same material that is still available for archaeologists to study:

> This is a contextual archaeology which attempts to preserve the context of social reproduction over time and space but does not depend on discovering 'ideas in people's heads' ... Instead of attempting to read back from modern archaeological remains to meanings in the past, a better proposal is to explore the implications of particular material conditions for the structuring of specified social relations (Barrett 1987, 471).

Turning back to tell sites and their interpretation, the starting point of this discussion, we see, in the Carpathian Basin and beyond, from the 5th millennium BC onwards a characteristic social 'cycling' with adjustments within the structural limits of broadly tribal societies (Parkinson 2002; 2006), but with little 'progress' in terms of social differentiation and political hierarchisation far into the Bronze Age (Kienlin 2012b; 2015a; Duffy 2014): from the Late Neolithic tell sites, via a dispersed Copper Age pattern and the reappearance of settlement mounds during the Early and Middle Bronze Age, and on to the differently organised fortified sites of the Late Bronze Age, situated on the hilltops of the Carpathian ranges as well as in the lowland marshes, some of them of truly impressive size but occupied for a limited period of time only when compared to the previous tell sites in the area. We see, here, social change *and* the recurrence twice of settlement mounds, and this finding is insufficiently understood if one follows the traditional top-down approach of Bronze Age archaeology with its predominant interest in the evolution of stratified society and the socio-political impact of metalworking *etc.*

Archaeology should try to establish an understanding of such historically specific constellations of tell-living, without on the other hand introducing a rigid Neolithic versus Bronze Age divide. The evidence from both periods is multi-faceted, and in many aspects there was continuity. We should not deliberately restrict ourselves to the study of Bronze Age communities in terms of 'political economy', supra-regional elite exchange and political hierarchisation. Rather than competition and the attempt to establish or reproduce political hierarchies, in the Bronze Age, as in the previous Neolithic, we also see a concern with communal values. Traditional notions of the world, of the self *and* the community, were encouraged rather than setting a premium on the aggressive aggrandising behaviour of select 'alpha' males only, which so tend to fascinate us. What we see is the long-term stability of a traditional way of life rather than Bronze Age communities fundamentally different from everything that had come before. There was continuity in the norms and values structuring the life of these communities and their social space in contrast to 'foreign' (*i.e.* Mediterranean) models of hierarchical society and their spatial correlates (*e.g.* palaces, central storage or workshops), if such were in fact known during a later phase in the existence of our Bronze Age tells. And there was, on the internal side of things, resistance in the face of the ever-present individual ambition to become more equal than the others.

Unlike the reductionist macro-perspective of mainstream social modelling and consequent talk of 'proto-urban' or 'chiefly' tells as centres dominating the Bronze Age landscape, inspired by practice theory we should move towards a fine-grained contextual understanding of the specific materiality of life on tell sites, Neolithic and Bronze Age, of their respective spatial and architectural settings that guided perception and that were available to be drawn upon in social action. We should take aim at an account that allows for what is truly remarkable about such sites – be they Neolithic or Bronze Age – and what we can infer from them about the way of life they once framed and enabled. For throughout different tell-'building' groups of both periods, on the one hand we see a strong normative conception of how the social and material world should be organised, and in terms of their spatial layout most sites feature the 'classic' elements of a tell or tell-like 'core', a more or less massive ditch and an outer settlement beyond. Yet, on the other hand, the exact manifestation of these parts, their development through time and their relation *vis-à-vis* each other clearly was often different from site to site, and subject to change and negotiation (for a case study see Kienlin 2018). There is a tension, then, between an explicit emphasis on the adherence to a traditional way of life, most prominent of course the fact of living on a mound that developed on top of previous generations of houses itself, and the effect of 'agency' on that 'structure' (= 'structural' or rather 'structuring' properties = rules and resources pace Giddens 1979; 1984) and social (and material!) space, *i.e.* spatial 'structures' – discursive and physical – realised in action, but also structuring that action (in extension to Löw 2016).

On the one hand, we are confronted with a somewhat 'conservative' attitude to community, social space and architecture that discouraged deviation and conflict, while on the other hand we see adjustments going on, for example, in the allocation and 'ambitions' of households to an 'on-tell' or 'off-tell' position *etc.* Their 'status' in terms of settling down in different sections of the site and potentially their corresponding role in their community with all the consequences this may have entailed was partly fluid and under negotiation. Similarly, the relative size and possible importance of the various parts of the settlements can be seen to change through time and differ from site to site. In detail, different solutions were found regarding the spatial arrangement of settlements and the organisation of society. However, this clearly took place within structural confines that did not – typically – allow putting the cohesion of the entire community at risk. An overarching 'identity' was maintained for quite some time that – among other aspects of social life and materiality – in its explicit emphasis on tell-'living', on direct architectural continuity *etc.* differs markedly from social life as it had unfolded during the preceding Copper Age and the beginnings of the local Early Bronze Age prior to the re-emergence of tells, as well as ever after during the local Late Bronze and Iron Ages.

In terms of the practice approach outlined in this paper, it is important here to recall that the 'social' is never a static given but is in permanent flux. All social life is situated in space and time, where it constantly unfolds anew. The social, then, is a process, and the above contention of a 'conservative' attitude on our tells to community and the organisation of space, stability and the absence of change in the sense that tell-'life' persisted, decidedly must not be taken to imply that social reproduction had somehow come to an end, nor that there ever was anything in existence like ahistorical 'tell society' as such. Rather, stability and the apparent lack of change on a macro scale, are specific features of the social field, in a given region and for a specific period of time. They come about as the result of social life unfolding in a specific way, and not another, that leaves the total nexus of practices – *i.e.* the doings and sayings organised by norms and understandings – *and* the material 'arrangements' that together make up human sociality (*pace* Schatzki 1996; 2002) seemingly unchanged in outward appearance.

In a community thus characterised, favouring tradition over change, norms and shared ends not only link and 'orient' actions into practices, as they always do, but may effectuate the broadly speaking 'unchanged' persistence of traditional practices and discourage 'deviation' by social actors, without ever reducing them, of course, to mere 'dummies'. Similarly, in such a situation, the *material* world which is always both the outcome of action and structures that action in the context of organised practices, by virtue of its longevity and apparent 'givenness' may come to prefigure the social future in likeness of the past more consistently than is 'normally' the case. The social process, however, will always remain fundamentally open and indeterminate, as social actors *do* have agency and intentionality in pursuit of their notion of life well accomplished, because there are limits, on the other hand, to their discursive penetration and attempts at manipulating social 'reality', and because their knowledgeability is always 'bounded' and all kinds of unintended consequences feed back into future action (Giddens 1979). So both apparent stability and change always have to be understood as contingent upon specific historical contexts and as being 'a product of the actual concrete state of the social site' (Schatzki 2002, 222–223), including 'traditional' practices, their material setting and human intentionality. They are not an inherent, given property of this 'type' of society or social structure or that:

> Practices and fields are inherently open; they can always be perpetuated through further actions, even if they evolve in the process. Practices can also cease, of course; for example through elimination, as when their practitioners are murdered, or through fragmentation as when ends, projects, actions, and rules that organize them are absorbed into the organization of different practice complexes (Schatzki 2019b, 59).

For our tells, it is argued here, the latter development, fragmentation and an end to their constitutive practices or rather bundles of practices, was delayed, by and large, until the onset of the local Late Bronze Age. However, underneath the specific identity or manifestation of sociality maintained, we clearly do see social practices and corresponding material arrangements being negotiated and adjusted. It is suggested that archaeology should take an interest in such processes on the 'micro' scale rather than succumb to the temptation of neat macro history and great narratives aloof from the material remains of past lives.

Referring back to Barrett and the above discussion, we should not be essentialising from a rich and diverse range of evidence however indirectly linked to past knowledge, action and intentionality. We should also not be equating cultural manifestations that are historically unique and the material possibilities they provided, when instead we should be trying to develop an understanding of what is specific about the groups or phenomena studied. Rather than subsuming the evidence at hand to some preconceived idea of the type of society encountered, it is suggested we allow for what is unique and seek to develop an understanding of the actual material remains of a historically specific social and cultural configuration that has come upon us in the archaeological record. The result may be less captivating than the grand narratives still told much too often, but for exactly this reason it may also be more consonant with the lives we want to study as they were once lived in the more or less contingent course of events that unfolded as people carried forward their programmes of understandings and intentions in the organised field of practices and reworked the materialities at their disposal. Or, to let Schatzki have the final say here:

> I believe that one noteworthy outcome of writing histories and analyzing contemporary phenomena with these experientially resonant concepts is that history and the contemporary world seem less systematic or ordered and more labyrinthine and contingent than they do when described and analyzed through the conceptual armature of many other theories (Schatzki 2010, 146).

Notes

1   In this sense both Giddens and Bourdieu are not adherents of a flat ontology in practice theory as outlined by Schatzki (2016; 2019a, 32–33).
2   In general accordance with Giddens' anti-essentialist perspective, Bourdieu as well argues against overarching social totalities determining human action and perception – centrally through his concept of 'habitus' that seeks to bridge the gap between 'structure' and 'agency', and introduces a recursive understanding of both sides instead of the dichotomies previously assumed (*e.g.* Bourdieu 1977, 78–87; 1990, 52–65). Habitus, that is to say, mediates between structure and agency, it brings about and orientates individual and collective practices by providing 'systems of durable, transposable dispositions' (Bourdieu 1990, 53) that guide action and make certain choices and proceedings appear more desirable and natural than others. It accounts for the evident consistency and orchestration of the social – without recourse required to abstract rules that determine the course of social life – by ensuring instead 'the active presence of past experiences, which, deposited in each organism in the form of schemes of perception, thought and action, tend to guarantee the "correctness" of practices and their constancy over time, more reliably than all formal rules and explicit norms' (Bourdieu 1990, 54).
3   'As I shall employ it, "structure" refers to "structural property", or more exactly, to "structuring property", structuring properties providing the "binding" of time and space in social systems. I argue that these properties can be understood as rules and resources, recursively implicated in the reproduction of social systems' (Giddens 1979, 64).
4   On the *Raumvergessenheit* of traditional sociology, criticised by proponents of the so-called 'spatial turn', see for example Schroer (2006, 17–28) and Delitz (2009, 11–15).
5   M. Löw (2016, 26–32) takes aim at a related point with her critique that Giddens' space is essentially what she calls a 'container space', the external setting or frame in which social interaction happens or social practices are located.

6   This in itself from the perspective of Schatzki, and others, of course, is a shortcoming since it makes up for an incomplete account of the social only: 'The networks of actor-network theory closely resemble what I call "arrangements". Both are composed of interrelated material entities. Arrangements, however, are only one of the two principle sorts of phenomena that make up social phenomena. The second is practices, which have no pendent in actor-network theory ... Actor-network theory thereby fails to capture a key feature of human social life, namely, the practices that are tied to arrangements and help constitute social phenomena' (Schatzki 2010, 134–135).

7   See also Barrett (2006; 2012; 2014; 2016a; 2016b). Broadly the same concern is currently expressed by Ribeiro (2016, 233): 'agency has to be perceived as those knowledgeable choices which actors are actually free to make. These choices can only exist within a *social context* in which an actor understands what choices can be made. It is only in this framework that the notions of both "agency" and "context" make sense' (see also Ribeiro 2019).

8   See, for example, Barrett (1994, 3): 'This requires that we recognize, in the fleeting and the momentary occurrences of human action, the expectation that those actions were appropriate and would be effective, that they made sense according to some recognizable order and logic in the world which they addressed and to which they also contributed. Structures are both the means by which socially recognizable actions are achieved, and their consequences.' Barrett, for obvious reasons, is following here Giddens' theory of structuration (1979; 1984), not the subsequent Schatzki (1996; 2002) version. The consequent understanding of the social is much the same.

References

Barrett, J.C. (1987) Contextual archaeology. *Antiquity* 61, 468–473.

Barrett, J.C. (1994) *Fragments from Antiquity. An Archaeology of Social Life in Britain, 2900–1200 BC.* Oxford, Blackwell.

Barrett, J.C. (2006) Archaeology as the Investigation of the contexts of humanity. In D. Papaconstantinou (ed.), *Deconstructing Context: A Critical Approach to Archaeological Practice*, 194–211. Oxford, Oxbow Books.

Barrett, J.C. (2012) Agency. A revisionist account. In I. Hodder (ed.), *Archaeological Theory Today* (2nd edition), 146–166. Cambridge, Polity Press.

Barrett, J.C. (2014) The material constitution of humanness. *Archaeological Dialogues* 21, 65–74.

Barrett, J.C. (2016a) Archaeology after interpretation. Returning humanity to archaeological Theory. *Archaeological Dialogues* 23, 133–137.

Barrett, J.C. (2016b) The new antiquarianism? *Antiquity* 90, 1681–1686.

Bergerbrant, S. & Sabatini, S. (2013) *Counterpoint: Essays in Archaeology and Heritage Studies in Honour of Professor Kristian Kristiansen.* Oxford, British Archaeological Report S2508.

Blanton, R.E., Feinman, G.M., Kowalewski, S.A. & Peregrine, P.N. (1996) A dual-processual theory for the evolution of Mesoamerican civilization. *Current Anthropology* 37, 1–14.

Bourdieu, P. (1977) *Outline of a Theory of Practice.* Cambridge, Cambridge University Press.

Bourdieu, P. (1990) *The Logic of Practice.* Stanford CA, Stanford University Press.

Brück, J. (2005) Experiencing the past? The development of a phenomenological archaeology in British prehistory. *Archaeological Dialogues* 12, 45–72.

Childe, V.G. (1950) The urban revolution. *Town Planning Review* 21, 3–17.

Delitz, H. (2009) *Architektursoziologie. Themen der Soziologie.* Bielefeld, Transcript.

Delitz, H. (2010) *Gebaute Gesellschaft. Architektur als Medium des Sozialen.* Frankfurt am Main, Campus.

Dietler, M. (2010) *Archaeologies of Colonialism. Consumption, Entanglement, and Violence in Ancient Mediterranean France.* Berkeley CA, University of California Press.

Dobres, M.-A. & Robb, J.E. (2000) *Agency in Archaeology.* London, Routledge.

Duffy, P.R. (2014) *Complexity and Autonomy in Bronze Age Europe. Assessing Cultural Developments in Eastern Hungary.* Budapest, Prehistoric Research in the Körös Region 1.

Dünne, J. (2006) Soziale Räume. Einleitung. In J. Dünne & S. Günzel (eds), *Raumtheorie. Grundlagentexte aus Philosophie und Kulturwissenschaften*, 289–303. Frankfurt am Main, Suhrkamp.

Earle, T. (2002) *Bronze Age Economics. The Beginnings of Political Economies.* Boulder CO, Westview.

Earle, T., Ling, J., Uhnér, C., Stos-Gale, Z. & Melheim, L. (2015) The political economy and metal trade in Bronze Age Europe: Understanding regional variability in terms of comparative advantages and articulations. *European Journal of Archaeology* 18, 633–657.

Gardner, A. (2008) Agency. In R.A. Bentley, H.D.G. Maschner & C. Chippindale (eds), *Handbook of Archaeological Theories*, 95–108. Lanham MD, AltaMira Press.

Gibbon, C. (1993) Comment: O'Shea on Hodder's *Domestication*. *American Anthropologist* 95, 711–714.

Giddens, A. (1979) *Central Problems in Social Theory. Action, Structure and Contradiction in Social Analysis.* Basingstoke, Macmillan.

Giddens, A. (1984) *The Constitution of Society. Outline of the Theory of Structuration.* Berkeley CA, University of California Press.

Gogâltan, F. (2010) Die Tells und der Urbanisierungsprozess. In B. Horejs & T.L. Kienlin (eds), *Siedlung und Handwerk – Studien zu sozialen Kontexten in der Bronzezeit*, 13–46. Bonn, Habelt.

Gogâltan, F. (2017) The Bronze Age multilayered settlements in the Carpathian Basin (ca. 2500–1600/1500 BC). An old catalogue and some chronological problems. *Journal of Ancient History and Archaeology* 4, 28–55.

Hänsel, B. (2002) Stationen der Bronzezeit zwischen Griechenland und Mitteleuropa. *Bericht der Römisch-Germanischen Kommission* 83, 69–97.

Hansen, S. & Krause, R. (2018) *Bronzezeitliche Burgen zwischen Taunus und Karpaten. Beiträge der Ersten Internationalen*

LOEWE-Konferenz vom 7. bis 9. Dezember 2016 in Frankfurt/M. Bonn, Habelt.

Harding, A. (2013) World systems, cores, and peripheries in prehistoric Europe. *European Journal of Archaeology* 16, 378–400.

Hodder, I. (1990) *The Domestication of Europe. Structure and Contingency in Neolithic Societies.* Oxford, Blackwell.

Hodder, I. (2012) *Entangled. An Archaeology of the Relationships Between Humans and Things.* Chichester, Wiley-Blackwell.

Horn, C. & Kristiansen, K. (2018) *Warfare in Bronze Age Society.* Cambridge, Cambridge University Press.

Johnson, M.H. (2012) Phenomenological approaches in landscape archaeology. *Annual Review of Anthropology* 41, 269–284.

Kalthoff, H., Cress, T. & Röhl, T. (2016) Einleitung: Materialität in Kultur und Gesellschaft. In H. Kalthoff, T. Cress & T. Röhl (eds), *Materialität. Herausforderungen für die Sozial- und Kulturwissenschaften*, 11–41. Paderborn, Wilhelm Fink.

Kienlin, T.L. (2012a) Beyond elites: An introduction. In T.L. Kienlin & A. Zimmermann (eds), *Beyond Elites. Alternatives to Hierarchical Systems in Modelling Social Formations*, 15–32. Bonn, Habelt.

Kienlin, T.L. (2012b) Patterns of change, or: Perceptions deceived? Comments on theiInterpretation of Late Neolithic and Bronze Age tell settlement in the Carpathian Basin. In T.L. Kienlin & A. Zimmermann (eds), *Beyond Elites. Alternatives to Hierarchical Systems in Modelling Social Formations*, 251–310. Bonn, Habelt.

Kienlin, T.L. (2015a) *Bronze Age Tell Communities in Context – An Exploration Into Culture, Society, and the Study of European Prehistory. Part 1: Critique. Europe and the Mediterranean.* Oxford, Archaeopress.

Kienlin, T.L. (2015b) All heroes in their armour bright and shining? Comments on the Bronze Age 'other'. In T.L. Kienlin (ed.), *Fremdheit – Perspektiven auf das Andere*, 153–193. Bonn, Habelt.

Kienlin, T.L. (2017) World systems and the structuring potential of foreign-derived (prestige) goods. on modelling Bronze Age economy and society. In A.K. Scholz, M. Bartelheim, R. Hardenberg & J. Staecker (eds), *ResourceCultures. Sociocultural Dynamics and the Use of Resources – Theories, Methods, Perspectives*, 143–157. Tübingen, Universität Tübingen.

Kienlin, T.L. (2018) Borsod Region Bronze Age settlement: 'Diversity in uniformity'. In T.L. Kienlin, K.P. Fischl & T. Pusztai (eds), *Borsod Region Bronze Age Settlement (BORBAS). Catalogue of the Early to Middle Bronze Age Tell Sites Covered by Magnetometry and Surface Survey*, 11–91. Bonn, Habelt.

Kristiansen, K. & Earle, T. (2015) Neolithic versus Bronze Age social formations: A political economy approach. In K. Kristiansen, L. Šmejda & J. Turek (eds), *Paradigm Found. Archaeological Theory Present, Past and Future. Essays in Honour of Evžen Neustupný*, 234–247. Oxford, Oxbow Books.

Kristiansen, K. & Larsson, T.B. (2005) *The Rise of Bronze Age Society. Travels, Transmissions and Transformations.* Cambridge, Cambridge University Press.

Lindstrøm, T.C. (2015) Agency 'in itself'. A discussion of inanimate, animal and human agency. *Archaeological Dialogues* 22, 207–238.

Ling, J., Earle, T. & Kristiansen, K. (2018) Maritime mode of production. Raiding and trading in seafaring chiefdoms. *Current Anthropology* 59, 488–524.

Link, Th. (2006) *Das Ende der neolithischen Tellsiedlungen. Ein kulturgeschichtliches Phänomen des 5. Jahrtausends v. Chr. im Karpatenbecken.* Bonn, Habelt.

Löw, M. (2016) *The Sociology of Space. Materiality, Social Structures, and Action.* London, Palgrave Macmillan.

Meller, H. (2017) Armies in the Early Bronze Age? An alternative interpretation of Únětice culture axe hoards. *Antiquity* 91, 1529–1545.

Miller, D. (1985) *Artefacts as Categories. A Study of Ceramic Variability in Central India.* Cambridge, Cambridge University Press.

Miller, D. (2005) *Materiality.* Durham NC, Duke University Press.

Ortner, S.B. (1984) Theory in anthropology since the sixties. *Comparative Studies in Society and History* 26, 126–166.

Parkinson, W.A. (2002) Integration, interaction, and tribal 'cycling': The transition to the Copper Age on the Great Hungarian Plain. In W.A. Parkinson (ed.), *The Archaeology of Tribal Societies*. 391–438. Ann Arbor MI, Archaeological Series 15.

Parkinson, W.A. (2006) *The Social Organization of Early Copper Age Tribes on the Great Hungarian Plain.* Oxford, British Archaeological Report S1573.

Reckwitz, A. (2008) *Unscharfe Grenzen. Perspektiven der Kultursoziologie.* Bielefeld, Transcript.

Reckwitz, A. (2016) *Kreativität und soziale Praxis. Studien zur Sozial- und Gesellschaftstheorie.* Bielefeld, Transcript.

Renfrew, C. (1998) Mind and matter: Cognitive archaeology and external symbolic storage. In C. Renfrew & C. Scarre (eds), *Cognition and Material Culture: The Archaeology of Symbolic Storage*, 1–6. Cambridge, McDonald Institute.

Ribeiro, A. (2016) Against object agency. A counterreaction to Sørensen's 'Hammers and nails'. *Archaeological Dialogues* 23, 229–235.

Ribeiro, A. (2019) Against object agency 2. Continuing the discussion with Sørensen. *Archaeological Dialogues* 26, 39–44.

Rowlands, M.J. (1994) Childe and the archaeology of freedom. In D.R. Harris (ed.), *The Archaeology of V. Gordon Childe: Contemporary Perspectives*, 35–54. London, UCL Press.

Schäfer, H. (2016a) Einleitung. Grundlagen, Rezeption und Forschungsperspektiven der Praxistheorie. In H. Schäfer (ed.), *Praxistheorie. Ein soziologisches Forschungsprogramm*, 9–25. Bielefeld, Transcript.

Schäfer, H. (2016b) Praxis als Wiederholung. Das Denken der Iterabilität und seine Konsequenzen für die Methodologie praxeologischer Forschung. In H. Schäfer (ed.), *Praxistheorie. Ein soziologisches Forschungsprogramm*, 137–159. Bielefeld, Transcript.

Schatzki, T.R. (1996) *Social Practices. A Wittgensteinian Approach to Human Activity and the Social.* Cambridge, Cambridge University Press.

Schatzki, T.R. (2001) Introduction. Practice Theory. In T.R. Schatzki, K. Knorr Cetina & E.v. Savigny (eds), *The Practice Turn in Contemporary Theory*, 1–14. London, Routledge.

Schatzki, T.R. (2002) *The Site of the Social. A Philosophical Account of the Constitution of Social Life and Change.* University Park PA, Pennsylvania State University Press.

Schatzki, T.R. (2010) Materiality and Social Life. *Nature and Culture* 5, 123–149.

Schatzki, T.R. (2016) Practice Theory as flat ontology. In G. Spaargaren, D. Weenink & M. Lamers (eds), *Practice Theory and Research. Exploring the Dynamics of Social Life*, 28–42. London, Routledge.

Schatzki, T.R. (2019a) *Social Change in a Material World.* London, Routledge.

Schatzki, T.R. (2019b) On plural actions. In A. Buch & T.R. Schatzki (eds), *Questions of Practice in Philosophy and Social Theory*, 49–64. New York, Routledge.

Schroer, M. (2006) *Räume, Orte, Grenzen. Auf dem Weg zu einer Soziologie des Raums.* Frankfurt am Main, Suhrkamp.

Shanks, M. & Tilley, C. (1987) *Social Theory and Archaeology.* Cambridge, Polity Press.

Shanks, M. & Tilley, C. (1992) *Re-Constructing Archaeology: Theory and Practice.* London, Routledge.

Sørensen, M.L.S. & Rebay-Salisbury, K. (2013) *Embodied Knowledge. Perspectives on Belief and Technology.* Oxford, Oxbow Books.

Stein, G.J. (1999) *Rethinking World-Systems. Diasporas, Colonies, and Interaction in Uruk Mesopotamia.* Tucson AZ, University of Arizona Press.

Tilley, C. (1994) *A Phenomenology of Landscape. Places, Paths and Monuments.* Oxford, Berg.

Tilley, C., Keane, W., Küchler, S., Rowlands, M. & Spyer, P. (2006) *Handbook of Material Culture.* London, Sage.

Vandkilde, H. (2016) Bronzization: The Bronze Age as pre-modern globalization. *Prähistorische Zeitschrift* 91, 103–123.

Wynne-Jones, S. & Kohring, S. (2007) Socialising complexity. In S. Kohring & S. Wynne-Jones (eds), *Socialising Complexity. Structure, Interaction and Power in Archaeological Discourse*, 2–12. Oxford, Oxbow Books.

13

Architecture, Power and Everyday Life in the Iron Age of North-eastern Iberia. Research from 1985 to 2019 on the Tell-like Fortress of Els Vilars (Arbeca, Lleida, Spain)

Joan B. López, Emili Junyent and Natàlia Alonso

Joan B. López left us during the last days of preparation of this article. Nothing presented in this study would have been possible without him. He is infinitely missed professionally and personally.

Introduction

The fortress of Els Vilars is in the south of the Pre-Pyrenees in the epicentre of the Central Depression of the Western Catalan Plain on land belonging to the Municipality of Arbeca (Lleida, Catalonia, Spain). Its geographical coordinates are: UTM 31N/ETRS89; X: 329410; Y: 4603892 and its altitude is 301.7 m above sea level (ICGC 2019-06; Topographic base 1:5000) (Fig. 13.1). It is linked respectively to the Mediterranean and Continental Europe by the Segre and Francolí Rivers.

The site has been the subject of uninterrupted archaeological campaigns since 1985 by the Grup d'Investigació Prehistòrica of the University of Lleida. Work over the years has yielded its entire layout and evolutionary sequence. It has gained scientific interest at both the national and international level, and in 1998 was declared a *Bé Cultural d'Interès Nacional* (*BCIN*: Site of Cultural Interest). More recently (2016), it was the object of an exhibition 'The Vilars d'Arbeca Fortress: Land, Water and Power in the Iberian World' commemorating its 30 years of excavations. This exhibition's catalogue (Junyent & López 2016) includes a complete bibliography of the site. Past and daily news can also be followed on its website: http://www.vilars.cat.

This chapter presents an overview of the research, methodology and main historical-archaeological, social and economic findings of the site's almost 500 years (775–300 cal BC). It also sheds light on the contributions of this research in defining a new regional model of territorial structure during the First Iron Age and the Iberian Period.

Els Vilars: A partially mutilated tell

Although known since 1975, the first archaeological interventions did not take place until 1985–1986 in the form of rescue campaigns due to the threat of agriculture. The earliest fieldwork only focused on a narrow strip of land, a sort of baulk about two–three m high and 30 m in length, which divided two agricultural properties (Fig. 13.2, a–c). The features unearthed were the corners of a few houses of a settlement from the Middle Iberian period (425–300 BC) like many others in the area (Fig. 13.2, d–e). What was anomalous was its setting in the plain, contrasting with most Iberian settlements occupying elevations. A few trial trenches at the foot of the baulk before the end of the initial campaign uncovered more structures that ultimately served to initiate a wider programme of fieldwork.

Today we know that Els Vilars is a spectacular fortress with an oval layout enclosing a residential area with up to four successive phases of urban remodelling limited to a surface of barely 60 × 45 m (Fig. 13.3 and 13.5, a). The site's stratigraphic sequence can be broken down into five

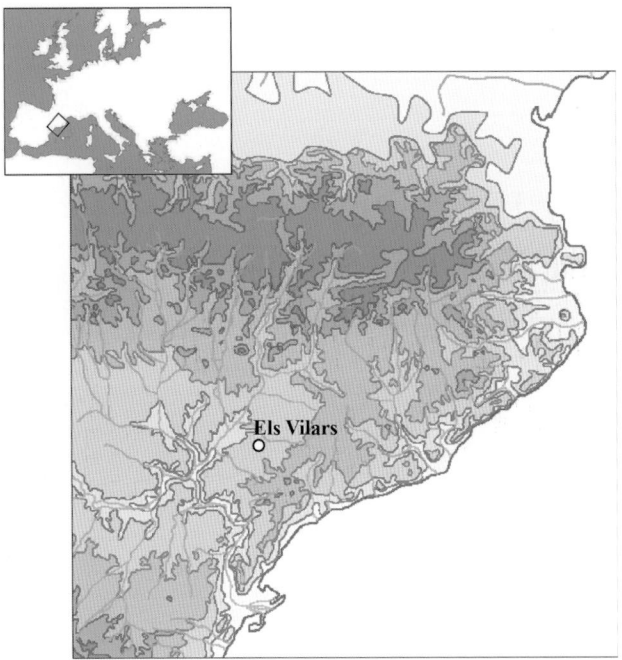

Figure 13.1 Map of the north-east of the Iberian Peninsula with the position of the Fortress of Els Vilars (Arbeca, Lleida, Catalonia).

A remarkable aspect of this site is that the perimeter of its initial enclosure (Vilars 0) was never modified and the different overlapping phases of construction led to the formation of an authentic tell with a very thick stratigraphic sequence (Fig. 13.2). Agricultural activity, especially intense since its mechanisation in the mid-20th century, mutilated the original tell, destroying its final phases (Vilars III and Vilars IV). The sole feature of the later phase is a monumental well-cistern (Vilars III) in the enclosure's centre cutting through the layers of the preceding phases. Fortunately the earliest phases of occupation, in particular Vilars 0 and Vilars I, were spared and practically intact (Figs 13.3 and 13.5a).

The dynamics of sedimentation and occupation immediately beyond the initial enclosure followed a diametrically opposite direction materialised by a continuous expansion of the defensive system (Figs 13.4 and 13.6). This consisted initially of a wall with a single facing with 11 towers (Vilars 0) which was subsequently reinforced (Vilars I) with new curtain walls and walls attached to the initial structure, as well as by a barrier of multiple standing stones (*chevaux-de-frise*) (Fig. 13.5c) and a first segmented moat protecting the East Gate (Fig. 13.5b).

This moat very soon became obsolete and during the following phase (Vilars II) a second perimeter moat was dug that partially annulled and sectioned the existing *chevaux-de-frise*. This coincided with a new system of access through a new gate raised on the northern side (Fig. 13.5d). Observations of this new system of defence are only partial and its width remains unknown because during the subsequent phase (Vilars III) it was absorbed into a newer and more spectacular moat more than 20 m wide and 3 m deep. The new moat also led to refurbishments to the access ramp to the enclosure through the North Gate, which was reinforced by small vertical trenches (Fig. 13.4). The defences at this time were also expanded

major phases based on the finds and radiocarbon dates (Table 13.1). These are as follows:

- First Iron Age
  Vilars 0: 775–700 BC
  Vilars I: 700–550 BC
- Iberian period
  Vilars II: 550–450 BC (Early Iberian)
  Vilars III: 450–325 BC (Middle Iberian)
  Vilars IV: 325–300 BC (Middle Iberian)

Table 13.1 List of the C14 datings and schema of the chronological sequence of the Fortress.

Laboratory reference number	14C yr BP	±	cal BC 1-sigma (IntCal13)	cal BC 2-sigma (IntCal13)	Dated material	Context	Phase
Beta-72610	2670	70	900 - 796	1008 - 591	charcoal	House	Vilars 0
Beta-72611	2640	60	894 - 778	929 - 555	charcoal	House	Vilars 0
Beta-92278	2580	50	813 - 591	834 - 541	human bone	House	Vilars 0
Beta-92277	2460	50	752 - 489	762 - 414	human bone	House	Vilars 0
Beta-145298	2620	40	823 - 786	895 - 674	equid bone	House	Vilars I
Beta-145299	2540	40	795 - 566	802 - 541	equid bone	House	Vilars I
Beta-267445	2220	40	361 - 208	387 - 196	charcoal	Moat	Vilars III
Beta-267447	2280	40	399 - 235	404 - 208	charcoal	Well-Cistern 75/76	Vilars III
Beta-267446	2210	40	359 - 205	382 - 183	charcoal	Well-Cistern 35/36	Vilars III

Radiocarbon dates (AMS) have been calibrated using the CALIB Program v.7.1 (Stuiver et al. 2017)

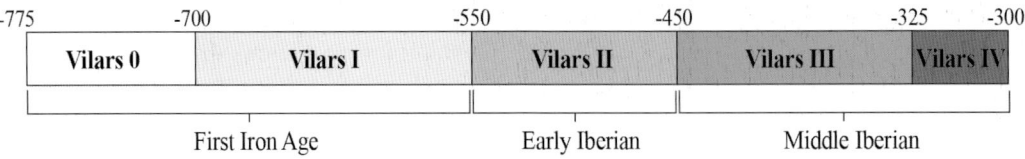

Figure 13.2 Views of the baulk: a: detail prior to the excavation; b: view at the outset of the excavation; c: view from 1991 of the excavations with the baulk to the right (photograph: Paisajes Españoles); d–e: views of features along the summit of the baulk from the Middle Iberian period.

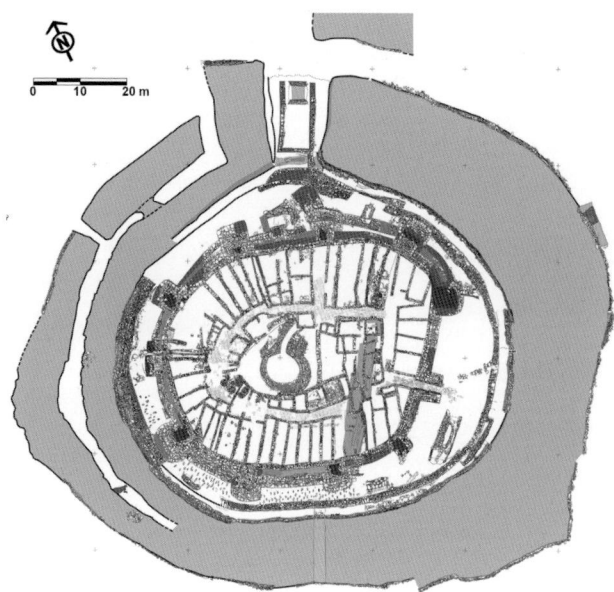

Figure 13.3 Plan of the Els Vilars Fortress in 2019.

at this point by the digging of a second segmented moat that hindered the approach to the fortress. The only feature that is known now of this second structure is its interior escarpment, as the other part of the construction is beyond the limits of the property owned by the Municipality of Arbeca. A significant aspect worth highlighting within the whole of this process is that the site's layout in its final phases (Vilars III–IV) had a surface area of more than 8000 m^2 intended for defence and only 2400 m^2 for domestic activities.

The interior of the tell's enclosure indeed suffered a drastic and brutal 'mutilation' whose positive outcome is that today, after 34 years of fieldwork, we benefit from the entire layout of a First Iron Age fortification that would have remained concealed. The characteristics of this mutilated tell with its multiple overlapping phases conditioned the means adopted to present it to the public. The process had to follow four requirements. The first was to offer an easy, intelligible reading of the features. This forced us to display relatively large areas with a single phase of occupation and avoid areas with a superposition of structures. The second was, nonetheless, to offer a view of all the site's phases, assessing their significance and the state of preservation. The third was to preserve the long section extending through the tell and take advantage of its stratigraphy to reveal the different sequences. The fourth was to retain unexcavated zones, scientific reserves, for future research (Junyent & Casals 2013).

The combination of the site's historical-archaeological characteristics with its designation as a *BCIN* and the objective of a social use led to applying a model of presentation following a preservationist tradition based primarily on three concepts: 'musealised open air romantic ruins', 'minimal intervention' and 'recovery of elevations'. The aim of this triple design seeks to gain citizen empathy by means of authenticity, presenting only structures that are rigorously recorded and recovering both positive (raising the preserved wall's height) and negative (excavation of the pits) features. The fortress's structures allow it to be an object of a natural preservation, a departure from preventive and curative types of consolidations, thus avoiding converting it into either a 'romantic ruin' or a 'reconstruction in style' (Junyent 2015a).

The gestation of a project

The Grup d'Investigació Prehistòrica (GIP) was created in 1987 at the University of Lleida subsequent to the initial rescue interventions. The collegiate group, led by Dr Emili Junyent, then embarked on a first research project focusing on the First Iron Age and the Iberian Period in the Western Catalan Plain. The project, pioneering in many ways due to its methodology, considered it necessary to undertake an extensive excavation and adopt a digital registration system adapted from that in use at *Lattara* (Lattes, Hérault, France; Garcés *et al.* 1991) and, perhaps most importantly, incorporating a multitude of interdisciplinary studies. Indeed, the palaeoeconomic and palaeoecological reconstruction of the settlement was considered fundamental to this integrative interdisciplinary research (Alonso *et al.* 1996; Junyent & López 2016).

An intense programme of reconstruction also took place from the 1990s. A plan (Pla Director Vilars 2000. Projecte d'excavació arqueològica, ordenació, consolidació i restauració de la Fortalesa dels Vilars d'Arbeca, les Garrigues, Lleida; Alonso *et al.* 2000a) was commissioned by the Generalitat de Catalunya with the intention of consolidating and restoring structures to minimise the risks of extensive excavation. An asphalted access, parking lot, reception point and a perimeter fence with security cameras were put in place in 2010–2011 to promote visits. Visits were also facilitated by an itinerary with explanatory panels.

The site has also been the object of multiple actions aimed at the dissemination and socialisation of heritage. In 1999 it formed part of the *Ruta del Ibers* (*Itinerary of the Iberians*) promoted by the Museu d'Arqueologia de Catalunya. This coincided with the publication of the first 3D and virtual reality materials (Alonso *et al.* 2000b). The association *Amics de Vilars* (Friends of Vilars), created in 2005, has contributed decisively to spreading knowledge as to its heritage by the inhabitants of Arbeca and the Garrigues region (Associació Amics de Vilars & GIP 2007; Vidal & Junyent 2007). Since then, activities of different types organised by the association (concerts, performances, races, meetings of riders, cyclists, astronomy, *etc.*) have served to reinforce scientific dissemination, especially at local and regional levels.

Furthermore, two site guides were published in 2005 and 2010 in the Museu d'Arqueologia de Catalunya series and several itinerant exhibitions, notably *Cavalls i poder en el món ibèric. El cas de la Fortalesa d'Arbeca* (2009) and *Dones de la plana... Dones de la muntanya* (2014), travelled to dozens of locations in Catalonia and beyond. More recently, the exhibition *La fortalesa dels Vilars d'Arbeca. Terra, aigua i poder en el món iber* (2016) and its catalogue (Junyent & López 2016) commemorating the 30 years of research at Vilars was organised by the Museu de Lleida and later in the Museu d'Arqueologia de Catalunya (Barcelona). Moreover, an APP offering complementary visiting information is available for smart phones.

Social recognition of the site is also noted by its continual presence in the media. It was the subject of episodes of the TV3 primetime programme *Sota Terra* (2010) (emulating the highly successful *Time Team* of the British Channel 4) and *El Reportero de la Historia* (2010) on the TVE, as well as four episodes of *La Aventura de la Historia, El Túnel del Tiempo* (2016) and a documentary *Arqueomanía, La nave de Tharsis* (2017).

In short, the strategy of balancing conservation, socialisation and research has been key to the fortress having become today a national (Junyent 2018) and European reference both scientifically, through its contributions to the study of the First Iron Age and the Iberian Period, and from the point of view of heritage, its magnitude, beauty and spectacular nature. The site is now spreading more and more regional roots while simultaneously receiving numerous visits of many nationalities.

The sequence of a fortress spanning almost 500 years

The First Iron Age

This period consists of the fortification's *ex novo* founding (Vilars 0) and its subsequent remodelling (Vilars I) affecting both its interior and its defensive system.

Vilars 0: 775–700 cal BC

The initial phase was designed with a single stone enclosure wall 1 m thick marked by 11 solid quadrangular or slightly rectangular towers (5–6 m in thickness) (Fig. 13.4, a). Its main gate was to the east, at the greater end of the oval, below a large tower. The opposite side had a second gate flanked by a bastion and a tower.

The gates led to an interior perimeter street parallel to the wall stretching between the facades of a series of contiguous houses and another circle of structures delimiting a central open-air space. It is possible that this great central 'square' had a cistern, a communal structure typical of the earliest settlements of the Segre-Cinca Cultural Group (heretofore GSC) during the last third of the 2nd millennium cal BC (López 2001; Junyent 2003; Junyent & Moya 2011). This remains unclear as the digging during the Middle Iberian Period of a monumental well-cistern (see below), recently restored, destroyed all the potential traces of earlier features.

The whole perimeter of houses remains and three- quarters of their surfaces have been excavated. The remaining urban features of this phase, toward the centre of the enclosure, remain either under later levels or were also destroyed during construction of the large well-cistern.

The houses, delimited by walls of stone and adobe, are single-celled. Most of their accesses feature an antechamber or porch defined by the extension of the house's side walls (Fig. 13.7). Spacious and featuring a central hearth, their study is currently in progress. Recent research nonetheless reveals significant differences in size (20–30 m^2) as well as in their interior fittings, which include running benches, distribution of roof supports, and even main room partitioning. It remains to be seen to what extent this diversified architecture responds to mere functional aspects or if they betray differences of social rank.

Ancestral ritual practices such as perinatal burials beneath the houses (Agustí *et al.* 2000) bolster the notion of continuity of certain ideological values from the earlier GSC period. However, the staging of the fortification itself, which also developed an incipient local iron working (see

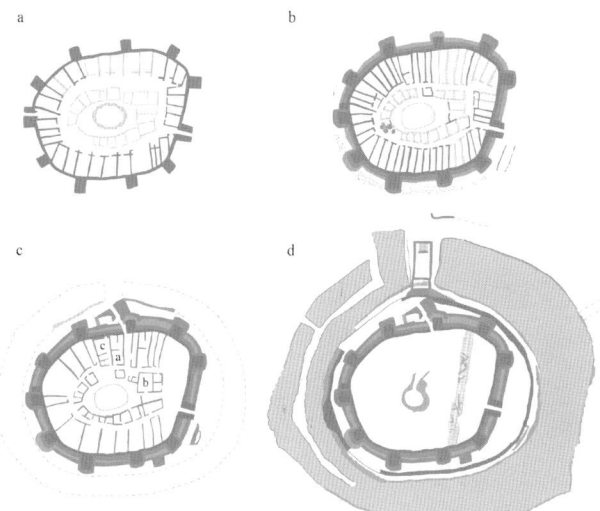

Figure 13.4 Sequence of the Fortress: a: Vilars 0, First Iron Age (775–700 cal BC); b: Vilars I, First Iron Age (700–550 cal BC); c: Vilars II, Early Iberian phase (550–450 BC) with (a) 'blacksmith's house'; (b) 'assembly hall'; (c) 'temple'; d: Vilars III, Middle Iberian phase (450–325 BC).

Figure 13.5 a: Aerial view of the Fortress (north to the top) and details of the b: East Gate; c: Chevaux-de-frise; d: North Gate.

Figure 13.6 Reconstructions of the Fortress: a: Vilars 0, 775–700 cal BC; b: Vilars I, 700–550 cal BC; c: Vilars II, 550–450 BC; d: Vilars III, 450–325 BC (GIP: J.R. Casals).

Vilars I: 700–550 cal BC

This phase witnessed significant gradual changes throughout the whole of the fortification (Figs 13.4, b and 13.6). The oldest wall, on the one hand, began to be reinforced with the addition of three successive new walls of mixed technique (stone and adobe) attached on its outer face. Their overall width at certain points attains almost 6 m and forms, along its top, a sort of parapet increasing the enclosure's defensive capacity. The towers were likewise simultaneously lined with new walls (two at certain points) and acquired a rectangular, rounded angle, form. This not only ensured their stability but prevented them from being embedded in the curtain walls and losing their flanking function.

The most significant feature of this phase is the *chevaux-de-frise,* a defensive barrier consisting of multiple vertical pointed slabs (Fig. 13.5c). Although identified along the entire southern and western facades and in part to the northwest, it most likely originally surrounded the entire enclosure. Its discovery at the outset of the excavation was a novelty on an international level given its dating, appearance and location in the Iberian Peninsula (Alonso *et al.* 2003). However, the lifespan of this feature was very brief as it fell into disuse at the outset of the Early Iberian Period. This phase nonetheless saw the construction of the earliest segmented moat, with two escarpments protecting access to the East Gate (Fig. 13.4, b).

It is necessary to highlight the sealing in the urban area of the West Gate and, above all, the changes that affected the floors of the houses. Features of these new houses are preserved in the southern, northern and western quarters. They were constructed by dividing the existing houses in two and advancing their facade toward the street, absorbing the earlier space interpreted as antechambers. This generated a new, narrower and more elongated layout and led to an expansion of the volume of these structures through the construction of an upper storey in the rear of the buildings (Fig. 13.7), archaeologically inferred from the presence of supports intended for sturdy wooden posts. As there was no significant difference between them and the new design, this construction could simply have been a response to the needs of the community's growing population.

The transformations of the enclosure appear to coincide, in turn, with the appearance of the earliest horse foetus burials under the houses, although it cannot be ruled out that the tradition stems from an earlier phase (Fig. 13.8, b). The symbolism of this rite is of the utmost importance as it demonstrates that horses possessed a social value transcending their function as a mere element of labour. In any case, equine breeding must have been an added value for the local powers (Nieto *et al.* 2010).

Finally, a remarkable feature forming part of this phase, due to its uniqueness and social significance, is the open-air communal bread making area in the western quarter, consisting of five domed ovens (Fig. 13.9, a). They serve

below), is a tangible indicator of an unusual process of centralisation of power and territorial hierarchy that became capital in the subsequent centuries.

as indicators of a centralised management of production processes and the existence of agents (chieftains?) exercising control.

The Iberian Period
Villars II; Early Iberian period: 550–450/425 BC

The site's first direct or indirect contacts with the Mediterranean world, although tentative, took place in the middle of the 6th century BC as evidenced by ceramics and metals (Castellano 2017). A process was initiated at this time whose source, either internal developments or external factors, is very difficult to quantify. What is certain is that the fortress underwent significant changes that affected both its own urban planning and defensive system, as well as the other spheres of social, economic and ideological nature (Fig. 13.4, c).

The levels of the Vilars II phase are unevenly conserved as they were completely destroyed by agricultural work in the eastern area and highly damaged to the west. Even so, these levels, due both to their quality and quantity, amount to the most important reference for this period in Western Catalonia. The field work distinguished three subphases, with sharp differences in their disposition, architecture and material culture: Vilars IIa (550–500 BC), Vilars IIb (500–475/450 BC) and Vilars IIc (475/450–425 BC) (GIP 2005, 655–656). This sequence, preserved unevenly, cannot be addressed in detail in this study and will be described as a whole. As noted above, the site's occupation never exceeded the limits defined by the perimeter of the initial wall and the different modifications of the urban plan of its interior overlapped generating an archaeological tell. However, an expansion of the space immediately beyond the wall did take place the Early Iberian period.

The first important modification affected the accesses and defences (Junyent *et al.* 2009): A new gate to the north was opened and a first perimeter moat was dug (Figs 13.4, c and 13.5, d). What then became the sole gate was raised tangent to one of the existing towers, which was reinforced with a solid bastion attached to its front. A new empty tower was raised (possibly a guardhouse) on the opposite flank. Both features were arranged with a diagonal orientation (northwest to southeast) with respect to the wall's face creating a corridor, inaccessible head-on. This first appears to emulate the characteristic gates of fortifications found elsewhere in the Mediterranean and secondly demonstrates an explicit desire to monumentalise the fortress's main access, another expression of the hegemony it boasted over the territory. Details of the moat of this phase are very meagre as it was absorbed by a later moat from the Middle Iberian period. The same appears to occur with the ramp crossing built within the framework of the same construction process. What is visible of its design suggests it enabled mounting a counter-attack (Junyent *et al.* 2009; Junyent & Moya 2011). Despite the presence of the moat, the remains of an inner escarpment are preserved to the east of the new gate. These types of external defences during the Early Iron Age were also likely present at Molí de l'Espígol (Tornabous, l'Urgell; Escala *et al.* 2018) and clearly identified at other more distant sites in the Ebro Valley such as Cabezo de la Cruz (La Muela, Saragossa; Picazo & Rodanés 2009). The new gate affected the interior of the enclosure as it led to the building of a new street, a feature that nonetheless did not affect the layout of the older, main perimeter street. New dwellings were also raised in the space occupied by the earlier houses, at times levelling the ground and demolishing certain features. However, the general structure of the internal urban fabric did not undergo significant modifications, at least not in the excavated area, except for those deriving from the raising of the new North Gate. This required construction of a new section of street linked to the perimeter street and the suppression of the old southwest square with the communal ovens, now absorbed by new constructions (Junyent & López 2016). Even so, the domestic architecture betrays important conceptual changes. On the one hand, there appears to be a differentiation between residence and workspaces. The dwellings, moreover, undergo remarkable transformations in both size and internal organisation with a greater specialisation of spaces.

There appear to be three different construction models (Fig. 13.4, c):

- Houses with two living spaces: a large rectangular room and a narrower lateral room, possibly in certain cases, a patio, corresponding to 'ordinary' dwelling spaces.
- More complex houses with three living spaces: a large room toward the front and two smaller toward the back, corresponding in this case to workshops or craftsmen residences.
- Single-cell dwellings and small buildings that appear to correspond to spaces linked to production and/or storage, without discarding their use as stables for small or medium-sized animals.

The first two types are arranged attached to the wall and built above the houses of the Vilars I phase. A tripartite building known as the 'blacksmith's house' stands out to the west of the new street overlooking the North Gate. It covers an area of about 50 m^2 and features an iron forging hearth in its front room (see below; Junyent & López 2016, 46) (Figs 13.4, a (a), 13.7 and 13.10b).

The third model of dwelling is to the other side of the perimeter street and around the central square. Its surfaces range between 2.5 and 15 m^2 and its exact function is unclear despite the evidence of milling and possibly a mica workshop. Worth highlighting is the physical separation of

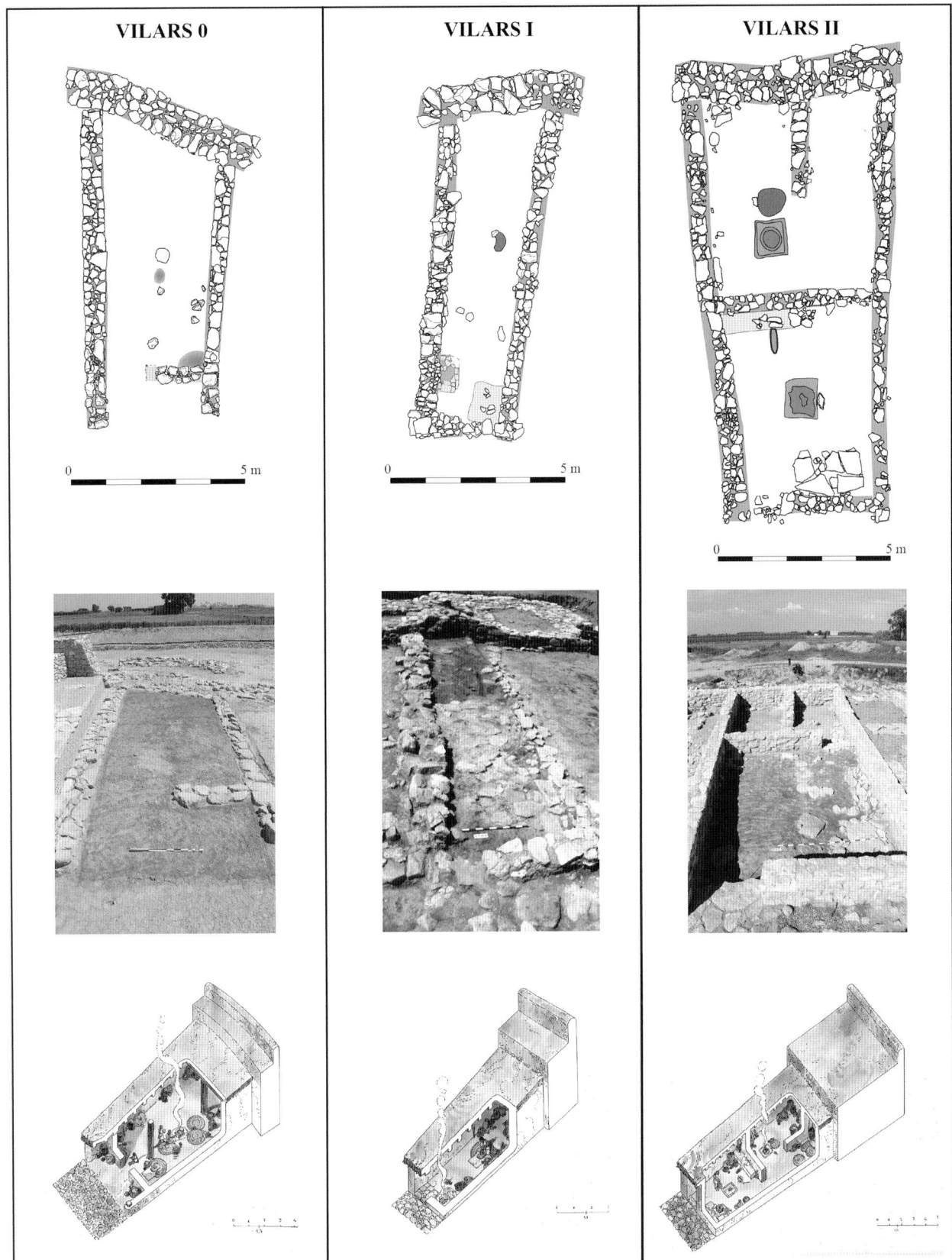

Figure 13.7 Houses. Ground plans, photographs and reconstruction of the different types of houses: Vilars 0, 775–700 BC; Vilars I, 700–550 BC; Vilars II, 550–450 BC (drawings by F. Riart).

living spaces rendering it difficult to distinguish between private and communal uses.

Finally, the most significant novelty so far, and surely the clearest evidence of the social and ideological changes taking place in this period, is the presence of public buildings. Two were unearthed bearing characteristics that allow them to be interpreted as communal spaces of a political or religious nature (see GIP 2005 for their detailed description and study).

The first, to the northeast of the central space, was not completely excavated due to the overlap of the site's central baulk (Fig. 13.4, c (b)). It corresponds nonetheless to a large quadrangular construction whose interior presents a unique organisation with two adobe benches along the north and south walls circumscribing a large central hearth in the shape of an oxhide. Two pits were detected in the preparation levels, one of which contained the almost complete remains of a young adult pig. The other held the head of a consumed pig of similar age and the remains of a young ovicaprid, also consumed (Nieto 2012, 262). Both the structure of the building and its internal features allow us, therefore, to assume that the space fulfilled a special function. The most plausible hypothesis is that of a room for 'meetings' or other social actions of supra-family nature. The deposition of consumed pigs surely reflects the celebration of ritual banquets prior to its construction.

The second structure also corresponds to a large building with a surface of about 55 m^2 (Figs 13.4, c (c) and 13.9, b) in the northern quarter, west of the 'blacksmith's house'. It has a trapezoidal floor plan, divided into three rooms communicated by three doors aligned along the eastern wall. Its first two rooms are small while that serving as a vestibule is compartmentalised to the west. The back room (39 m^2) is the most spectacular and presents a series of unique elements. Its back wall reveals a feature clad in clay that juts out forming a shelf about 50 cm high. The wall also presents an interruption near the room's northeast corner forming a sort of small cupboard. On the floor was a handmade ceramic cup. Toward the centre of the space, but avoiding the axis of the opening of the gate, there were up to three large superimposed hearths associated with three successive pavement levels. The first is rectangular with an attached semi-circular feature forming a small cavity filled with ashes. The other two are oxhide shaped, similar, albeit slightly smaller, to that in the previous building. To the northeast of the hearths was an earthen base or quadrangular platform holding a sort of circular column made with fragments of adobe and small stone (possibly an altar) near a clay cylinder 20 cm in diameter. Finally, the base of a jar or *pithos* placed in a small pit was next to the eastern wall of the room. This vessel, repaired *in situ* with plaster, contained a small bronze chain.

All these features bore carefully applied coats of clay plastering and their pavements, walls and lime finishings

Figure 13.8 Ritual deposits: a: triple human perinatals; b: horse foetus; c: pig; d: goat; e: sheep.

alternate with thin black layers of soot, a material confirmed by physicochemical, micromorphological and palynological analyses. The analyses also indicate that the soot corresponds to burn shrubs. In short, there was here an intense and enduring combustion, which led to successive refurbishments and the whitewashing of walls and pavements to maintain them in optimal conditions.

These finds leave no doubt as to a ritual/sacred function of the building, which becomes the earliest Iberian 'temple' in the Western Catalan Plain. Its ceremonies remain arcane despite the presence of faunal remains and artefacts such as a fragment of *thymiaterion* (censor) (Castellano 2017, 133, fig. 15.9). Oxhide hearths, although quite exceptional, are nonetheless found in dwellings devoid of special architectural connotations at other sites in the area such as Molí d'Espígol (Escala *et al.* 2018, 278, fig. 9) and Sant Joan Vell de Térmens (Vàzquez *et al.* 2014).

Vilars III–IV, Middle Iberian period: 450–300 BC

As noted, agricultural work since the 1950s destroyed part of the tell's structures, in particular the final phases of the sequence within the enclosure and the great moat. The exceptions are certain domestic features and the well-cistern.

THE MIDDLE IBERIAN MOAT (VILARS III–IV)

This construction was an undertaking of such magnitude that it surely played out over an extended period of time (Junyent

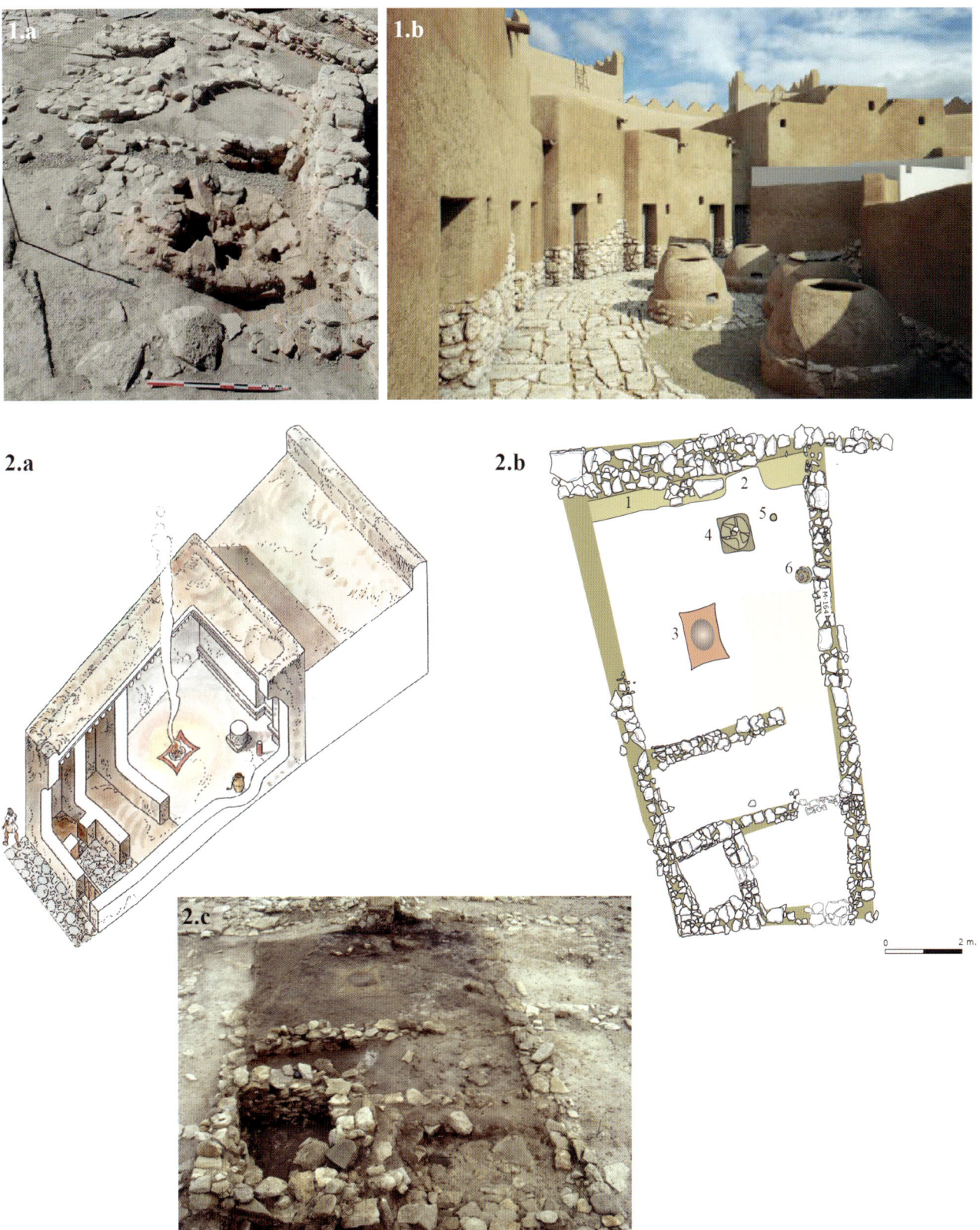

Figure 13.9 Communal features and public buildings: 1: Open-air bread ovens of Vilars I phase (1.a) and 3D rendering by J.R. Casals (GIP) (1.b); 2: Sacred building, artistic rendering by F. Riart (2.a); plan of this building (2.b) containing a clay shelf (1), a small cupboard (2), an oxhide-shaped hearth (3), an altar (4), a clay cylinder (5) and a jar base (6); photo of this construction (2.c).

Figure 13.10 Iron working: a: smelting furnace (Vilars 0, 775–700 BC); b: smithy hearth (Vilars II: 550–450 BC); millstone manufacture: c: upper stone of an Iberian pushing rotary mill (Vilars II, 550–450 BC); d: mill podium (Vilars III, 450–325 BC).

& Moya 2011). It must have required constant refurbishment, remodelling and maintenance. Unlike the few remains of the older Iberian moat, this more recent feature endured until the last stages of the settlement. With it the fortress attained its maximum complexity.

It took on the form of a vast oval almost completely surrounding the slightly higher platform of the walled enclosure's foundation (Figs 13.4 and 13.5, a). Its continuity was only interrupted to the north by a feature serving as the base of the fortified access to the North Gate (Fig. 13.5, d). It is clearly identified with a second moat and, quite possibly, other advanced constructions (Fig. 13.6). It is defined by a scarp with a minimum perimeter of 240 m and a counterscarp with a maximum perimeter of 373 m, equivalent to an area surpassing 8000 m^2. Its width varies so the walls of the escarpment and the counterscarp are separated by a minimum of 14 m and up to a maximum of 29 m. As in the case of its width, its depth is also not constant. Its depth from the base of the wall to its shallowest point is at least 2.3 m while its deepest point is 3.8 m.

In general, the moat comprises a large empty basin whose base slopes downward from its northeast end. Here is where the water possibly entered, flowing in a clockwise direction toward the southwest angle (Junyent & Moya 2011). Hence the deepest area of the moat is toward the west, in particular in the southwest quadrant marked by two large elongated pools.

The moat's archaeological sedimentation sequence clearly reveals two major processes. There is, on the one hand, a series of clayey grey and greenish sediments revealing signs of oxidation and reduction. These levels stem from the dynamics of an aquatic environment and correspond to accumulations during the moat's use. Its flooding cannot be put into doubt as these conditions are evident from the sediment's micromorphology and the calcium carbonate accumulations.

The second major phase, above these deposits, is marked by a few brownish clay strata corresponding to collapses and layers of gravels stemming from the natural filling and erosion of the feature's slopes, the collapse of its stone structures and depositions after sudden torrents from the Aixaragall River ravine. This second sequence characterises the moat's filling process subsequent to the abandonment of the fortress when the moat ceased to have a stable function.

THE WELL-CISTERN
The well-cistern of Els Vilars (Fig. 13.11), although heir of an urban tradition of the end of the 2nd millennium BC in the Ebro Valley and the Western Catalan Plain, differs from other cases by its dimensions, its splendid masonry, its steps leading down to the water, and the sophisticated construction

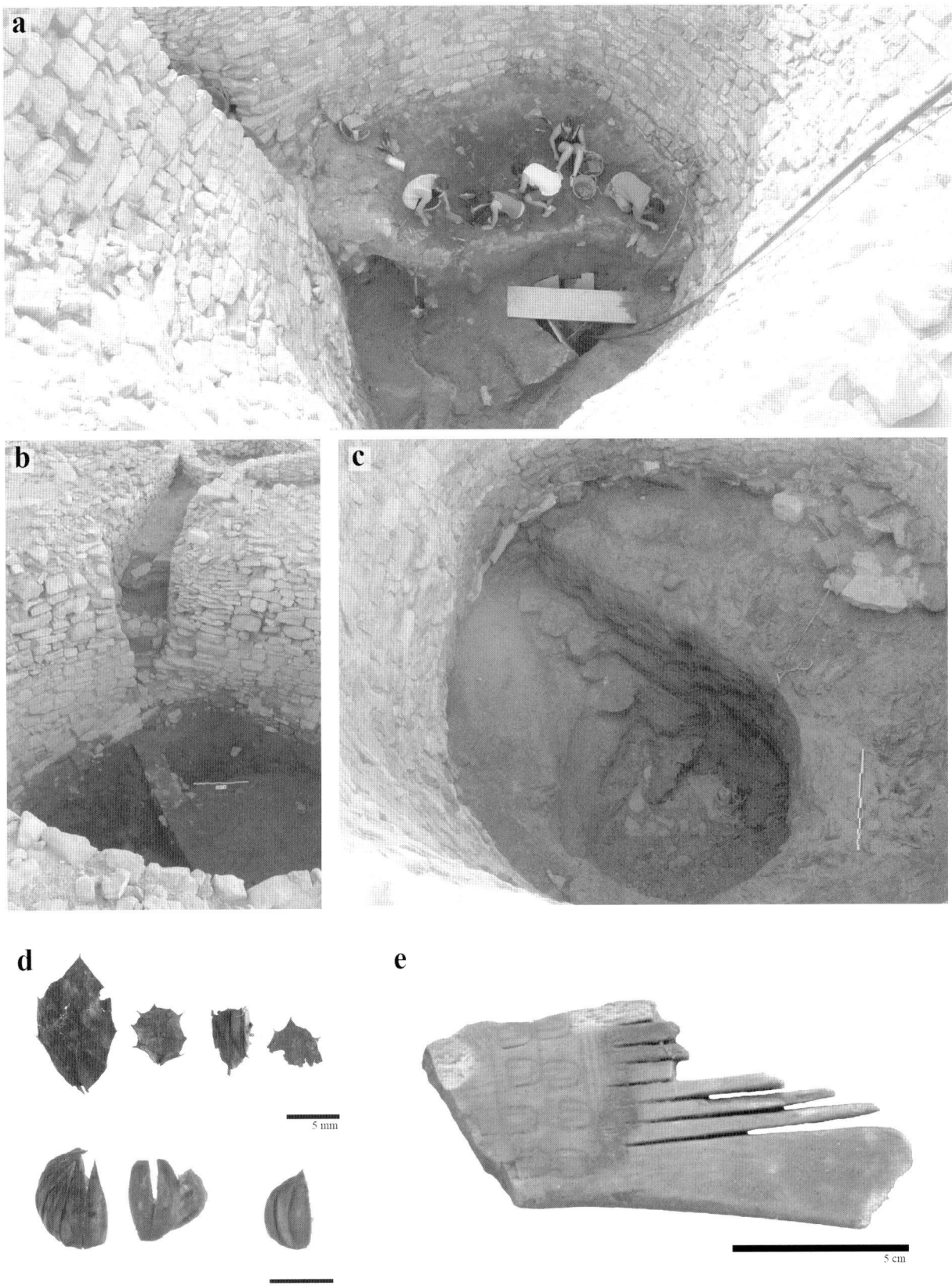

Figure 13.11 Well-cistern: a: excavation of its base; b: access ramp; c: shaft cut through the bedrock; d: waterlogged plant remains: oak/kermes leaves, top, and flax capsules, bottom; e: decorated comb fragment carved from common boxwood.

at its base of a horizontal conduit to increase its capacity. Its use-life was nonetheless short. It was built around 425 BC and shortly before 300 BC it was already serving as a rubbish well before its final sealing. The present study cannot go into the details as to how it collected water, its relationship with the moat and pools, and its significance in the framework of the schema of defence, aspects explored in other articles (Junyent & Moya 2011; Junyent et al. 2012).

Its interior reveals three large sedimentary packages: a) deposits toward its base linked to its operation; b) intermediate levels of use as a tip; and c) a heterogeneous upper level of stones and earth evidencing its disuse at the site's abandonment. Its two deeper packages offer an exceptional amount of data and an exorbitant volume and variety of artefacts compared to the usual dynamic of the site. The fill alone contained 15,000 fragments of pottery (360 kg) tantamount to a minimum of 1270 individuals (vessels). They serve as an unprecedented source of information to define the basic characteristics of the Vilars III and IV cultural facies (Bernal 2019). A compelling aspect is that a large part of this fill remained flooded over time leading to an extraordinary preservation of organic matter (Fig. 13.11, d–e). It was sieved entirely, leading to recovery of all the archaeological remains. These included waterlogged organic materials such as white pine, oak and elm logs, a decorated boxwood comb, grape and fig pips, flax capsules, acorn domes, holm oak or kermes oak leaves, numerous archaeozoological macro-remains (Nieto et al. 2018), and dog and ovicaprid coprolites.

Among the exceptional finds, due to its novelty in a hinterland settlement, are the vertebrae and scales of small marine fish (*Sparidae*, *Centracanthidae* and *Mullidae*) (Piquès, under study) that could have arrived at the fortress either dried, salted, smoked or as *garum* or *allec*. The introduction of these products into the Iberian Peninsula transited through southern or Ibizan Phoenician and Punic workshops that marketed them throughout the Mediterranean. They are also known to have been traded by Greek merchants. It is still unclear in which state these fish arrived at Vilars. There is nonetheless no doubt that they were exchanged and that they were luxury products, reflecting the splendour of the fortification's power in the Middle Iberian period, phases that remain a mystery due to their destruction by modern agriculture.

The main economic activities

The previous sections have evoked economic aspects linked to certain phases of the site. What follows is a succinct and general view of the most relevant. Reconstruction of the palaeoclimatic and palaeoenvironmental conditions throughout the centuries of life of the fortress has been the subject of multidisciplinary approach. Identifying the environmental sequence of the last 3000 years was carried out by a combination of samples collected from the Estany d'Ivars-Vilasana, a small lake a few kilometres away, and sediments from the well-cistern and the moat (Currás 2012). The findings of the lake sediment assessment point to an unstable water level throughout the 1st millennium BC marked by oscillations of wet and dry periods. Isotopic carbon discrimination ($\Delta^{13}C$) studies carried out on archaeological charcoals elsewhere throughout the Western Catalan Plain also reveal a period of relative aridity during this millennium despite an average rainfall greater than that of today (Ferrio et al. 2006). The exploitation of its environment throughout the c. 500 years of occupation provoked drastic changes to the landscape. The cutting of forests for cultivation and pasture, and to exploit timber for construction, tools and firewood, put a great pressure on the forests that changed over time (Currás 2012; Vila 2018). Anthracological analyses indicate how the exploitation of wood for fuel varied throughout the site's different phases (Vila 2018). Woodlands most commonly represented by oak and holm/kermes oak, were the type most often exploited throughout all the phases. There is nonetheless evidence of the substitution of holm/kermes oak by oak between Vilars 0 and Vilars II (the data for Vilars III are scarce and less precise). This may be due to a progressive clearing of the site's surroundings leading to a search for fuel in somewhat more distant catchment areas, a factor which would entail even greater planning. At the same time, secondary substitution communities such as Aleppo pines grow faster than oaks or holm oaks in open spaces ensuing from human activity, especially since the Early Iberian period. This timeframe also saw an increase of shrub vegetation closer to the fortress indicating more intensive exploitation.

Agriculture

The study of agricultural processes is one of the main lines of research of the Vilars project (Alonso 1999, 122–139; Alonso et al. 2008; Alonso & Pérez-Jordà 2019). Cereal cultivation was one of the basic strategies of subsistence throughout the sequence. The most common cereal was hulled barley (*Hordeum vulgare*) followed by bread wheat/durum wheat (*Triticum aestivum/durum*). Emmer (*T. dicoccum*), by contrast, play a lesser role from the First Iron Age. Spring cereals (foxtail millet, *Setaria italica*, and millet, *Panicum miliaceum*), in turn, experience significant growth, in particular in the Early Iberian period. The crops reached the fortress already semi-clean, and there is evidence that inside the enclosure only fine sieving was carried out to definitively separate the grain from the chaff and weeds (Alonso et al. 2008).

Pulses, mainly lentils (*Lens culinaris*) and broad beans (*Vicia faba*), are poorly represented. Their feeble representation coincides with that of archaeobotanical finds of other sites of the Western Plain. Of note are the seeds and non-carbonised flax capsules (*Linum usitatissimum*) found in the well-cistern. This plant could have served for both oil and textile production (Junyent & López 2016)

Fig (*Ficus carica*) and grapes (*Vitis vinifera*) are detected as of the Early Iberian period (Alonso *et al.* 2008). Although already known in the area in the form of harvested fruits, the novelty now is that they are locally cultivated. In fact, it is very possible that a stone press recycled as construction material in a wall from the Vilars III phase hails from the end of the Early Iberian period when it could have played a role in wine production (Junyent & López 2016, 130). In any case, the numerous grape pips in the fill of the well-cistern signal that this activity continued during the Middle Iberian period.

Livestock

Animal breeding at Vilars as in almost all proto-historic settlements of the Western Catalan Plain, was a basic subsistence activity and took on a diversified form (Nieto 2012). Despite certain variations during its different phases, livestock consisted essentially of ovicaprids (sheep and goats), cattle and pigs. There is also evidence of other domestic animals such as dogs, or special status cases such as equidae. Hunting, although secondary and sporadic, continued mainly in the form of lagomorphs (rabbits and hares) and big game such as deer. Deer hunting was probably a social act linked to prestige.

From the point of view of general livestock management, it is possible as early as the Early Iberian period to observe an important decrease among ovicaprids in the rate of slaughter of younger animals (2–6 months) and an increase of keeping subadult animals and adults. This could be indicative of intensive exploitation of secondary products (wool and milk) and a greater use of meat. The exploitation of goats appears to be geared toward an intensive obtaining of milk followed by a secondary intention toward tender meat (young animals). Sheep are meanwhile exploited preferably for tender meat, followed by milk and wool.

Pig management reveals a greater nurture of adult specimens, evidenced by frequency peaks between 12 and 24 months yielding more meat. Sacrifice rates are more spaced and the elimination of the surplus is carried out more progressively in spite of a significant number of sacrifices between 6 and 12 months. This strategy offered more guarantees for reproduction and greater growth. Finally, as regards cattle, there is an important peak of sacrifice of individuals under 2 years (to obtain tender veal) and another between 2 and 4 (optimum yield of meat).

Otherwise, the remains of consumed domestic horse are unearthed in settlements of the Western Catalan Plain since the Early Bronze Age. Horse riding is not recorded in general until the First Iron Age. This animal is often linked to the funerary world and ritual practices (see below) and certainly bore different symbolic meanings. Its high cost demonstrates that it served as a sign of wealth among the Iberian aristocracy.

Iron and bronze working

As noted, Vilars reveals evidence of continual iron working. The most significant cultural and technological element of the Vilars 0 phase is, without a doubt, the discovery of an iron bowl-type reduction furnace containing a metal nodule (Agustí *et al.* 2000; GIP 2003; Rovira 1998) (Fig. 13.10, a). Its function has nonetheless been questioned (Rovira Llorens 2000) due to the absence of slag and pyrometallurgical debris in the surroundings. Such an absence can be relativised, however, when considering that only the lower part of the structure is preserved, only half of the workshop is currently excavated and, above all, it was common during refurbishments at the time to clean the pavements thoroughly before laying down new ones. Artefacts recovered in the houses throughout all the phases are quantitatively low, almost anecdotal, when compared to those usually unearthed at most of these types of sites. The main iron object so far in the Vilars 0 phase is a fragment of a shank, which, considering the large excavated area, represents an early foray in iron working as this technology was not consolidated at Vilars until the Early Iberian period.

The dating of this structure from its archaeological context remains imprecise as the other artefacts recovered in the workshop do not differ from those appearing in contemporary houses of Vilars 0. The few iron reduction furnaces in the northeast of the Iberian Peninsula either date to the Middle Iberian contexts (Rovira 2000) or at most, although of different typology, to the 6th–5th centuries BC as in the case of those of Valdestrada (Seno, Teruel) in the Lower Aragón (Martín *et al.* 2003). Moreover, the earliest iron objects identified in the region are of little help in this regard. What is known as to the introduction of iron working in Western Catalonia suggests that it took place at least since the middle of the 8th century BC, according to the findings of sites in the Languedoc and Aquitaine in France (Junyent 1992).

The problem posed by the Vilars furnace, however, goes much deeper. This discussion is not geared to identifying the agents responsible for the introduction of specific objects, but that of the iron technology itself and, in this context, whether its arrival preceded that of manufactured goods. Elsewhere, artefacts currently linked to the production and use of iron (slag and objects) date to the late 7th century cal BC at the Serra del Calvari (Valencia) (Vàzquez *et al.* 2005) and even to the outset of the 8th century cal BC as at Cabezo de la Cruz (La Muela, Zaragoza) in the Middle Ebro Valley (Picazo & Rodanés 2009). Iron objects, however, are scarce. The Early Iberian phase (Vilars II), phase in which an iron forging hearth has been found (Fig. 13.10, b), offers the greatest number of better-preserved objects. These include a mattock, a knife and two ferrules that, due to their small size, could be related to canes or similar objects more than with javelins (Junyent & López 2016, 137, 139, 149). Another iron object of the Middle Iberian, a plough clamp, was recovered in the well-cistern (Junyent & López 2016, 138), while yet another Early Iberian iron weapon can be indirectly identified due to an ivory pommel (Junyent & López 2016, 135). It could represent a Fronton-type sword bearing a spike with a circular section.

No structure at the site directly indicates bronze metallurgy. Indirect confirmation of bronze working can nonetheless be gleaned from moulds. One corresponds to the proximal part of a bivalve of a tubular axe with a square mouth while the other is a bivalve of a tubular chisel with trimming of conical type often linked to woodworking (Junyent & López 2016, 150–151). The bronze objects, nonetheless, probably stem from exchanges. They include four arrowheads of Late Bronze/First Iron Age tradition and several more or less well-preserved objects linked to clothing such as fibulae and pendants formed by chains with different terminal motifs (spheroidal, 'pacifiers', rattles, tubular *etc.*). These types of pendants appear in the northeast of the Iberian Peninsula during the second half of the 7th century BC in contexts containing Phoenician materials.

Food production: rotary querns

One of the main contributions of the Els Vilars project at the international level stems from two different types of rotary mills found in an intermediate phase of the Early Iberian period (525–475 BC). The first is a circular lower stone about 40 cm in diameter hewn from bioclastic limestone, a rock typical of the Miocene from the area of Tarragona and exploited at relatively distant quarries such as Mèdol and Lorito. It therefore arrived at the fortress in a finished form, possibly within the framework of a commercial exchange. The second is the upper stone (runner) of a larger mill (50 cm in diameter; 27 cm in height) of local porous limestone (Fig. 13.10, c).

Nobody disputes that the arrival of rotary mill, apart from improving the method of grinding and increasing the yield of flour, was transcendental on a scale like that of the potter's wheel and that it replaced the older to-and-fro hand quern. The continuous motion of the new models also forms part of the principle of all subsequent industrial machinery. The quern and millstone finds at Vilars have opened a debate of international scope leading in many directions (Alonso 1999; 2002; Alonso *et al.* 2011; 2016; Alonso & Frankel 2017). In sum, research at Vilars proves, on the one hand, that the rotary mill is an Iberian invention. On the other hand, there was at Vilars, besides the smaller 'classic' rotary quern operated by a single individual by means of a wooden handle or similar fitting (ultimately the smaller model that spread throughout the Mediterranean), a larger mill manufactured locally which required a wooden rig to drive its upper stone by one or two standing individuals (Fig. 13.10, c). This larger model, baptised as the 'Iberian rotary pushing-mill', appears to have been distributed exclusively in the Iberian Peninsula and the specimen from Vilars is among the oldest (Alonso *et al.* 2016; Alonso & Frankel 2017). This mill in the framework of the site's economic activities is also significant as it could indicate that grinding during the Early Iberian may not have been exclusively domestic, but a communal activity restricted to specialised spaces.

Power, territory, ideology and rituals

The fortress was the central residence of a chieftain who exercised a dominion over a territory and inhabitants dispersed in smaller dependent communities. The main archaeological indicators of this reality stem from the site's fortification, an excess of architecture of power, the territorialisation and hierarchy of settlements, the relation of domination and subordination of certain communities defended by powerful walls and others without walls, and their interdependency. Although the indicators from the interior of the enclosure do not appear to offer as blunt a reading of military architecture, the presence of the well-cistern nonetheless points to the same degree of organisational and coercive complexity required by a defensive system. Likewise, the warehouses and productive activities such as iron working and millstone manufacture reveal the existence of specialist craftsmen, albeit not autonomous workshops, manned by individuals detached from participating in other economic subsistence activities. There is evidence, nonetheless, of a differentiated architecture, undoubtedly of communal character (cultual enclosure and large room with an Orientalising oxhide-shaped hearth, communal ovens, large mills), suggesting a complex social and political life. Trade with the coastal towns and Mediterranean merchants is evidenced by imports of Phoenician and Greek pottery and Punic jewellery, fish sauces, certain millstone types, bronze objects such as fibulae with bilateral springs, and chains and pendants characteristic of the Palaeo-Iberian cemeteries of the mouth of the Ebro. There are also exogenous materials such as amber and ivory (Alonso 1999; Junyent & López 2016; Castellano 2017).

The leadership also maintained control of the ideology (that is, the beliefs, cults, ceremonies and rituals), as well as the architecture, iconography and military prestige, powerful and indispensable instruments to ensure social cohesion. Power induces, through identification with material and ideological symbols, respect, acceptance of authority and affirmation of the community's identity. The power structure, in turn, guarantees its members the reproduction of material and social life. Although there is little direct material evidence of the practices accompanying these beliefs, the symbolic world was without doubt very complex. This is garnered from the building raised and dedicated to communal cult and, in the domestic sphere, the practice of a variety of rituals such as the burial of perinatals, horse foetuses, or total or partial depositions of goat and sheep (Nieto 2013) (Fig. 13.8).

The ritual placing of horse foetuses beneath house floors, a practice also evidenced at the nearby settlement of Tossal del Molinet (Junyent & López 2015), is exceptional, unknown to date in contemporary sites of the Iberian Peninsula and Europe. Although the rite is well recorded with 12 of the 15 cases of the Early Iberian period (Vilars II), little is known as to its origins. They correspond to natural abortions between 4 and 6 months (Fig. 13.8, b). The fact that this rite does not apply to the foetuses of other animals such as goat, sheep, pig, ox or dog, and that it is identical to that of perinatal humans, offers a glimpse as to the symbolic value bestowed on horses.

On the other hand, the population of the Western Catalan Plain underwent great changes in settlement patterns and their distribution throughout the territory during the centuries prior to the site's founding (Alonso *et al.* 1998; López 2001; Junyent & López 2016). The small closed settlements from the end of the 2nd millennium BC are mainly found on hills closest to the Segre River Valley or at the headwaters of its tributaries. The beginning of the 1st millennium BC then saw a decrease in the number of settlements as the populations began to concentrate yielding a new settlement model with a more common occupation of the lateral valleys. It is during the First Iron Age when this colonisation became more stable and a process of hierarchy of the territory was set in motion, directed from fortified main nuclei such as Els Vilars and subsidiary villages.

During the 8th, 7th and much of the 6th century – the First Iron Age prior to the Iberian Civilisation – the territory appears to be articulated by these fortified residential centres competing with each other. These small political entities controlled a few hundred square kilometres and the communities residing in subsidiary non-fortified settlements (Tossal Molinet, in the Poal; Tossal del Seba and l'Estany, in Arbeca) comprised populations of between 500 and 1000 people. This is suggested by the regular distance of 10–20 km between the fortresses of Castell del Albi (Albi), Els Vilars (Arbeca), Molí de l'Espígol (Tornabous) and Vell Pla (Guissona) (Junyent & López 2016, fig. 19).

This panorama contrasts radically with that of the 4th and 3rd centuries BC when the archaic Ilergete State represented by the sites of *Atanagrum/Itirta* under the rule of Indíbil and Mandonio dominated more than 10,000 km^2 and a population of over 130,000 inhabitants (Junyent 2015b). Obviously, the interest of these figures deduced from the size of the armies raised by the Ilergete regimes according to Greco-Latin authors is not their accuracy, but the difference of scale from one reality to the other and in the profound transformations between the two. These transformations can also explain the reason for the fading away of the old fortress of Els Vilars.

Acknowledgements

We thank the members of the *Grup d'Investigació Prehistòrica* for their constant and generous contributions. Research on the Els Vilars fortification is currently financed by the *Generalitat de Catalunya* (CLTOO9/18/00039) and the *Ministerio de Economía y Competitividad* (HAR2016-78277-R and PID2019-110022GB-I00) in the framework of the project *Grup Consolidat 3DPatrimoni* (2017SGR1714). The English translation is the work of T.J. Anderson.

Figure 13.12 View of the Fortress and its moat after the flood of 2019.

References

Agustí, B., Alonso, N., Garcés, I., Junyent, E., Lafuente, A. & López, J.B. (2000) Una inhumación múltiple de perinatales en la Fortaleza de Els Vilars (Arbeca, Lérida) y las prácticas de enterramiento en hábitat durante la Ia Edad del Hierro en el Valle del Segre (Cataluña). In B. Dedet, P. Gruat, G. Marchand, M. Py & M. Schwaller (eds), *Archéologie de la mort, archéologie de la tombe au premier Âge du Fer. Actes du XXIe Colloque International de l'Association Francaise pour l'Etude de l'Âge du Fer. Conques – Montrozier, 8–11 mai 1997. Thème spécialisé*, 305–324. Lattes, Monographies d'Archéologie Méditerranéenne 5.

Alonso, N. (1999) *De la llavor a la farina. Els processos agrícoles protohistòrics a la Catalunya Occidental*. Lattes, Monographies d'Archéologie Méditerranéenne 4.

Alonso, N. (2002) Le moulin rotatif manuel au nord-est de la Péninsule Ibérique. Une innovation technique dans le contexte domestique de la mouture de cereals. In H. Procopiu & R. Treuil (eds), *Moudre et Broyer. L'interprétation fonctionnelle de l'outillage de mouture et de broyage dans la Préhistoire et l'Antiquité*, 11–127. Paris, Université de Paris.

Alonso, N. & Frankel, R. (2017) Survey of ancient milling systems in the Mediterranean. *Revue Archéologique de l'Est* 43, 461–478.

Alonso, N. & Pérez-Jordà, G. (2019) Elites and farmers in Iberian Iron Age cities (7th–2nd centuries BC). Storage and processing of agricultural products. In D. Garcia & R. Orgeolet (eds), *Country in the City. Forms and Functions of Agro-pastoral Activities in Mediterranean Pre-Classical Cities (Aegean and Western Mediterranean Protohistory)*, 7–22. Oxford, Archaeopress.

Alonso, N., Pérez, G. & López, D. (2016) Les moulins rotatifs poussés du monde ibérique. Caractéristiques et utilisation. In L. Jacottey & G. Rollier (eds), *Archéologie des moulins hydrauliques, à traction animale et à vent, des origines à l'époque médiévale*, 559–578. Besançon, Presses Universitaires de Franche-Comté.

Alonso, N., Junyent, E., Lafuente, A. & López, J.B. (1998) Chronométrie de l'Âge des Métaux dans la basse vallée du Segre (Catalogne, Espagne) à partir des datations 14C. In J. Evin (ed.), *Actes du 3ème Colloque International 14C et Archéologie. Lyon 6–10 avril 1998*, 287–292. Paris, Mémoires de la Société Préhistorique Française XXVI.

Alonso, N., Junyent, E., Lafuente, A. & López, J.B. (2003) *Chevaux-de-frise i fortificació en la primera edat del ferro europea. Reunió Internacional. Lleida, 27–29 de març de 2003*. Lleida, Universitat de Lleida – Consell Comarcal del Segrià.

Alonso, N., Junyent, E., Lafuente, A. & López, J.B. (2008) Plant remains, storage and crop processing inside the Iron Age fort of Els Vilars d'Arbeca (Catalonia, Spain). *Vegetation History and Archaeobotany* 17, 149–158.

Alonso, N., Aulinas, M., García, M.T., Martín, F., Prats, G. & Vila, S. (2011) Manufacturing rotary querns in the 4th century BC fortified settlement of Els Vilars (Arbeca, Catalonia, Spain). In D. Williams & D. Peacock (eds), *Bread for the People. The Archaeology of Mills and Milling. Proceedings of a Colloquium held in the British School at Rome, 4th–7th November 2009*, 55–65. Oxford, British Archaeological Report S2274.

Alonso, N., Junyent, E., Lafuente, A., López, J.B. & Tartera, E. (2000a) La fortaleza de Arbeca. El proyecto Vilars 2000. Investigación, recuperación y socialización del conocimiento y del patrimonio. *Trabajos de Prehistoria* 57(2), 161–173.

Alonso, N., Garcés, I., Junyent, E., Lafuente, A., López, J.B., Miró, J.M., Ros, M.T. & Rovira, C. (1996) L'assentament de Els Vilars (Arbeca, les Garrigues). Territori, recursos i activitats productives. In J. Rovira i Port (ed.), *Models d'Ocupació, Transformació i Explotació del Territori entre el 1600 i el 500 a.n.e. a la Catalunya Meridional i Zones Limitrofes de la Depressió de l'Ebre. Actes de la Taula Rodona, Sant Feliu de Codines, 18.–19. de novembre de 1994*. Gala 3-5, 319–339. Sant Feliu de Codines, Museu Arqueològic Municipal.

Alonso, N., Junyent, E., Lafuente, A., López, J.B, Lorés, J., Muñoz, D., Pérez, M. & Tartera, E. (2000b) Virtual Reality as an extension of the archaeological record. Reconstruction of the Iron Age fortress Els Vilars (Arbeca, Catalonia, Spain). In J.A. Barceló, M. Forte & D.H. Sanders (eds), *Virtual Reality in Archaeology*, 225–231. Oxford, British Archaeological Report S843.

Associació Amics de Vilars & Grup d'Investigació Prehistòrica (2007) L'Associació Amics de Vilars. Anàlisi i balanç en el seu primer aniversari, In N. Alonso, E. Junyent, A. Lafuente, J. López, E. Tartera & A. Vidal (eds), *Associacions d'Amics del Patrimoni Arqueològic. Funció i rol social en el segle XXI*, 149–171. Lleida, Edicions de la Universitat de Lleida.

Bernal, J. (2019) *La ceràmica ilergeta del segle IV a.n.e. Aportacions per a la caracterització de l'Ibèric Ple a la Ilergècia a través de l'estudi dels materials ceràmics recuperats en les cisternes dels Vilars (Arbeca, les Garrigues) i de les Roques de Sant Formatge (Seròs, el Segrià)*. Unpublished PhD dissertation, Universitat de Lleida.

Castellano, A. (2017) Aproximació a la caracterització de l'horitzó Ibèric Antic (segles VI–V ane) a la fortalesa dels Vilars (Arbeca, les Garrigues). *Revista d'Arqueologia de Ponent* 27, 117–145.

Currás, A. (2012) *Estudio sobre la evolución de los paisajes mediterráneos continentales en Lleida y Guadalajara durante los últimos 3000 años a partir de la secuencia polínica de Ivars, Somolinos y Cañamares*. Unpublished PhD dissertation, Universitat de Barcelona.

Escala, O., Moya, A., Piqué, G., Principal, J., Tartera, E. & Vidal, A. (2018) Darreres novetats al Molí d'Espígol (Tornabous, Urgell). El projecte de l'1% cultural. L'excavació arqueològica i els treballs de consolidació i restauració del jaciment. *Tribuna d'Arqueologia* 2014–2015, 265–301.

Ferrio, J.P., Alonso, N., López, J.B., Araus J.L. & Voltas J. (2006) Carbon isotope composition of fossil charcoal reveals aridity changes in the NW Mediterranean Basin. *Global Change Biology* 12(7), 1253–1266.

Garcés, I., Junyent, E., Lafuente, A. & López, J.B. (1991) Sistema de registro y tratamiento automático de la información en el yacimiento protohistórico de Els Vilars (Arbeca, Lleida). *Complutum* 1, 189–210.

Grup d'Investigació Prehistòrica (GIP) (2003) Caballos y hierro. El campo frisio y la fortaleza de 'Els Vilars d'Arbeca' (Lleida, España), siglos VIII–IV a.n.e. In N. Alonso, E. Junyent, A. Lafuente & J.B. López (eds), *'Chevaux-de-frise' i fortificació en la primera Edat del Ferro europea*, 233–274. Lleida, Universitat de Lleida.

Grup d'Investigació Prehistòrica (GIP) (2005) Dos hogares orientalizantes de la fortaleza de Els Vilars (Arbeca, Lleida). In S. Celestino & J. Jiménez (eds), *Actas del III Simposio Internacional de Arqueología de Mérida, Protohistoria del Mediterráneo Occidental. El Periodo Orientalizante (Mérida, 5–8 de mayo de 2003)*, 651–667. Mérida: Anejos de Archivo Español de Arqueología, XXXV.

Junyent, E. (1992) Els orígens del ferro a Catalunya. *Revista d'Arqueologia de Ponent* 2, 21–36.

Junyent, E. (2003) L'albada de la civilització i els temps ilergets. In E. Junyent & A. Pérez, *Història de Lleida. L'antiguitat, d'Iltirta a Ilerda*, vol. 1, 11–184. Lleida, Pagès Editors.

Junyent, E. (2015a) Reflexions sobre criteris arquitectònics d'intervenció en jaciments arqueològics. Els casos del Dolmen de Reguers (Seró-Artesa de Segre) i de la Fortalesa dels Vilars (Arbeca). In X. Company, I. Puig, C. Montgay & S. Machetti (eds), *El gran valor de les lletres i les humanitats. Homenatge al Dr. Frederic Vilà i Tornos*, 147–154. Lleida, Universitat de Lleida.

Junyent, E. (2015b) L'evidència arqueològica en la definició de la societat estatal arcaica ilergeta. In M.C. Belarte, D. García & J. Sanmartí (eds), *Les estructures socials a la Gàl·lia i a Ibèria. Actes de la VII Reunió Internacional d'Arqueologia de Calafell (Calafell, 7 al 9 de març de 2013)*, 165–191. Barcelona, Arqueomediterrània 14.

Junyent, E. (2018) 775–300 a.C. Terra, aigua i poder en el món iber. In B. de Riquer (dir.), *Història Mundial de Catalunya*, 56–65. Barcelona, Edicions 62.

Junyent, E. & Casals, C. (2013) La Fortalesa dels Vilars d'Arbeca. Conservació i socialització. In D. Gordillo (ed.), *Fortificaciones. Intervenciones en el patrimonio defensivo. Actas de XXXIV Jornadas Internacionales sobre la intervención en el Patrimonio Arquitectónico. Barcelona y Tortosa, 15 al 18 de diciembre de 2011*, 49–58. Madrid, Ministerio de Educación, Cultura y Deporte.

Junyent, E. & López, J.B. (2015) Les excavacions dels anys 1973–1974 i 1980 al Tossal del Molinet (el Poal, Pla d'Urgell). Una aldea de la primera Edat del Ferro i època ibèrica, Mascançà. *Centre de Recerques del Pla d'Urgell* 6, 73–98.

Junyent, E. & López, J.B. (2016) *The Vilars d'Arbeca Fortress. Land, Water and Power in the Iberian World*. Lleida, Catàlegs 3.

Junyent, E. & Moya, A. (2011) Els fossats de la Fortalesa dels Vilars d'Arbeca (Catalunya, Espanya). *Revista d'Arqueologia de Ponent* 21, 93–120.

Junyent, E., Poch, R.M. & Balasch, C. (2012) Water and defense systems in Els Vilars fortress (Arbeca, Catalonia, Spain). A multiproxy approach. *Cypsela* 22, 49–70.

Junyent, E., López, J.B., Moya, A. & Tartera, E. (2009) L'accés fortificat i les portes en el sistema defensiu de la fortalesa dels Vilars (Arbeca, les Garrigues). *Revista d'Arqueologia de Ponent* 19, 307–334.

López, J.B. (2001) *L'evolució del poblament protohistòric a la Catalunya occidental. Models d'ocupació del territori i urbanisme*. Unpublished PhD dissertation, Universitat de Lleida.

Martín, A., López, V. & Gabaldón, A. (2003) El conjunto minero-metalúrgico del término municipal de Seno (Bajo Aragón). Un ejemplo del origen y difusión de la siderurgia protohistórica en el Levante español. *Salduie* 3, 257–267.

Nieto, A. (2012) *Entre el consum i l'afecte. La interacció entre els animals i les comunitats protohistòriques de la plana occidental catalana (segles VII–VI a.C.)*. Unpublished PhD dissertation, Universitat de Lleida.

Nieto, A. (2013) Porcs, cavalls, ovelles i infants. Noves aportacions a les pràctiques rituals de la Fortalesa dels Vilars (Arbeca, les Garrigues). *Revista d'Arqueologia de Ponent* 23, 127–162.

Nieto, A. Gardeisen, A. Junyent, E. & Lopez, J.B. (2010) Inhumations de foetus d'équidés dans la forteresse du premier âge du Fer de Els Vilars (Arbeca, Catalogne). In A. Gardeisen, E. Furet & N. Boulbes (eds), *Histoire d'équidés. Des textes, des images et des os*. Monographies d'Archéologie Méditerranéenne 4, 125–148. Lattes, Ed. de l'Association pour le Développement de l'Archéologie en Languedoc-Roussillon.

Nieto, A., López, J.B., Gardeisen, A. & Junyent, E. (2018) Votive well or refuse tip? Chronicle of an abandonment. Taphonomic study of the faunal remains of an Iron Age well-cistern. *Historical Biology* 30(6), 894–915.

Picazo, J.V. & Rodanés J.M. (2009) *Los Poblados del Bronce Final y Primera Edad del Hierro. Cabezo de la Cruz (La Muela, Zaragoza)*. Zaragoza, Gobierno de Aragón.

Rovira, M.C. (1998) Le travail du fer en Catalogne du VIIe au Ier s. av. n. ère, In M. Feugère & V. Serneels (eds), *Recherches sur l'économie du fer en Méditerranée nord-occcidentale*, 65–75. Montagnac, Monographies Instrumentum 4.

Rovira, M.C. (2000) Los talleres de herrero en el mundo ibérico. Aspectos técnicos y sociales, In C. Mata & G. Pérez (eds), *Ibers. Agricultors, artesans i comerciants. III Reunió sobre Economia en el Món Ibèric (València, 24–27 noviembre 1999)*, 265–270. Valencia, Saguntum Extra 3.

Rovira Llorens S. (2000) Continuismo e innovación en la metalurgia Ibérica. In C. Mata & G. Pérez (eds), *Ibers. Agricultors, artesans i comerciants. III Reunió sobre Economia en el Món Ibèric (València, 24–27 noviembre 1999)*, 209–221. Valencia, Saguntum Extra 3.

Vàzquez, M.P., González, J.R., Medina, J. & Escuder, X. (2014) Sant Joan Vell de Térmens. Molins més enllà de la mòlta a la protohistòria de la plana occidental catalane. *Revista d'Arqueologia de Ponent* 24, 347–362.

Vàzquez, M.P., González, J.R., Medina, J., Mata, J.M. & Rodríguez, J.I. (2005) Actividades siderúrgicas en yacimientos de la primera Edad del Hierro próximos a la confluencia de los ríos Cinca, Segre y Ebro. In O. Puche & M. Ayarzagüena (eds), *Minería y metalurgia históricas en el sudoeste europeo (Madrid, 23–27 junio 2004)*, 129–145. Madrid, Sociedad Española para la Defensa del Patrimonio Geológico y Minero – Sociedad Española de Historia de la Arqueología.

Vidal, A. & Junyent, E. (2007) El Patrimonio Arqueológico Inmueble de la demarcación geoturística 'Terres de Lleida'. Criterios de evaluación y modelos de actuación. In V. Campos (ed.), *IV Congreso Internacional sobre Musealización de Xacementos Arqueolóxicos Conservación e presentación de xacementos arqueolóxicos no medio rural. Impacto social no territorio – IV Congreso Internacional sobre Musealización de Yacimientos Arqueológicos: Conservación y presentación de yacimientos arqueológicos en el medio rural. Impacto social en el territorio*, Santiago de Compostela, 13–16 November 2006, 323–330. Santiago de Compostela, Xunta de Galicia.

Vila, S. (2018) *L'explotació dels recursos vegetals a la plana occidental catalana durant la protohistòria a partir de l'anàlisi antracològica (III–I millenni)*. Unpublished PhD dissertation, Universitat de Lleida.

PART 3

CONCLUDING REMARKS

14

Then, Now, to Come – A Commentary*

John Chapman

I suppose that the editors of this volume about tells – Antonio Blanco-González and Tobias Kienlin – had invited me to write a commentary because I had been working away at tells for over 30 years and had (allegedly) gained some expertise in the topic. My initial emotions on reading the 13 chapters were shock, followed by pleasure – at the extreme diversity of research represented here. I had no concept that an Iron Age fort in Iberia could have had tell-like characteristics! This diversity embraced all aspects of the topic – the approaches to the material, the theoretical underpinnings (if any) of the work, the time-places discussed, the interpretations of the phenomena under dissection and, above all, the interests in such a superabundance of aspects of tells.

How did such diversity arise amongst contemporary scholars? For Naumov (Chapter 8), the question relates to local and regional differences in data and the variety of approaches to these data. The best support for this view comes from López *et al.* (Chapter 13) on Iron Age Els Vilars which is unlike all other sites discussed in this volume because of its cultural foundations in Catalunya but which does indeed resemble a tell. But the issue is more complex than that. One obvious source has been the increased number of researchers targeting tells – the notion of 'a small cast of actors', which Robin Boast once used to characterise researchers into the Beaker phenomenon (Boast 1997), has clearly undergone substantial expansion and, with expansion, comes diversity. Another causal agent may have been the variety of the researchers' backgrounds – with almost half of the projects represented here coming from international teams ('foreigners' to a Brexiteer) and just over half from 'local teams'. But it seems to me that the principal factor in such diversity arises from the amazing variability in basic theoretical preconceptions which the authors have brought to the table. I am reminded of Roland Fletcher's (1989) conclusion that archaeology has not undergone a series of paradigm replacements as was described *e.g.* for physics by Thomas Kuhn (1970) but, rather, has accumulated new paradigms (New, processual, cognitive-processual, post-processual, New Materialism, symmetrical, *etc.*) while never discarding any old ones. Like hoarders who cannot bear to throw away anything of possible future value, archaeologists have kept the culture-historical flame burning just in case it had residual value,[1] or maintained processual tool-boxes such as GIS despite post-processual castigation (Thomas 1993). Thus, this volume represents a *smorgasbord* of theoretical (and atheoretical) approaches to tells, revealing itself to be a creature of the late 20th century into the 2000s.

Every collection of essays from as diverse a set of authors as this acts as a timemark[2] on the intellectual landscape dotted with tells and other sites. The essays form conversations between each other, with dominant voices occasionally rising above the hubbub (am I thinking 'Tower of Babel'?). The most important debate concerns the shift from the view of tells as a generic site type with a series of distinctive characteristics (physical, spatial and social) which form a more or less stable (?some would say 'static') core definition to the view of tells as a site type of enormous variability, whether this was expressed internally (intra-site) or at the inter-site level. Another facet of this shift is the move from a top-down interpretation of tells as a form of socio-spatial order to a bottom-up question of how to discern the everyday practices to sustain life on a tell – a re-formulation of the tension between structure and action. To borrow a metaphor from Andrew Fleming,[3] does the term 'tell' subsume such a broad church of conflicting views that it cannot avoid a roof collapse? In other words, what holds the site type of 'tell' together as a coherent entity? Is it indeed a coherent entity?

One important way to distinguish tells as a coherent entity is to make a comparison with flat sites. The traditional approach began by noting that all tells started off their lives as flat sites (Chapman 1989) – a position with which several contributors to this volume concur (Staniuk *et al.*, Naumov and Souvatzi). My sharp distinction between tells and flat sites made on the basis of landscape visibility, ancestral depth and different Built-to-Unbuilt (BUB) space ratios, with low BUB ratios limiting the range of social practices possible on tells, was criticised by Evans (2005), provoking a more positive view of flat sites with their larger areas of open space for herding, gardening, pyrotechnology, rituals and meeting (Chapman in press). Nonetheless, the distinction between the two site types was maintained, with an interesting kinship dimension added by Souvatzi (Chapter 9) who proposes unilinear descent groups for tells and bilateral kinship for flat sites, with a mixture for sites with both elements (*e.g.* Sesklo). This volume marks a stronger emphasis on similarities between tells and flat sites than earlier, whether because of combinations of both elements on the same site (*e.g.* Csőszhalom), lengthy occupation spans (*e.g.* Nea Makri: Souvatzi, Chapter 9), shared morphologies (especially Souvatzi, Chapter 9) and comparable ranges of depositional practices. Moreover, there is the thorny classificatory question of what distinguished a 'tell' from a 'tell-like' structure (see Gogâltan *et al.*, Chapter 6; Füzesi *et al.*, Chapter 10) or, in Bulgarian prehistory, a 'multi-layer settlement' – with some intermediate types closer to flat sites than tells. The question becomes dramatically more relevant in considering Els Vilars – a heavily defended fortlet full of structures for residence and production, whose occupations were defined by a 4–5 m stratigraphy contained within the same 60 × 45 m defended space for almost 500 years. At first sight, this was like no tell in the Balkan Peninsula but comparison with North Bulgarian Copper Age tells such as Poljanica or Ovcharovo shows similarities in size, multiple enclosure features and high density of occupation. I predict that this will be an interesting space to watch, with more interpretative differences emerging soon in response to this question.

Another major question concerns the similarities and differences between Neolithic/Chalcolithic tells and Bronze Age/Iron Age tells. Although this volume contains research on tells from both periods, there is not a single chapter in which comparisons are made between the two.[4] It seems as if we are perpetuating chronologically watertight debates where the participants do not listen to views over the fence – hence the pressing need for volumes such as this. But this means that, at present, we cannot provide an overall reply to what makes tells different from flat sites in either the Neolithic/Chalcolithic or the Bronze Age/Iron Age or, indeed, what makes these sites similar or different in each period. The two criteria of landscape visibility and ancestral depth remain the most obvious points of difference – traits which may have been drawn upon in a plethora of different ways on different sites.

Then, now

The contents of the papers in this volume can be summarised and structured in a time – space grid (Fig. 14.1) with a *vertical* scale marking biographies, from creation through use, with changing uses through time, to abandonment and a *horizontal* scale moving from an entire landscape, to site clusters, to individual sites (tells and flat sites) and on to houses and individual use contexts. With the exception of Kienlin's chapter on practice theory, most chapters address several parts of the grid, with the chapter on Els Vilars touching upon as many as *nine* different sectors – mostly the uses of the entire site and individual contexts but also their abandonment and their landscape context. Equally, Sofaer *et al.* (Chapter 11) on the Százhalombatta tell consider all aspects of the tell, from individual contexts up to the whole site through time, with many changes in use and including a discussion on abandonment. By contrast, Krahtopoulou *et al.* (Chapter 3) focus on the landscape of the Kambos area of Western Thessaly and one tell within that landscape. I hope that the figure gives a useful diagrammatic representation of the contents of the volume. I shall use its parameters as a guide to new ideas and interpretations.

All of the chapters dealing with landscapes focus on palaeo-hydrology and its effects on (mostly Neolithic) settlement distributions. While Füzesi *et al.* use the 18th century AD Austrian Military Map to reconstruct palaeo-meanders in relation to Late Neolithic site clusters in Eastern Hungary, Naumov, Krahtopoulou *et al.* and Souvatzi identify the importance of long-disappeared wetlands and lakes to the founding of settlements – mostly tells – in their respective areas.[5] Many projects have identified the significance of palaeo-hydrology in the spread of the Neolithic, from John Nandris's (1970) study of water table as a factor in Early Neolithic Körös settlement in Southeast Hungary to the more recent Çatalhöyük palaeo-environmental studies (Ayala *et al.* 2017). Here, more emphasis could have been laid on the taphonomic impact of alluviation on the low rate of discovery of Neolithic sites in Western Thessaly. The Els Vilars study discusses lake-level fluctuations and aridity phases based on the local lake of Estany d'Ivars-Vilasana but without relating these fluctuations to the site development.

The paucity of studies of site clusters – represented in only three chapters – appears to be a function of embedding projects in intensive, systematic fieldwalking research. The Neolithic example around the Öcsöd tell-like site derived from 1990s fieldwalking projects and earlier settlement research (Kalicz 1957), while research by Gogâltan *et al.* included fieldwalking to identify Bronze Age tells in Western Romania and the site clusters related to Naumov's palaeo-wetlands research were discovered in extensive village-based survey in the 1970s. There is huge potential in relating individual site studies to their settlement context,

Figure 14.1 Time-place foci of chapters in this volume, with numbered circles referring to each chapter and placed according to the principal research focus/foci of the chapter. NB Chapter 12 by Kienlin does not figure in this image because it is a high-level analysis of interpretations of social practice on tells. Legend to the graphic: Chapter 2. Molist et al.; Chapter 3. Krahtopoulou et al.; Chapter 4. Steadman & Ross; Chapter 5. Staniuk et al.; Chapter 6. Gogâltan et al.; Chapter 7. Klinkenberg; Chapter 8. Naumov; Chapter 9. Souvatzi; Chapter 10. Füzesi et al.; Chapter 11. Sofaer et al.; Chapter 13. López et al.

not least the use of the site cluster approach to the 440 Thessalian Neolithic tells known to date for diachronic land-use capability research.

The greatest advances in the volume are found in the focus on an individual tell, which is found in the majority of chapters. These studies cover the full range of tell biographies, from their creation through their often multiple uses to their abandonment. The use of Jennifer Birch's hypothesis of 'coalescent communities' to explain the origins of Öcsöd from a suite of local groups to a single nucleated co-resident central site could be effective for many tell contexts, just as it has been for the long-term, flat, persistent place of Alsónyék in Western Hungary (Bánffy *et al.* 2016).

Our understanding of the use-life of tells, and settlement in Old Europe in general, has been transformed by the recent florescence of large-scale geophysical surveys. This advance is well illustrated by chapters by Krahtopoulou *et al.*, Staniuk *et al.*, Gogâltan *et al.*, Naumov, Souvatzi, Füzesi *et al.* and Sofaer *et al.* Exemplary in these new plans is the 2018 Öcsöd survey showing three new semi-circular interrupted ditches round the tell-like centre, the ditches ranging from 1.7 m to 2.9 m deep, 250 m, 400 m and 500 m in diameter and comprising 20–30 m long segments made by small groups contributing their labour to the communal effort before the rapid backfilling which emphasised that performance was the ultimate goal. But, as we found in the Trypillia megasites Project (Chapman *et al.* 2014; Gaydarska 2020), the methodological advances of geophysical investigation will be vitiated without corresponding theoretical changes in our understandings of site temporality and spatial order. One extraordinary contrast that stems from the new generation of geophysical plans is the huge variability of tell spatial layouts in both the Neolithic (Füzesi *et al.*, Chapter 10) and Bronze Age (Gogâltan *et al.*, Chapter 6) periods, based upon the combination and recombination of three or four key elements, in comparison to the markedly traditional plans of Trypillia megasites, with the regular use of the same four or five planning principles. As exemplified also in Souvatzi's chapter, this difference requires new theorisation of temporalities and spatial order to improve our understanding of the empirical geophysical data.[6]

Two chapters with a markedly different theoretical background focus on the role of material culture in tells through time. Steadman and Ross (Chapter 4) examine three ways in which later – usually Late Bronze Age/Early Iron Age – residents drew upon the resources of earlier, Chalcolithic, dwelling phases at Çadir Höyük, a Central Anatolian tell occupied discontinuously from 5200 BC to the Byzantine period. The denial of ancestral links in favour of a long-term attachment to place seems 'out of place' for the reinvention of a dark burnished ware potting tradition, the reuse of sherds as tools and the re-use of wall foundations in later buildings. Whether or not the ancestors were known or identified, use of far older remains is framed in a similar relationship to the deep past as an ancestral link. A comparable example is the collection and reuse of Neolithic lithics from the Late Neolithic Csőszhalom tell by residents on the Bronze Age tell of Kenderföld 1200 m away from, and intervisible with, the ancestral tell.

The other project, at the Százhalombatta tell, is concerned with inventing a new vocabulary which we do not yet possess for describing the everyday in order to write more detailed stories about tell life. Sofaer and her co-authors (Chapter 11) show how changes in outdoor space were typical for the tell, whether from an area full of houses to a cart-track complete with wheel-ruts and then an outdoor working area. Here continuity in material culture sustains social memory and maintains social traditions in the face of changes in houses and use of outdoor space. While house orientation, size and proportions showed long-term stability, other aspects of houses were subject to change, like the two-roomed houses converted into two one-room houses. Dirty, messy areas full of rubbish located outside the houses were considered as 'liminal areas' lacking social regulation and used tactically by individuals for refuse disposal. There were specific horizons where 'the tell did not behave as it should', when veneration of ancestral houses was almost totally abandoned. This extract from a complex, varied tell narrative is light years away from the top-down 'political' naming of tells as 'mediaeval castles', with their chiefly courts, standing armies and proto-states – strongly criticised in the chapters by Sofaer *et al.* and Kienlin but resonating with the Els Vilars Iron Age study, replete with chieftains, fortlet moats and *cheveaux-de-frise* defences. Kienlin's chapter (Chapter 12) stands out from the remainder in taking the theoretical high ground and posting a significant challenge to recent Bronze Age narratives, through the use of practice theory grounded in the American philosopher Th. Schatzki.

A further contribution by Sofaer *et al.* deals with the abandonment of the Százhalombatta tell in terms of the growing tendency of *ad hoc* decisions and increasing spatial disorder on the tell well before abandonment. This is comparable to the increasing entropy found in the late Level XI of Tell Ovcharovo, in northeast Bulgaria, also well before the final, spatially disordered occupation horizon (Chapman & Gaydarska 2019). Few contributors have met the challenge of explaining how their tell met its end and there are clearly advances in understanding to be made in this task (but see below for Els Vilars).

In addition to the forms of everyday practice discussed by Sofaer *et al.*, larger-scale, communal work has also been discussed at the intra-tell level. The most obvious of these is the construction of enclosing banks and ditches (see chapters by Souvatzi, Molist *et al.* and Füzesi *et al.*) as well as embankments and retaining walls (Molist *et al.*, Chapter 2). Earth-moving also appears in two accounts (Krahtopoulou *et al.* and Sofaer *et al.*), with earth being brought cyclically from places in the landscape onto the Prodromos II tell and earth being moved across the Százhalombatta tell from the edge of the site to level areas of the tell. Füzesi *et al.* (Chapter 10) discuss the segments of the three ditches round Öcsöd in terms of the meaning of digging, with the implication that we can understand something of the affordances of digging. This is one of the rare examples in the volume of an approach, albeit indirect, to the agency of sites, features or objects and, for this, it is welcomed. Other examples of discussions of the agency of pit-digging include Chapman (2000c), in which pits dug into earlier dwelling levels were considered as an exchange with the ancestors, while pits dug into 'natural' soil were conceived of an exchange with 'nature'.

It is impossible to do justice to the Els Vilars fortlet without characterizing the labour-intensive construction of the five-fold sequence of defensive structures, which culminated in the Middle Iberian construction of a massive moat covering some 8000 m^2 and ranging in depth from 2.3 m to 3.8 m. At this time, the area covered in defensive structures exceeded the area of residential space by a factor of three or four – underpinning the local chieftain's power base with monumental visual effects which are beautifully illustrated by López *et al.* (Chapter 13). Here, it is the defences which dominate the landscape rather than the growing height of the tell-like mound. Nonetheless, the aggrandizing defensive features could not save the fortlet from eventual abandonment in the 4th century BC, when political nucleation into massive central places and large territorial polities made the tiny Els Vilars irrelevant.

Returning to intra-site practices, the Öcsöd chapter includes the example of deliberate fragmentation of an elaborately decorated 72 cm high anthropomorphic storage-vessel,

20 of whose fragments were placed together in a single deposit, while a further 66 sherds were dispersed across the site. This still left other parts of the vessel missing – presumably moved to more remote parts of the site, if not off-site. The off-site removal of most of a second anthropomorphic storage-vessel is more likely, since only 12 sherds were found in another deposit on the tell. These impressive vessels would have symbolised both the personal, as *dividuals*, and the collective body and present an excellent example of deliberate intra-site fragmentation (Chapman 2000a).

The final example of intra-site practices discussed here is Klinkenberg's chapter on the Late Bronze Age *dunnu* of Tell Sabi Abyad.[7] The chapter begins with the provocative assertion, which I have spent many years disputing (Chapman 2000b; 2000c, *etc.*), that all artefacts are refuse unless placed in a Pompeii-like context.[8] Thus the methodological framework for the chapter is a combination of Schifferian deposition with Wilk and Rathje's household archaeology. The author focuses on the clay tablets from the *dunnu* archive, recognising that the tablets are not in themselves the archive but deliberately discarded elements of an archive. The analysis shows two forms of depositional bias – temporal bias when deposition occurred far later than primary tablet use, and spatial bias, with the tablets deposited away from their original place of use. The overall conclusion that complex discard practices typify a tell environment has been well exemplified.

To come

I have commented on the most salient issues discussed in the tell volume. I now focus briefly on what is missing from this collection. Three themes stand out for their absence – sex and gender, social memory and the agency of the tell.

As a primary referent for tell-dwellers, sex and gender cannot be ignored in any nuanced discussion of tells. The general literature on this topic is vast and yet the implications of family composition and sex and gender roles are routinely ignored in this collection. Only Souvatzi tackles the important issue of kinship, but she does not fully tease out its implications for sex and gender. Surprisingly there are no references to the important approach of maintenance activities to sex and gender relations (Alarcón García & Sánchez Romero 2010) and to their significance in the formation of household identities (Hendon 2006). The investigation of both Neolithic and Bronze Age tells offers the opportunity to interrogate Robb & Harris' (2018) claim that gender relations were fundamentally different in these periods. I look forward to more attention paid to this theme in future tell research.

Social memory has emerged as a key topic in the last two decades (Hendon 2010; Adam & Kemp 2019). Although Sofaer *et al.* touch upon social memory at Százhalombatta, the topic is otherwise widely ignored. Social memory played an important role in all tells, where vertical superposition of houses (Bailey 1996) and other features was typical, betokening the trans-generational links which underpinned the material continuity of tell living. It is axiomatic that previous spatial (dis)order formed one set of pre-conditions to the form of the next dwelling horizon and that social memory kept alive previous layouts, practices and timemarks on the tell. The ultimate source of these memories was the community of ancestors who had earlier dwelt on the tell (Chapman 1989; see Souvatzi, this volume). It is difficult to see a renewed understanding of the meaning of tells without taking the ancestors into account more creatively than appeared in this volume.

The third neglected topic certainly poses the greatest theoretical challenges to authors researching tells – the question of the agency of tells (and, indeed, flat sites). The reader does not have to be fully-paid-up subscriber to the 'object itineraries' approach (for a recent review and literature, see Bauer 2019) to accept that Stonehenge, 10 kg cast copper shaft-hole axes or LBK longhouses have an agency of their own separate from that of their creators. Each and every settlement could be visually differentiated from the surrounding landscape by the form and density of its occupation, especially with the building of two-storey houses, although the Els Vilars defences made a bigger impression than the mound. The gradual vertical growth of tells provided an added differentiation, acting as the basis for visual tell agency which proclaimed the ancestral relations of the site – the higher the mound, the longer the ancestral time-depth. But there was also a moral agency to sites, which rested on the association of an occupant with the site she occupied, with personal reputation resting on one's place of dwelling (Wilson 1988). In the case of tells, the moral value shared by person and place increased with the time-depth of the settlement and the range of ancestral associations, as consolidated through social memory (see above) – a process that could well have explained the lengthy life of the Els Vilars fortlet. These forms of tell agency were generalised agencies, not necessarily dependent on the changing everyday practices which characterised tells but more a part of the structural conditions of dwelling held in tension with everyday action. Here is a third area of future research which could prove important in our full understanding of the phenomenon of tell-living.

In conclusion

Tells and their coeval flat sites provide a continuing challenge not only to our theoretical and methodological approaches to the topic but also to our ability to *imagine* different pasts, pasts based upon principles and practices that may have been utterly alien to our modern values. I once spent half an hour trying to convince an eminent economist – then a

Vice-Chancellor of a British university – of the existence of deliberate fragmentation in the past. I clearly failed in my persuasion to imagine a practice so utterly uneconomic that it could not possibly have happened (at the time, I did not have access to the Öcsöd example!). It is the same with tells – places where past, present and future met in ways that are not at all obvious to us. If our vocabulary for telling everyday narratives is deficient, as Sofaer *et al.* claim, one source of new inspiration may be the sort of imaginary tales that Ruth Tringham told about life in the Neolithic (Tringham 1991; 1994). The editors informed me that the absence of a chapter on the small mounded Iberian sites known as 'motillas', which I, perhaps naively, conceptualise as tells, was because the narratives of their excavation reports did not permit a discussion in terms of the interpretations of the tells which were presented in this volume – another lack of appropriate vocabulary. But just as the form of the memoir has been changed for ever with the publication of Karl Ove Knausgård's (2008–2018) extraordinarily detailed six-volume account of his life, '*My struggle*', so we can expect the emergence of new structural forms and narratives about tells, replete with new vocabulary about the everyday. To the extent that this volume has helped the debate in this direction, and for all of the insights into tells from Europe and the Near East, we should be grateful to the editors and the authors for their refreshing research.

Acknowledgements

I am very grateful to Antonio and Tobias for inviting me to offer a *digestif* for this volume on tells – a settlement form that has always intrigued me since I first excavated on the Neolithic tell of Knossos in summer 1970 with Professor John D. Evans. Thanks, too, to all of the authors who gave me so much food for thought and such a varied menu. And a final word of gratitude to Bisserka for company, stimulation and critical vigour.

Notes

* Two parts of the title derive from Peter Fowler's Inaugural Lecture as Professor of Archaeology at Newcastle University (entitled Then, Now, delivered in the University on 26/1/1986), which resulted some years later in a book The Past in Contemporary Society: Then, Now (Fowler 2002).
1 And who can say that they were in error? Note the way in which the mainstays of culture history, such as migration, which were severely criticised by Processualists, have made a comeback on the back of new methods such as ancient DNA and isotopic analysis.
2 A timemark can be thought of as analogous to a landmark but in a temporal trajectory – a moment which is marked out as somehow special for present and future generations (Chapman 1998; 2012).
3 Andrew Fleming used this metaphor in relation to the diversification of views sheltering under the roof of 'Processualism' (Fleming 1990).
4 It should be noted that Steadman & Ross' chapter on Çadir Höyük (Chapter 4) compares pottery and architecture in both periods rather than a discussion of what was happening on the different tell occupations.
5 While Naumov and Souvatzi provide a map showing palaeo-hydrology and tells, the Western Thessalian chapter has no such map, which would have been very useful. The Els Vilars chapter also lacks a map of the site showing the location of the nearby lake.
6 It is interesting to note that Session 446 at the EAA Virtual Meeting in Budapest (2020) will consider open, empty spaces in settlement planning.
7 Although about a tell, this chapter does not really belong in this volume – the analysis could have been carried out on any kind of site.
8 Klinkenberg makes no mention of the recent useful addition to the range of depositional forms made by Kuna (2015).

References

Adam, B. & Kemp, S. (2019) Time matters. Faces, externalised knowledge and transcendence. In S. Souvatzi, A. Baysal & E.L. Baysal (eds), *Time and History in Prehistory*, 210–228. London, Routledge.

Alarcón García, E. & Sánchez Romero, M. (2010) Maintenance activities as a category for analysing prehistoric societies. In L.H. Domassnes, T. Hjorungdal, S. Montón-Subías, M. Sánchez Romero & N.L. Wicker (eds), *Situating Gender in European Archaeologies*. Budapest, Series Minor 23, 261–282.

Ayala, G., Wainwright, J., Walker, J., Hodara, R., Lloyd, J.M., Lend, M. & Doherthy, C. (2017) Paleoenvironmental reconstruction of the alluvial landscape of the Neolithic Çatalhöyük, central southern Turkey: The implications for early agriculture and responses to environmental changes. *Journal of Archaeological Science* 87, 30–43.

Bailey, D. (1996) The life, time and works of House 59, Tell Ovcharovo, Bulgaria. In T. Darvill & J. Thomas (eds), *Neolithic Houses in Northwest Europe and Beyond*, 143–156. Oxford, Neolithic Studies Group Seminar Papers 1.

Bánffy, E., Osztás, A., Oross, K., Zalai-Gaál, I., Marton, T., Nyerges, É.Á., Köhler, K., Bayliss, A., Hamilton, D. & Whittle, A. (2016) The Alsónyék story: towards the prehistory of a persistent place. *Bericht der Römisch-Germanisch Kommission* 94, 283–318.

Bauer, A.A. (2019) Itinerant objects. *Annual Review of Anthropology* 48, 335–352.

Boast, R. (1997) A small company of actors. A critique of style. *Journal of Material Culture* 2(2), 173–198.

Chapman, J. (1989) The early Balkan village. *Varia Archaeologica Hungarica* 2, 33–53.

Chapman, J. (1998) Objects and places: their value in the past. In D.W. Bailey (ed.), *The Archaeology of Prestige and Wealth*, 106–130. Oxford, British Archaeological Report S730.

Chapman, J. (2000a) *Fragmentation in Archaeology: People, Places and Broken Objects in the Prehistory of South Eastern Europe*. London, Routledge.

Chapman, J. (2000b) 'Rubbish-dumps' or 'places of deposition'?: Neolithic and Copper Age settlements in Central and Eastern Europe. In A. Ritchie (ed.), *Neolithic Orkney in its European Context*, 347–362. Cambridge, MacDonald Institute.

Chapman, J. (2000c) Pit-digging and structured deposition in the Neolithic and Copper Age of Central and Eastern Europe. *Proceedings of the Prehistoric Society* 61, 51–67.

Chapman, J. (2012) The negotiation of place value in the landscape. In J.K. Papadopoulos & G. Urton (eds), *The Construction of Value in the Ancient World*, 66–89. Los Angeles CA, UCLA Cotsen Institute of Archaeology Press.

Chapman, J. (in press) *Forging Identities in Balkan Prehistory: Dividuals, Individuals and Communities, 7000–3000 BC*. Leiden, Sidestone Press.

Chapman, J. & Gaydarska, B. (2019) Concepts of time and history on Chalcolithic tell settlements and Trypillia megasites. In S. Souvatzi, A. Baysal & E.L. Baysal (eds), *Time and History in Prehistory*, 147–171. London, Routledge.

Chapman, J., Videiko, M.Y., Hale, D., Gaydarska, B., Burdo, N., Rassmann, K., Mischka, C., Müller, J., Korvin-Piotrovskiy, A. & Kruts, V. (2014) The second phase of the Trypillia mega-site methodological revolution. A new research agenda. *European Journal of Archaeology* 17(3), 369–406.

Evans, J. (2005) Memory and ordination: environmental archaeology in tells. In D. Bailey, A. Whittle & V. Cummings (eds), *(Un)settling the Neolithic*, 112–125. Oxford, Oxbow Books.

Fleming, A. (1990) Pretentious – moi? In F. Baker & J. Thomas (eds), *Writing the Past in the Present*, 83–86. Lampeter, Saint David's College.

Fletcher, R. (1989) Social theory and archaeology: diversity, paradox and potential. *Mankind* 19(1), 65–75.

Fowler, P.J. (2002) *The Past in Contemporary Society: Then, Now*. London, Routledge.

Gaydarska, B. (2020) *Early Urbanism in Europe: The Trypillia Mega-sites of the Ukrainian Forest-steppe*. Berlin, De Gruyter.

Hendon, J.A. (2006) The engendered household. In S.M. Nelson (ed.), *Handbook of Gender in Archaeology*, 171–198. London, Altamira Press.

Hendon, J.A. (2010) *Houses in a Landscape: Memory and Everyday Life in Mesoamerica*. Durham NC, Duke University Press.

Kalicz, N. (1957) *Tiszazug őskori települései*. Budapest, Régészeti Füzetek 1.

Knausgård, K.O. (2008–2018) *My Struggle*. New York, Harvill Secker.

Kuhn, T. (1970) *The Structure of Scientific Revolutions*. Chicago IL, University of Chicago Press.

Kuna, M. (2015) Categories of settlement discard. In K. Kristiansen, L. Šmejda & J. Turek (eds), *Paradigm Found. Archaeological Theory – Present, Past and Future*, 278–292. Oxford, Oxbow Books.

Nandris, J. (1970) Ground water as a factor in the FTN settlement of the Körös region. *Zbornik Narodnog Muzeja Beograda* 6, 59–71.

Robb, J. & Harris, O.J.T. (2018) Becoming gendered in European prehistory: was Neolithic *gender* fundamentally different? *American Antiquity* 83(1), 128–147.

Thomas, J. (1993) The politics of vision and the archaeologies of landscape. In B. Bender (ed.), *Landscape: Politics and Perspectives*, 19–48. Oxford, Berg.

Tringham, R. (1991) Households with faces: the challenge of gender in prehistoric architectural remains. In J.M. Gero & M. Conkey (eds), *Engendering Archaeology*, 93–131. Oxford, Blackwell.

Tringham, R. (1994) Engendered places in prehistory. *Gender, Place and Culture* 1, 169–203.

Wilson, P. (1988) *The Domestication of the Human Species*. Cambridge, Cambridge University Press.